MEMOIRS

OF A

MARYLAND VOLUNTEER.

MEMOIRS

OF A

MARYLAND VOLUNTEER.

WAR WITH MEXICO,

IN THE YEARS 1846-7-8.

BY

JOHN R. KENLY.

PHILADELPHIA:
J. B. LIPPINCOTT & CO.
1873.

LIPPINCOTT'S PRESS,
PHILADELPHIA.

TO THE MEMORY

OF

MAJOR-GENERAL ZACHARY TAYLOR,

WHO, WHILE LIVING, WAS A TRUE TYPE OF THE AMERICAN SOLDIER,

THIS WORK

IS AFFECTIONATELY DEDICATED.

CONTENTS.

CHAPTER XII.

CHAPTER XIII.

CHAPTER XIV.

CHAPTER XV.

CHAPTER XVI.

CHAPTER XVII.

CHAPTER XVIII.

CHAPTER XIX.

CHAPTER XX.

CHAPTER XXI.

CHAPTER XXII.

CHAPTER XXIII.

CHAPTER XXIV.

CHAPTER XXV.

CHAPTER XXVI.

CHAPTER XXVII.

CHAPTER XXVIII.

CHAPTER XXIX.

CHAPTER XXX.

CHAPTER XXXI.

CHAPTER XXXII.

CHAPTER XXXIII.

CHAPTER XXXIV.

CHAPTER XXXV.

CHAPTER XXXVI.

MEMOIRS

OF

A MARYLAND VOLUNTEER.

CHAPTER I.

PRELIMINARY.

THE recognition of the independence of Texas, and its subsequent annexation, may have been the proximate cause of the war with Mexico; but for years there had been smouldering embers, which the evolution of time alone would have fanned into active warfare against the Mexican people. It was not alone because the sympathies of the Americans were with the Texans in their brave and heroic struggle for liberty from Mexican military domination, that the military chieftains of the pseudo-republic were so bitter in their hostility to the United States; and it was not alone because the early settlers of Texas were our own race and blood that we felt so keenly their massacre at Mier, and their triumph at San Jacinto. No! there were deep-seated causes of hostility between the two peoples. The one, an antagonism of race upon the borders of the two countries, which was instinctive and involuntary, as much so as between the Red Man and the Western Pioneer; another, a long continuance of outrages upon the persons and property of American citizens by Mexican officials, and redress either positively refused or vexatiously and willfully postponed; another, the watchful jealousy with which the officials of Mexico had been regarding the expansive growth of the United States,—a jealousy from which sprang at first distrust, then hatred. These were continuously exhibited.

General Jackson, the then President of the United States, in a Message to Congress on the 8th of February, 1837, said, "The wanton character of some of the outrages upon the persons and property of our citizens, upon the officers and flag of the United States, independent of recent insults to this Government by the late Extraordinary Mexican minister, would justify, in the eyes of all nations, immediate war." Still no war.

I was cognizant of some of these outrages. Mr. Edward Hoffman, a merchant of Baltimore, after having paid duties on his merchandise at Santa Fé, to the custom-house officers there stationed, and obtained regular permits for the importation of his goods into Mexico, was deliberately robbed of the same permits by the custom-house officials at Chihuahua, deprived of his goods, and imprisoned in a loathsome dungeon, until he bought himself out of their hands by money obtained from his friends.*

The simple narration of the outrages done to other Americans by Mexican officials, which he witnessed,

* His claim for losses was allowed after the war, by the Commission provided for by the Treaty of Peace.

filled one with indignation; and well-authenticated accounts of the continuous wrongs done our citizens were published throughout the country.

Notwithstanding the independence of Texas had been recognized by most of the European powers, and the utter inability of Mexico to re-establish her authority over it,* yet the Mexican Government and people, including Antonio Lopez de Santa Anna, insisted upon their right of sovereignty over Texas, and declared that no quarter would be given to any *foreigner* taken fighting against the troops of Mexico. This was from 1841 to 1844.

On the 3d of March, 1845, the joint resolution for the admission of Texas into the American Union passed both Houses of Congress, and, being signed by the President on the same day, became a law. This, however, did not consummate the measure; the consent of the people of Texas was required, and it was supposed by some that the President of the Lone Star State might listen to propositions from the representatives of England and France, who endeavored to defeat the measure.

All these attempts signally failed. On the 23d of June, 1845, the Government of Texas, by the unanimous vote of both Houses, and the approval of the Executive, gave its consent; and the convention to which the matter had been finally referred, by its ordinance of July 4, 1845, assented to it, and annexation was consummated. From this time the senti-

---

* See a letter from Hon. Daniel Webster to Nicholas Biddle, dated September 10, 1838, published in the Life of Webster, by George Ticknor Curtis, 1870, vol. i. p. 579.

ment of the people of Mexico was nearly national,* that the "*Barbarians of the North*" should be chastised for their presumption; and the movement of Taylor's troops to the west of the Nueces culminated in the murder of Colonel Cross, the defeat of a party under Lieutenant Porter, the capture of Captain Thornton's squadron of dragoons by the Mexicans on this side of the Rio Grande, and the Act of our Congress of the 13th of May, 1846, recognizing the existence of a state of war.

In the President's Message to Congress, which preceded by two days the passage of the above Act, he told the people of the United States "that American blood had been shed upon American soil, and that, by the acts of her generals, Mexico had proclaimed that hostilities had commenced."

Was the country between the Nueces and the Rio Grande American soil? The whole *casus belli* turns on this. I say it was: and this assertion is made after much reading on the subject. If the province of, or republic of, Texas ever owned to the left bank of the Rio Grande, we were in, under the terms of annexation; and that she did so claim, after the treaty with the Mexican generals in 1836, is not

* There were some exceptions. The President, Herrera, was opposed to war; and I was told in the city of Mexico in 1848, by an eye-witness of the affair, that in January, 1846, on the day that Herrera was compelled to resign by Paredes and his adherents, when Herrera left the palace the people in the plaza made way for him as he passed alone through the crowd, and with tears in their eyes prayed God to protect and bless him, so highly was he esteemed by all classes.

disputed. Besides this, I think the probabilities are that as a province or state of the Mexican confederation, the Rio Grande, or Bravo del Norte as they also termed it, was its natural western boundary,* as no other State of the Mexican republic was lying east of this river but Texas.

After the victories of the Texans, they drove the Mexicans across the Rio Grande, and on the banks of this river the Texan leaders deliberated upon the boundaries of their future republic. Many of them were well acquainted with the rich valley of the Rio Grande west of that river, and urged that the mountains of the Sierra Madre, lying about a hundred miles back, should be the western limits of their State. This would have given to the Texans the Mexican State of Tamaulipas, rich in cotton- and sugar-lands, and a natural boundary line much preferable to the Rio Grande.

It is related as a fact that every officer of the Texan army present at this conference was in favor of this boundary, with the single exception of their com-

* I admit there is Mexican authority for the claim made by some geographers that the Nueces was the eastern boundary of the State of Coahuila; but General Almonte, high Mexican authority, said that this was an error. France claimed by the discovery of the Mississippi all the country to the Rio Grande. This is a natural geographical division. When we bought Louisiana from Napoleon in 1803, we claimed under its grant to the Rio Grande. By our treaty with Spain in 1819 we abandoned our claim to all the territory west of the Sabine River. Texas now took up what our statesmen had abandoned, and the victory of San Jacinto, with its sequences, removed all doubt as to whom the territory belonged on the 4th day of April, 1846.

manding officer, General Sam Houston. He overruled the decision of the officers, and insisted that the Rio Grande River should be the line from its mouth to the 39th parallel of north latitude,* and thus it was established by Act of the Congress of the republic of Texas in 1836; so that, when Texas came into the Union, she brought with her the boundary on the west gained by her people in their war of independence.

On the 4th of April, 1846, the Mexican General Arista was ordered by his Government to cross the Rio Grande, and attack and destroy the American army by every means in his power; and he immediately announced to General Taylor, on this side the river, that he considered hostilities as having commenced. On the 25th of April General Torrejon did cross the river, and killed Lieutenant Mason, with a large proportion of Thornton's squadron United States Dragoons, and captured the balance.

The war had commenced; Arista followed Torrejon, and, on the left bank of the Rio Grande, in the State of Texas, fought and was defeated by General Taylor on the 8th and 9th days of May, 1846.

The news of the battles of the 8th and 9th of May—PALO ALTO and RESACA DE LA PALMA—caused the liveliest rejoicing throughout the United States, and the victories of our gallant little army of regulars raised the military enthusiasm of the nation to the highest pitch.

By the Act of May 13, 1846, the President was authorized to call forth volunteers in any number not

---

* Doniphan's Campaign.

exceeding 50,000, to serve for the period of one year or during the war. Prior to the passage of this Act, a considerable number of volunteers from Louisiana had been called for by Generals Gaines and Taylor for three months' service, and had marched with alacrity to the support of the army in the field.

Soon after the news of the battles on the Rio Grande had been received in Baltimore, I went to the city of Washington, provided with a letter of introduction to the President of the United States from an influential citizen of Baltimore,—Mr. Francis Gallagher,—and had an interview with Mr. Polk. I solicited from him an appointment to the regular army; he told me that he purposed calling for volunteers—would take some from Maryland, and that then I would have an opportunity to respond to the call of my country with higher rank than he could give me.

Continued my efforts to enter the regular army until the 1st day of June, when after a conversation with Lieutenant-Colonel Wm. H. Watson, I determined to raise a company of volunteers for a battalion which he was organizing for twelve months' service.

On the next day, the 2d of June, opened a rendezvous in the armory of the Eagle Artillery Company (of which company I was the First Lieutenant), and another at Trades' Union Hall, corner of Baltimore Street and Tripolett's Alley. Volunteers came in with extraordinary rapidity, and on the morning of the 4th day of June I carried to the city of Washington, by railroad, two officers and fifty-eight men, the whole having been recruited by me in less than thirty-six hours. Prior to leaving my rendezvous in

Baltimore Street, I was honored and gratified by being presented with a sword and sash by Captain George P. Kane, the commanding officer, on behalf of the Eagle Artillery Company, with which I had been connected as private and officer for several years.

On reaching Washington we were met by the volunteers from Baltimore who had preceded me, and escorted to the War Department, from whence we marched to the Marine Barracks, where quarters had been assigned my recruits.

On the next day sent Lieutenants Francis B. Schaeffer and Oden Bowie back to Baltimore to bring more men, who, I had been informed, were anxious to join the company. They returned on the 7th, and on the next day, the 8th day of June, 1846, we marched to the War Department, and were mustered into the service of the United States by Lorenzo Thomas, Major and Assistant-Adjutant-General United States Army, for twelve months, my company consisting of three officers and eighty-four non-commissioned officers and privates.

The following is the roll of the company, which was known as "Baltimore's Own":

Captain, John R. Kenly.

First Lieutenant, Francis B. Schaeffer.

Second Lieutenant, Oden Bowie.

Sergeants: William E. Aisquith, William Hickman, George O. Lansdale, Thomas Tyser.

Corporals: Benjamin F. Brand, James H. Mansfield, James A. Beacham, James Tibbles.

Privates: John Andrews, John F. Alexander, John Allen, Wm. Allen, Lemuel Atkinson, George W.

Bowie, John A. Billington, Wm. A. Butler, Wm. Bannister, Samuel Beaston, John Boyd, Edward Boulanger, Jacob Baker, Edward I. Byram, Richard H. Belt, James B. Canning, George N. Collins, De Azro A. B. Cutting, Jacob Degomp, Francis M. Dobbin, Joseph H. Dick, Henry I. Elding, Charles Fischer, Louis Fuller, Henry Forbush, Francis Fisher, George Gordon, Samuel Gelston, Vincent Henxler, John H. Hipkins, James Henry, Barney Hawkins, George T. Hugo, Charles Hill, George Healey, Wm. S. Hatch, Charles Johnson, John S. Johnson, David Johnson, Leroy Knight, Thomas Leyburn, Thomas Leveuton, Francis A. Labédie, John Loughry, Samuel Lockhart, William Macready, George Macnelly, Joseph B. Millard, James H. Merton, Jacob Morris, John Magness, Charles W. Matchett, John McGunnell, Edward Myers, Henry P. Norris, Francis Louis Nettan, Franklin B. Nimocks, Josiah Pregg, Charles Pratt, James Peregoy, Seth S. Rogers, John Reese, Joseph B. Richardson, Wm. M. S. Riley, Andrew I. Ritter, Wm. Rapley, John K. Robinson, James W. Sullivan, John Smith, Thomas T. Stansbury, Wm. H. Sibley, John W. Turner, Joseph Wharry, Daniel Williams, Wm. Wilson, and Ernest Tressel.

The following were subsequently mustered into the company, viz.:

Privates: John Creamer, Armistead Henderson, Alexander Ramsay, Henry Heft, and Chas. Heidelbach.

Under the Act of Congress before referred to, the field and company officers of the volunteers accepted under the call were to be appointed and commissioned according to the laws of the State from whence they came; and I, with my two lieutenants, were commissioned by his Excellency, Thomas G. Pratt, Governor of the State of Maryland.

The organization to which I was attached was designated "THE BATTALION OF BALTIMORE AND WASHINGTON VOLUNTEERS," and which became subsequently widely and well known as "THE OLD BALTIMORE BATTALION." It was composed of six companies of infantry; four of them having been recruited in Baltimore, and two of them in the city of Washington, District of Columbia. They were officered as follows:

Company A, from Baltimore: Captain, James E. Steuart; Lieutenants, Benjamin Ferguson Owens and Samuel Wilt; add'l. Second Lieutenant, David P. Chapman.

Company B, from Baltimore: Captain, James Piper; Lieutenants, Lawrence, Dolan, and Marcellus K. Taylor; add'l. Second Lieutenant, Isaac H. Marrow.

Company C, from Washington: Captain, Robert Bronaugh; Lieutenants, Phineas B. Bell, William O'Brien, Thomas M. Gleason.

Company D, from Washington: Captain, John Waters; Lieutenants, Wm. I. Parham, Eugene Boyle, Edward Murphy.

Company E, from Baltimore: Captain, John R. Kenly; Lieutenants, Francis B. Schaeffer and Oden Bowie; add'l. Second Lieutenant, William E. Aisquith.

Company F,* from Baltimore: Captain, James Boyd; Lieutenants, Joseph H. Ruddach and Robert E. Haslett; add'l. Second Lieutenant, James Taneyhill.

---

* Chesapeake Rifles.

The whole under the command of Lieutenant-Colonel William H. Watson, its only field officer.

My commission bore date the 4th day of June, 1846; and on the 13th of the same month I was on board the transport steamer Massachusetts, bound for the seat of war in Mexico, with as brave a set of men as ever wore the uniform of the United States army. The battalion was of the best material for the service and the country in which it was to be engaged, but lacked trained officers to set it up and make soldiers of its rank and file. This, time and the effect of war brought about, and I lived to see the battalion second to none in the volunteer arm of the service in appearance and efficiency.

The thread of my memoirs is now taken up from notes, letters, and diary, mostly made and written as the events occurred.

June 10, 1846. The battalion was ordered by the Secretary of War to leave the Marine Barracks, where it had been quartered, for Fort Washington, on the banks of the Potomac River, seven miles below the town of Alexandria. The cause of this unexpected order was an application from the mayor of the city of Washington, who had been incensed at the bad behavior of some of the men, and who, as it was alleged, had entered into a personal quarrel with them, in which, as may well be supposed, he was not much the gainer.

June 13. Left the fort, and embarked on board the steamer Powhattan, and at 8 o'clock P.M. arrived alongside the steamer Massachusetts, lying in the river, which had been chartered by the Government to convey our battalion and a large amount of stores to Point Isabel, in the Gulf of Mexico. It had been raining hard all day, and suddenly five hundred men were thrown upon a steamer of seven hundred tons' burden, whose hold and deck were filled and covered with forage and other military stores. A scene of indescribable confusion ensued, which the darkness seemed to swell and magnify; and no repose was had on that night of chaos, except that which was obtained through pure exhaustion.

June 14. We were in such a condition to-day that, although it was Sunday, we were forced to drop down the river about two miles below Alexandria, in order to make an effort to clear the decks of the ship, and keep the men on board from the allurements of their friends, male and female, who had followed them from Washington and Baltimore. Berths had been prepared for two hundred men; these were in the main hold, over the bulk of the Government freight; no accommodations whatever were provided for the balance of the troops. Carpenters were now put to work, and a series of bunks were constructed on the main deck, running from the quarter deck, on either side of the ship, forward to the forecastle, which were constructed so as to contain the largest number of soldiers, and yet permit the seamen to work ship. These bunks were a frightful source of disorder, and were the cause of much trouble on the voyage, between the soldiers and the sailors. We had a very riotous night; but, all the officers being put upon guard duty, we managed to hold our own, although it was rough work.

June 15. Every preparation being made to weigh anchor; all hurry, bustle and confusion. An effort was made to clear the ship by mustering all that were to sail on the upper deck—my men behaving (as I afterwards learned soldiers become) more like children than grown men; one wanted a pen, another a sheet of paper, one wanted me to read a letter just received, another wanted me to write one for him, another wanted me to send his money home, another wanted me to keep it for him, one wanted a wafer, another ink, one complained that his uniform was too large, another that *his* was too small, one said that he was sick and wanted me to give him medicine, another that he couldn't find the surgeon—not to be wondered at, for in the mob that was at that time on board that ship one's own identity was almost lost.

June 16. Our ship got under weigh at 8 o'clock this morning, and immediately a change for the better came over every man on board the Massachusetts. Hurra! we are fairly started for the seat of war! such was the joyous greeting which fell from the bright faces and smiling lips of all those who now crowded the decks of the transport. At 9 A.M., abreast of Mount Vernon. Hats off, boys! SILENCE, fore and aft! and thus we floated past the grave of WASHINGTON.

At 6 P.M. we were off Piney Point, and fired a salute as we entered the Chesapeake. Our officers still keeping guard, we had a more quiet night.

June 17. At 9 A.M., off the capes, the pilot left us, carrying a large bag of letters. A delightful morning, but a long swell rolling in is making the landsmen among our soldiers (there were many seamen among them; in my own company there were five men who had been several years in the United States naval service before volunteering with me) feel the premonitions of sea-sickness. To-day our decks were scoured, well washed, and some degree of military discipline attempted.

June 18. At 10 o'clock last night we were off Cape Hatteras—that dread of all mariners; we gave it a wide berth, though we could distinctly see its lighthouse. At 4 A.M. the moon rose, and the sea looked like a mass of molten gold; nothing disturbed its repose in my morning watch but the play of dolphins and the dance of Mother Carey's chickens, the petrel of the wide Atlantic. A fine run to-day, using both wind and steam to urge us forward.

June 19. Delightful breezes, and making rapid progress. At 9 A.M. saw a large vessel, which made signals to close; bore away for her, and all was excitement, an opinion being prevalent that she was a letter of marque, with a Mexican commission. No one could doubt the earnest wish of our men that she might prove to be an enemy, but, on speaking, she turned out to be an American ship. At 3 P.M. a beautiful pilot boat, No. 2, came gracefully alongside, and asked if we wished a pilot for Charleston; large shoals of porpoises around us this afternoon. At 6 P.M., wind increasing, all sail was set and steam dispensed with; during the night the wind increased to a hurricane, and the rain descended in torrents; passed several vessels flying before the wind; during the blow, I was called upon to quell a serious fight among my own men. Knives were used, blood spilt, and we arrested the offenders. Rum was the cause of all the trouble.

June 20. Calm this morning, and the decks covered with sea-sick soldiers, that last night's pitching had placed *hors du combat;* dolphins playing around the ship, as if to charm us with their freedom and grace. At 4 P.M. the wind suddenly commenced blowing violently, causing the ship again to pitch frightfully. During the night, despite the rolling of the ship, a pretty general free fight occurred in the hold among the men, which was difficult to quell; but the officers uniting and mutually assisting each other, were, backed by their authority, too strong for the rioters. We now saw the impolicy of having had the men paid their advance-money (some twenty dollars to each volunteer) before we sailed from Alexandria. There was a large quantity of liquor *somewhere* on board, and the subaltern officers of the steamer, either directly, or indirectly through the sailors, sold quantities to our men, which made them mutinous and disorderly; it would not have been the case had there been no money to buy whisky with.

June 21—Sunday. Progressing finely. At 12 o'clock, noon, latitude 30° 9′ north, and laying our course for Abaco, one of the Bahama Islands; ship rolling, and decks literally jammed full of sea-sick soldiers; saw that misery did not like company.

June 22. A heavy squall this morning, which laid the ship over and wet everything; got sick to-day, but ascribed it to sympathy for others; the wind being adverse, had to resort to our propeller, which screwed us along nobly. At 6.30 P.M. a topsail schooner came bearing down upon us, and the feverish excitement incident to the beginning or first stages of a war, which had made our newspapers filled with rumors of *privateers* swarming in the Gulf of Mexico, was now very apparent among our raw soldiers. *Of course* she was a privateer, but this was a very cowardly one; for as soon as those who had charge of her made out the number of men about our decks, a change was made in her course as swiftly as possible; she went about, and ran with all the speed that was in her. We pursued with steam, and overhauled her, when, with a backed topsail, she threw out the Cross of St. George, and the meteor flag of Old England was floating over the schooner Evander, from Nassau for New York. She was a beautiful craft, and I never saw anything on the sea more attractive than the picture presented as she rolled gracefully on the long swell of the ocean—the setting sun mellowing everything, and sea and sky in harmony with their glowing, yet dissolving and varied, colors, chasing each other into the shadows of night. She was loaded with fruit, and the captain of the steamer permitted his mate to visit her to make purchases. Nearly every man had a commission for him to execute, and the mate returned with his boat filled with pineapples and bananas, for which he had to give, as he said, a *sea-price:* four dollars a bunch for bananas, twenty-five cents apiece for pineapples. I gave a lot of the bananas to such of the men as had no money, and to those who were sick.

June 23. Our captain this morning said that we

had *lost sixty miles* easting, and that we would reach Abaco to-night; calm all day, and delightful weather; the sick getting well, and all in good spirits.

June 24. At 4 A.M., off the revolving light on Abaco. We had passed the "Hole in the Wall," a rock at one of the points of the island, before it was day enough to make out, but I saw where it *ought* to be. The sea was as smooth and polished as a mirror this morning, and the island lay in all the beauty of the tropics, its undulating shores, wooded to the beach, reflected and reproduced upon its bosom, while heavy clouds, piled like mountains in the background, were being gilded, burnished, and made gorgeous, with the rays of the rising sun. At 6 A.M. we were in sight of Berry Island, another of the Bahama group; beautiful water-fowl were floating about us on the smooth surface of the sea and shoals, or rather flocks of flying-fish were leaping and sporting in the two elements of air and water. At 9 A.M. we were east of the Berry Islands, and a negro man came off in a boat to us, bringing fresh fish, milk, eggs, sponge, and shells for sale, which were soon all disposed of. The fish were curious to us in shape and color, and made excellent pan-fish, as we all agreed, in *this* matter at least, at dinner time.

So far all had gone well, but a fearful danger was in close proximity. At 2 o'clock P.M. we were going along with a nine-knot breeze, when two large rocks hove in sight, which proved to be a couple of *keys*, known by the name of "Little Isaacs," the breakers tossing madly over them. The men commenced looking over the sides of the ship in excited nervous manner, talking loudly, and it was soon generally known that we were running with our keel pretty close to the bottom of the sea; large rocks were plainly discernible beneath the water, and an uneasy feeling spread through the ship. Still we flew along, little dreaming that our captain was utterly lost, as he subsequently admitted that he was, when, being just abreast of the Little Isaacs, our ship *struck.* Again she struck, still harder, bringing every man to his knees who had been standing upon his feet, and producing a panic terror such as I hope never again to see. Again she struck, and this time remained hard and fast upon the rocks beneath us, except, being lifted by the swell of the ocean, she would settle again, with a thump which strained every timber in her, and every human being on board, to their utmost tension. The captain screamed and shouted, the men cried, prayed, and ran wildly about the decks; some jumped into the quarter-boats which hung upon the davits, others stripped themselves of clothing, no one doubted but that she would go to pieces. The captain threw himself upon his knees in the most abject terror. I both saw and heard him crying that all was lost.

No one assumed command, no one issued an order; every instant we expected the masts to go over the sides, and our bottom to be crushed in; when, no one can tell how it *was* done, but the men, that is, our soldiers who had been men-of-warsmen, lowered a sail on the mizen mast, called a spanker, which being immediately filled by the wind, the ship *rolled off*—I can describe the sensation I felt in no other way—the rocks upon which we had been imbedded, and glided into deeper water. We were still in great danger from these hidden perils, and all confidence was lost in the navigation of the ship. The wind increased in violence, yet we had to carry every rag of canvas in order to weather the "Great Isaacs," another group of keys some thirteen miles from where we had struck; it commenced raining very hard, and by 6 P.M. it was perfectly dark, the ship rushing like a race-horse through the water, with her bulwarks careened to its surface, under the force of the gale which was blowing. It was an awful night, and I realized for the first time the indescribable sensation and effect caused by darkness and the vicinity of danger, when men are massed together. About midnight the captain, who had somewhat recovered his lost manhood, said that he thought we were now safe and clear of the keys. Under the mercy of the Almighty, we owed our safety to those who had built the Massachusetts; it was her strong timbers and sound hull that had saved us from a frightful end. We all felt, and all said, that we owed our lives to the steamer Massachusetts, and our imminent peril to those who navigated her.

June 25. At 4 A.M. I went on deck, the ship still reeling on the heavy sea, though the wind had abated its violence. The sun rose like a globe of fire, casting an angry glance on the turbulent waves, and a large ship down to the leeward added to the grandeur of the scene. It soon began to rain, and the wind rose again: we progressed rapidly, and about 12 o'clock, noon, we saw land on our lee-bow; it was the "Carysford Reef," upon which a light-boat was riding at anchor; at 4 P.M. we were sailing slowly along the shores of Florida, still anxious about weathering these well-known and dangerous reefs, the current drifting us nearer and nearer to the shore as the wind died away.

June 26. On coming to the deck this morning I found it raining, and the vessel moving quite rapidly under steam-power, which had been resorted to during the night by reason of the calm and our proximity to the shore; at noon we were off Key West, whose houses and shipping were visible as we lay off and on waiting for a pilot. The sea was now as smooth as glass, and the heat of the sun oppressive; Key West and its island home, floating upon the bosom of the Gulf as Venice amid its lagoons; and three or four large cotton-ships were in our vicinity, lazily yielding to the gentle motion of the tide.

While we were at dinner one of the soldiers caught a dolphin, and I gazed with pain at its unrivaled colors. It was four feet in length, and looked as if it had been gilded, then spotted with blue globes of glass; as it flapped out its existence on the deck of our dirty transport, the gold and blue would fade, and then reappear with almost their original lustre and beauty, until the discoloration of death closed my first (as it will certainly be my last) view of the dying dolphin. It was a painful sight to me.

The pilot who came on board told us that the port of Tampico had been blockaded by our fleet, and we sent by him a package of letters for home.

At 4 P.M. we were once more out of sight of land,—

the sea still smooth, no wind,—and making good progress, under steam, across the Gulf of Mexico.

June 28—Sunday. We have been making good headway for the past twenty-four hours, the sea still smooth; and we have thus been able to use our propeller, which, it seems, as we have been suspecting, don't work when the sea is rough. The heat is very great, the thermometer (Fahrenheit) ranging from ninety to ninety-one degrees in the coolest place on the ship, while it stands several degrees higher in the cabin: we, the officers, all sleep on deck without any covering. We have had a good deal of trouble about the allowance of water to the men; the whole arrangement was very bad, and constant quarrels, with hard fighting, have been going on for the past forty-eight hours. We are all now just as anxious to get out of the ship as we were to get on board.

June 29—six o'clock P.M. Since yesterday there has not been much change in the atmosphere, ocean, or anything else, except perhaps a greater desire to get on shore. It is exceedingly hot, and the crowded state of our decks (there are upwards of six hundred men on board this ship of seven hundred tons), with a tropical sun blazing upon us, and the heat engendered by the fiery furnaces in the ship, with the fear that our water will give out,—the men already fighting for their turns to obtain their rations,—and the sick list swelling at a fearful rate, make us anxious and apprehensive; for if our steam-power were to fail us the thing would be up, as there is no doubt but that our water is being rapidly exhausted. Our ship has been twice on fire from the cooking arrangements of the men *on deck*, there having been no places provided for fires to cook with prior to leaving on our voyage, and those improvised being very insecure and a constant source of apprehension, and justly as it turned out to my mind.

I believe that I have heretofore said our men were paid an advance of some twenty dollars each before leaving Alexandria. I estimate that about one-half of the sum paid them, say five thousand dollars, was brought on board the Massachusetts. From the first hour they came on board until the present time, by day and by night, except when we were in such peril on the reefs, *gambling* has been going on under every shape and device that skill can suggest; and it has been a curious subject of study and interest with me to watch how rapidly the gold and silver was passing from the many to the few. In less than a week nearly all the money was in the hands of about fifty men; now I am sure that the bulk of the five thousand dollars is in the pockets, or belonging to, not more than twenty of our battalion, if so many. So that in two weeks the money belonging to say three hundred and fifty men (some one hundred of our men did not gamble), confined upon one ship, had been won or got from them by not more than a dozen of their comrades, and from my observation I am sure that, had the voyage lasted another week, *all* the money of those who gambled would have been possessed by two or three. Surely there is an affinity more or less strong between certain men and money.

It may be asked, why was this gambling suffered, as it was the fruitful cause of the almost continuous fighting in the hold of the ship? The answer is plain: what else were they to do in the crowded pen they were shut up in? Positively there was barely space or room to lie down anywhere, and those who kept awake playing cards gave room to the others, and opportunity to get a little sleep. Taking into consideration all the discomforts which the men suffered, and the unwarrantable scantiness of the supplies, they behaved well, and generally speaking were respectful to their officers. If they had been forbidden to play, the order could not have been enforced in the hive which swarmed on board our ship.

June 30. Hot, hotter, hottest! Not a breath of wind, but steaming ahead rapidly; all day long we have been panting under the burning rays of the sun, but indulging in hopes that land would soon be in sight, so that at least we might not famish for want of water. We are told that we will make the mouth of the Rio Grande some time to-morrow, should no accident happen to our machinery or ship. The little remaining water in our tanks smells worse than it is possible to imagine any fluid could smell, yet we wish there was more of it. My goodness! it seems so strange to me *now* that any one should ever waste water.

CHAPTER II.

ARRIVAL AT THE BRAZOS SANTIAGO.

July 1. After seventeen days' confinement, there is now a prospect of a happy release from this ship. The island of Brazos is now in sight. At 3 P.M. we anchored outside of the breakers, which were wildly dashing on the sandy beach. A Government steamer came out an hour after our arrival, and took three companies of our troops on shore. This was my last night on board the steamer, and a magnificent one it was in the heavens above and the earth and the sea around and about us, and I was about being gratified in the earnest longing of my heart—to be a soldier.

July 2. At this 6 A.M. a steamer came alongside, under the management of Major Lyons, of the Louisiana Brigade, and my company was transported to the island, upon which I landed, and, forming on the beach under a burning sun, which peeled me as soon, and as if done with, scalding water, marched under orders a short distance up the beach, and halted on some sand-hills, where, having as yet no shelter, we passed the night upon the sand, supperless, bedless, with a foretaste of what was in store for us.

I had worked very hard this day, though but partially successful, trying to get my stores, tents, and company property ashore, and the heat of the sun had nearly prostrated me; but I was full of life and of health, and my whole heart was in the business I had undertaken. Fortunately we had found water, although brackish, by digging into the sand and sinking wells not far from the edge of the Gulf, and the men generally were as full of life and spirits as I was; so my first day in the *field* was one of good hope, despite the grumbling and discontent of some.

July 3. I had time to look round me this morning, and found the island a small sand spit, lying a few miles north of the mouth of the Rio Grande, and at the outlet of the Laguna—or *bay* as we would call it —del Madre, and distant a mile or so from the mainland. Immediately north is another but larger island, named Padre Island, between which and the mainland the waters of this Laguna or Bay del Madre make in from the Gulf of Mexico, and pass out by the Brazos Santiago, lying as before said at its mouth. Point Isabel is in sight, distant three miles up the lagoon. Upon this point is the Government depot of supplies for the army of General Taylor. Upon the island not a blade of grass or vegetation is growing—nothing but sand, and seaward the wrecks of five vessels add to the general misery of the landscape. Small as is the area, several thousand volunteers from Missouri, Tennessee, Alabama, Mississippi, and Louisiana are lying with us, waiting for orders. Though the sun was gathering strength hourly, from the heated rays reflected from the burning sands there was no shelter whatever for my men, and most of them threw themselves into the breakers, which tumbled with unceasing roar upon the beach, for the grateful luxury of a bath. Here I had the misfortune to lose one of my men, drowned in the breakers despite the desperate efforts made by his comrades to save him. His name was Richard H. Belt, from Carroll County, Maryland; and his body neatly sewed up in a blanket we buried, after the burial service of the Episcopal Church had been read by me, in a grave scooped out of the sand-hill on the edge of the Gulf. Three volleys fired by a platoon of soldiers closed the funeral ceremonies, and next morning not a sign could we perceive of the grave or of the hill in which it had been dug, —all blown away by the wind, which shifts these hills as it does the snow-drifts of northern climes.

July 4. This day one year ago I was playing soldier at Westminster, Maryland, with the Eagle Artillery Company of Baltimore; now, to say the least of it, things are very different; busy, very busy, issuing arms and accoutrements, ammunition, mess-pans, and the other etcetera known to captains of companies. The heat of the sun almost unsupportable, but not as much shelter from its rays as a blade of grass would afford,—no tents yet. We buried one of Captain Piper's men to-day in the sand.

July 5. Slept on an arms-chest last night, and arose this morning feeling very unwell; but I kept at work during the day, and shoved off a spell of sickness. After nightfall we buried in the sand one of Captain Steuart's men; this time the grave was hollowed at the top of the hill, around whose sides clustered the members of his company. A fire had been built in the vicinity, to give light. The sea was tumbling in on the beach with deafening roar, whilst the moon would now and then burst from behind a bank of clouds, lighting up, with the rays from the fire, the men who with uncovered heads were trying to catch the words of the burial service, which it was impossible to hear for the noise of the surf. It was a solemn and impressive scene, producing a marked effect upon the rough men gathered around the grave of a comrade, thus cut off away from home and kindred, and thus buried where to-morrow no one might find his final resting-place.

July 6. I paid a visit, by boat, to Point Isabel, on the other side of the lagoon. I found the troops here in excellent order, very different from our state on the Brazos. Things looked tidy and military. Visited the hospital, and was much affected by the appearance of the wounded Mexicans, they looked so sad and pitiable, and will not soon forget the look of gratitude which one gave me when I brushed off from his wounded stump, to which the sheet was fastened with clotted gore, the flies which had settled upon it. I also whilst here got copies of the following

PROCLAMATIONS ISSUED BY THE MEXICANS.

Shortly after arriving opposite Matamoras, the following proclamation was circulated through the American camp.

" *The Commander-in-Chief of the Mexican Army to the English and Irish under the American General Taylor.*

" KNOW YE : That the Government of the United States is committing repeated acts of barbarous aggression against the magnanimous Mexican nation ; that the Government which exists 'under the flag of the stars' is unworthy the designation of Christian. Recollect that you were born in Great Britain, that the American Government looks with coldness upon the powerful flag of England, and is provoking to a rupture the warlike people to whom it belongs, President Polk boldly manifesting a desire to take possession of Oregon as he has already done of Texas. Now then come with all confidence to the Mexican ranks, and I guarantee to you, upon my honor, good treatment, and that all your expenses shall be defrayed until your arrival in the beautiful capital of Mexico.

"Germans, French, Poles, and individuals of other nations! separate yourselves from the Yankees, and do not contribute to defend a robbery and usurpation which, be assured, the civilized nations of Europe look upon with the utmost indignation. Come, therefore, and array yourselves under the tri-colored flag,* in the confidence that the God of Armies protects it, and that it will protect you, equally with the English.

"PEDRO DE AMPUDIA.

"FRANCISCO R. MORENO, Adjutant of the Commander-in-Chief.
"Head-Quarters upon the road to Matamoras, April 2, 1846."

On the twenty-first of the same month, April, the following proclamation was also circulated among the American soldiers, intended, like the former, to make them betray their country.

"HEAD-QUARTERS AT MATAMORAS,
"April 20, 1846.

"SOLDIERS! You have enlisted in a time of peace to serve in that army for a specific time; but your obligations never implied that you were bound to violate the laws of God, and the most sacred right of friends. The United States Government, contrary to the wishes of a majority of all honest and honorable Americans, has ordered you to take *forcible* possession of the territory of a *friendly* neighbor, who has never given her consent to such occupation. In other words, while the treaty of peace and commerce between Mexico and the United States is in full force, the United States, presuming on her strength and prosperity, and on our supposed imbecility and cowardice, attempts to make you the blind instruments of her unholy and mad ambition, and *force* you to appear as the hateful robbers of our dear homes, and the

* The Mexican flag was red, white, and green.

unprovoked violators of our dearest feelings as men and patriots. Such villany and outrage I know is perfectly repugnant to the noble sentiments of any gentleman, and it is base and foul to rush you on to certain death, in order to aggrandise a few lawless individuals in defiance of the laws of God and man.

"It is to no purpose if they tell you that the law for the annexation of Texas justifies your occupation of the Rio Bravo del Norte, for by this act they rob us of a great part of Tamaulipas, Coahuila, Chihuaha, and New Mexico; and it is barbarous to send a handful of men on such an errand against a powerful and warlike nation. Besides, most of you are Europeans, and we are the *declared friends* of most of the nations of *Europe*. The North Americans are ambitious, overbearing, and insolent as a nation, and they will only make use of you as vile tools to carry out their abominable plans of pillage and rapine.

"I warn you in the name of justice, honor, and your own interests and self-respect, to abandon their desperate and unholy cause, and become *peaceful Mexican* citizens. I guarantee you in such a case a half-section of land, or three hundred and twenty acres, to settle upon gratis. Be wise then, and just, and honorable, and take no part in murdering us who have no unkind feelings for you. Lands shall be given to officers, sergeants, and corporals, according to rank, privates receiving three hundred and twenty acres as stated.

"If in time of action you wish to espouse our cause, throw away your arms and run to us, and we will embrace you as true friends and Christians. It is not decent or prudent to say more. But should any of you render important service to Mexico, you shall be accordingly considered and preferred.

"(Signed) "M. ARISTA,
"Commander-in-Chief of the Mexican Army."

July 9. Took up our line of march for the invasion of Mexico, and reached the Rio Grande, or Rio Bravo del Norte, distant eight miles from where we had landed on the Brazos. We crossed the Boca Chica, an arm of the sea, about 500 yards wide, which separates the island of Brazos Santiago from the mainland, and which makes in from the Gulf of Mexico to the Laguna del Madre, and through which also the waters of the latter communicate with the Gulf.

Our road lay for two miles through a desert of sand, the sun blazing down upon us with an intensity of heat never before experienced; we then struck the beach, upon which, the sand being harder, the men marched with more ease; we forded the Boca Chica, the water averaging about three feet in depth. The sea was very grateful to our parched skin, but it was very difficult to advance through, and the line of troops became straggling and disordered. Another hour's marching brought us to the river, within fifty yards of which we bivouacked, in rear of a Tennessee regiment. This was our first march, and no one who made it will ever forget it. I felt as if I were on fire, my nose being one blister, and my hands apparently scorched, and feeling just that way.

July 10. Face much swollen this morning; so much so that my eyes are nearly closed, and face feels as if it were burning; a good deal alarmed, until our surgeon told me it was only an effect of the fatigue and exposure of yesterday. The mosquitoes troubled us all a good deal last night, and the men, generally, out of sorts to-day.

July 12—Sunday. Still at the mouth of the Rio Grande, or Boca del Rio, as the Mexicans call it, which means mouth of the river; and a very picturesque place it is. But this cannot account for the halt in our advance. Last night I went wolf-hunting, but saw none, though we heard plenty. Shot a couple of plover by moonlight, and ate them this morning for breakfast. There appears to be a great deal of game in this country, and various kinds of fish are found in the lagoons, some large enough to be *bayoneted* by the men, and some are knocked in the head with clubs*—all good eating; at any rate the soldiers prefer them to salt beef and pork.

July 16. Still at the mouth of the Rio Grande; and we are well enough satisfied, but can't account for the unexpected delay to our advance. There is one serious trouble here, and that is the mosquitoes. We really get but little sleep, and our camp at night is filled with men wandering about for shelter from these intolerable pests, and filling the air with imprecations upon their ruthless assailants. No kind of clothing is proof or protection against their bites; they pierce through, with their stings, pantaloons, drawers, stockings, and (some deliberately assert) boots. All night long, without the slightest intermission, they continue their attacks, and the assertion of many that they are nearly driven crazy is not much exaggerated.

This morning three companies of the Tennessee volunteers, encamped with us, left for up the river, and we are in hopes that our turn will soon come. Already this place shows the advance of the Anglo-Saxon race: steamboats and schooners arriving and departing daily, discharging provisions, stores, and troops for the "army of occupation," as some have been pleased to call Taylor's troops. To-day a company of strolling

* This is a camp *fish story.*

players, bound for Matamoras, and hailing from New Orleans, stopped at the landing. I must confess to looking upon them with much interest, and—must I say it?—with pity. The *ladies* of the troupe gratified the men of our troop by casting bottles of wine from the steamer's deck into their midst, whilst to add to the *hilarity of the occasion*, they graciously sang for them a few of their favorite airs. Ah, me! poor women! Though full of apparent gayety, my heart bled for them.

July 18. I crossed the river this morning in a ship's quarter-boat, and stepped upon undisputed Mexican soil. There was quite a little town here once, called Bagdad (I wonder if the Tigris were ever such a river as this angry, muddy, crooked Rio Grande!) but some seventeen years ago a hurricane destroyed it, with two thousand of its inhabitants. It is still called after its name, but instead of houses there are but wretched cabins, in which dwell fifty or sixty natives, called in the language of the country *rancheros*, whose business, from all I could learn, was herding or having in charge herds of cattle, which grazed in the neighborhood. When we got back we learned that a corporal of a company of regulars stationed at the landing had been murdered during our absence, by a prisoner of his own company whom he had under guard; his burial took place this evening—this is the fourth since we landed.

July 19. This morning it commenced raining, accompanied with a violent wind, and in a short time our low land was completely flooded; directly in front and rear of my company the water collected in pools of from one to two feet deep, whilst everything in my tent was rendered damp and disagreeable by the incessant rain. The wind howled around us, and the surf thundered on the shore; large flocks of sea-birds flew overhead, and the ponds of water within a few yards of our camp were covered with plover, snipe, and curlews. In the course of the day we had to change the location of some of the tents, as they were flooded with water.

July 20. Still raining; but before noon the sun came out, and we dried our clothing and blankets. A regiment of Alabama volunteers arrived to-day, and encamped upon our left; they are a fine-looking set of men.

July 22. A regiment of Louisiana volunteers arrived to-day, from Matamoras, en route for home; it is a portion of the volunteers called forth by General Taylor, whose term of three months' service is about expiring; the officers were very indignant that the General would not accept their offer to continue in the service and re-volunteer for twelve months.

July 23. Left the mouth of the river, and, ascending the left bank, after a distressing march of fourteen or fifteen miles over a country flooded by the recent rains and a rise of the Rio Grande, reached our camping ground opposite to the Mexican town of Burita.

July 24. Our camp was pitched upon a ridge well covered with chaparral and well filled with rattlesnakes; we cleared out both, and our men, having got up their tents and killed some wild cattle, were soon comfortable with fresh beef and rest.

July 25. The delay in obtaining transportation

for army purposes has compelled General Taylor to postpone his advance; and, to preserve the health of his troops, whose numbers are daily increasing from the continuous arrival of twelve months' men, he has ordered their encampment upon the highlands skirting the river between this and Matamoras. It is a wilderness upon which the foot of man has rarely trod; wild cattle and horses are running over the prairie lands which skirt this ridge on either side to the river, and the lagoons which chequer the flats are filled with red-winged flamingo,—the ibis of the Egyptians,—wild geese, duck, and other aquatic fowl; on the long branches of the willow-like trees were birds swarming, and warbling their peaceful melodies, and the open grounds were flowered with all variety of cacti and the Spanish bayonet-plant. The background of the open vista wore the ever-varying colors of the dense chaparral, while the broad and swollen torrent of the Rio Grande flowed between us and the town of Burita, around whose adobe houses the white tents of our volunteers were pitched, adding interest by their contrast to the novel country in which we were now sojourning.

July 26—Sunday. Having received an invitation from Captain Arnold, Second United States Dragoons, I crossed the river to Burita, and dined with him. Here I met my old friend Randolph Ridgely, of Baltimore, now a lieutenant in the late Captain Ringgold's Battery of Light Artillery, and who had particularly distinguished himself in the battles of the 8th and 9th of May—Palo Alto, and Resaca de la Palma. After dinner we had a horse-race between Colonel Bailie

Peyton, of the Louisiana Volunteers, and Randolph Ridgely, in which Peyton's horse won: which he would not have done, as Ridgely laughingly said, if the race-course had been the road towards the enemy.

July 28. Our camp was the scene of a fearful riot to-day, and one which came near being a bloody battle between our battalion and the First Ohio regiment of volunteers. The difficulty commenced on the banks of the river, about a catfish which had just been caught, and was claimed by men of both regiments. A fight ensued, when Colonel Mitchell, the commanding officer of the Ohio regiment, interfered, and, drawing his sword, cut one of our men in several places. His sword was soon taken from him, broken in pieces, and he came to camp. I saw him approaching, heard him order his men to parade with ball-cartridges, and they were soon hurrying in large numbers, without any semblance of formation, to the river bank, loading their muskets as they ran. At the same time the cry was raised, "Turn out, Baltimoreans!" in our camp; the men seized their guns, loaded them, and singly and in squads hastened down to the river after the Ohio men, to help our men there who were armed. Some of our officers, seized with the same frenzy as the men, behaved in the most outrageous manner, issuing cartridges in person, and inciting their companies to hurry into the approaching battle. Colonel Watson was absent, and somehow or other I took the whole responsibility on myself; keeping my own company in their company street, with the assurance that if the fight commenced they should go to help their comrades. I ran among the most violent, and between those who were about to fire into each other, and, by commands and entreaties, kept them from firing. I knew that one shot would be the signal of a bloody struggle, and fortunately at this moment Lieutenant-Colonel John B. Weller, of the Ohio regiment, came upon the ground. I shall never forget how his behavior relieved me; I saw him coming, and feared that he was as crazy as the others; and if he had been, there's no telling where would have been the end of that day's work. His first order was for the men to go back to camp, and that the officers of the two regiments would settle the difficulty; this brought our ranking officer, Captain James E. Steuart, and Colonel Mitchell, to the front, and they were personally friendly. Soon other officers joined the group, and, forming a line between the two bodies of men (who by this time had arranged themselves in order of battle), we got them away from their lines, and finally back to camp.

On the same night Colonel Mitchell proceeded to Matamoras, to lay a complaint before General Taylor against the Baltimore Battalion; thereupon Colonel Watson ordered Captain Steuart and me to go there also, to rebut any charges which Mitchell might make.

July 29. Crossed over to Burita, and bought a mustang pony for six dollars, to ride to Matamoras; but, a steamer coming along, preferred that way of travelling as not being quite so dangerous, apart from all other reasons. Went on board the steamer Virginia, and ascended the Rio Grande to Matamoras. I had seen and heard tell of the crookedness of this grand river, but there is no way of showing how tortuous is its course except by the illustration given by an Alabama volunteer; he said "he had seen a crow fly from the top of a tree, follow up the course of the river for fifteen minutes, then light; and it *lit* on the same tree it had started from."*

For several miles above Burita both banks were lined with the white tents of the volunteers scattered along at intervals, where good camping-ground was to be found; soon, however, these disappeared, and were succeeded by groves of plantain, willow-cotton, and other southern trees. We "pulled up" for the night at a rancho on the river bank, at about thirty miles by the river below the city. It was at this point the Mexicans, four thousand strong, had crossed the river to intercept and cut General Taylor's communications with Point Isabel.

July 30. Arrived at the city of Matamoras, and, accompanied by Lieutenant Randolph Ridgely, who had kindly volunteered to introduce us, proceeded at once to General Taylor's quarters. We found the old

---

* The windings of the Rio Grande are remarkable. There is one hacienda on its banks which a boat passes in front of seven times after coming in sight of, and before actually reaching it, —the river making seven close convolutions east and west in perhaps twelve miles of country; and there is one of the turns where you pass a long low bank for five miles, and can look over and see the river again not one hundred feet from you on the other edge. Thus, after sailing in reality ten miles along the voyager has actually only advanced two hundred yards. The same writer says that the river at Camargo presented the same appearance as it did a thousand miles above.—*A Campaign in New Mexico*, by Frank S. Edwards.

general writing in a tent, around which was strewed large numbers of newspapers, and before which—I was struck with the fact—no guard was stationed. He came out to receive us, when Ridgely, after introducing us, left the place. I opened the business, and gave our version of the difficulty with the Ohio volunteers. As I progressed, the general looked very black, and I argued very unfavorably for the success of our mission; but when I told him that my company had been kept in camp, and had not participated in the riot (although, in point of fact, it was commenced by one of my own soldiers; of this, however, I was ignorant at the time), his countenance lightened up a little. When I had got through with my statement, the general said "it was an unfortunate occurrence, but inasmuch as the whole matter would be referred to a court of inquiry, Colonel Mitchell having preferred charges against some of our officers and men, he would wait until their finding was made known before he would take any further notice of it—and to hold ourselves in readiness to march to Camargo in eight or ten days."*

The conclusion of his reply—"to hold ourselves in readiness to march"—so warmed my heart to the general, that he made me his friend at that instant; for it should be remarked that rumor had it we were to be disbanded. I was much taken also with his simplicity of manner, the total absence of all preten-

* No court was ever ordered, as far as I know, and the whole matter was dropped *officially;* but the embers of discontent remained smouldering, and at times manifesting themselves, between the two regiments, as long as we were in the service.

sion in dress and address, and the unmistakable regret which he showed that he felt, at this serious difficulty between the volunteers of his army.

We returned to Ridgely's tent, where we dined, and then walked from camp into the city. Matamoras is an old Spanish town on the right bank of the Rio Grande, about forty miles from its mouth, and, though bearing marks of decay, is still the second town in importance in Northern Mexico. It covers about two miles square, but is not compactly built as are American cities, every house, except in the main plaza or public square, having a large garden surrounding it. All the windows of the houses in the business part of the town are grated from top to bottom with iron bars, which gives them the appearance of prisons.

The plaza, in the centre of the city, has on three of its sides very respectable blocks of houses, occupied by the merchants, and on its other side a cathedral, which, though unfinished, presents a venerable, church-like look. After leaving the plaza the houses decrease in size for some distance, until the small reed and thatched huts terminate in the suburbs. All of the more wealthy inhabitants had fled the city after the defeat of their army at Resaca, for it swarmed with the robbers and desperadoes cut loose from the military bands, and now organized for plunder. All military and civil law ended with the defeat of Arista, and the inhabitants of Matamoras suffered more horrors from these outlaws than they would have done from a long siege.

The stores on the plaza were now occupied by American merchants, sutlers, *tavern-keepers*, billiard-rooms, etc., which were crowded with soldiers; and the indescribable bedlam which the picture presented will not soon be forgotten. Many of the houses show the effect of our cannonading from Fort Brown on the other side of the river, and I saw two thirty-two-pound balls lying in a yard, where, after passing entirely through several houses, they were now lying quietly side by side, as harmless as the dead.

I went into the market, and here the scene was entirely native. A row of women were sitting on their haunches, with crocks of milk before them, from which they sold the milk by the cupfull to their purchasers; others in the same position, selling little parcels of eggs,—three in a pile,—red peppers, peaches, melons of several varieties, and many kinds of vegetables unknown by name or sight. Game of various kinds was being carried about for sale and the prices cried out with melodious voices. Others were engaged cooking for the hungry, while the men were busy buying and selling horses (all in the same market), cows, sombreros, corn, hay, bread, and meat, which latter looked as well butchered as any in our markets. The place was crowded with our volunteers, and groups of Mexicans, clustered together, were eyeing them with no friendly gaze, while the demeanor of their women was gentle, peaceful, and apparently confiding; there was no look or appearance of alarm in any of the women. After leaving the market, I went into several stores still kept by their Mexican shopkeepers, and finally got into one which bothered me: persons seemed not only to be buying, but also selling, with scarcely a word uttered by buyer or seller. I inquired the price of an article, and after a good deal of difficulty of interchanging my good (as I thought) for their bad Spanish, I found out that I was in a *pawnbroker's* shop. We went into General Ampudia's house and got some refreshments from its American occupant, then into the house of the late prefect of the city, to play billiards, and finally into the "Fonda del Commercio" to supper, on rabbits, eggs, kidneys, and coffee. After supper we went to the theatre, and recognized our quondam friends whom we had met at the mouth of the river. Such an audience! The Texan Rangers were there, pistols and knives in their belts, many with swords at their sides, others with long rifles, while drunken volunteers from nearly every southern State of the Union were mingled with regulars of the horse, foot, and artillery arms of the service, in a medley of wild, riotous dissipation and confusion. I do not believe that anybody ever did know what was being played that night in that theatre. On leaving the house, Steuart and I tried to find a lodging-place, and succeeded, *Calle Guanaxuato*, in finding room on a floor to lie down, as we had stood, with fifty or sixty snoring men around, some with, others, like ourselves, without, blankets.

August 1. We left Matamoras by a steamer which was going down the river, and had a disagreeable time, as we ran aground on a sand-bar, where we laid thirty-six hours, exposed to the merciless attacks of mosquitoes more virulent in their venom than those at the mouth of the river. We arrived at camp on the fourth, and I brought the glad tidings that we were to march.

August 5. It is high time that we should leave this camp; it has been raining hard here for the past three days, and it is nothing but muck and mire; besides, drinking the muddy water (yes, it is as muddy as that in any mud-puddle) of the Rio Grande is beginning to tell on the men. We have too many sick, mostly with the diarrhœa, for our numbers, and it is thought a considerable number will have to be discharged.

August 6. We received orders to march; two companies, with all the heavy baggage and stores, were to ascend the river in a steamer to Camargo, the other four companies to go by land; and it was to be determined by lot which companies were to *ride.* Chance decided in favor of Captains Steuart and Waters, and the footmen commenced getting ready to tramp.

August 7. The whole camp alive to-day. Companies A and D, Steuart's and Waters's, left by steamer for Camargo, distant by the river about two hundred and fifty miles, some say not more than one hundred and eighty miles. I sent my servant Ned by the steamer under care of Captain Steuart, and discharged four of my men, Boulanger, Cutting, Pratt and Turner, on account of inability to march, by reason of sickness.

August 11—Sunday. All the sick of the battalion that were discharged, numbering thirty-three, left for the United States, and were accompanied by Doctor Dove, of Washington, our surgeon, who also desired to return; their departure cast a good deal of gloom over those who remained, but as I had sent all my men who were unable to march up the river by the steamer, and had got relieved from the care of the sick, I was in good spirits and anxious to start.

August 13. On the evening of the 11th we crossed the Rio Grande in a steamer to Burita, and took up our line of march for Matamoras, which we reached this day about noon; distance variously estimated at from twenty-six to thirty miles. I lost a man from my company, named McGunnell, on the march, and was unable to account for his absence. Our road from Burita was mostly through the water, and we waded one lagoon of three miles wide, with an average of three feet of water in depth, and in some places four feet, without a halt; many of the men caught hold of each other for support, as the fatigue of this wading through such a depth of water for such a distance is inconceivable. For a distance of eighteen miles the road was a muck; and happy those who marched at the head of the column, for those at the rear had to go through a heavier mire on account of the footsteps of those in front. The recent overflow of the Rio Grande had made the roads impassable except for American volunteers.

August 14. We are now at Matamoras, and on the eve of important operations; let us take a retrospect, and also a glance at the present status and condition of affairs. After the battles of the 8th and 9th of May, General Arista recrossed the river and occupied this town with his shattered forces. Our troops commenced crossing the river on the 13th, preparatory to an assault. Arista asked for an armistice, which Taylor refused to grant, but said that he might withdraw his forces on condition of leaving the property of the city uninjured. When our troops had effected a crossing (their landing on the Mexican soil being undisputed), preparations were made for an assault; a parley, however, was sounded, when the authorities of the city answered that General Arista had abandoned the place with all his troops, and that the city of Matamoras was at the disposal of General Taylor. Our troops took possession, the American flag was hoisted, and the march to the "halls of the Montezumas" about to be undertaken.

Large numbers of volunteers were arriving to swell the little army of regulars into an army in fact, but supplies were not coming commensurate with the number of men, and the means of transportation were totally inadequate to move the large force now constituting General Taylor's "army of occupation."

Hence the delay on the Rio Grande, and the loss of precious time on its banks. In the meantime important movements and changes were taking place among the Mexican people and rulers. The defeat of Arista had rendered him unpopular, and a great deal of dissatisfaction and confusion of opinions prevailed among all classes. Toward the end of June an election was held throughout the States of Mexico, and General Paredes was *declared* elected President, over Herrera, and General Bravo Vice-President, of Mexico. The ultra war party had triumphed, and Arista and other revolutionists defied the authority of the new President, yet united with him in the *grito* (cry), *Guerra al cuchillo,* "war to the knife," against the Yankees. There is no doubt whatever in my mind that the sentiment of the Mexicans was unanimous for war.* They knew no more of what had brought an army of foreigners upon their territory, than did the natives of New Zealand. No press, no public opinion, constant revolutions and internecine strife, *how* were they to know what their rulers had been doing, or *what* the foreign relations of their Government?

General Taylor very wisely, I think, undertook to enlighten them, and before we left Matamoras issued the following proclamation to the inhabitants of Mexico, which had, however, about as much effect as the incendiary manifests of Ampudia and Arista. Still I thought it was right, and cordially approved its purpose; for that General Taylor was sincerely desirous of protecting all inhabitants of the country that would remain neutral during the impending conflict, I am abundantly satisfied.

"A PROCLAMATION.

"*By the General Commanding the Army of the United States of America, to the People of Mexico.*

"AFTER many years of patient endurance, the United States are at length constrained to acknowledge that a war exists between our Government and the Government of Mexico. For many years our citizens have been subjected to repeated insults and injuries; our vessels and cargoes have been seized and confiscated, our merchants have been plundered, maimed, imprisoned, without cause and without reparation. At length your Government acknowledged the justice of our claims, and agreed by treaty to make satisfaction by payment of several millions of dollars; but this treaty has been violated by your rulers, and the stipulated

---

* After a long sojourn in this country, I have seen nothing, heard nothing, to make me change the above opinion.

payment has been withheld. Our late effort to terminate all the difficulties by peaceful negotiation has been rejected by the Dictator Paredes; and our minister of peace, whom your rulers had agreed to receive, has been refused a hearing. He has been treated with indignity and insult, and Paredes has announced that war exists between us. This war, thus first proclaimed by him, has been acknowledged as an existing fact by our own President and Congress with perfect unanimity, and will be prosecuted with vigor and energy against your army and rulers; but those of the Mexican people who remain neutral will not be molested.

"Your Government is in the hands of tyrants and usurpers. They have abolished your State Governments, they have overthrown your federal constitution, they have deprived you of the right of suffrage, destroyed the liberty of the press, despoiled you of your arms, and reduced you to a state of absolute dependence upon the power of a military dictator. Your armies and rulers extort from the people by grievous taxation, by forced loans, and military seizures, the very money which sustains the usurpers in their power. Being disarmed, you were left defenceless and as an easy prey to the savage Comanches, who not only destroy your lives and property, but drive into captivity more horrible than death itself your wives and children. It is your military rulers who have reduced you to this deplorable condition. It is these tyrants and their corrupt and cruel satellites, gorged with the people's treasure, by whom you are thus oppressed and impoverished,—some of whom have boldly advocated a monarchical government, and would place a European prince upon the throne of Mexico. We come to obtain reparation for repeated wrongs and injuries; we come to obtain indemnity for the past, and security for the future; we come to overthrow the tyrants who have destroyed your liberties; but we come to make no war upon the people of Mexico, nor upon any form of free government they may choose to select for themselves.

* * * * * * * *

"We come among the people of Mexico as friends and republican brethren; and all who receive us as such shall be protected, whilst all who are seduced into the army of your Dictator shall be treated as enemies. We shall want from you nothing but food for our army, and for this you shall always be paid in cash the full value. It is the settled policy of your tyrants to deceive you in regard to the character and policy of our Government and people. These tyrants fear the example of our free institutions, and constantly endeavor to misrepresent our purposes, and inspire you with hatred for your republican brethren of the American Union. Give us but the opportunity to undeceive you, and you will soon learn that all the representations of Paredes were false, and were only made to induce you to consent to the establishment of a despotic government. In your struggle for liberty with the Spanish monarchy thousands of our countrymen risked their lives and shed their blood in your defence. Our own commodore, the gallant Porter, maintained your flag upon the ocean; and our Government was the first to acknowledge your independence. With pride and pleasure we enrolled your name on the list of independent republics, and sincerely desired that you might in peace and prosperity enjoy all the blessings of free government.

"Mexicans! we must treat as enemies, and overthrow, the tyrants who, whilst they have wronged and insulted us, have deprived you of your liberty; but the Mexican people who remain neutral during the contest shall be protected against their military despots by the republican army of the Union.

"(Signed) "Z. TAYLOR,
"Brevet Major-General U. S. A. Commanding."

CHAPTER III.

THE RIO GRANDE.

THE river Rio Grande, or Bravo del Norte, finds its sources in the sierras of the Rocky Mountains in about 40½° north latitude, and, running a southeasterly course of nearly two thousand miles, flows a mighty torrent into the Gulf of Mexico. This flood of waters, meeting the swell and tides of the Gulf, causes a bar, shifting and dangerous, at the mouth of the river. With our command of the sea, the river necessarily became the base of General Taylor's objective movements, and, despite the bar at its mouth, steamers drawing not less than six to eight feet were carrying by its means his supplies some two hundred to three hundred miles into the interior.

To cut loose from this base, and advance through a hostile country comparatively unknown, in pursuit of an enemy whose power of endurance was undisputed, and whose numbers were known to be large, required courage of a high order and self-reliance in an equal degree.

General Zachary Taylor possessed both, and he had now mapped out in his own mind a campaign which, in the end, gave great lustre to the American arms. His first move now was to concentrate all the troops, regular and volunteer, that he proposed to use for his advance, at Camargo, a town on the banks of the San Juan River, a few miles above where it empties into the Rio Grande. It is worthy of remark, in demonstrating that a soldier's value is in proportion to his experience, that the steamers first purchased by the Government in New Orleans were of too heavy draught of water to cross the bar at the mouth of the river, and those that could be procured of sufficiently light draught it was deemed unsafe to trust to cross the Gulf of Mexico; so that the delay which had occurred was owing in fact to an ignorance of detail, the responsibility for which rested *nowhere*. Finally light-draught steamers ventured across the Gulf, and, with the wrecks of some half-dozen of their number lying on the bar, they found their way into and up the river to Camargo, distant two hundred and fifty miles from its mouth, and our future depot of supplies. Strange, that an army operating in this valley of the Rio Grande should have to look for its subsistence to the great valley of the Mississippi, which had been, as this now was, the extreme western limit of hardy enterprise and daring.

In the meantime the Texan Rangers had cleared the small posts held by the Mexicans between Matamoras and Camargo of all their armed defenders, and, with a regiment of our volunteers at Reynosa, the enemy had gradually been driven back from the river, and was somewhere concentrating at the base of the Sierra Madre mountains.

On the 14th day of August our battalion was brigaded with six companies of Kentucky volunteers, called the Louisville Legion, and twelve companies of Ohio volunteers, making a brigade of about two thousand men.

August 15. Left Matamoras, to march with the brigade to Camargo, distant from 130 to 150 miles, by what was called the mountain road.

Our march was over a desert rather than a mountainous country; from the time we left the Rio Grande at Matamoras, until we struck the San Juan River on the 23d of August, not a stream, rivulet, brook, or spring, did we see or hear of, the only water to be had being found in ponds or *tanks*, as they were called, in which rain-water had been collected for the use of the cattle. We suffered very much, and our march was more that of a routed army of stragglers than the advance of a well-organized brigade.

The distance from Matamoras to Camargo, by my calculation, was one hundred and thirty miles, and of this we marched seventy-eight miles in four days' continuous marching. On the first day of the march we made ten miles, on the second day eleven miles, on the third day twenty-six miles, on the fourth day but five miles, the men being completely exhausted from the preceding days' fatigue and suffering; on the fifth day twenty miles, on the sixth day eighteen miles, on the seventh day seventeen miles, and on the eighth day twenty-three miles; total, one hundred and thirty miles in eight days. This would have been excellent marching over good roads, but through the country of our route it was a shameful mismanagement, and reflected but little credit upon all concerned in the movement. The excuse was that our guides had misled the commanding officer, being themselves ignorant of the scarcity of water, and of the very road which we traveled. We marched in the middle of the day, with a burning sun overhead, and burning sand beneath our feet; not a drop of rain had fallen in this section of the country for months, and the dust raised by the tramp of so many men hung over our heads with a smothering denseness from which there was no escape. When we reached a pond, which was nothing but a hog-wallow, men and horses rushed pell-mell frantically into it, all semblance of rank and organization forgotten and disregarded.

At noon of the third day we reached a pond, in

the water of which large numbers of cattle were standing to escape the heat of the noon-day, and the swarm of flies which annoyed them. For how many days these cattle had stood in this water we know not; but very few of us who drank it kept it *down* after it was swallowed, and the taste of that water was remembered for a long time with nausea and disgust. On this day's march I fell in the road utterly broken down, and I saw men toward night frantically digging with their bayonets in the dry bed of a water-course, in the vain hope of finding water beneath the surface, but all was as dry as the arid country around. For miles our command was straggling along, day after day, some reaching camp long after nightfall, inviting attack by their looseness of array, and scorning the commands of superior officers, through the utter demoralization which prevailed. Curses and imprecations loud and deep were heard, and a vindictiveness was manifested, rarely I expect ever shown by American troops. I saw men fall down in convulsions on this march, frothing at their mouths, clutching the sand with their hands, and left to lie until nature and the shadows of night restored them to consciousness and strength. Kentuckians, Ohio men, and Baltimoreans, were all mixed together; the strongest and best walkers pressing to the front, the weak and the weary lagging behind. No word of encouragement, none of command, was heard, perhaps none was needed, for all who were able to march could be found at the tanks, and to reach the river was the leading, the only, object of that brigade on its memorable march to Camargo.

August 24. We found here, upon our arrival yesterday, the two companies of our battalion which had escaped the march by coming up the river on a steamboat. Our sick, camp and garrison equipage, and my servant, were awaiting us, and after getting my company into some sort of comfort, I walked into Camargo to take a look around me. I found it a much more Spanish-looking town than Matamoras, judging from pictures I had seen of Spanish towns. It was, to use the expression of one of my men I found wandering through the streets, a *rocky-looking* place. It has of course a plaza, and a rather dilapidated cathedral church. It boasted once of having two thousand inhabitants; now I am sure there are not more than one thousand, with nearly an equal number of dogs and chicken-cocks. The houses are low heavy stone buildings, with flat roofs, and, having been completely inundated last June by an overflow of the San Juan, the appearance of the town was not clean or attractive. It is the residence of General Canales, a lawyer by profession, and somewhat noted as a partisan leader. I found that he was very popular here, and when he left, which he did on the approach of our troops, he carried with him a considerable number of its fighting population.*

I found General Taylor here with his headquarters, and an army of regulars and volunteers, including several regiments of Texans. The main plaza is the camp of a regiment, and all the larger

---

*I have read in a book, since the war, that the arrival of our troops was welcomed by the inhabitants of Camargo, as a relief from the tyranny of Canales; this is not the fact.

houses are filled with quartermaster and commissary stores. Everything and everybody is busy and bustling, and the excitement of an advance and an approaching battle is increasing hourly. General Worth, with a couple of regiments, has gone to Mier, forty miles off; General Smith left this morning, and Randolph Ridgely told me that he expects to march with his battery this week. Having seen and heard enough for one day, I returned to camp, the fatigues of the past week already forgotten in the enthusiasm engendered by the martial scenes I had witnessed.

August 26. I suppose it always has been so in all armies, ancient and modern, it certainly is so in the "army of occupation," that a vast quantity of *rumors* are flying around. In the absence of newspapers, soldiers in the field are very fond of gossip, and that gossip is confined to the narrow limits of the *next march*, or the plan of campaign. From morning till night, this is the talk.

The weather ceased to be a topic of conversation from the hour of our arrival on the Brazos, and now, from the next to the highest in rank down to the enlisted man, at all hours of the day and night you may hear a thousand rumors, but all tending to the same point, or in the same direction. No one can tell from whence they come; the hardiest has not dared to say General Taylor said so and so, but rumor says we are going to Monterey. And where that is, and how we are going to get there, rumor, as yet, knoweth not. The Mexicans with whom I have talked say the same thing; they have their rumors, which point in the same direction; they say that their army has retired to Monterey, and that it will fight us there, *mucho fandango*, at Monterey. So I have concluded that we *are* going to Monterey, wherever that may be, and that we will fight a battle there; feeling ashamed, however, that I didn't know where it was,—for I used to be a little vain of my knowledge of geography,—but of a town called Monterey, this side of the one thus named on the California coast of the Pacific Ocean, I was as ignorant as a heathen. Not having seen an American newspaper for more than a month, and not having the acquaintance of an army correspondent, I fed upon rumors, satisfied with that pabulum, and an innate soldierly contentment in the discharge of my own duties.

August 30. I have learned by experience the truth of a famous saying which Shakspeare makes one of his characters use, "Uneasy lies the head that wears a crown." I have never been a king, but the symbol of authority, whether it be a crown or the shoulder-straps of a Captain of volunteers, carries with it so much unrest and anxiety that it is strange men will seek such trappings. It has been a very trying time the past few days. Orders were received that our battalion would be mustered to-morrow for payment, and that each Captain should have prepared and ready for that day four full rolls containing the names of all the members of his company, present and absent, where mustered, when mustered, when last paid, the amount of clothing each man had received, the value of the equipments, arms, and accoutrements received by each, the amount due the sutler, and a recapitulation showing the number present for duty, those that were present sick, those that were absent sick, those on extra duty, those in arrest or confinement, those on detached service, those absent without leave, the number joined by transfer, the number joined from desertion, the number discharged by expiration of service, or for disability, the number that had deserted, the number that had died, etc., etc. I looked at the blank forms, and my military enthusiasm was oozing perceptibly through my pores. No help for it; the work had to be done. So, selecting some half-dozen of the best clerks in my company, I went at it. We labored hard, for no one officer or soldier in the command had ever had anything of the kind to do before. Labor as we did, however, I could not make my account *balance*,—that is the only way to express it; in other words, I could not make *this* roll correspond with the original one made at Washington on the 8th of June, when we were mustered into the army, by reason of the numerous changes which had taken place since that time. Finally the mustering-officer came along, and I told him my difficulties. Though an entire stranger, he sat down alongside of us and kindly assisted and explained, until I grasped what was before me, and was enabled to complete satisfactorily my rolls. To First Lieutenant William A. Nichols, of the Second Regiment of Artillery, United States Army, I owe my thanks for his courtesy, and gratitude for his instruction.

August 31. This day, looked forward to by me with as much apprehension, if not more, than if we were going to fight a battle, was the day of muster, and all the troops here were mustered for payment.

Thanks to Lieutenant Nichols my rolls were nearly correct, and I had but little trouble in getting them accepted after the parade. As before said, each commanding officer of a company had to prepare four rolls. Of these four, one is sent direct to the Adjutant-General of the United States Army at Washington, by which means the Government is informed of the numbers present and absent of its armies in the field; two are given to the paymaster, who calculates the pay due each soldier, and the amount is placed against the name of the soldier upon each roll, and signed by the soldier at the time of payment. One copy of the rolls is retained by the company commander, as a basis for his roll at the next muster. By these means the condition of an army is verified, and all changes occurring are noted upon each successive muster, until the final one at the end of the term of service, when every man borne upon the original muster-in roll must be accounted for. If a Captain can only prepare his first rolls correctly, he will have but little thereafter to trouble him. A mistake in this, however, leads to successive and increasing blunders. It does not follow that troops are immediately paid after these musters for payment, and we were not; but, our company rolls being in, the Captains were free from the responsibility of delay.

None other than a man who has been the Captain of a volunteer company can appreciate this feeling of responsibility. In the regular army, there is not the same closeness of relation between the enlisted man and his Captain, for he has been assigned to the command and may be transferred at any time; but in the volunteer service, the men have been, generally speaking, enlisted by the Captain, and to him alone they look for their pay. Without pay, a soldier is one of the most disagreeable beings on earth, and without pay, soldiers are not easily commanded. As a general rule, no amount of pay will make men take up arms in a cause for which they have no sympathy; at the same time experience has demonstrated that, without pay, soldiers won't fight—saints would not do it, if they were soldiers.

My troubles for the day were not yet over, for, being in hourly expectation of orders to march, the sick of my company gave me great concern. Two months in this climate, and two such marches as those from Burita* to Matamoras, and from thence to Camargo, had frightfully depleted the strength of the volunteer regiments. In my own company eighteen men were on their backs, unmistakably not fit for the field, and what to do with them was the question now uppermost in my mind. I went to see Colonel Watson, and gave him a faithful account of the condition of our sick. The matter was so grave that he went at once to head-quarters and had an interview with General Taylor, which resulted in an order being issued that such of the sick as were thought unfit by the surgeon to march should be left in the general hospital at Camargo. I left eighteen, of whom the following were discharged on surgeon's certificate of disability

* The Countess de Burita was the heroïne of the first defence of Saragossa, when besieged, in 1808, by the French, under General Lefebvre Desnouettes. I presume this town was named in her honor.

as soon as they were examined: Corporal James Tibbles; Privates John F. Alexander, James B. Canning, Jacob Degomp, Francis Fisher, George Gordon, Barney Hawkins, Charles Johnson, David Johnson, Samuel Lockhart, William Macready, Josiah Pregg, James Peregoy, Ernest Tressel, and William C. Wilson; the proportion of sick in the other companies of the battalion being about the same, while in some other regiments it was much larger. In the First Tennessee a large number died, and the general opinion was that we were in a very unhealthy camp. No one can tell whence the name came, but already in speaking of Camargo the men would invariably call it the *graveyard.* Captain W. S. Henry, of the United States Army, in writing from here at this time, says: "The volunteers continue to arrive. They have suffered a great deal at their encampment at the mouth of the river, and at the Brazos Santiago, that barren and sandy island where the sand drifts in clouds. Diarrhœa, dysentery, and fevers, have been very fatal. Discharges are numerous, and the great majority are pretty well disgusted with the service. My only surprise is that people so suddenly transported from a high to a low latitude in the midst of summer should have so few cases of disease. They may consider themselves very fortunate."

CHAPTER IV.

CAMARGO.

September 1, 1846. At Camargo.

To comprehend this campaign of the Rio Grande it will be necessary to go back a few weeks, in order to learn what were the plans, if any, which the Government had formed for the prosecution of the war. Major-General Winfield Scott, the eminent soldier, was the commanding general of the army of the United States, but he had written himself into disfavor with both the President and the Secretary of War, the Hon. William L. Marcy. General Scott's views had no controlling influence upon the campaign, and for the present we must leave him where I am inclined to think he preferred being left, a watchful observer of the course of events and the conduct of the war. His reputation as a general officer was well established, that of Taylor's comparatively unknown,—certainly far below that of Scott's; for as yet the laurels gathered at Palo Alto and Resaca had been ascribed more to the steady gallantry of the "regulars" than to the military capacity of Taylor.

The Government propounded this question to General Taylor, "Shall the campaign be conducted with the view of striking at the city of Mexico, or confined, so far as regards the forces under your immediate command, to the northern provinces of Mexico?"* On the 2d of July the general answered "That it was his intention of moving with a column of six thousand men upon an experimental expedition as far as Monterey. He considered that six thousand men was the maximum force which could be employed on the expedition, having regard to their subsistence and the resources of the country in pack-mules and transportation generally. That from Camargo to the city of Mexico was a line little short of one thousand miles in length; the resources of the country, to say the best, not superabundant, and over long spaces of the route were known to be deficient. That the road as we advanced south approached both seas, yet the topography of the country and the consequent character of the communications forbid the taking up a new line of supply from Tampico or the Pacific coast;" and concluded by saying, "Except in the case, deemed improbable, of the entire acquiescence, if not support, on the part of the Mexican people, I consider it impracticable to keep open so long a line of communication. It is therefore my opinion that our operations from this frontier should not look to the city of Mexico, but should be confined to cutting off the northern provinces,—an undertaking of comparative facility and assurance of success."

On the 9th of July Mr. Marcy wrote to General Taylor as follows: "If, from all the information which you may communicate to the Department, as well as

---

* Letter from Hon. W. L. Marcy, Secretary of War, to General Taylor, dated War Department, Washington, June 8, 1846.

that derived from other sources, it should appear that the difficulties and obstacles to the conducting of a campaign from the Rio Grande, the present base of your operations, for any considerable distance into the interior of Mexico, will be very great, the Department will consider whether the main invasion should not ultimately take place from some other point on the coast, say *Tampico* or some other point in the vicinity of *Vera Cruz.* This suggestion is made with a view to call your attention to it, and to obtain from you such information as you may be able to impart. Should it be determined that the main army should invade Mexico at some other point than the Rio Grande,—say in the vicinity of Vera Cruz,—a large and sufficient number of transport vessels could be placed at the mouth of the Rio Grande by the time the healthy season sets in,—say early in November. The main army, with all its munitions, could be transported, leaving a sufficient force behind to hold and occupy the Rio Grande and all the towns and provinces which you may have conquered before that time. In the event of such being the plan of operations, your opinion is desired what increased force, if any, will be required to carry it out with success. We learn that the army could be disembarked a few miles distant from Vera Cruz, and readily invest the town in its rear, without coming within range of the guns of the fortress of San Juan d'Ulloa. The town could be readily taken by land, while the fortress, being invested by land and sea, and all communication cut off, must soon fall. From Vera Cruz to the city of Mexico there is a fine road, upon which the diligences or stage-coaches run daily. The distance from Vera Cruz to the city of Mexico is not more than one-third of that from the Rio Grande to the city of Mexico. Upon these important points, in addition to those mentioned in my letter of the 8th of June, your opinions and views are desired at the earliest period your duties will permit you to give them. In the mean time, the Department confidently relies on you to press forward your operations vigorously, to the extent of your means, so as to occupy the important points within your reach on the Rio Grande and in the interior."

To this, General Taylor replied on the 1st of August, from Matamoras: "As to the military operations best calculated to secure an early and honorable peace, my report of the 2nd of July will have put the Department in possession of my views touching operations in this quarter, and I have now little to add to that report. Whether a large force can be subsisted beyond Monterey must be determined by actual experiment, and will depend much upon the disposition of the enemy toward us. If a column (say ten thousand men) can be sustained in provisions at Saltillo, it may advance thence upon San Luis Potosi, and, I doubt not, would speedily bring proposals for peace. If, on the other hand, a column cannot be sustained beyond Monterey, it will be for the Government to determine, from considerations of state, whether a simple occupation of the frontier departments (including Chihuahua and New Mexico), or, in addition to such occupation, an expedition against the capital by way of Vera Cruz, would be most expedient. I cannot give a positive opinion as to the practicability of an expedition against Vera Cruz, or the amount of force that would probably be required for it. The Department of War must be much better informed than I am on that point. From the impracticable character of the routes from Tampico, particularly that leading to Mexico, I should judge an expedition against the capital from that point to be out of the question. The simultaneous embarkation of a large body of troops at Brazos Santiago, as proposed in the Secretary's communication, would be attended with great difficulty, if we may judge from the delays and danger which accompany the unloading of single transports, owing to the almost perpetual roughness of the bar and boisterous character of the anchorage. It may also well be questioned whether a force of volunteers, without much instruction (more than those now here can receive in season for such an expedition), can prudently be allowed to form the bulk of an army for so delicate an operation as a descent upon a foreign coast, where it can have no proper base of operations or supplies."

From the above correspondence it will be perceived that the War Department, whilst making inquiries of General Taylor, gave him no positive instructions, except that he should press forward his operations vigorously, so as to occupy the important points within his reach on the Rio Grande and in the interior, given to him by Secretary Marcy in his letter of the 9th of July; while as early as the 2nd of the same month General Taylor had informed the War Department that it was his intention of moving with a column of six thousand men upon Monterey.

We were now, at the 1st day of September, 1846, at Camargo, and General Taylor was ready to move forward. These were his arrangements: the regular troops of the army were organized into two divisions; the first, under the command of General Twiggs, consisted of the Second Dragoons, the First, Second, Third, and Fourth Regiments of Infantry, and Bragg's and Ridgely's Batteries; the Second, under General Worth, of the Artillery Battalion, the Fifth, Seventh, and Eighth Regiments of Infantry, Duncannon's Battery, and Captain Blanchard's company of Louisiana volunteers. Of the twelve months' volunteers that were to form part of the column, they were organized into a field division under the command of Major-General Butler, of Kentucky, with Brigadiers-General Hamer, of Ohio, and Quitman, of Mississippi (the latter was born in the State of New York). A large number —about six thousand—twelve months' men were to be distributed at Camargo and the several posts on the river which it was deemed necessary to hold. The following paragraph of "Orders No. 108" expresses a great deal: "The limited means of transportation, and the uncertainty in regard to the supplies that may be drawn from the theatre of operations, imposes upon the commanding general the necessity of taking into the field, in the first instance, only a moderate portion of the volunteer force now under his orders."

Of the force thus to be left, the whole was to be under the command of Major-General Robert Patterson, of Pennsylvania.

In the course of the preceding week and since our arrival here, the Baltimore Battalion had been brigaded in three several commands, but on this day we had the honor, owing to the personal efforts of Colonel Watson, of being attached to General Twiggs' (First) Division of Regulars, and brigaded in the Fourth Brigade with the First Regiment of Infantry, under the command of Lieutenant-Colonel Henry Wilson, of the United States Army. I was delighted.

The Baltimore Battalion, as it was generally called (without any disrespect to our friends and comrades of the two Washington companies), was dressed in the regular blue uniform and equipments of the regular troops of the line of the army, and was the only command of volunteers thus equipped that I am aware of, at this time. Its character was that of being disorderly and riotous, which reputation it had brought from Washington, and had been added to on the Brazos, at Camp Belknap, and at Matamoras; but I say as a soldier that its behavior was as orderly, and that it was more obedient and its appearance more soldier-like, than that of any volunteers I have seen in the country. The reason why, frequently, its conduct was considered disorderly, was owing to the facts that nearly every man in it was from the cities of Washington and Baltimore, many of whom had been sailors, others members of fire-companies, fishing-clubs, etc., and they were a wild, frolicksome, reckless set, full of fun and hard to keep in camp. They were forever wandering about, and frequently came into collision with volunteers from other States, who, being mostly from the rural districts, had some curious-looking uniforms and hats, and would not understand the character or take the fun of these city fellows, particularly as they were dressed in army uniforms. This assignment of the battalion to a brigade of regulars was regarded as a great feather in our caps.

The field division of volunteers under the command of General Butler consisted of the First Mississippi, Colonel Jefferson Davis; the First Tennessee, Colonel William B. Campbell; the First Ohio, Colonel Alexander M. Mitchell; and the First Kentucky, Colonel Stephen Ormsby: regiments of volunteers. Two regiments of Texan cavalry under Colonel James Pinkney Henderson completed the force of the column. Before we left Camargo, and on this 1st day of September, under the authority of the Act of Congress and instructions from the headquarters of the army, an election was held in the several companies of our battalion for an additional second lieutenant. In my company it resulted in the choice of Orderly Sergeant William E. Aisquith,* of the city of Baltimore, and he was subsequently duly commissioned. He was my choice, and the whole subject is worthy of a few reflections. Perhaps in the history of the

* On the afternoon before I left Baltimore with my company, Mr. Robert M. McLane came to the rendezvous and asked me to do him a favor by accepting Aisquith as a volunteer, and giving him a place as one of my officers; which I declined to do, as I had already determined who were to be my Lieutenants; but after he told me that Aisquith was the son of Captain Aisquith, who at the battle of North Point, in command of a company of sharpshooters, had rendered efficient service and behaved with much gallantry, and that he was a graduate of the United States Military Academy at West Point, I replied, that I would give him the place of Orderly Sergeant of my company, and give him a chance for promotion; and this I did.

whole world, and of its armies, no such spectacle had ever been seen before as the right of suffrage or vote by ballot being given to the soldiers of an organized army in the field, for the selection of their officers. It must be borne in mind that, by the militia laws of several States of the Union, the company officers were selected by the men, and in some of the States the field officers were likewise thus elected. It was so I am sure in Maryland, that company officers were thus elected; and inasmuch as the Act of Congress which authorized the Government to accept twelve months' volunteers, provided that the company officers should be commissioned by the Governors of the respective States from which they were accepted, it followed that the additional lieutenant allowed to each company should be elected and commissioned as had been the others from the same State. If I had been asked at the time I raised my company whether I would have permitted the men to select their officers, I should have given up its command before I would have consented to it; but now, after two months' arduous and active field service, I believed the men would select the most competent and trusty of their number; and, as far as our battalion was concerned, they generally did so. In my own company it was emphatically so; for although the opponent of Sergeant Aisquith was a well-drilled soldier, of very pleasing address, generous and popular, he received but six out of the sixty-seven votes cast. True it is that my influence aided Mr. Aisquith, but the large vote he received was due to the consciousness which the men now had that playing soldiers at home and practicing it here were two very different things, and that their lives and their comforts would mainly depend upon the skill and discretion of their officers.

CHAPTER V.

CAMPAIGN OF THE RIO GRANDE.

On the afternoon of September the 1st we bade farewell to the sickly environs of Camargo, crossed the San Juan River, and encamped with the First Regiment of Infantry, under orders to march to Seralvo, some seventy miles distant. In lieu of wagons for the transportation of our baggage, eight mules on an average were given to each company; the orders being, to every eight men a mule, and one to the company officers. All the wheel-transportation which General Taylor had at his disposal was being used to carry supplies of all kinds forward to Seralvo, which was established as an *entrepot*, and at which a portion of General Worth's division was already posted for its protection. No doubt was now entertained by any one that heavy work was before us; and the tread of the courageous, and the step of the faint-hearted, were as marked and as different as day from night.

September 2. The larger portion of this day was spent in getting our baggage packed upon the backs of the mules that were driven into our camp for this purpose. Their appearance created a profound sensation, and the laughter with which they were received and appropriated by the various squads rang loud and joyously through the valley of the San Juan.

If there be any one thing which requires patience, good humor, and skill, it is to properly load a mule so as not to put too much weight upon him, and that that which is put shall be equally balanced on either side, and carefully fastened to the pack-saddle. It amounts to an art.

I watched the process daily with great interest, and each day admired more and more the good qualities of the Mexican arriéros or muleteers. You have but to know that tents, tent-poles, kettles, mess-pans, axes, picks, coffee-mills, boxes of ammunition, etc., were to be daily put on and off a mule's back, to be carried safely over hill and dale, through thicket and through flowing water for miles and miles of toilsome march, to appreciate the knowledge requisite to do the work well. It *was* well done, and I learned to have affection for the mule and its keeper, despite the many annoyances incidental to this species of army transportation. From the very first, our men took kindly to the muleteers, and to the end of the march the utmost harmony and good will existed between them. It may seem strange to say that, notwithstanding they knew not a word of each other's language, they understood each other; but I have seen them talking together and laughing heartily over the subject of conversation. Owing to the delay in getting ready, it was nearly nightfall when we had marched three or four miles, so we halted and bivouacked for the night.

On the 3d, we marched fourteen miles, crossing the Arroyo Salado; on the 4th passed the picturesque-looking town of Mier, rendered famous by the desperate battle fought here four years ago between the Texans and Mexicans. On the 5th reached the *Alamo** River, a swift running stream, whose name was fresh in the memory of the Texans, and gave fierceness to their well-known battle cry, "*Remember the Alamo!*" and on the 6th reached Puntiaguda, distant fifty-five miles from Camargo. Here we halted for the main body of the troops to join us.

We had left the State of Tamaulipas, whose eastern boundary is the Rio Grande and Gulf of Mexico, and had entered the State of Nuevo Leon. The appearance of the country was very different from what we had in a measure become familiar with; instead of the sands, the cactus, the unwholesome water and enfeebling atmosphere, we were in a well cultivated country, with clear running streams, and gardens and fields blooming with the fig and the pomegranate. The air was delightful, and the sweet water of running mountain brooks was delicious to the palate, which for two months had been nauseated with the muddy fluid of the Rio Grande. The roads over which we had marched were good, and the manner and order of the march were grateful to men who had been driven in confusion through the lagoons and the mire, over sandy deserts and burning plains, from the Gulf to

---

* The town of Mier is on the banks of this river.

the banks of the San Juan. I was beginning to learn my profession, not the least of whose requirements is the knowledge of the proper way to march troops, and was learning in the only mode by which it could be acquired. A very marked change was perceptible in our ranks; we were being instructed in guard-mounting, picket- and outpost-duty, by those who were competent to teach, and as we approached the vicinity of the enemy the martial spirit of the men revived. Our health and strength were being regained in this salubrious climate, and the novelty of the ever-varying scenery through which we passed cheered and brightened the countenances of all.

I was much pleased with this little village of four hundred inhabitants, through whose streets the head-waters of the Alamo were rushing over their rocky bed to join and mingle with the torrent of the Bravo del Norte.

On the 7th, General Taylor came up with the main body, and after resting for two days, we all marched on the 9th to Seralvo, distant fifteen miles, which we reached the same night. Here we found General Worth's division; and the army of occupation was concentrated to take breath, fill cartridge-boxes and haversacks, and then to march to Monterey.

During our halt at Puntiaguda, word was brought from General Worth that a large force of cavalry was in his vicinity; and while I was gazing in awe and in silence at the wonderful phenomenon of a lunar rainbow I was startled with the drums beating an alarm. We were held in readiness to move to the support of Worth, but the affair which caused this first stampede* proved to be but a fight on that day between Captain McCullough's company of Texan Rangers and a portion of General Canales's cavalry. It was deemed advisable, however, to proceed with caution, and we awaited the arrival of General Taylor, when we moved forward with his troops. Camp rumor, after vacillating and fluctuating between the thousand-and-one stories heard daily and hourly since we had left the San Juan, was now settled and unanimous that fight we must at Monterey. I had become satisfied of this from the information given to me by the muleteers, one of whom told me he *knew* that they were fortifying the town, and General Ampudia had marched into it with a large army. I could not disbelieve the positive statements of this man; his truthfulness was stamped on every lineament of his honest countenance.

This town of Seralvo is one of considerable size and importance, beautifully situated in a valley surrounded by mountains, and in the centre of a highly cultivated rich and productive country. A tributary to the Alamo flows through it, which supplies water to the inhabitants, and, by means of ditches, to the gardens which surround every house in the town, and which are by it kept in perennial verdure and bloom. Several handsome bridges cross this clear bold stream in different parts of the town, and on its banks the lemon, the orange, and the grand pecan, invite, by their beauty and foliage, the ladies of Seralvo to the

---

* This word means everything from a downright running away to a merely being hurried or startled without flight.

luxury of their shade. We found plenty of fruit here, and enjoyed the fig, the peach, and the pomegranate, fresh plucked from the tree, and that delicious drink, limonada, made from limes taken by myself from the branches upon which they had grown. It is not only by far the most attractive, clean, and picturesque town I have yet seen in Mexico, but the refreshing coolness of its thick-walled dwellings was the constant theme of those who had been so long exposed to the heat of the sun. They not only afforded shade, but there was an indescribable atmosphere within their walls which gave a sense of pleasure and repose to the weary and foot-sore officer fortunate enough to find this rest. In the far distance the lofty Sierras, overlooking the valley of Monterey, loom up grandly on the western horizon, and the bare cliffs to the north indicate where the once celebrated silver mines of Seralvo were worked for the conquering Spaniard, by the helpless natives. It is with its surroundings a beautiful country, and for the few days that we were here nothing whatever occurred to disturb the friendly relations which existed or seemed to exist between the people and our army. Fandangos, monté, limonada, with a dash now and then of vino de Parras, made our halt pass swiftly and pleasantly, so that when the bugles sang truce, and the reveille was followed by the generale on the morning of the 13th of September, we marched from Seralvo with regret, and the first pleasant memory of Mexico had effected a lodgment in our breasts. The following were our orders:

"HEADQUARTERS, ARMY OF OCCUPATION,
"Seralvo, September 11, 1846.

"*Orders No.* 115.]

"I. As the army may expect to meet resistance in the further advance towards Monterey, it is necessary that the march should be conducted with all proper precaution to meet attack and to secure the baggage and supplies. From this point the following will be the order of the march until otherwise directed.

"II. All the pioneers of the army, consolidated into one party, will march early to-morrow on the route to Marin, for the purpose of repairing the road and rendering it practicable for artillery and wagons. The pioneers of each division will be under a subaltern, to be especially detailed for the duty; and the whole will be under the command of Captain Craig, Third Infantry, who will report at headquarters for instructions. This pioneer party will be covered by a squadron of dragoons and Captain McCulloch's company of rangers. Two officers of topographical engineers, to be detailed by Captain Williams, will accompany the party for the purpose of examining the route. Two wagons will be provided by the quartermaster's department for the transportation of the tools, provisions, and knapsacks of the pioneer party.

"III. The First Division will march on the 13th inst., to be followed on successive days by the Second Division and the Field Division of Volunteers. The headquarters will march with the First Division. Captain Gillespie with half of his company will report to Major-General Butler; the other half, under the First Lieutenant, to Brigadier-General Worth. These detachments will be employed for outposts and videttes, and as expresses between the columns and headquarters.

"IV. The subsistence supplies will be divided among the three columns, the senior commissary of each division receipting for the stores and being charged with their care and management. The senior commissaries of divisions will report to Captain Waggoner for this duty.

"V. Each division will be followed immediately by its baggage train and supply train, with a strong rear-guard. The ordnance train, under Captain Ramsay, will march with the Second Division, between its baggage and supply trains, and will come under the protection of the guards of their division. The medical supplies will in like manner march with the first division.

"VI. The troops will take eight days' rations and forty rounds of ammunition. All surplus arms and accoutrements resulting from casualties on the road will be deposited with Lieutenant Stewart, left in charge of the depot at this place, who will give certificates of deposit to company commanders.

"VII. The wagons appropriated for the transportation of water will not be required, and will be turned over to the quartermaster's department for general purposes.

"VIII. Two companies of the Mississippi regiment will be designated for the garrison of this depot. All sick and disabled men unfit for the march will be left behind, under the charge of a medical officer, to be selected for this duty by the medical directors.

"By order of Major-General Taylor,

"W. W. S. Bliss,

"A. A. G."

"Headquarters, Army of Occupation,

"Seralvo, September 12, 1846.

"*Orders No.* 108.]

"I. Pursuant to orders of yesterday from headquarters, the First Division will be ready to move at daylight to-morrow in the following order:

"1st. Dragoons.

"2d. Ridgely's Battery.

"3d. Third Brigade.

"4th. Fourth Brigade.

"5th. The baggage trains, in the order designated for the corps to which they belong.

"6th. The medical supplies.

"7th. Supply trains.

"8th. Rear guard of two companies of infantry, to be furnished by the brigades alternately, commencing with the Third.

"II. The dragoons and the artillery will be foraged, to include the Fourteenth.

"III. The guards for the night will mount an hour before sunset, and will consist of four companies of infantry, two from each brigade, to be turned off by the brigade officer. Each brigade will, with its two companies for guard, furnish a captain of the day detailed from this office, who will have the superintendence of the whole and will report at these headquarters for orders immediately before guard-mounting.

"By order of Brigadier-General Twiggs,

"D. C. Buell,

"A. A. A. G."

Information has been received which places it beyond a doubt that General Ampudia marched into Monterey on the 31st of August, and that a large force is actively engaged fortifying the town. I took a look at General Taylor as he passed us on horseback while we were marching to-day, and I was satisfied that, whatever might be ahead of us, we would go on until *he* gave the order to halt. Ampudia certainly will have to make battle if he expects to hold Monterey, for go there General Taylor will. This is what I thought.

We marched along steadily and compactly all day a west-south-westerly course, keeping the mountains on our right and making apparently for a gorge in the sierra. Our division was in the advance, preceded by the Texan cavalry and followed by Worth's division and Butler's volunteer division. I was struck with the elasticity of the spirits of the men, which, notwithstanding the withering heat of the sun, found vent in song and laughter as they stepped solidly on to the front. The victories at Palo Alto and Resaca had given a confidence to these men which was communicated to the volunteers, and I could not but reflect on the value that the prestige of success gave to our raw troops, and the good policy which guided our being brigaded with the regulars.

We saw but few people to-day, though the country was filled with fields of cane and corn, inviting the labor of the husbandman. We saw no cattle ; a few frightened long-legged hogs scampered away at our approach, and everything indicated, as forcibly as do certain signs on the ocean, that a storm was brewing ahead of us.

We marched to-day about fourteen miles, and bivouacked on a deep and rapid stream whose name we could not learn. To-night rumor was rampant through our camps; a courier had come in from our cavalry advance, from Colonel Henderson to General Taylor, that four thousand of the enemy's cavalry were in front of him, and that he wanted assistance. We had something to sleep on, and those who didn't sleep, to talk about, until the reveille was beaten on the morning of

September 14. We were up before light, and on the march by daybreak. It was cold, and we moved briskly; soon the sun lighted up the conical mountain peaks on our right, and the tops of the ridges, with his glorious coloring, and the freshness of a new day gave additional interest to the beautiful country we were traversing. All was excitement, for McCullough had had a fight with the enemy this morning, and a wounded prisoner was sent to General Taylor's headquarters for examination; this was fact, and not rumor, so we hurried forward. We were going too fast, for our mules could not keep pace with the hasty tramp of the men, and it wasn't good management to let there be a gap between us and our supplies, with cavalry in our front, and why not on our flanks or rear? We halted now every few miles, and leisurely forded two streams which crossed our line of march. This was the first day since my landing on the Brazos in which I had not suffered from the heat of the sun; for two months and a half I had been constantly exposed to its burning rays, and the sense of cold experienced last night sent a chill through my blood which was exceedingly disagreeable. The cool air from the slopes of the adjacent mountains, and the elevation we are attaining, have rendered the temperature so pleasant that we feel as if we could march thirty miles a day with more ease than twenty lower down the country. We have now approached so close to the mountains on either side, as we near the gorge at the head of the valley, that we can see the foliage upon the trees which cover them; and I regret to say that our road is becoming so rough and stony that my feet are getting tender. So we go, complaining of the sand because it was hot, and now of the mountain-side because it is rocky! We halted after having marched fourteen miles, and bivouacked with our lines drawn, to stand to our arms in military array, whether it were necessary by night or by daylight.

September 15. I was in charge of our advance guard to-day, and, marching at the head of the column, perfectly reveled in the enjoyment of the magnificent scenery of the mountains and the valleys, and the military enthusiasm with which I was in a blaze. All was beautiful that was in sight, the air sweet and bracing, the sun comfortably warm, and the enemy known to be but a few miles distant. I knew not where our cavalry was, but I knew that our army was behind me, and the enemy in front. I pushed on, and, ascending a mountain over which our road lay, we hastened to reach its crest, for we thought that perhaps we might see the long-talked-of *Lancers.* What a prospect burst upon our view! a valley lay below us completely surrounded by mountains: through this valley ran a river, making in its course the graceful curve of Hogarth's line of beauty, and nestling on its banks a town was lying, just being lighted up by the sun's rays from over the eastern sierra. No famed valley of the Tyrol could be more beautiful, no valley hamlet on the banks of the Susquehanna more at repose; it was the repose of death. Gazing long upon this panorama, which nature and man had made so interesting, I was roused from my reverie by hearing the sound of horses' feet rapidly approaching from the rear. One glance was sufficient,—it was General Taylor, his staff, and a small escort of cavalry: dismounting, he approached and did me the honor to recognize me by a pleasant smile and an extended hand. He said that he remembered our interview at Matamoras, and then asked if I had anything to report: I replied that we had not met, nor had we seen, a living being since we had left camp at daybreak, and that not a creature could be seen moving in the valley below, nor in the town at our feet, from which I inferred that the enemy could not be far off. He said nothing for perhaps a minute or two, looking steadily toward the valley while thus silent, then suddenly said: "Captain, move forward cautiously, and if you can, continue your march through that town" (pointing to it as he spoke) "and halt on the other side until the column gets up." My command was on the march immediately, silently descending the mountain-road, which we could soon discover led right through the town of Marin. I was the first, of course, to enter its main street, and no man that ever entered a recently deserted town will ever forget the effect it produced upon him. We saw almost instantaneously—I might say we *felt*—that the town was abandoned; the men huddled together, and pressed on me from the rear as if hurrying forward. Not a word was uttered. Our tramp resounded from the house-walls on either side, amid the quiet, the unnatural stillness, the sense of danger. What is that? a dead man was lying in our track, his feet in a doorway, his body stretched toward the middle of the street, and a pool of blood about where his head lay. I saw as we passed that he was dead and had been recently slain, but when or by whom, or for what, who could tell? So we passed on through the town, and—I can speak for myself—drew a long breath of relief when we got into the open country; but there, sure enough, was the enemy.

At the distance of about three-fourths of a mile, a body of cavalry, with pennons fluttering on their lances, were at halt, seemingly (at least I thought so) uncertain what to do. They had evidently passed through the town ahead of me, and irresolution was apparent in their actions. Suddenly they resumed their march slowly, having seen, as I judged, the head of our column making its appearance over the mountain; and it was so, for I soon heard the coming up of our leading battalions.

Receiving no further orders, I remained where I was for several hours, the army gradually getting up to the town: it was evident that something more than ordinary kept us in check; finally General Twiggs, the commanding general of our division, with his staff, rode through the town, and presently a staff-officer came from him with orders for me to follow him, that the division was going into camp. This was very unusual, as it was not yet noon, and we had marched but a few miles. The meadow selected for our camp was a charming one on the banks of the San Juan River (there are three or four rivers of this name in Northern Mexico—it is a sort of fancy name with the Mexicans, this of *Saint John*), and here we remained until the 18th, the army again being concentrated, its different divisions refitted, and its material of war replenished and carefully inspected.

We are now within twenty-five miles of Monterey, and the rumors which are upon the lips of the entire camp are not based as usual upon *guesses* made by the army gossips, but upon reports received directly from the enemy's camp, and more or less reliable. A large force is at Monterey preparing to hold it, and dispute by battle our further advance into their country. Nine thousand men, it is said, are in the city, about one-third of whom are regular troops, the other two-thirds militia of the country,—perhaps—why not?—volunteers. The regulars are the remains of the army that fought on the Rio Grande, and my opinion is, that men who fought as bravely as they did in a fair stand-up fight, without breastworks, exposed to the destructive fire of our light artillery, will make a stubborn fight behind works which they have had ample time to construct, *mucho fandango,* at Monterey! I confess that these words were continually ringing in my ears, and likewise confess that I hoped we would not be disappointed. We were two thousand miles away from home, but not a thought or a wish was backward; *en avant!* was the individual and united sentiment of General Taylor's entire army. There is no mistake about this..

We remained here all of the 16th and 17th days of September. They were busy days; yet, even amid the bustle and excitement, the beauty and grandeur of the scenery was the theme of general and wide-spread admiration.

September 18. The army moved this morning, the three divisions following each other at intervals of an hour's march, the First Division still in the advance. We passed through the village of Agua Frio, and just beyond it saw the enemy's cavalry; it was doubtless the same force which had preceded us all the way from Seralvo, and was said to be the cavalry of General Torrejon. I had noticed that our arriéros had changed their appearance and demeanor very materially within the past two or three days. From some knowledge of their language, I was enabled to make myself understood by them and could gather the purport of what they said, and was on pleasant terms with the chief of those attached to our battalion. At first he was cheerful and communicative, but since our halt at Marin was taciturn and gloomy.

I was near him when he caught a glimpse of his countrymen, the cavalry of Torrejon, and upon my soul I pitied him. He was very much alarmed; and what could I say to him by way of encouragement? I was not surprised to hear during the day that a number of these muleteers had made an effort to escape, by leaving their mules and their cargoes to shift for themselves, and taking to the chaparral; but Colonel Kinney, of Corpus Christi, who was the contractor, and chief of the *mule corps,* headed them off and brought them back to the care of their companions in trouble, the patient, oppressed, but ever-faithful mules. We made eighteen miles to-day, and went into camp upon the hacienda or farm of San Francisco, seven miles from Monterey.

September 19. We resumed our march this morning at 8 o'clock, and were near the head of the column when, at about 10 o'clock, while we were marching very rapidly, the heavy boom of a cannon was heard reverberating with a thousand echoes among the mountains; presently another sullen roar was heard, and then another. Every pulse fluttered, and many a long breath drawn; we still hurried on: a halt was ordered, and our astonishment was great when we saw General Taylor and staff slowly countermarching, and Paymaster Major Kirby, of Taylor's staff, carrying in his hands a twelve-pound ball which had been fired at the party and fallen near the feet of the general. We also countermarched and encamped in a wood about three miles from Monterey, and made preparations for the battle, which, no one now questioned, was to be a deadly struggle.

The Baltimore Battalion, after a long, weary, and fatiguing march of a little upwards of three hundred miles from the Brazos Santiago, was now in the presence of the enemy.

All day long the firing from heavy guns continued, with an occasional rattle of musketry. The Texan Rangers were skirting the environs of the town, and engineer officers were already making reconnaissances; against these the fire of the Mexicans was directed, and as I watched their fire, and the movements of our cavalry from the edge of the wood in which our troops lay, I thought that I had never before beheld anything as interesting or attractive. We were just out of the range of their guns, and large numbers of the men gathered to witness the spectacle which was being exhibited upon the plain that extended from our camp to the town. On our right was a large stone citadel, upon the ramparts of which guns were mounted in barbette, and from which jets of flame and smoke issued, soon followed by the heavy boom of explosion. Immediately in front was the city, upon a lofty tower in which the flag of Mexico was flying, but its colors were undistinguishable at this distance. On our left a large number of mounted men were either idly clustered in squads, or else galloping to and fro in reckless disregard of the cannon balls ricochetting over and among them. Not a sound could be heard from the town, not a creature could be seen, not a single drift of smoke to indicate that it was inhabited. There it lay, its outline clearly marked by lines of earthworks, curtains and bastions—against the hazy blue of the mountain-side in its rear. Volumes of smoke were being carried from above the citadel, and shaped by a light wind into fantastic figures which were repeated upon the earth's surface by the sun, which shone with resplendent power through all these clouds of men and things, as if in mockery of their littleness. Now a cheer would ring from the citadel as a well aimed shot would produce some confusion among the Texans; then a yell from their side, in defiance, would roll down to our hearing. The discharge of loaded fire-arms in our own camp, preparatory to inspection of arms, was mingled with the beat of drums and bugle-calls of a well ordered force. Guards were being marched to their posts, artillery horses being led to water, staff-officers were galloping to and fro, cook-fires being lighted, wagons corralled, mules unharnessed, and all the indescribable machinery of an army on the eve of battle was in the hands of—military discipline. During the afternoon we pitched our tents as leisurely, and went through the ordinary routine of camp duty as quietly, as we did at Matamoras, but at tattoo roll-call I thought that I noticed an unusual degree of quiet and a clearer response as each name was called by the orderly sergeant upon my company parade. It was a clear, cold night; that is, it was cool enough for the men to desire to approach the fire, which they did, and I noticed also that they remained up later, and there were more of them in a body, than usual. Otherwise nothing indicated that before morning we might be on our way to storm the town, as was pretty generally thought would be the case.

September 20—Sunday. It was late this morning

before the sunlight made its way into our camp where we had passed the night. I arose refreshed by a good night's sleep, and ready for the duties of the day. All was quiet until after breakfast, when rumors announced important movements at hand, and orders were received to hold ourselves in readiness to march. During the morning, I heard that General Worth's Division would be ordered to turn the works on the west of the town, and was about marching. I stepped over to its camp and saw it leave; the men were in excellent spirits, and that division of regular troops presented an appearance which will never be effaced from my mind. It was thoroughly military and soldierlike; they looked so clean, their arms and accoutrements in such beautiful order, that all my enthusiasm for soldiers was greatly gratified. The artillery battalion especially attracted my attention; the red-legged infantry (as they were called from the broad red stripe running down the seams of their blue pantaloons) never on dress parade appeared to better advantage. Duncan's battery of flying artillery looked superb; the guns were as polished as those I had seen on Sunday's inspection at Fort McHenry, when Ringgold had brought this arm to the value now accorded it; and General Worth, the beau ideal of a gallant soldier, rode at the head of the column, as if conscious of the pride he had reason to feel in commanding such a body of troops. Colonel Jack Hayes's regiment of Texans, and McCullough's and Gillespie's companies of Rangers, accompanied the Division.

Returning to my own camp, I ascended a tree which

commanded a view of the city, and here I remained for some hours, watching the movements of the Texans, who, apparently without any orders, and certainly without any semblance of organization, were scouring over the plain, inviting the fire of the citadel, which answered at intervals by throwing a shot at these daring men without doing them any damage. The town still lay in its death-like repose; as yet not a sound could be heard from it. The only show of resistance or of activity was at the fort, which was called by us either the *black fort*, from the dark-looking stone of which it was constructed, or the *citadel*, from its size and strength. At four o'clock in the afternoon the long roll of the drums called the First Division to arms, and we fell into ranks fully believing that the hour had come for battle. We marched out from camp into the plain, and found Butler's volunteer division, Ridgely's and Bragg's batteries of flying artillery, and Webster's regular battery of twenty-four-pound howitzers, ready to move with us. General Taylor and staff were also there. We marched toward the city, halted within a mile of its works, and formed line of battle; not a shot fired, not a sound heard save the word of command. Even the black fort was hushed, and the sun went down behind the lofty mountain ridge on our right, leaving us in an amphitheatre of loveliness, and the peaks of the Comanche Saddle Mountain on our left, tinged with the gorgeous coloring of our own autumn evenings.

The town was directly in front of our line; its houses, its churches, its defenses,—all lying in the stillness and beauty of that Sabbath evening; nothing between us and its people but a few hundred yards of open plain.

It was evident to all that this movement of ours was in connection with Worth's; but what that was, or ours, a Captain of Infantry knew no more on this field than if he were at home. Still standing to our arms, night fell upon us, and with it a deluge of rain; now commenced the ringing of church bells in the town, the barking of dogs, and the flashings to and fro of lights, rockets, and alarms. Orders were passed down our ranks to maintain complete silence, with permission for the men to sit down in their places. Suddenly the clangor of bugles and brass bands was heard in the city, or emerging from it, and we were on our feet in the twinkling of an eye. It was profoundly dark, and the rain still fell in torrents; no enemy came, but we heard in the stillness of the night the hurried movements and activity in the town,—they had taken the alarm caused by the approach of Worth from an unexpected quarter.

We remained here until between ten and eleven o'clock, when we marched back to camp, learning on our way that a mortar battery had been constructed by our troops while we were lying in the plain; and that the howitzer battery had likewise been put in position.

Before the assault, let us take a look at the town, its garrison, and its defenses.

CHAPTER VI.

MONTEREY.

Monterey, the capital of New Leon, a city of eight to ten thousand inhabitants, would be considered a handsome town in any part of the world. The city itself is built upon a plain on the northern side of a small river called the San Juan, with a rivulet running through it which empties into the San Juan to the east of the town. The main road from the Rio Grande to the city of Mexico passes through Monterey, then on by way of Saltillo and San Luis Potosi to the capital. East, west, and south of the town, in close proximity, spurs and ridges of the Sierra Madre mountains limit the area of the plain, which opens to the north, and was the road by which we approached it. Just outside of the town, on its north-west front or angle, was what we called the black fort,—a square work with dry ditches and embrasures for thirty-four guns; there were but ten or twelve mounted, of various sizes from fours to eighteens, but chiefly twelves. Within the area of the walls was an unfinished cathedral, which rose to a considerable elevation above the parapets, and was occupied by infantry as a strong redoubt in support of the batteries *en barbette*.

General Ampudia had thrown himself into the town about the 14th of August, with about three thousand troops of the line, and the number of the troops had been daily increased by additions of regular and irregular forces until he had ten thousand fighting men of all arms under his command. With these men, and reliefs of citizens, an elaborate system of works had been constructed for the defense of the town. From the citadel a stream of water ran in an easterly course through the suburbs into the city, and which then emptied into the San Juan beyond the town on the east, as I have before stated. Its banks were in some places steep and deep; irrigating ditches extended from it to the north. This branch was crossed near the middle of its course by a pretty stone bridge, called La Purisima. There was a strong work, or *tête du pont*, on the south side of the bridge, and two long earth breastworks were on the southern bank of this stream *within the city;* on the east corner of the town a redoubt named Fort Teneria, mounting five guns—two sixes, one nine-, one twelve-pounder, and one howitzer,—connected by any number of ditches, hedges and barricades with the line of defense of the stream; while immediately in its rear, perhaps a little south-west of it, was another fort, called El Diablo, with three guns, and still another with four guns a little to its west, all of which were connected with and supported each other by curtains, ditches, and breastworks. Every street was barricaded,—many with embrasures for guns,—and every house and house-top was an arsenal of arms and missiles. All along the streets leading into the town from the north, in addition to the barricades, there were sand-bag parapets on the house-tops, behind which a large number of infantry were posted. No network of defense could have been much better prepared; and into it we got precisely by the way they who constructed it would have wished us to come.

I am not so familiar with the defenses on the western side, although I have visited and examined them. On the hill *Independencia*, overlooking the Saltillo road, was a large, venerable-looking building, called by us the bishop's palace (it was formerly the seat of the bishop of this diocese), which was strongly fortified and lined with troops and artillery. This hill fell off precipitously to the plain on its eastern side, and the citadel before spoken of commanded all the approaches from this direction: the Saltillo road, which was a prolongation of the main street of the city, running west, was defended by lines of barricades and the grenelled walls of a cemetery until they connected with the works that I have referred to—of the eastern defenses. In the centre of the city was the cathedral, with a large square or plaza in front; all the streets leading into it were strongly barricaded, and all the houses in its vicinity strengthened with every appliance of military engineering within the means of the garrison. In front of the town the plain was cut up by numerous quarry-pits from which stone had been taken for building purposes, and these pits were fringed with low chaparral bushes. With these details, and the knowledge that the road by which we had marched from Marin entered the city from the north through our present camp, a pretty fair idea may be obtained of our field of battle.

General Pedro de Ampudia was in chief command, having among his subordinates Brigadiers Torrejon,

Ortega, Requena, Méjia, Conde, and the Governor of the State of New Leon, Don Manuel M. Llano.

On the 14th day of September, while our army was at Seralvo, General Ampudia issued the following proclamation, of which I have a copy, and think it worthy of preservation, as its style is eminently Mexican:

"*The General-in-Chief of the Army of the North, to his companions-in-arms.*

"SOLDIERS! The enemy, numbering only two thousand five hundred regular troops, the remainder being only a band of adventurers without valor or discipline, are, according to reliable information, about advancing upon Seralvo to commit the barbarity of attacking this most important place; we count nearly three thousand regulars and auxiliary cavalry, and these will defeat them again and again before they can reach this city. Soldiers, we are constructing fortifications to make the base of our operations secure, and hence we will sally forth at a convenient time, and drive back this enemy at the point of the bayonet.

"Soldiers! Three great virtues make the soldier worthy of his profession: discipline, constancy under fatigue, and valor. He who would at this moment desert his colors is a coward and a traitor to his country. Our own nation, and even foreign countries, are the witnesses of your conduct. The question now is, whether our independence shall be preserved, or forever lost; and its solution is in your hands.

"I have assured the supreme Government of the triumph of our arms, confiding in your loyalty and enthusiasm; and we will prove to the whole world that we are worthy sons of the immortal Hidalgo, Morelos, Allende, Iturbide, and so many other heroes who knew how to die combating for the independence of our cherished country.

"Soldiers! Victory or death must be our only device.

"PEDRO DE AMPUDIA.

"HEADQUARTERS, MONTEREY, September 14, 1846."

CHAPTER VII.

STORMING OF MONTEREY.

September 21, 1846. I was awakened this morning before daylight, by an orderly who brought a message that Colonel Watson desired to see me. I dressed hurriedly and went to his tent. He was dressing by candle-light, and, as soon as I entered, told me that he had received orders to march with the First Division to storm Monterey; that he was troubled with one paragraph of the order which directed him to leave one company of his battalion as a camp-guard, and he wished to consult with me as to the company that he should detail. We talked the matter over whilst he was dressing, and he determined that Captain Robert Bronaugh's company should remain in camp. I should further say that one company of each regiment in the division was likewise detailed under the same orders as Colonel Watson had received; the large force of the enemy's cavalry making it dangerous to leave our camp without a strong guard. Before he had finished dressing, the Colonel, holding in his hands a pair of heavy new boots with cork soles, sent to him as a present from some of his friends of the Baltimore Bar, asked me whether he should wear those or a lighter pair, then lying on the floor of his tent. I replied, jestingly, that the lighter pair would be more suitable, as I thought there would be some running done to-day: he laughed heartily, and saying that he had the advantage of me, as he was mounted, put on the heavy boots. It was by these boots as much as by anything else that I identified his remains when they were disinterred to send to Baltimore for burial. The reveille soon sounded throughout our camp, the slumbering fires of the past night were replenished with wood, coffee was cooked, and by sunrise our men had breakfasted. Before eight o'clock we were in line, and the orders detailing Captain Bronaugh's company published on the parade. He behaved as I would have done, I expect, under the same circumstances—badly; and sharp and angry words passed between him and our Colonel. We moved out of the woods, fell in with the rest of the division, halted, a detail of Lieutenant Owen of Steuart's company with two enlisted men from each company was made to report for picket duty, resumed our march toward the city, and halted again where we had been in line of battle the preceding evening. The mortar, which had been then placed, was now discharged, and we witnessed the flight of the shell and its explosion in the air over the town; several others succeeded with very uncertain flight, when, from the citadel, two twelve-pound balls were sent in our direction, but they fell short. After half an hour's halt, the Fourth Brigade, consisting of our battalion, four companies of the First Infantry, with six companies of the Third Infantry, marched by file to the left, and after thirty minutes' hard marching, emerged from a cornfield at the distance of five hundred yards from and directly in front of a fort (Teneria), which opened upon us immediately.

We had been marching by a flank through the cornfield, but now moved forward into line, which threw the Third Infantry on the right, the First Infantry in the centre, and the Baltimore Battalion on the left. We advanced toward the fort with steadiness and rapidity, receiving its fire of round and grape shot, and the musketry of its infantry supports, when there came across our line of advance, and apparently in close proximity, the sound of an eighteen-pound ball sent from the citadel. *We were being enfiladed.* Still we advanced; another shot from the citadel, and the leg of Lieutenant Dilworth, of the First Infantry, was taken off as he stepped. If the gun which had fired that shot had been aimed the eighth of an inch more to the left, there is no telling how many would have been crippled. Still we advanced, notwithstanding this additional fire on our exposed flank, until we were within a little less than one hundred yards of the fort, until two of the guns were abandoned by their gunners, when, just at the moment the fruits of our gallant charge were within our grasp, our brigade commander committed the unpardonable blunder of changing the point of attack, and attempting to move by the right flank by file left, into a street of the town which debouched into the plain, about opposite the right of our line—our battalion being directly in front of the fort on its left. I was looking at the embrasure of the now silent gun, through which I purposed to go into the redoubt, when I observed a great deal of confusion on our right, which in a second was communicated to the whole line, and the impetus of our charge was gone. No orders could be heard; the din was deafening, shot crashing through our ranks; but it was evident what was contemplated, by the direction which our right was taking, and our battalion followed the Third and First Infantry into the street.

Our brigade commander was a very brave man,—I saw this now, and repeatedly afterwards during the day,—but he was no soldier, for he lacked the natural instinct of a soldier.

If there had been any faltering in his troops, if there were any impassable obstacle in our front, then there might have been some excuse for changing the direction of the brigade; but, going with the speed that we were, the hesitation caused by all not comprehending the movement was of itself sufficient to break the *élan* of the charge, without any regard to the severity of the fire to which the men were exposed at the moment. The dumbest soldier in that brigade *felt* that we had made a false and fatal step.

General Garland told me that his purpose was, in entering the town, "*to take the fort in reverse.*" He did not seem to think that those who had put the fort where it was would be likely to put a line of defenses to its *reverse* as well as to its front; he found it out before the day was over, and my own opinion is he got this idea from what it was said Captain Bacchus, of the First Infantry, subsequently did.

Let us see what is said about this matter by others.

I cite from Major R. S. Ripley's History of the War with Mexico, vol. i. page 206, etc.

"When Garland's Division moved from off the batteries (the mortars), Major Mansfield, with other reconnoitering officers, having two companies of infantry as the immediate escort, advanced into the suburbs of the town in search of a point of attack, and, after a short reconnaissance, sent a request to Garland to come forward. Whether he intended that he should come forward in person to examine the position, or that he should move up his troops to engage them, Garland understood him in the latter sense. While Mansfield had been employed in reconnaissance, Garland had halted the main body of his command out of range. Upon receiving the message, he moved forward in line, keeping to the left of the main road. By following the route which Mansfield had pursued, he gave his right flank to the citadel, while Fort Teneria was upon his left and front. The latter of these works soon opened heavily upon the command, and the citadel followed its example with a destructive enfilading fire. Still the Americans moved steadily forward until reaching the scattered buildings and inclosures of the suburb, which broke their formation; but, although in confusion, the advance was rapidly continued, for it was thought that Fort Teneria might be turned and taken in reverse. The Mexican fire from both citadel and Fort Teneria was kept up with vigor; and as the command approached the rivulet through the suburb, the masked breastworks on its southern bank received it with another destructive fire, which increased the confusion. Neither officers nor men knew anything of their position. Mansfield, who had led the assault when the troops had reached him, although wounded, pressed on, pointing out positions for attack, and there was no lack of brave officers to lead and brave men to follow; but from the gardens, from the neighboring house-tops, as well as from the masked breastworks, an unseen foe pelted the troops with musketry, while the heavy fire from Fort Teneria and the citadel kept rolling in on their flanks. Movements against a seemingly practicable point only brought a greater slaughter; and after many officers and men had fallen, still ignorant of their locality, the troops paused, and finally took shelter in a neighboring street."

It will be observed that Major Ripley ascribes our formation being broken to our reaching the scattered buildings and inclosures of the suburb. This is an error, as is also another statement made by him, that but three officers and some seventy men of our battalion kept to its work during the assault. Major Ripley was not with us, but was engaged gallantly fighting in Worth's Division on the other side of the town; and I will show farther on how this misstatement originated, for, up to the period of entering the town, not a man had shrunk from the assault.

To resume the thread of my narration: I have said the Third and First Infantry were on our right, and necessarily by the flank movement preceded us into the street leading into the heart of the town, and they caught the severity of the fire of the Mexicans lying in wait for our advance. It was a terrific fire from all sides, and as we hurried up the street we passed the dead, the dying, and those who were seeking shelter of the two leading battalions. I was well up with the head of our battalion, and did not look behind, but I have no doubt that men of ours sought shelter as had those who preceded them. I say, however, that the mass of our men followed as far as the mass of the brigade, and that was as far as brave men could go. There was no going any farther; the brigade was gone as an organization, and the last order given in that town by Colonel Garland, prior to the order to retreat, was obeyed by some twenty or thirty officers and men; the rest were unable to fight or do more than they had done, and were lying in the streets by which we had reached the shambles in which we were now cooped. I am wrong in saying this was all that remained of the brigade; I did not know at the time, and I believe it was not known to the commanding officers, that Captain Bacchus of the First Infantry had crossed the rivulet, and, with men of his own company and others, was in possession of a building which looked into Fort Teneria, and was firing upon its garrison. I have been told this by those who were present, and believe it to be true, because I had got some men in a house and was firing from its rear windows upon the Mexicans at the bridge head, when I was ordered out, and felt for the instant, by the tone of the order, as if I had been caught skulking; and I have a right to say that it was not known Bacchus was in a building, or *he* would have been ordered out of it.

Garland was on foot, Watson was on foot, Major Bainbridge was on foot;* Lieutenant-Colonel Henry Wilson, commanding the First Infantry, cool and collected, was on horseback; the dead and the dying were lying very thick, when there came tearing up to this point, designated the shambles, a section of Bragg's Battery, under Lieutenant John F. Reynolds; it had come in by the way we came, and met with a rough reception; it looked as if it had, and where it now was not much would have been left of it in a few minutes if not ordered out, which was done. To turn the leading piece was difficult in the narrow street; this was effected by lifting the gun-carriage jam up to the wall of the house, in front of which it had halted, by officers and men of the Baltimore Battalion. This gun disengaged, the other followed it out into the plain.

The Fourth Brigade was gone, but its commanding

---

* They had been dismounted by the enemy's fire.

officer was at his post. As angry as I was, I could not but admire the courage of Colonel Garland, for even in that storm of missiles he seemed unwilling to withdraw. Finally he said to the few about him, "We must retreat." Watson, turning to me, asked which way I was going. I replied, "With the men." He said, "I am going this way," and crossed to an open gateway on the north side of the street, entered it, and this was the last I saw of him. My second lieutenant, Oden Bowie, followed him; and I, with my lieutenants Schaeffer and Aisquith, took the streets by which we had entered—there was no difficulty in finding our route, it was painfully marked—to the plain outside the town. We were followed by our men, of both regular and volunteer battalions, who joined us in the retreat at every step, from the shelters they had sought. They were strung along from the suburbs up to the spot where Garland gave the order to retreat. As we emerged from the town, the citadel opened upon us with redoubled fury, and a portion of the men, both regulars and volunteers, continued their retreat until they got out of the line of fire; and this is the foundation of Major Ripley's statement.

The Baltimore Battalion went into action with about two hundred and thirty men, there being but five companies of us, and heavy details (among others, one of twelve men for Ridgely's battery) had reduced our present for duty to about this number. I carried forty-two muskets into action, and my company was one of the strongest in the battalion; so that if there were but seventy men, as Ripley says, it was a pretty fair proportion, after what had been done. But there were more; I rallied about one hundred and eighty officers and men, and made so respectable a front that Garland ordered me to unite with the fragments of the First and Third, which were being formed under Captain Miller, of the First Infantry, to support Bragg's Battery against a body of Lancers which had shown itself in the field, and whom we drove off with loss. I had with me Second Lieutenant Samuel Wilt, of Company A; First Lieutenant Laurence Dolan and Second Lieutenant M. K. Taylor, of Company B; First Lieutenant Eugene Boyle and acting Lieutenant John Truscott, of Company D; Lieutenants Schaeffer and Aisquith of my own Company E; and Captain James Boyd, with Second Lieutenant Robert E. Haslett and acting Lieutenant James Taneyhill, of Company F. (I am quite positive that I saw Captain James Piper in the town, and was told by those who had a right to know, that Captain James E. Steuart was also there. First Lieutenant Joseph H. Ruddach, a brave and efficient officer, was not with his Company F, being absent, sick at Seralvo.) With the Baltimore Battalion as thus organized I shared the fortunes of the First Division, under very trying circumstances, until night put an end to the conflict for the day.

Again let us hear from Ripley; he says, pages 208–9:

"In the meantime, Bragg's Battery had been advanced into the suburb, and had opened; but a few discharges proved the inefficiency of his guns in the position. His men and horses fell rapidly under the fire of the unseen enemy, and against the heavier metal of Fort Teneria in embrasure he was powerless;

and, finally, this first attempt at a demonstration was consummated by the whole command being ordered to fall back out of range."

There are two grave errors here. The first, intimating that the section of Bragg's Battery to which I have referred halted in the suburbs; it did not, it was brought far up into the town. The second error is in alleging that it opened fire; it did not; and the reason given by Ripley is why it was not unlimbered and put into action,—" his men and horses were falling rapidly." Garland did right in ordering it out of town; it was powerless there at that time.

I thank Major Ripley for saying that "the whole command was ordered to fall back out of range," for it was this very order, which I did not hear, that justified those officers and men of the Baltimore Battalion, and abundantly refutes the charge of their "having fled beyond the range of fire." They always told me that they were not only ordered to retire beyond the range of fire, but that they were led in doing so by officers other than their own.

After having repulsed the Lancers, we were ordered to shelter ourselves under the earthworks of Fort Teneria, which had been carried while we were in the town by a battalion of the Fourth Regular Infantry and Quitman's Brigade of the First Mississippi and First Tennessee regiments of volunteers. It must be borne in mind that the guns of the citadel were still sweeping the plain, and the capture of Fort Teneria enabled us, for the first time on that day, to find any shelter from its fire.

Here Brigadier-General Hamer came with the

shattered fragments of his brigade, and here Randolph Ridgely's Battery was somewhat protected, the riders and gunners being dismounted.

Now I can explain the death of Watson. When General Taylor heard the heavy volleys with which the appearance of our brigade in town was greeted, he sent forward a part of Butler's Volunteer Division to our support. These entered the city by several streets to the right (west) of the one by which we entered. Its leading regiment was Colonel Mitchell's, the First Ohio Volunteers,—our old friends of the Rio Grande,—and being met with the same reception as had been given to us, it was forced to retreat, and came out of town a good deal broken up. If Garland could have held on longer, as he wanted to do, or Hamer had arrived sooner, it is more than probable we could have held our own; but we just passed each other, Hamer coming in as Garland was going out. When Watson left me, inclining to the left, he met these troops coming in, and, joining them, fell dead in the charge. None of us had seen or heard anything of Hamer's Brigade until we saw them retreating from the town, and it was from them that the distressing fact was made known to me. Up to this time I was in momentary expectation of seeing him, and was imagining the pride he would feel when I turned over to him the command of his battalion, whose gallant conduct at that time was on the lips of every soldier of the First Division who had been in the town. "We will fight with the brave Baltimoreans," was heard on every side on that morning of the 21st of September, after the repulse of the first assault.

There was a dry ditch about Fort Teneria; and in this ditch and around and in the redoubt a large number of troops were collected of the First, and Butler's Volunteer Division. Brigadier-General Hamer ordered the men to form, but upon its being attempted, the fire from the citadel was directed against the mass, and, at the same time, the guns of Fort Diablo opened upon us. General Taylor now arrived, and going into the redoubt in company with him and Captain Randolph Ridgely, I saw the latter, aided by those who were around, train the guns of this fort, which had been captured, upon Fort Diablo, and its fire materially diminished by the fire from our guns in this fort. Our men were now enabled to form without being so much exposed, and another assault was made into the town with the same result as the former.

Again I cite from Ripley; he says, pages 211, 212, 213:

"So soon as the event was known, fragments of the different regiments, and Bragg's and Ridgely's field batteries [I did not see Bragg's Battery here; I am sure it was not whilst I was] were collected about the captured work [Fort Teneria]. General Taylor determined to hold his position in the town, and attempts were made to advance. General Butler first led the Ohio regiment to the left of the former attack, with the intention of assaulting Fort Diablo; but that work was stoutly defended, and could not immediately be taken. Butler, accordingly, fell back, but not until he had been wounded and lost many men. Meanwhile Taylor had ordered the main force of the First Division (still under Garland, although General Twiggs had come up from the camp to the captured work*) to extend to the right and

---

* I will explain this matter after I shall have got through with the extract.

endeavor to penetrate the town, with the idea of making way by an extended circuit to the rear of Fort Diablo. This was attempted, and although severely cut up by the fire of the Mexicans as they crossed the streets, especially from the *tête de pont* of La Purisima, the troops passed beyond the bridge-head, and, although in confusion, entered the yards of the street next the rivulet, driving the Mexicans from the adjacent houses; but further advance was impracticable. Directly in front lay a street swept by the fire of the *tête de pont*, and beyond, the deep ditches and high banks of the rivulet: while the Mexicans occupied the parapet of the bridge and a low wall which extended on the southern bank, whence they plied their musketry with unceasing vigor. But still the officers, though falling with the men at every moment, called on them to maintain their ground, while they searched in vain for a practicable point to pass the stream. Captain Ridgely brought up a section of his battery, but his fire was ineffectual against that of the heavy metal of the enemy from behind his parapets, and the battle in this quarter continued without any advantage to the Americans. The Mexicans were nevertheless pressed closely, and a heavy battalion of infantry from the interior of the town was sent to support the garrison of the *tête de pont*. It came down the street leading to the bridge, but before it could gain shelter it had to pass under the American fire from the houses and yards on the northern bank of the stream, which was delivered with so much effect that the column was driven back into the town. The Mexican artillery was then placed in position to bear upon the Americans, and, opening from the distance, beat through the walls of the houses and yards, whence they delivered their fire and rendered the position untenable. After a continued occupation of the exposed point, the attempt to pass the rivulet was given up as impracticable, and the troops were withdrawn to Fort Teneria.

"While the various operations had taken place in the suburbs, the Mexican Lancers had made many demonstrations of attacking the American troops in rear and cutting up the camp-guard at the wood of San Domingo,* though none of the demonstra-

---

* Our camp.

tions had been serious except that upon the detached companies of Garland's retreating command. The main body of the Lancers had come down at one time upon the Ohio and Mississippi regiments [I was in the town when *this* attack was made], which had been withdrawn from Fort Teneria; but these regiments had fallen back against a chaparral fence, whence they delivered a fire, and the Lancers had retreated. Bragg's Battery was sent in that direction from the captured work, and a few discharges effectually dispersed them. The captured guns of Fort Teneria were served from time to time upon Fort Diablo, until one of the howitzers was brought forward from the first position of the batteries. But the principal operations of the day upon the eastern front of Monterey were finished. During the afternoon the main body of the troops remained in and about the captured work, collecting the dead and wounded, and strengthening the position. The enemy made no direct attempt to dislodge them, but kept up a cannonade from Fort Diablo whenever any were exposed, which was replied to from a howitzer and with musketry. A movement of Lancers on the southern bank of the San Juan beyond the town was opposed by Ridgely's Battery, and a few shots drove them back. When night fell, the First, Third, and Fourth Infantry and Ridgely's guns were detailed to guard the captured work, and the remaining troops were ordered to the camp at the wood of San Domingo."

It would be very difficult for any one writer to have detailed more faithfully than Major Ripley has done the events embraced in the above extract from his history; the only material error is in including in the second assault some matter of description which belongs to the first assault, and connected therewith. I doubt much whether a more correct description was ever given of the incidents of a day's battle.

I said that I would explain the matter about General Twiggs's arrival at the captured work, and why it was that Garland still commanded the First

Division. I should, before this, have said that Colonel Garland was the next senior to General Twiggs, and took command of the division in his absence I saw General Twiggs when he came upon the field riding from the direction of the camp, but well out of the range of the guns of the citadel. This was, I think, about noon; it might have been a little earlier, but it was after the repulse of our first assault. I was so struck with his coming almost alone and in such very unmilitary garb, that he noticed me, and, approaching, said, "I expected a battle to-day, but didn't think it would come off so soon, and took a dose of medicine last night, as I always do before a battle so as to loosen my bowels; for a bullet striking the belly when the bowels were loose might pass through the intestines without cutting them." I was very much interested at hearing all this from so old a soldier, but still it didn't satisfy me; and I wasn't astonished when I heard subsequently that General Taylor had quietly ignored his being present, and suffered the command of his division to remain with Garland. He, however, remained in and about the field, although I did not see him again until late in the evening, when he appeared to have assumed command, and ordered the division, with the exception of the regiments before mentioned, to return to camp.

Among the many officers who had strenuously exerted themselves during the day, after the first assault, to reorganize the broken troops of both divisions, my attention was particularly attracted to one by reason of his *voice;* it was so clear, so distinct, so encouraging, and commanding, that when I first heard it I looked toward him and inquired who he was, and was told that he was Colonel Albert Sydney Johnston, of Texas, serving on the staff of Major-General Butler. I was sorry when my command was taken from him, as he was the first officer that had succeeded in bringing some degree of order out of the confusion which prevailed.

In recalling the effect produced upon me by the voice of Colonel Johnston, I cannot refrain from giving expression to the cheering influence of the manner and words of Captain Randolph Ridgely. When we were entering the town at the second assault, Ridgely came tearing along with his section, his head slightly bent forward, with his face to the right, as if meeting a storm of sleet, instead of iron, rain, and leaden hail, as it was; while in this position, passing me, marching forward with the Baltimore Battalion, his whole face lighted up with a smile, and he cried out, "Kenly, what do you think of this?" it seeming to do him good to know that I was in the same predicament with him.

Of this day's fighting, Major Ripley says truly, there were not wanting "brave officers to lead, or brave men to follow;" and we had lost three hundred and ninety-four men killed or wounded, including one general officer, eight field officers, seven captains, and eighteen lieutenants.

We dragged our weary limbs back to camp, and then I realized most painfully the irreparable loss we had sustained in the death of Colonel Watson, and I almost reproached myself at not having grieved more during the day; he was not only my commander, he was my friend, and I mourned his death.

September 22. A heavy cannonading was kept up all last night, and the rockets from the town illuminated the mountains in the rear to such an extent that the scenery was grand, almost sublime. At reveille we were ordered to be ready to leave at a moment's warning, and the stiffened limbs of the men yielded unwilling obedience to orders to fall in. During the morning it was reported that the Mexicans were assembling on the plain, and the division was formed, when my company was detailed to move to the front to support Bragg's Battery, near the city. I left the camp with my men, and once more took the road to the town. We soon perceived that there was heavy firing on the hill next the Loma Independencia, upon which was the bishop's palace, and we saw the soldiers fighting; it was the most exciting scene I had ever beheld, for now they were advancing to the assault on the palace. How my heart beat! for I felt that if they could carry the palace, the town was ours. On rushed the Americans, in full view as we marched, met with the fire from the Mexicans; but still they pressed on, and now they were getting in the works. Almost simultaneously with the entry of the Americans, we saw the Mexicans leaping from the windows, and running from the rear of the palace down the hill toward the city. We saw the Mexican flag lowered, and such a cheer as we sent up was never heard before on that plain; it was taken up by other troops, and the first flash of victory filled our breasts with inexpressible exultation.

The bishop's palace carried, it was clear that the

town was gone, for this hill entirely commanded Monterey and its environs, and it was only a question of time as to when it would surrender. All the dangers and fatigues of the preceding day were forgotten, and we moved forward almost forgetting the black fort, until a well-known sound reminded us that its heavy metal was paying its respects to us. I took my position on the left of the battery, which was in a slight hollow under the brow of a hill, and there we lay for two long hours exposed to an uninterrupted firing from the citadel, its twelve- and eighteen-pound balls flying over us in direct flight, or else made to ricochet so as to plunge in our midst. We lay with our heads toward the fort, with intervals of several feet between each man, and the horses and the guns were likewise separated by intervals, so that the rise of the hill protected us from the fire; but many of the ricochet shot plunged through, tearing up the earth in furrows, and scattering sand and gravel over us; but not one man was struck. Only the arm-chest of one of the limbers was shattered, the chips from which, flying in the air, were greeted by a loud cheer from the fort; and they never ceased firing as long as we remained there. Finally one by one the guns were withdrawn, and then in single file we ran as fast as we could until we got under shelter from the never-to-be-forgotten sound of those cannon-balls. I made the experience that nothing is so demoralizing to troops as exposure to an artillery fire of solid shot. I saw our very best troops on the preceding day quail under this fire, and to-day I noticed the dread with which our artillerymen regarded it as they made ready to withdraw from our position.

We had been thrown out to check any demonstration from the city, but the capture of the bishop's palace and the advance of Worth's troops gave the Mexicans enough to attend to in town.

Our division was now allowed to take some much-needed rest, and we lay listening to the sounds of the battle raging in Monterey, with that interest which it is impossible to portray, and which will be forever unknown, except to those who had gone through the fiery baptism of the preceding day. With us, every volume of sound was scrutinized, whether it were *ours* or *theirs*, every phase of the roar of musketry or booming of guns was discussed as to its locality and probable effect, the numbers engaged were counted over and over again, and the movements of the morrow determined, with an assurance of success that the fall of the bishop's palace had now given to every man in our army.

CHAPTER VIII.

THIRD DAY OF THE BATTLE.

At reveille on the morning of Wednesday, September 23d, we were again ordered to hold ourselves in readiness to leave, as a final attack was to be made on the town by the whole of the two divisions. At 8.30 the long roll sounded and the troops sprang to their arms; at 9 o'clock A.M. we marched from our camp, still in the wood of San Domingo, but called by us Walnut Springs, and followed our well-known road to the city; we halted within half a mile from the town, when the First Division moved forward into line of battle, and the command was given, "*In place, rest.*" This looked like work, and we had reason to believe that it was before us, for the town was shrouded in a canopy of smoke, within whose folds a sanguinary combat was raging. We were comparatively safe from fire, and our interest and excitement increased every hour; bombs were flying continually from either side; volleys of musketry, lighting up the smoke with a lurid glare, were mingled with the dull heavy roar of cannon flashing their jets of flame through the dark cloud enveloping friend and foe, and rolling down upon us, reeking with the smell of battle. I would have given an arm to have been ordered to the attack, and all were alike excited. As the fighting continued, I never beheld men in such a condition as ours; it was impossible to keep them in the ranks. They would jump up and sit down, fix and unfix bayonets, open their cartridge-boxes, unbutton their coats, stamp with their feet, swear the most horrid oaths, and it needed but one single cry of "Forward!" to have thrown that division like a torrent into the city, to aid their hard-pressed comrades. Still we waited for the order, still the fight raged in the town; hour after hour passed, *hearing* a battle and we doing nothing. We had been kept so long momentarily expecting the order to advance, that we had got worked up in the excitement to almost imagining that we were in position to participate, expecting to see the Mexicans making a sortie; and this was precisely what we were doing, and what we were placed here to do, although we were not aware of it at the time.

We must now take a glance at what Worth has been doing in this great drama, still continuing, and see where his troops are on this third day.

As we have seen, he left our camp at Walnut Springs on the afternoon of Sunday, the 20th, and after a sharp skirmish on the Saltillo road with a large force of Mexican cavalry and infantry, succeeded in turning the left or western defenses of Ampudia, and was on the night of that day in rear of the town. On the 21st, by a series of brilliant movements, he had effected such results that the capture by assault of the bishop's palace on the 22d, and the pursuit of its fleeing garrison into the western part of the town, followed as necessary consequences from these initial steps. His troops, advancing from the west, were now on this third day pressing the Mexicans toward the fire of the Americans, working their way from the east.

That General Worth handled his troops with consummate skill, and that his division behaved with great gallantry, no one has ever questioned. They gained great credit, and deservedly won the praise and the confidence of our country; but it would be to ignore facts if it were not admitted that General Taylor's operations on the eastern and northern fronts had contributed most materially to Worth's successes. In fact, Taylor did the work, and our losses had been Worth's gain, our little brigade losing more men on the 21st than Worth's whole division in the three days' fighting; and this is the way it happened. The Mexican General was outgeneraled, outwitted, and outmanœuvred from first to last. He had failed in every single instance to divine the object contemplated by us, and in no single instance did he display sufficient military judgment to take advantage of our mistakes. With a superior force of infantry, he failed to make a single sortie after our repulses; and with a superior force of cavalry, he failed to make a single successful demonstration upon our broken troops.

When, on the night of Sunday, Taylor lay in front of Monterey to cover Worth's flank movement, Ampudia was taken by surprise, and, without sufficient reflection, believed that ours was the real column of attack, and Worth's but a feint. When on the next morning he found Taylor had gone and Worth advancing, he threw his heavy masses of infantry to the line of his western defenses, but to be hurried back as soon as he saw Taylor's column advancing to his eastern works. He was now sure that Worth meant only a diversion in favor of Taylor, and that his original opinion was correct and had been well founded. This mistake, while it operated to his destruction, was near proving ours, for he threw at least six thousand infantry against us and *kept* them pelting away with but little regard to Worth's action. The consequences were that though he drove us out of town, he failed to support Fort Teneria, which was carried, while the Fourth Brigade was fighting the unequal contest and keeping his troops engaged as already narrated; and, having effected a lodgment, Taylor's position was so threatening on his right flank that he kept under the delusion that his danger was most imminent here, and kept the masses of his troops of the line confronting us. The bishop's palace was thus shamefully neglected by him, and when it fell, as I have already described, on the 22d, he awoke to the startling realities of his false calculations.

But one step remained for him to take, and that was to recapture the palace if it cost him his last man; he had plenty of troops and to spare to do it with, and he only made an abortive demonstration on the night of the 22d.

Thus it will be seen, as is unmistakably the fact, that Taylor had been fighting, up to this time, the bulk of the Mexican army; and the losses of the respective Divisions demonstrate it.

Now, on this third day, the advance of Worth's Division from the west relieved considerably the pressure on Taylor, and the whole army was concentrating its cordon around the garrison of Monterey. On the west, the guns from the bishop's palace were throwing shot and shell; on the south, a single gun was plunging solid shot into the main plaza; on the east, Fort Teneria was hurling its missiles toward the cathedral; and on the north lay our Division, an unbroken line of tried troops,—a dangerous neighbor in this hour of battle.

All this grand panorama was passing before our eyes, and until dark, without hunger, and without thirst, we waited. The curtain was up, and we were ready dressed to play our part. The call was not sounded, for we had been performing all that our commanding general had wanted us to do; for *he* knew where the

First Division of his army was, and *he* knew what he was doing when he put it there.

As night approached, the firing gradually dropped off, save that now and then a whizzing, which seemed more spiteful because less in quantity, might be heard cutting the air as the missile sped on its flight; now and then the explosion of a single bomb lit up the darkness of cloud and smoke with a thousand pictures of light and shadow; but as the cold shades of evening fell upon us, a silence, heavy and profound, was over camp and field, town and mountains, the living and the dead.

We returned noiselessly to the wood of San Domingo for rest, in order to gather strength for another day of unrest.

September 24—Thursday. The first information I received this morning was, that an armistice had been agreed upon for the twenty-four hours from the past midnight until the next; all was excitement and speculation as to the probabilities of an evacuation of the city by the Mexicans. During the day several heavy guns were heard, and we thought that hostilities had recommenced. At 5 o'clock in the afternoon the long roll beat, and we fell in hurriedly, not knowing what was to be done next; our whole brigade marched out of camp under command of Colonel Garland, and took the road to the fort which he had attacked on Monday morning the 21st. As we marched along, every eye was turned toward the old gray citadel; there was the same grim artillery looking from over the parapets, and each instant we expected to see the fire belch forth from its open mouths. No man would dare to deny the relief he felt when, filing from the main road, we obliqued to the left and were under cover from its range. We reached the well-remembered locality, and learned that we were to relieve General Hamer's brigade in holding Fort Teneria and adjacent works.

As we neared the redoubt, the stench from the buried and unburied dead was so offensive, that many of the men were made sick to vomiting. The four companies of the First Infantry under Lieutenant-Colonel Wilson were stationed in the main fort, and he did my company the honor to request that it might be detailed to strengthen his battalion. Not knowing what work was before us, we had left camp to go into battle without overcoats, and bringing with us neither rations nor blankets; it grew very cold, and there was nothing but the bare ground to lie upon. Just as they were dressed at midday, the men now lay huddled together, with their loaded muskets (which they were ordered to keep in their hands) sadly interfering with efforts to afford each other a little warmth. We knew not at what moment we would be attacked, and the entire absence of rumor kept us in such suspense, that, with the dreadful stench, increasing every hour, I think that no one fell asleep. Not less than thirty Mexicans had been covered up in a breastwork or curtain which extended and ran from the fort in which we were, to a distillery near by that had been converted into a redoubt; upon some of these bodies the earth was very thin, while our own dead were adding to the lesson of the day, and preaching to the living, as never priest taught in meeting-house or minster, that "this corruptible must put on incorruption."

I was on guard, and, as I could not have slept, was rather glad of it; there was no necessity to visit my sentries on post—they were wide awake. About midnight I heard the sharp challenge of the most distant sentinel, and the next moment the rattling of sabres and the noise as if of a body of horse moving rapidly toward us. Not a doubt was in my mind but that it was a body of Lancers at the head of a sally from the town. I gave the alarm instantly, and every man was on his feet. Captain Webster, who with his two twenty-four-pound howitzers was within the fort, pointed his guns, matches were lighted, and everything was made ready to meet the coming shock. No one smelt the dead, but the chill of the night air caused many a brave man to shiver with the cold as we stood in the darkness, hours of time concentrated in the running of a few minutes. Colonel Garland came into the fort, told Lieutenant-Colonel Wilson that the noise which had alarmed us was "General Taylor and staff leaving the city, escorted by a regiment of Mexican cavalry; *that all was settled, and that a capitulation had been agreed upon.*"

So sudden was the transition in our feelings, so sudden the unexpected intelligence of a cessation of hostilities, that the exultation, which otherwise would have been natural, was smothered by a dumb sense of wonder and astonishment.

In the startling alarm of approaching Mexicans in the dead of night, we had lost smell of the stench; we now lost all feeling of cold in the variety of emotions caused by the knowledge lighting up our minds that a great victory had crowned our arms with the success we had fought so continuously to win.

September 25—Friday. As daylight approached, the ramparts were crowded with the soldiers, anxious to see the evidence of the town being in our hands. Never did the glorious sun shine on a more beautiful prospect than was lying stretched around and about us. Nature was in unison with our feelings, and the happy termination of days and weeks of toil and danger added to the delight which a smiling landscape awakens in the dullest of human beings.

Within an hour, hundreds of women came to the fort, some sobbing, some smiling, to see the prisoners who were confined in the distillery building: they were admitted, and it was so affecting an interview that I had to go away.

We still waited to see our flag thrown to the breeze, but we waited in vain; the whole town seemed as if dead, so quiet was everything, and rumors started as if by magic from all quarters (in the fort and works we were holding) that the capitulation was a mere ruse, and done to gain time; that if *they* had been old Taylor, *they* wouldn't have granted an armistice—not a minute; *they* knew how it would be all along, etc. etc. etc.

We had got some ship-biscuits and salt beef, and the most of us were champing away at our hard tack, when, at 1 o'clock P.M., there came a flash of fire so suddenly, followed by such a density of volume of sound like the crash of thunder, that we sprang to our feet simultaneously. "They have begun again," was the general exclamation of officer and man; and all eyes were directed to the old gray castle. Behold! the American flag was being hoisted on that staff, from which the Mexican ensign had so proudly—yes, and gallantly—waved. One deafening shout followed, as sudden and as overpowering in volume as had been the salute which the Mexicans had paid to their flag when lowered at the citadel; three times three was huzzaed by every company and regiment of Taylor's army; and the flag of the Baltimore Battalion was hoisted on Fort Teneria as Captain Webster's guns, under command of Lieutenant James L. Donaldson, of Baltimore, fired a national salute in honor of the storming and capture of Monterey.

CHAPTER IX.

CAPITULATION OF MONTEREY.

"*General Orders.*

"TERMS of the capitulation of the city of Monterey, the capital of Nueva Leon, agreed upon by the undersigned commissioners, to wit: General Worth, of the United States army; General Henderson, of the Texan Volunteers; and Colonel Davis, of the Mississippi Riflemen, on the part of Major-General Taylor, commanding in chief the United States forces; and General Requena and General Ortega, of the Army of Mexico, and Señor Manuel M. Llano, Governor of Nueva Leon, on the part of Señor General Don Pedro Ampudia, commanding in chief the Army of the North of Mexico.

"ARTICLE 1. As the legitimate result of the operations before this place, and the present position of the contending armies, it is agreed that the city, the fortifications, cannon, the munitions of war, and all other public property, with the under-mentioned exceptions, be surrendered to the commanding general of the United States forces now at Monterey.

"ARTICLE 2. That the Mexican forces be allowed to retain the following arms, to wit: The commissioned officers, their side arms; the cavalry, their arms and accoutrements; the artillery, one field battery, not to exceed six pieces, with twenty-one rounds of ammunition.

"ARTICLE 3. That the Mexican armed forces retire within seven days from this date beyond the line formed by the pass of the Rinconada, the city of Linares, and San Fernando de Pusos.

"ARTICLE 4. That the citadel of Monterey be evacuated by the Mexican and occupied by the American forces to-morrow morning at 10 o'clock.

"ARTICLE 5. To avoid collisions, and for mutual convenience, that the troops of the United States will not occupy the city until the Mexican forces have withdrawn, except for hospital and storage purposes.

"ARTICLE 6. That the forces of the United States will not advance beyond the line specified in the third article before the expiration of eight weeks, or until the orders of the respective governments can be received.

"ARTICLE 7. That the public property to be delivered shall be turned over and received by officers appointed by the commanding generals of the two armies.

"ARTICLE 8. That all doubts as to the meaning of any of the preceding articles shall be solved by an equitable construction, and on principles of liberality to the retiring army.

"ARTICLE 9. That the Mexican flag, when struck at the citadel, may be saluted by its own battery.

"(Signed) "W. J. WORTH,
"Brigadier-General United States Army.
"J. PINKNEY HENDERSON,
"Major-General commanding Texan Volunteers.
"JEFFERSON DAVIS,
"Colonel Mississippi Riflemen.
"J. M. ORTEGA,
"T. REQUENA,
"MANUEL M. LLANO.

"Approved. { "PEDRO AMPUDIA,
"Z. TAYLOR, Maj.-Gen. U.S.A. Commanding.

"Dated at MONTEREY, September 24, 1846."

Prior to this capitulation, a flag of truce had arrived at our camp without my knowledge early on the morning of the 24th, although I was early informed that an armistice for twenty-four hours had been arranged. The flag bore the following letter from General Ampudia to General Taylor:

"*D. Pedro Ampudia, General-in-Chief, to Major-General Taylor.*

"HEADQUARTERS AT MONTEREY,
September 23, 1846, 9 o'clock P.M.

"SEÑOR GENERAL,—Having made the defense of which I believe this city is susceptible, I have fulfilled my duty, and have satisfied the military honor which, in a certain manner, is common to all armies of the civilized world.

"To prosecute the defense, therefore, would only result in distress to the population, who have already suffered enough from the misfortunes consequent on war; and taking it for granted that the American government has manifested a disposition to negotiate, I propose to you to evacuate the city and its fort, taking with me the *personnel* and *matériel* which have remained, and under the assurance that no harm shall ensue to the inhabitants who have taken a part in the defense.

"Be pleased to accept the assurance of my distinguished consideration.

"PEDRO DE AMPUDIA.

"To Señor Don Z. TAYLOR,
"Commander-in-chief of the American Army."

To this, General Taylor sent the following answer:

"HEADQUARTERS ARMY OF OCCUPATION,
CAMP BEFORE MONTEREY,
September 24, 1846, 7 o'clock A.M.

"SIR,—Your communication bearing date at 9 o'clock P.M. on the 23d instant has just been received by the hands of Colonel Morena.

"In answer to your proposition to evacuate the city and fort, with all the *personnel* and *matériel* of war, I have to state that my duty compels me to decline acceding to it. A complete surrender of the town and garrison, the latter as prisoners of war, is now demanded. But such surrender will be upon terms; and the gallant defense of the place, creditable alike to the Mexican troops and nation, will prompt me to make those terms as liberal as possible. The garrison will be allowed at your option, after laying down its arms, to retire to the interior, on condition of not serving again during the war or until regularly exchanged. I need hardly say that the rights of non-combatants will be respected.

"An answer to this communication is required by 12 o'clock. If you assent to an accommodation, an officer will be dispatched at once, under instructions to arrange the conditions.

"I am sir, very respectfully,
"Your obedient servant,
"Z. TAYLOR,
"Major-General U.S.A. Commanding.

"Señor D. PEDRO DE AMPUDIA,
"General-in-chief, Monterey."

During the day a cessation of hostilities took place, and, at the request of Ampudia, an interview took place between the two commanding generals, which resulted in the capitulation, and to which I have heretofore referred.

Before I refer to the terms granted to the Mexicans, and which occasioned wide-spread comment and dissatisfaction both at Washington and in the army,—in the latter, a reflex of the former,—I shall give extracts from the official report of General Taylor:

"Upon occupying the city it was discovered to be of great strength in itself, and to have its approaches carefully and strongly fortified. The town and works were armed with forty-two pieces of cannon, well supplied with ammunition, and manned with a force of at least seven thousand troops of the line and from two thousand to three thousand irregulars. The force under my orders before Monterey was four hundred and twenty-five officers and six thousand two hundred and twenty men.

Our artillery consisted of one ten-inch mortar, two twenty-four-pound howitzers, and four light field batteries of four guns—the mortar being the only piece suitable to the operations of the siege.

"Our loss is twelve officers and one hundred and eight men killed; thirty-one officers and three hundred and thirty-seven men wounded.* That of the enemy is not known, but is believed to considerably exceed our own."

The following is a list of the officers killed or those who died from their wounds, and the list of the wounded, in the operations about Monterey:

Captain Williams, Topographical Engineers.
Major W. W. Lear, Third Infantry.
Lieutenant J. C. Terrett, First Infantry.
Lieutenant R. Dilworth, First Infantry.
Captain L. N. Morris, Third Infantry.
Captain G. P. Field, Third Infantry.
Captain and Brevet-Major P. N. Barbour, Third Infantry.
Lieutenant D. S. Irwin, Third Infantry.
Lieutenant R. Hazlitt, Third Infantry.
Lieutenant C. Hoskins, Fourth Infantry.
Brevet-Lieutenant J. S. Wood, of the Second Infantry; serving with the Fourth Infantry.
Captain H. McKavett, Eighth Infantry.
Lieutenant-Colonel Wm. H. Watson, Baltimore Battalion.
Lieutenant Hett, First Ohio Volunteers.
Captain Allen, First Tennessee Volunteers.
Lieutenant Putnam, First Tennessee Volunteers.
Captain Gillespie, Texas Rangers.

Among the wounded officers were

Major-General Butler, slightly; Lieutenant-Colonel McClung, of the First Mississippi Rifles, severely; Colonel Mitchell, of the

* The total loss in Worth's Division, killed and wounded, in the operations about Monterey, was fifty-five, which of course is included in the above aggregate of four hundred and eighty-eight.

First Ohio Volunteers, slightly; Major Mansfield, of the Engineer Corps; Major J. S. Abercrombie, of the First Infantry; Captain J. H. Lamotte, of the First Infantry; Major H. Bainbridge, of the Third Infantry; Lieutenant R. H. Graham, of the Fourth Infantry; Lieutenant N. B. Rossell, of the Fifth Infantry; Captain R. C. Gatlin and Lieutenant I. H. Pollet, of the Seventh Infantry; and Lieutenant C. Wainwright, of the Eighth Infantry.

The following is the list of the killed or who died from their wounds, and the wounded, of the battalion of Baltimore and Washington Volunteers, in the operations about Monterey, Mexico, September 21st, 22d, and 23d, 1846:

Lieutenant-Colonel Wm. H. Watson, Commanding Battalion, killed.

Orderly Sergeant and Acting Lieutenant John Truscott, Company D, killed.

Sergeant George A. Herring, Company F, killed.
Private Wm. J. Alexander, Company A, killed.
" Robert Caples, Company A, killed.
" Patrick O'Brien, Company B, killed.
" Alexander Ramsay, Company E, killed.
" Joseph Wharry, Company E, killed.
" William Kelly, Company F, killed.

WOUNDED.

Private Joseph Files, Company A, lost an arm.
" William Lee, Company A, shot through the body.
" Robert Donnelly, Company A, slightly.
Orderly Sergeant Wm. F. Powelson, Company B, slightly.
Private George Harrold, Company B, slightly.
" Charles Yeck, Company D, slightly.
" Andrew J. Morris, Company D, slightly.
Color Sergeant Albert Hart, lost an arm.
Color-Guard Corporal Jacob C. Hemmick, slightly.
Orderly Sergeant G. Oliver Lansdale, Company E, slightly.
Private John Allen, Company E, slightly.

Private James Henry, Company E, severely.
" Harry I. Elting, Company E, slightly.
" Henry Gifford, Company F, slightly.
" Melvin S. Stone, Company F, slightly.
" Edward Stephenson, Company F, slightly.

Total: Killed, nine; wounded, sixteen; aggregate, twenty-five.

"The battle is over: the army, both regulars and volunteers,—or more properly speaking, Americans,—have proved themselves invincible. Both officers and men, with death staring them in the face, did their duty without flinching, and with a bravery worthy of all praise."—*From "Campaign Sketches," by Captain W. S. Henry, Third Infantry.*

A meeting of the officers of the battalion was held in camp, on September 27th, for the purpose of expressing the regret felt by the battalion, and the loss it had met with, in the death of Lieutenant-Colonel William H. Watson, of Baltimore, its late commanding officer. Resolutions were passed, eulogizing the character of the deceased, and manifesting deep sympathy for his bereaved family; a committee was also appointed to prepare suitable resolutions for transmission to the newspapers of Baltimore City, for publication, so that the sense of the meeting might be made known to the people of Maryland.

Before I give place to the report of Captain James E. Steuart, the senior captain of the battalion, I transcribe the following congratulatory order of General Taylor:

"Headquarters Army of Occupation,
"Camp near Monterey, September 27, 1846.

"*Orders No.* 123.

"The commanding general has the satisfaction to congratulate the army under his command upon another signal triumph over the Mexican forces, superior to us in numbers, strongly fortified, and with an immense preponderance of artillery. They have yet been driven from point to point, until forced to sue for terms of capitulation. Such terms have been granted as were considered due to the gallant defense of the town, and to the liberal policy of our own government.

"The general begs to return his thanks to his commanders, and to all his officers and men, both of the regular and volunteer forces, for the skill, the courage, and the perseverance with which they have overcome manifold difficulties, and finally achieved a victory, shedding lustre upon the American arms.

"A great result has been obtained, but not without the loss of many gallant and accomplished officers and brave men. The army and country will deeply sympathize with the families and friends of those who have thus sealed their devotion with their lives.

"By order of Major-General Taylor.

"W. W. S. Bliss,
"A. A. G."

Official Report of Captain James E. Steuart, commanding officer of the Battalion of Baltimore and Washington Volunteers.

"Camp near Monterey, Mexico,
September 26, 1846.

"The battalion of Maryland and D. C. Volunteers, under the command of Lieutenant-Colonel Watson, connected with the First Regiment of Infantry, the whole under the command of Lieutenant-Colonel Wilson, were ordered to march at about 8 o'clock on the morning of the 21st inst., for the attack on Monterey. The battalion were out in their full strength, save Company C, Captain Bronaugh, which was ordered to remain on guard-duty at camp, and Lieutenant Owen, of Company A, with a detachment of twelve men, were ordered on picket-guard by General Twiggs. The battalion marched towards the city, and charged in the most gallant manner on a battery, under a galling fire in which it sustained some loss. The point of attack was then changed by order of Colonel Garland, and we entered the city exposed to a destructive fire from several batteries, supported by a large number of infantry, which raked the streets.

"We remained in the city for nearly half an hour, when we

were ordered to retire; in doing so, the battalion became separated. Colonel Watson fell by a musket-shot, whilst gallantly leading on to a second assault on the city.

"A portion of the battalion was then formed under Captain Kenly, and remained on the field of battle until it was ordered back to camp by General Twiggs, having been under a heavy fire nearly nine hours, losing in action: killed, six; wounded, eighteen.*

"I take pleasure in noticing the gallant conduct of the battalion throughout.

"(Signed) "JAMES E. STEUART,
"Captain Commanding."

It will be observed that this report bears date the 26th day of September. On the preceding day I had handed to Captain Steuart my report of the operations on the 21st inst., in which I reported that I had rallied the battalion after we had come out of the town, and, finding myself the senior officer present, had assumed command, had kept it in action, and fought with it, until ordered at nightfall to return to camp. I also reported the names of the officers who were present with their companies, and their gallant conduct during the day.

I was on friendly terms with Captain Steuart, had seen him behave with as much bravery as any man in the brigade in the assault on the fort, and never dreamed that he would do me the wrong to withhold from the commanding general the official knowledge of my conduct on the 21st.

He did withhold it, and also his own official report, until it was too late for me to remedy the wrong; and

* Three of these were mortally wounded, and two of them were dead at the date of this report.

the consequence was, my name was not mentioned in general orders from the headquarters of the army.

The bare mention of this behavior will convey to a soldier, after reading Captain Steuart's own report, a proper sense of the grievous and irreparable wrong done me.

A few days after the capitulation, an officer came to me, direct from General Taylor's tent, and in a surprised manner asked me why no report had been received from the Baltimore Battalion. I was confounded. He said, moreover, that General Twiggs and General Taylor had *both* sent to Captain Steuart, saying that they were waiting for his report.

I hurried to the tent of Steuart, and, in as quiet a manner as I could, inquired if he had not sent in his official report to headquarters. He hesitated, and then answered that he had done so. I then asked if he had mentioned my name. He replied that he had done so.

I told him that I had heard differently, but must content myself with his assurance. Still not satisfied, I called upon him again in the course of the day, when he again assured me that he had sent in his report and had mentioned my conduct.

It never occurred to me at the time to inquire by whom he had sent it, but subsequent events gave me good reason to believe that, even if sent, it had been destroyed by the messenger, as it never reached General Twiggs's headquarters.

There was one very bad man and bad counselor about Captain Steuart's headquarters.

If I had only had the presence of mind to have

gone further, and traced the report,—for it was undoubtedly *written*, as Steuart said,—I would yet have been in time for General Taylor's report; but unfortunately it never entered my thoughts.

The foregoing report, from the copy in the Adjutant's office, was subsequently published in the Baltimore newspapers, and to some extent satisfied my friends.

The report is strictly and literally true, as far as it goes, except that we remained in the city longer than Captain Steuart reports; but nothing whatever is said of the movements of the battalion on the second and third days, although he led the battalion on the third day and was present for duty on the second day of the battle; and everything done by the battalion on the first day after the fall of Watson, except that I formed the battalion and remained on the field, is quietly ignored.

CHAPTER X.

CAPITULATION OF MONTEREY.

In his dispatches to the government, General Taylor wrote concerning the *terms* granted the garrison by the capitulation:

"It will be seen that the terms granted the Mexican garrison are less rigorous than those first imposed. The gallant defense of the town, and the fact of a recent change of government in Mexico believed to be favorable to the interests of peace, induced me to concur with the commission in these terms, which will, I trust, receive the approval of the government. The latter consideration also prompted the convention for a temporary suspension of hostilities. Though scarcely warranted by my instructions, yet the change of affairs since those instructions were issued seemed to warrant this course. I beg to be advised as early as practicable whether I have met the views of the government in these particulars."

The Honorable William L. Marcy, Secretary of War, replied in a letter dated "War Department, Washington, October 13th, 1846" (see Ex. Doc. No. 60, page 355, etc.):

"Your communications of the 22d, 23d, and 25th ult., detailing the operations of the army under your immediate command at Monterey, have been received. The skill, courage, and gallant conduct displayed on that occasion by the troops under your command, both regulars and volunteers, have added glory to our arms, and merit from the government and people of the United States the warmest expressions of gratitude and praise.

"In relation to the terms of the capitulation of Monterey, the President instructs me to say that he regrets it was not deemed advisable to insist upon the terms which you had first proposed. The circumstances which dictated doubtless justified the change. The President, uninformed of these circumstances, does not know in what degree the recent change in the government of Mexico may have contributed to this result. Certain it is, however, that the present rulers of that republic have not yet given any evidence that they are 'favorable to the interests of peace.' Of this you will have already been informed by my dispatch of the 22d ult.

"The government did not contemplate, as you will perceive by the tenor of the dispatches from this department, that there would probably happen any contingency in the prosecution of the war in which it would be expedient to suspend hostilities before the offer of acceptable terms of peace."

As this subject of the capitulation was the general topic of conversation after the fall of Monterey, I have chosen to present the views of the government before making any reflections of my own.

The army was very much divided in opinion; those opposed to its terms as being too lenient increased in numbers with the number of days elapsing from the surrender of the town. At that time, and when the terms granted the garrison were first made known, I hazard the assertion that not one hundred men thought them too liberal, although a very large number became dissatisfied when they saw the Mexicans marching out, carrying with them the very battery of twelve-pounders from the citadel which had caused us so much loss. I confess that I did not like this, and felt uncomfortable at the sight; but I had been, was, and am now unequivocally of the opinion that General Taylor's wisdom in securing the surrender of the town and fortifications of Monterey was as great as his courage and boldness in the attack upon it. Aside from the claims of humanity, the helpless condition of the women and children, our own disparity of force and distance from base of supplies, I saw enough of the Mexican troops when they marched out, to satisfy me that they only lacked one daring leader to have made their escape or a successful defense. They went out sullenly, defiantly, and their attitude was such as to create a well-founded apprehension that a collision would occur between them and our troops who lined the roadside. This behavior increased the feeling against the capitulation; and when it became known that the administration had manifested its disapproval, its opponents largely outnumbered its defenders. Another cause, to which I shall hereafter refer, added to the clamors against General Taylor and fault-finding with his conduct toward the Mexicans; but it came from those who would not have followed him when he bared his breast in the shock of battle, and who were too heartless to appreciate the nobility of character possessed by their chief. It is worthy of note that I met with no one who had been in the assaults of the first day on the eastern defenses that found fault with the terms, and I could tell, as soon as I heard an opinion expressed, what part the speaker had taken, and to what corps he belonged, in the battles which resulted in the surrender of Monterey.

It was a long time after this before I became acquainted with the views of the general; and, as I have never seen them in print except in a public document, it is due to his memory to aid in their preservation.

I give the letter entire, as it can be found in the Executive Document before referred to, pages 359, 360.

"HEADQUARTERS ARMY OF OCCUPATION,
"CAMP NEAR MONTEREY, November 8, 1846.

"SIR,—In reply to so much of the communication of the Secretary of War, dated October 13th, as relates to the reasons which induced the convention resulting in the capitulation of Monterey, I have the honor to submit the following remarks:

"The convention presents two distinct points:

"*First.*—The permission granted the Mexican army to retire with their arms, etc.

"*Secondly.*—The temporary cessation of hostilities for the term of eight weeks. I shall remark on these in order.

"The force with which I advanced on Monterey was limited, by causes beyond my control, to about six thousand men. With this force, as every military man must admit who has seen the ground, it was entirely impossible to invest Monterey so closely as to prevent the escape of the garrison. Although the main communication with the interior was in our possession, yet one route was open to the Mexicans throughout the operations, and could not be closed, as were also other minor tracks and passes through the mountains. Had we therefore insisted on more rigorous terms than those granted, the result would have been the escape of the body of the Mexican force, with the destruction of its artillery and magazines; our only advantage the capture of a few prisoners of war, at the expense of valuable lives and much damage to the city. The consideration of humanity was present to my mind during the conference which led to the convention, and outweighed in my judgment the doubtful advantages to be gained by a resumption of the attack upon the town. This conclusion has been fully confirmed by an inspection of the enemy's position and means since the surrender. It was discovered that his principal magazine, containing an immense amount of powder, was in the cathedral, completely exposed to our shells from two directions. The explosion of this mass of powder, which must have ultimately resulted from a continuance of the bombardment, would have been infinitely disastrous, involving the destruction not only of the Mexican troops, but of non-combatants, and even our own people, had we pressed the attack.

"In regard to the temporary cessation of hostilities, the fact that we are not at this moment (within eleven days of the termination of the period fixed by the convention) prepared to move forward in force, is a sufficient explanation of the military reasons which dictated this suspension of arms. It paralyzed the enemy during a period when, from the want of necessary means, we could not possibly move. I desire distinctly to state, and to call the attention of the authorities to the fact, that, with all diligence in breaking mules and setting up wagons, the first wagons in addition to our original train from Corpus Christi (and but one hundred and twenty-five in number) reached my headquarters on the same day with the Secretary's communication of October 13th, viz., the 2d instant. At the date of the surrender of Monterey, our force had not more than ten days' rations; and even now, with all our endeavors, we have not more than twenty-five. The task of fighting and beating the enemy is among the least difficult that we encounter; the great question of supplies necessarily controls all the operations in a country like this. At the date of the convention I could not, of course, have foreseen that the department would direct an important detachment from my command without consulting me, or without waiting the result of the main operations under my orders.

"I have touched the prominent military points involved in the convention of Monterey. There were other considerations which weighed with the commissioners in framing, and with myself in approving, the articles of the convention. In the conference with General Ampudia, I was distinctly told by him that he had invited it to spare the effusion of blood, and because General Santa Anna had declared himself favorable to peace. I knew that our government had made propositions to that of Mexico to negotiate, and I deemed that the change of government in that country since my last instructions fully warranted me in entertaining considerations of policy. My grand motive in moving forward with very limited supplies had been to increase the inducements of the Mexican government to negotiate for peace. Whatever may be the actual views or disposition of the Mexican rulers, or of General Santa Anna, it is not unknown to the government that I had the very best reason for believing the statement of General Ampudia to be true. It was my opinion at the time of the convention, and it has not been changed, that the liberal treatment of the Mexican army, and the suspension of arms, would exert none but a favorable influence in our behalf.

"The result of the entire operation has been to throw the Mexican army back more than three hundred miles to the city of San Luis Potosi, and to open the country to us as far as we choose to penetrate it, up to the same point.

"It has been my purpose in this communication not so much to defend the convention from the censure which I deeply regret to find implied in the Secretary's letter, as to show that it was not adopted without cogent reasons, most of which occur of themselves to the minds of all who are acquainted with the condition of things here. To that end I beg that it may be laid before the General-in-Chief and the Secretary of War.

"I am, sir, very respectfully,

"Your obedient servant,

"(Signed) "Z. TAYLOR,

"Major-General U. S. A. Commanding.

"To the Adjutant-General of the Army, Washington, D. C."

Whilst I fully agree with the plain but cogent reasons so simply stated by General Taylor to be laid before the Secretary of War, I cannot and did not coincide with the view entertained by him, "that the liberal treatment of the Mexican army, and the suspension of arms, would exert none but a favorable influence in our behalf." I think that the general was clearly in error in this idea, and that his mistake arose from the impression which prevailed at his headquarters that the Mexicans were desirous of making peace. I have heretofore said, and now repeat it, that up to this time I had found none in favor of yielding one iota of the demand for the evacuation of their territory by our troops; but that Taylor gained more than did the Mexicans by the suspension of arms, is too clear for controversy, and the Mexicans, being deceived as to our supplies and means of transportation, were the losers by their own proposition, upon which Ampudia prided himself very much for his diplomacy.

But motives of state policy, though in the mind of General Taylor and duly considered, were not the main reasons for granting the terms he did; these were purely military, conjoined with a strong feeling of humanity. His sentiment of pity for the helpless inhabitants of Monterey coincided with his opinion, as a military chief, that the actual status of things justified letting go the garrison for the sake of the other and manifest advantages resulting to his arms from the acquisition of the city, its munitions, and its fortifications. Whatever might be the future policy of his own or the Mexican government, he had captured the capital of an important State of the Mexican Republic, had strengthened his base for further offensive movements, and had added very greatly to the prestige of American valor by inspiring confidence in the steadiness of his volunteer forces. How fully the latter view was sustained by the result of further operations, history is familiar with, and Buena Vista strengthened the confidence which those who knew him entertained for the judgment as well as the military capacity of General Taylor.

In this connection I beg attention to the official dispatch of General Ampudia, which must be read with the previous proclamations issued by him, to be properly appreciated.

"*Official dispatch of General Ampudia to the Mexican Secretary of War, announcing the surrender of Monterey.*

"MOST EXCELLENT SIR,—After a brilliant defense, in the course of which the enemy was repulsed with the loss of fifteen hundred men from various posts, he succeeded in possessing himself of the heights commanding the bishop's palace, and another to the south of it, and likewise a detached breastwork called the Teneria, and continuing his attacks through the houses, which he pierced in a direction toward the centre of the city, he succeeded in posting himself within half-gunshot of the principal square, where the troops were posted, who suffered much from the hollow shot. Under these circumstances I was requested by various principal officers to come to such terms as would diminish our losses; for to open our way with the bayonet, surrounded as we were by intrenched enemies, would have resulted in the dispersal of the troops, and nothing of the *matériel* would have been saved. These considerations having been weighed by me, I also took into view what the city suffered, and would suffer from the attacks by the piercing of the houses as well as the destruction by the bombs, the scarcity of ammunition which was beginning to be felt, the provisions which we were losing as the enemy's lines approached the centre, the distance from our supplies, and, finally, that to protract this state of things for two or three days, even if it were possible to do so, could not end in a triumph; and I consented to open propositions which resulted in the annexed terms of capitulation.*

"Your excellency will perceive that they preserve the honor of the nation and that of the army, and it is to be observed that if they do not grant us as much as was perhaps expected, that of itself proves the superiority of the enemy,—not in valor, which he displayed in most of the combats, but in his position within the squares of pierced masonry, which surrounded the square and cut off any supplies of provisions, wood, or other articles necessary to subsistence.

"With the greatest regret the army withdraws from their capital abundantly watered with its blood, leaving under the guaranties of the promises of the American generals the severely wounded and the neighboring population of the State, whose civil authorities will continue in the exercise of their functions. To-morrow I shall continue my march to Saltillo, where I will await the orders of the Supreme Government; and in communicating this to you I have the honor to reiterate the assurances of my highest respect.

"God and liberty.

"(Signed) "PEDRO DE AMPUDIA.

"HEADQUARTERS IN MONTEREY, September 25, 1846."

My desire has been to place this matter of the capture of Monterey and the incidents connected there-

---

* These have already been given.

with fairly on record; I have endeavored to do so, and upon review am willing to let it stand as true. Much of what I have written passed under my own knowledge, and when I consulted contemporaneous authority I sought that whose authenticity could not be questioned.

CHAPTER XI.

IN CAMP AT WALNUT SPRINGS.

General Taylor established his headquarters at Monterey in the woods at Walnut Springs, and the troops were camped pretty much as they halted for the bivouac of the 19th of September, in, around, and about this wood of San Domingo. The Baltimore Battalion selected a new camp a little distance from their bivouac, and not far from the modest tent of the general commanding the army of occupation. Immediately in front of the general's tent,—there being an open space of some extent,—the Mexicans from the surrounding country, who, with that instinct characteristic of all peoples, knew that Old Zack was their friend, had quietly established a market for the sale of their products directly under his eyes, and which he permitted to continue as long as we were in camp near Monterey. They felt that they were safe there; and I am sorry to say it was about the only safe place for them within a circuit of twenty miles. Already, within a few days after the surrender, a series of wanton outrages had been perpetrated upon the inoffensive inhabitants, which caused the liveliest sense of indignation among our best troops, and provoked bloody retaliation from the Mexicans. The matter was growing serious; it was no uncommon thing for several dead Mexicans to be found lying in the road, daily, between camp and town, and our men would be assailed on their way to camp from town, and several had been seriously wounded. My Second Sergeant, Benjamin F. Brand, was dreadfully wounded between town and camp by a gang of Mexican desperadoes; this was followed in a few days by a wholesale slaughter of Mexicans, but not by our men. The general sentiment of the army was one of horror, and a resolute determination to put an end to this state of things. In the mean time, Governor Morales, of Monterey, addressed a note to General Taylor, saying "that multitudes of complaint have been made to this government against excesses committed upon the persons and property of Mexicans, and that he had just been informed that three of their citizens had been killed," etc.

To this the general replied that it was with regret that he learned there was just cause of complaint, founded upon the grounds stated by his excellency; but that General Worth had been invested with authority to adopt measures to maintain order in the city, and he hoped all cause of further complaints would cease. I was an eyewitness to some of these transactions, and more than ever admired the character of Taylor for the active steps he took to prevent a continuance of these brutalities, both by friend and foe; and though not altogether successful, they became of less frequent occurrence, and a better feeling grew up between our people and the Mexicans.

It was the strong action taken by Taylor in this relation that, as I have before alluded to, added to the clamors on the part of some against the policy which dictated the terms of capitulation; but the old general was as firm in the camp as in the field, and he did what was right.

We soon commenced drilling, and, jointly with the regulars with whom we were brigaded, advanced in our military knowledge. Our camps were gradually brought into good condition, our guards well instructed, and picket duty carefully attended to. Each day added to the conviction that the war had but begun, and our duty as soldiers was now the business of the day. Our table was scantily supplied with government rations: this, however, made the delicious fruit which we got in abundance more prized. Bread, eggs, oranges, lemons, pomegranates, grapes, and bananas were brought daily into camp, and now and then a cow, and then a goat, were brought to be milked at the tent-door, to the great gratification of our men. It was growing cold, fires being very desirable at night, and, as we had no candles or oil, we passed our evenings around the camp-fires, talking and gossiping as only soldiers talk, and weaving that chain of *camaraderie* known only to soldiers and sailors.

We have just learned that Ampudia has halted at Saltillo, of course issued a proclamation, and, after calling on the people to take up arms, says that Santa Anna in person is coming to direct military operations against the invaders. So be it.

Our men begin to need clothing, particularly shoes; the long marches have been very destructive to the latter, and many of the men have made sandals from raw hide, which look right well; on parade, there are a good many without jackets, yet they look soldier-like and trim with their cross- and waist-belts.

We have just learned that a mail for our army has been captured by the Mexicans and sent to the city of Mexico. Rumor says, moreover, that General Taylor received a polite note from Ampudia, informing him of the fact. We have been for several days thinking of nothing but the arrival of this mail, as none of us had heard from home since our leaving there: our letters, we were constantly told, were lying at Point Isabel awaiting an escort; and now they were under the escort of the enemy. I think this day was a bad day for Mexicans; the general feeling being, what I heard a soldier say, "He would just like to have the eating of a Mexican." Don't take a soldier's letters if you want to keep on his best side.

It is getting *very* cold at night; still not a candle to be had for love or money, though there is very little of the latter. We are beginning to grumble, which is a good sign of health and progress in army life. We have no battalion drills, which is bad; company drills twice a day; squad drills at all hours; guard-mount, dress-parade, five daily roll-calls, then tattoo and taps; this is our routine.

Hurrah! I have received some prize-money, or rather loot, in the shape of cigars. I received two hundred cigars,—my share, as captain, of those taken at the capture of Monterey, and condemned as public property. I really think that at the time I would have preferred them to as many hard dollars; *now* I think differently.

Nothing can exceed the beauty of the surrounding scenery. The mountains are grand, especially at sunrise and sunset. I have seen the two peaks of the spur called from its shape the "Comanche Saddle," connected with a light strip of white cloud, and as the rising sun would strike it fleeces were thrown upward like the railing on a bridge, presenting the appearance of a hand-railing up a stairway, and making the whole look as if a bridge had been built up there for pedestrians to walk with safety across the chasm between the peaks.

May's Second Dragoons are now passing my tent; Bragg's Artillery are drilling on my left; the band of the First Infantry is practicing its usual morning exercises, while its drums and fifes are off in the chaparral at their lesson; the dead march is being played by the superior band of the Fourth Infantry at the head of one of the companies following a comrade to the grave; crowds of soldiers are passing and repassing with the listlessness of men off duty, and with the constant interchange of rumors remind me of the scenes I have witnessed in and around the old *Chronicle* office at Baltimore when we were waiting to hear from beyond the *Cayuga bridge,* in the old days of waiting to hear good news from New York, and which, by the by, rarely ever came to our wing of the political army.

On yesterday we buried Kelly, of Company F, who had died from the wounds received on the 21st ultimo. I had many reasons to feel very sad, and followed his remains, which were wrapped in a blanket, to their place of burial with more than usual mourning. Our single fife and drum were playing the dead march when we passed in front of the First Infantry Band practicing; it was playing "Dance, Boatmen, Dance," and involuntarily the escort and procession stepped off to the music of its quickstep, destroying the cadence if not the entire solemnity of the parade. How forcibly this incident struck us, and how painfully and rapidly the smile which it occasioned was changed to sternness of step and demeanor, will not soon be forgotten by those who were at that soldier's funeral. What a mockery to sing "A Soldier's Life is always Gay"!

CHAPTER XII.

SIGHT-SEEING IN MONTEREY.

I HAVE been into town, sight-seeing. As may be well supposed, my steps were first directed to the corner where I had seen so many officers and men fall. It looked very natural; the houses tenantless, doors open, walls torn and tattered, and all, save the dead and dying, the din and uproar of battle, very much as it appeared to me on the morning of the 21st. I found here some half-dozen American soldiers, who like myself had come to visit a well-remembered locality. They belonged to our brigade, and we spoke quietly together of incidents of battle which had been shared in common, and which had made us friends without knowing a difference of rank. From here I went up the street toward the bridge-head, and examined carefully the line of defenses, and more particularly the barricades. I learned a lesson in constructing them from these erected in the streets of Monterey. I do not think they could be improved or made more practically useful. I found the streets paved with square basaltic rocks, the sidewalks with large even flagstones. In many of the streets the pavement was torn up for defensive purposes, sand-bag parapets on every house, walls grenelled, breast-works and bastions at every corner. All who beheld these defenses were amazed that they were abandoned; it appeared to me, however, that they were *crowded* too much—too close together, and I was not surprised to learn, as I did to-day from a Mexican, that a large number of their infantry had not fired a shot. This is not improbable, looking to the number so imprudently massed about the centre of the city, and who were kept doing nothing for want of a general.

I visited the cathedral, and was surprised to find so large and imposing a church. Its exterior and interior are worthy of an extended visit. Some of the paintings appeared to me handsome, while others were ugly; the main altar was really grand, and that peculiar religious *tout ensemble* characteristic of Catholic worship was very perceptible in this venerable building. I also visited the pride of the town, the palace of General Arista, a very wealthy citizen of Monterey. Our wounded filled its corridors and marble-paved halls, around whose cots heavy curtains, mirrors, vases, paintings, etc. were hanging and arranged in careless profusion. The gardens and baths were fitted up in luxurious style, and the orange and the pomegranate mingled their perfume with the sweet rose of our own dear land. All was attractive, nay, enchanting.

I clambered up the hill on the west of the town to the building called the Obispada, or Bishop's Palace. I went to the window from which I had seen the first of the enemy leap when Worth's troops carried it by assault. The view from this window was charming, —the whole plain and the town nestling in its lap spread out before me; our camp and the road by which we had approached the city were also visible, and at my feet I could look into the old gray fort, whose guns had been carried off, but whose unmistakable visage was that of a veteran proud of his prowess.

It had a right to be, as all will bear witness who were within its range on the three days of last month.

The main plaza is, however, the great place of attraction. Here are already located billiard-saloons, restaurants, and drinking-saloons; in the centre a market is held daily, around which our soldiers are thronging, or else inspecting the cannon surrendered by the enemy, which are ranged on one of the sides of the square. Some of these pieces are of recent English manufacture and in excellent condition, as are also their carriages; others are old Spanish bronze or copper guns capable of good service; some are very old, and look as if they had been used by Cortez; altogether there are forty-two guns.

Having a twenty-four-hour leave of absence, I went to see an American circus to-night, the performance at which took place in the Mexican cockpit. There were a great many of our officers and soldiers present, —some few Mexicans; we had a grand *entrée* by the whole troupe, and then the usual ring ceremonies; but the feature of the evening was the riding by Dandy Jack upon the celebrated pony Comanche. The monkey's face was as familiar as if he were, or had been, in the ring at Front Street, and the shouts with which our men greeted his horsemanship must have been heard at camp. I noticed that the Mexicans were more interested in the contortions of the *india-rubber man* than in anything else exhibited. During the evening quite an uproar was occasioned by a heavy fall of rain; the galleries of the circus were uncovered,—open to the heavens; up here the rank and file were accommodated, and, as the rain began to wet them, they clamored for shelter. The manager agreed that they might find places beneath the *boxes* in which the officers were standing; they descended the ladder by which they had reached their elevation, and got under the plank flooring upon which we stood. Here they still complained of being uncomfortable, and a laughable scene of confusion ensued, the pit—in fact, the whole circus—becoming so tangled up that the clown announced from the now deserted gallery that, *owing to the inclemency of the weather*, the evening's performances were ended. They were for this place, but not—in town.

It is astonishing the number of men, non-combatants, that sprang up, as if by magic, around this army of occupation. Where they came from so suddenly after the surrender, nobody could tell, but really the place was filled with them. American stores, American goods, American drinks, and American faro had driven out Mexican shopkeepers and gamblers, and where, but a few days ago, none could be seen except in uniform, are now crowded civilians of every tongue and people. They follow the army, never precede it; they belong nowhere,—no, I am wrong: if asked where they are from, when soliciting permission "to open," they invariably answer, *New Orleans,* further than which no man knoweth to the contrary, and don't want to know, for you had better not press your question.

CHAPTER XIII.

DEATH OF CAPTAIN RIDGELY.

October 20, 1846. We have not heard from the United States since the news of the surrender must have reached there, and we are all anxiety to know what the government will do next. Rumors are very abundant, *not* of what we are going to do, but what the Mexicans are doing, and old stories revamped daily are flooding the camps. One day we hear that Santa Anna is within ten miles of Monterey with fifteen thousand men; on the next we hear that the Mexican Congress has made peace with the United States. Every shade and degree between these two extremes are hourly gossiped and discussed with an earnestness that would be laughable, were it not real.

On this day I wrote to my parents a letter, from which I make an extract verbatim, as it proved to be a prophecy:

"My own opinion is that the best plan (for conducting the war) will be to march to Tampico and operate in that quarter; for it would be suicidal to advance to San Luis Potosi with the army which we have; for there is no doubt but that a large force is there to oppose us, and, even if we should drive it before us, we would still be a long distance from the capital, where alone the terms of a peace can be dictated. The plan of the campaign should be to push on to Tampico, obtain the co-operation of the fleet, reduce this important town, and then, ho! for the city of Mexico by the way of Vera Cruz; and I should not be surprised if this were the very plan of operation adopted."

If I had been in the War Department at Washington, and in the councils of the government, at the time I wrote this letter, I could not have framed a more exact plan of what was subsequently done than is embraced above.

But as yet we had heard nothing, and the armistice was still in force.

October 31. I have a sad duty now to perform,—to record the death of my friend Captain Randolph Ridgely.

On last Sunday, the 25th inst., he sent over a horse to my camp and a message that he wanted me to accompany him to town, and I agreed to ride with him. In the course of the morning he told me that he had received an invitation to dine with Lieutenant Mackall, of the army, commanding a Battery of Light Artillery, and that I was also invited; he also informed me where Mackall's quarters were, so that, if we got separated, we might meet there.

Our horses had been put away in the yard of Mr. Lloyd Tilghman's sutler store, and when I went to get mine, I was told that Ridgely had just left and that I could overtake him, as he was on the road to Captain Mackall's Battery. I soon saw a crowd, and to my distress learned that Captain Ridgely had fallen from his horse. I have before said that the streets of Monterey were paved with basaltic rocks, and many had been torn up to form barricades; in the main street or road to Saltillo, the street through which Ridgely was riding, this was especially the case. One of these barricades had been thrown down, and the stones which formed it scattered loosely about; Ridgely's horse stumbled over one of these stones, and fell so quickly that Captain Ridgely was thrown, and his head striking the sharp corner of another of these rocks, his skull was fractured, and he remained insensible until his death, on last Tuesday night. I had parted with him not an half-hour previously, in the full enjoyment of life, health and strength, and now I could not realize that though living he was unconscious. Everything that friends and medical skill could do was done to save his life, for we knew that in his death one of the most gallant men of the army would have perished. He died, regretted and esteemed by the whole army; and the unprecedented respect paid to his remains, the touching tributes of affection showered upon his grave, evidenced the love and the admiration of men who had fought side by side with the hero. Every officer of standing—regular and volunteer — was present: Generals Taylor, Worth, Quitman, Hamer and Persifer F. Smith, with their respective staffs; artillery and infantry paraded, colors draped, drums beating the funeral march, and as the body was taken from the gun-carriage which had borne it, an audible sob heaved the breasts of his comrades. General Taylor stood immediately in front of me, and I saw him weeping, and his strong frame shaking with the extremity of his grief; so it was with many, and a more solemn occasion was never witnessed than the burial of Ridgely. Maryland has now given of her sons Ringgold, Watson and Ridgely! May those who have to follow them forget not her glory.

I give place now most willingly to the following handsome tribute, written by Captain William S. Henry, of the Third Infantry, and which may be found in his Campaign Sketches, pages 234–5:

"His body was brought out to the camp of his company, and buried with funeral honors on the evening of the 28th of October. His company escorted the remains, and the Baltimore Battalion attended as mourners. The procession was swelled by nearly all the officers of the army. Colonel Childs read the service for the dead, and three guns were fired over his grave. Dark clouds hung o'er the mountain tops; mists were in the valleys; and all nature seemed in mourning for the departed hero. Captain Ridgely graduated from West Point in 1837. He was a native of Baltimore, and from a family identified with the State of Maryland. He served with distinguished credit in the battles of Palo Alto and Resaca de la Palma, and in the storming of Monterey. For his gallantry in the action of the 9th of May, he was brevetted a captain and appointed an assistant adjutant-general; the latter appointment he accepted, the brevet he declined. He, as well as his friends, thought if he was deserving of a brevet for the 9th, he was equally so for the 8th of May.

It seems strange he should die by such means, after passing through three battles.

"If any officer has *particularly distinguished* himself, it is the lamented Ridgely. His dauntless courage and reckless exposure of person, combined with the most perfect coolness and judgment in the hottest fire, won golden opinions for him from all. Those who knew him in the social circle can well appreciate his loss. A bright star is extinguished! He will never return to pluck fresh honors for, and add new lustre to, the gallantry and chivalry of the service. Strange and unfathomable fate! He died from a fall from a horse, than whom none could ride with more grace and fearlessness, nor manage with more judgment and dexterity. He was probably the best rider in the world, an accomplished and polished gentleman, and one of the most heroic and gallant officers of the army."

CHAPTER XIV.

END OF THE ARMISTICE: GENERAL SANTA ANNA FOR WAR.

On the 2d of November, Major James Graham arrived at camp from the United States with dispatches from Washington. All was excitement, and rumor was trumpet-tongued; it soon became known that the government had officially notified General Taylor that it disapproved of the armistice, and it was supposed had instructed him to terminate it. On the 8th the following general orders were promulgated:

"Headquarters, Army of Occupation.
"Camp near Monterey, November 8, 1846.

"*General Orders, No.* 139.]

"Under instructions from the Department of War, the general-in-chief of the Mexican forces has been duly notified that the temporary cessation of hostilities agreed upon at the convention at Monterey will cease and determine from the 13th instant, after which date the American forces will be free to cross the line of demarcation established in said convention.

"Saltillo, the capital of the State of Coahuila, will be occupied by the United States troops."

* * * * * * *

Then follows the order of march.

On the 6th, Major Graham had been sent forward to give notice to the Mexican commanding general of the orders of our government; and on the 12th, just as General Taylor was preparing to march in the same direction, he received notice that a special bearer of dispatches was *en route* to Monterey. He awaited his arrival, and Major Robert M. McLane, of Baltimore, presented himself direct from the seat of government with important instructions to the general. These, however, did not prevent the contemplated advance toward Saltillo, and on the 13th General Worth marched with his division, accompanied by General Taylor.

As to the tenor of the dispatches, we know nothing positively, for old Taylor is as quiet as the grave; but rumor will have it that the army is to go to Vera Cruz, and that our division will remain on this line, as it was the most cut up in the capture of Monterey. We are at this time drilling three hours a day in battalion drill, with the four companies of the First Infantry, and one hour at company drill; our volunteers are pretty generally disgusted with *volunteering*, for it is no child's play, the daily labor now being done in earnest. Our camp is all bustle and activity, for although no one believes we will move for a week or so, we yet have orders to be ready to march at a moment's warning.

I was much astonished and gratified when I heard of the arrival of Major McLane, and immediately called on him. I was very much pleased to see him, and we had a pleasant interview; his citizen's clothes and city air brought *home* fresh to my heart, and his kind answers to my many questions made me very happy. My! my! this love of home! How strong a sentiment in the human breast!

General Taylor passed through our camp to-day, on his way to Saltillo; May's* Dragoons were his escort; as this small body of troops marched along, a general interest seemed manifested for Old Zack, as the men familiarly called him among themselves. There was an unmistakable anxiety felt for his safety, for the carelessness in the exposure of his person to danger was well known by the Baltimore Battalion.

Our sick list is increasing, and a very general desire to move prevails; the sun at mid-day is quite warm, the nights cold, hence fever and ague is abundant. The rumor of to-day was that Santa Anna is marching from San Luis Potosi toward Saltillo with twenty thousand men; he may have this many men, but he is not such a fool as to drive or attempt to drive Worth's Division back on Monterey. One of the

* Colonel Charles A. May: this gallant soldier was a native of the city of Washington, District of Columbia. He served in the Florida war: was brevetted major "for gallant service at Palo Alto," lieutenant-colonel "for gallant and highly distinguished conduct at Resaca de la Palma," and colonel "for gallant and meritorious conduct in battle of Buena Vista."

camp jests for the last fortnight has been to inquire, "When did you hear from General Wool?" there being an opinion prevalent that he is marching somewhere in the wilderness, hunting for the "army of occupation." The soldiers have got hold of it, and it amuses them greatly. I think from all I can learn that there is more truth than fancy in the story. It seems that he was sent out to effect a junction with Taylor for some ulterior object, but that the geography of the country was unknown, and a mistake made in the route of march. I expect that the soldiers have got hold of the right story, or they would not have so much fun in inquiring after him.

It is rumored to-day that the —— Regiment intends burning the town of Marin in revenge for the murder of two of their men; a heavy detail has just marched in that direction with five days' rations. A Mexican was shot dead in his own doorway yesterday; Lieutenant Bowie was passing a few minutes after the shot, and was called in to see him breathe his last.

We need General Taylor's presence all the time, and I hope he will soon return, for the bad feeling between the soldiers and country people is reviving; there are rumors of our communications with the Rio Grande being endangered, and that nearly every train is attacked on its way up.

General Taylor has returned from Saltillo, and we will soon move toward the sea; there seems no doubt about this, the only anxiety now is what troops will be left, and it has had one most excellent effect. It is well known that Taylor will *select* the troops to accompany him; he did this when he cut loose from the Rio Grande, and as there is almost a fever to leave Monterey the troops are on their very best behavior for fear that their corps will be left.

On his road to Saltillo, General Taylor received an answer to his communication informing the Mexicans of the cessation of the armistice. Sure enough, General Santa Anna was in command, for the note to Taylor was from him. The tone of this letter may be seen in the single extract that he (Taylor) "ought to discard all ideas of peace while a single North American treads in arms the territory of this republic, or while hostile squadrons remain in front of her ports."

From this it may be inferred that General Taylor had expressed a hope for peace; but Santa Anna's voice was still for war, and this was just the difference between the two men.

I went over to the market this morning to buy some oranges; having made my purchase, I was returning with an armful of the fruit, when hearing a call of "Captain," I looked and saw General Taylor sitting on a camp-stool in front of his tent. I approached him, and shaking me by the hand, he gave me a seat; I was so highly flattered that I hardly knew what I did, except that I gave him an orange. He asked me how we were getting on; I told him. He then said, "What could have induced Watson, yourself, and others to come so far from home to go through so many dangers and hardships?" I replied. He listened attentively, and when I had got through he shook his head, smiled, and said "he couldn't understand it." Before I left, General Twiggs came to where we were sitting, and made inquiry of

General Taylor as to when they would likely march, and whether he should take the Baltimore Battalion with him. General Taylor turned to me and asked whether I wished to go. I replied, "General, *we* always wish to follow you." He answered Twiggs, "Certainly, take them along." I waited to hear no more, but ran over to our camp to spread the joyous intelligence.

CHAPTER XV.

APPOINTMENT OF MAJOR R. C. BUCHANAN, U. S. ARMY, TO THE COMMAND OF THE BALTIMORE BATTALION.

NOVEMBER 24, 1846; an important day in the calendar of the Baltimore Battalion. On this day, by order of General Twiggs, commanding the First Division, Brevet-Major Robert C. Buchanan, of the Fourth Infantry, U.S.A., was assigned to the command of the Battalion of Baltimore and Washington Volunteers.

On assuming command, this gallant and accomplished soldier issued the following order:

"HEADQUARTERS BALTIMORE AND WASHINGTON BATTALION.
"Camp near Monterey, Mexico, November 25, 1846.
"*Orders No.* 1.]

"In obedience to special orders No. 5, dated Headquarters First Division Army of Occupation, November 24, 1846, the undersigned assumes the command of this battalion.

"Called to the command by the voluntary act of the officers belonging to it, his only method of showing his appreciation of the compliment will be by endeavoring to obtain for the battalion a name worthy of the State from which it comes.

"In this attempt he relies with confidence on the cordial co-operation of the officers and the good-will of the men for his success. With such assistance he has no fears for the result; without it he cannot hope to succeed.

"A native of Baltimore and a citizen of Washington, his only desire is to make the battalion worthy of the cities which sent it forth.

"(Signed) "ROBERT C. BUCHANAN,
"Brevet-Major Fourth Infantry, Commanding.
"F. B. SCHAEFFER,
"Adjutant."

This handsome inauguration of his command elicited the hearty approval of the battalion, and although there were some few who did not like a regular officer being placed over them, yet the feeling was almost unanimous in his favor. To Major Buchanan I am under lasting obligations; to him I owe a lesson which was very difficult for me to learn—that of obedience. It was *he* that made me a soldier, and the respect which I still entertain for him is based upon the knowledge of his integrity, his honor, and his high military capacity, acquired through hard service under his command and his teachings. A graduate of the Military Academy of West Point, a thorough soldier, a strict disciplinarian, a Marylander by birth, he possessed in addition just what was needed to qualify him for his new duties with a volunteer command—a remarkable equanimity of temperament. Before we left the service he had as handsome a command as a soldier need wish: all were in harmony with him, and all appreciated the value of the services he had rendered to every soldier of the battalion.

We had now been in the service six months, during three of which we had been in a brigade of regulars; and yet we were not soldiers. We were becoming so, and the fortunate advent of Buchanan marked the change into a higher grade of scholarship.

Drill, drill, drill; guard-mount and guard-duty; morning reports, provision returns, and inspection of arms. All these duties require attention, and with proper instruction they may be learned. We were taught to do them properly, and no more pride is felt in the acquisition of any knowledge than in that of the military art.

On the 9th day of December, Mr. Samuel S. Mills, of Baltimore, arrived in camp to convey the remains of Colonel Watson for burial in his native city. He brought with him an elegant coffin which had been provided by the generosity of his friends; and also, having learned at New Orleans the death of Captain Ridgely, a lead coffin for his remains.

On the next day I was directed by special orders to superintend the exhumation and the ceremony of parade. I found Watson's body in a tolerable state of preservation; he was lying the centre one of three bodies, the others were Lieutenants Hoskins and Wood, of the Fourth Infantry. I knew Watson by his two front teeth, beard, shoulder-straps, which were those of a major, and the new boots upon his feet; I had no doubt whatever of his identity. I took a button from his uniform coat, and his remains, inclosed in the coffin brought by Mr. Mills, were escorted by the Baltimore Battalion to the regimental parade ground, where a guard of honor was detailed to receive them. Here they remained until the exhumation of Ridgely's body, which was brought and placed side by side with that of Watson; our battalion and Ridgely's Battery forming the escort and working-party. The whole parade was solemn and interesting, witnessed by very large numbers of the troops in camp; and as the bodies were placed in the wagon for transportation homeward, a very general feeling of sadness marked the departure of all that was mortal of two of Maryland's gallant dead.

Before the arrival of Mr. Mills, Lieutenant Shover, of the army, and I, had made arrangements to send home the remains of Ridgely with those of Watson, and the thoughtful consideration of Mr. Mills had relieved us from a great deal of concern about the metallic coffin. Mr. Mills also brought coffins for the bodies of Herman Thomas, of Harford County, killed in the assault of the 22d of September, and George Pearson, of Baltimore, a member of our battalion, who had died from disease after our arrival at Monterey.

We are making preparations to march, though the orders are not yet out; another sifting process is going on, the last being on the banks of the Rio Grande three months ago. The sick and disabled are to be either discharged or sent into general hospital. The depletion now will not be so heavy as then, but still I expect to have to turn down some five or six of my company.

Time and exposure are thinning our ranks, but I am learning to be more economical in wasting the strength of the battalion by too many discharges. It costs the government too much to get a man here and fit him to be of some use, to let him go on frivolous pretence, and I have learned to judge of the sufficiency of the disability as basis for a discharge, without too much dependence upon the surgeon's opinion. There are two influences constantly at work in reference to these discharges, leaving out of consideration the soldier's claim: the one, the surgeon's wish to diminish the number of his sick; the other, the captain's *not* to diminish the strength of his company. I regard it as one of the most important of all the duties devolving upon the captain of a company, this, of the extent of his interference with the surgeons in matter of discharges. It is a very delicate responsibility, and army regulations do not meet my views upon this subject. If the surgeon and the captain were alike conscientious in sense of duty to their government, there would be no trouble about the propriety of a discharge; but I lean to the opinion, without questioning the skill to decide upon the sufficiency of cause, that the captain is nearer to the government and has a much better idea of the value of a soldier and of the use that may be made of him than the surgeon, and should have more controlling influence in granting the discharge than he now has.

It would be as well perhaps to make mention of our surgeon, Dr. Smythe M. Miles. He was, I believe, a native of the State of Georgia, and had been, I was told, an Assistant-Surgeon in the United States Navy. He became associated with our battalion on the Rio Grande the 8th day of August, 1846, by virtue of a contract made with Colonel Watson, at the pay of one hundred dollars per month, after the withdrawal of Dr. Dove, of Washington. There were a good many of these *contract* surgeons, as they were termed, now with the army, but I am sure none better than Dr. Miles. He continued with us until our end of service, and I had much confidence in his natural medical ability, if not in his acquirements.

CHAPTER XVI.

MARCH TO VICTORIA.

ON the 10th day of December an order was issued from the headquarters of the army of occupation, which transferred the Baltimore Battalion from the Fourth Brigade of the First Division to a volunteer brigade, consisting of the First Mississippi, the First Tennessee, and the First Georgia Regiments of Volunteers, commanded by Brigadier-General John A. Quitman, United States Army. A reorganization of the First Division was necessary in view of our contemplated march on Victoria, and we were very much gratified in being attached to Quitman's Brigade, as long as we had to leave our old friends of the First, Third, and Fourth Infantry; the látter regiment being left to hold the citadel of Monterey, the two former accompanying our column in the Fourth Brigade, commanded by Colonel P. F. Smith.

The First Tennessee and the First Mississippi were old friends of the Rio Grande in Hamer's Brigade, and we rejoined them with many a friendly shake of the hands. I was not personally acquainted with General Quitman, but esteemed him for his well-deserved reputation.

The order of march was issued on the 12th day of December, and on the 13th Twiggs's Division marched; on the 14th our brigade left its old camp, and the Baltimore Battalion, after nearly three months spent in the wood of San Domingo, near Monterey, took up its line of march for Victoria, distant some two hundred miles to the south-east.

General Taylor and headquarters of the army of occupation, marched with our brigade, and the initiative of a new campaign was taken. What might be its plan, or what was its object, was left to conjecture, as far as a captain of infantry was concerned.

General Worth, with his division, was at Saltillo. General Wool, having, as yet, not succeeded in finding Chihuahua, was somewhere about Parras or Monclova, in the same State of Coahuila. General Butler, with his division of volunteers and the Fourth U. S. Infantry, was at Monterey; General Patterson at Camargo, or on the line of the Rio Grande.

As yet we knew nothing of General Scott nor of his approaching arrival, nor of the transfer to him of the chief command of the armies in Mexico.

At 9 o'clock A.M. we left our huts, and, with almost a feeling of home-sickness, bade a final adieu to the grounds so long occupied by us. We took the old road to the city which we had followed on the morning of the 21st of September; before we reached the fort we passed the skeletons of a great many poor fellows who had been killed in the assault; their bones, flesh, and remnants of clothing were lying about exposed to full view, having been dug from the earth, where they had been buried, by the wolves.* We crossed the San Juan or Tigre River by wading, the depth being from two to three feet and the water very cold. We marched along a beautiful road, winding around the base of the mountain "Comanche Saddle," to the east of the city, and reached the most beautiful town I ever saw, named Guadalupe. Perhaps one reason why we all thought this such a pretty town was because a lovely Mexican señorita stood gazing at the troops as we passed; she excited universal admiration not only by reason of her beauty, but by her modest appearance and demeanor. She was the subject of our talk for the balance of the day's march, and many a soldier said he was coming back to Guadalupe, when the war was over.

The houses were generally built of cane, with thatched roofs, and a paling also of cane surrounding the gardens, in which bloomed the orange, the lemon, pomegranate, and banana. Outside of the tropics no such enchanting picture could be seen as in this little town, when the rays of the evening sun fell upon its beauties.

The road, after leaving Guadalupe, passed through a sugar-cane country of several miles in extent, and,

---

* I have not before noticed the number of wolves in the vicinity of Monterey; there were very many packs that seemed to den on the mountain sides in the environs of the city, and on one occasion a pack of at least fifty ran, in full cry, through our camp at night.

the cane being ripe, each officer and man was soon seen chewing and swallowing the sweetest of all fluids that ever touched the human palate. This sugar-cane juice, to the dry throat of a soldier who has been marching through clouds of dust, is the consummation of earthly enjoyments; as one of our men said, "There was no let up in it." As night approached, we struck the San Juan again; the crossing was quite difficult, as the river was deeper and more rapid than where we had crossed it in the morning. Many of the soldiers stumbled and fell into the water, which occasioned hearty peals of laughter from those who had successfully waded to the other bank.

We halted and bivouacked on the south bank of the river, the men being very much fatigued, though we had made but fourteen miles to-day. The sun about noon was very hot, and the road ankle-deep in dust; as night approached, it grew cold and camp-fires pleasant.

December 15. On the march by sunrise, our direction nearly due east, the road good but very dusty; the country arid until we approached the town of Cadarita, when it became good and highly cultivated, corn and sugar-cane fields alternating. We were told that the corn now in blossom was the *third* crop this year. The San Juan River was becoming a nuisance, as we had to cross it three times during the morning's march, and at each crossing the water was deeper than at the preceding, so that, with the water and dust, our pantaloons felt heavy and very disagreeable. The street of Cadarita through which we marched was lined with orange-trees loaded with fruit, to which we all helped ourselves *ad libitum*. In the plaza a column was erected, I could not ascertain for what purpose; on one of its sides a very large church was in ruins, whilst the several bells belonging to it were suspended not more than five or six feet from the ground. After passing for six miles through a succession of cane-fields, we again had to cross the river, making four times in this day's march. The men behaved badly to-day, the column being greatly scattered, the heat being intense and the marching very laborious. We had a long march of twenty-two miles, halting for the night on the banks of a race which fed a large sugar-mill. My feet were blistered; I suffered a good deal, yet I had to go on guard, and passed the night in watchfulness.

December 16. Stiff and sore, I was relieved from guard, and took my place at sunrise at the head of my company. I marched with difficulty; but it was not so hot as on yesterday, and the wind was blowing so that the dust did not hang upon us. We were traversing a belt of sterile country, and at 10 o'clock passed through a miserable hamlet, few people being visible; at 2 o'clock P.M. reached the Ramos River, a beautiful stream flowing east from the Sierra Madre; wading the river, we bivouacked on the sandy bed of its shore, having marched fourteen miles. Here rumors spread that we were cut off by the Mexicans, that a large force of the enemy was ahead and between us and the First Division. We soon found that we were halted to let a train close up, to be under the protection of our brigade.

December 17. Last night it was bitter cold, the

wind from the mountains sweeping down the river valley; we were aroused before daylight by the reveille, and stood up in ranks until 8 o'clock, before starting. Our battalion was thrown in the advance, and for eight miles we marched through a wood of moschete- or ebony-trees, which, by the by, had made us excellent fires the past night. At noon we ascended a mountain, on the top of which we found Generals Taylor and Twiggs, Colonel Smith, and their staffs. The road now descended rapidly; but we were ordered to move slówly and cautiously; couldn't think what was up, but we kept a sharp lookout; soon we saw a body of troops, which certainly were United States soldiers, and so they proved to be; a regiment of Tennessee volunteers were effecting a junction, having marched from Camargo. We are now in the vicinity of Monte Morelos, and have to wait until the train has been passed over the mountain. Fortunately our being in the advance saved us from great labor, as the rear regiments had to help the teams to pull the wagons up the hill. Our men were in huge spirits at this luck, and many of them went to see the little *mules* pull; many were the words of encouragement they gave to the Tennesseeans and Georgians, as they strained at the wagons.

Distance made to-day, fourteen miles.

December 18. In camp near the town of Monte Morelos, capital of the department of the same name, and called after a famous priest patriot, who distinguished himself in the Mexican war of independence. The town is small, Spanish-looking, with a very neat cathedral, inside and out. The mountains are all around, yet this is a centre of a large sugar trade with the miners in the adjoining State of San Luis; it is a flourishing well-built city, with well-paved streets and a decent-looking set of inhabitants. There are some fine stores, and altogether it has a well-to-do appearance. I noticed that the people seemed frightened, and there was unmistakably great excitement about headquarters; we couldn't make it out, or why we didn't march. Our astonishment was great when we saw the First Division of Regulars marching away from us and taking the road by which we had come. They left hurriedly, and we hastened to camp to learn that General Worth had sent for help, and that Taylor was on the march back to Monterey. Now for rumors, and they flew magnificently. There was no doubt about one thing,—we were left "in the mountains," and the next step was looked forward to with anxiety.

During the day orders were published that the First and Second Tennessee Regiments were to constitute one brigade under Colonel Campbell, of the First Tennessee; the First Mississippi, the First Georgia, and the Baltimore Battalion, another brigade under Colonel Jackson, of the Georgia Regiment; the whole constituting a field division, under Brigadier-General Quitman, and we were all ordered to continue our march on to-morrow.

The most reliable news we could get was that Santa Anna was threatening Worth, that Butler had left Monterey with all his disposable force to help Worth at Saltillo, and that Patterson was marching from the Rio Grande with the volunteers to occupy

Monterey. If all this be true, we are in rather an ugly dilemma, and to get out of this there is only one way, and that is to push on to the Gulf; *why* we did not return with Taylor, we learned as we marched. A body of troops were now *en route* to Victoria from the Rio Grande to meet our advance, and if we could not effect a junction with them they would be cut off.

We have had a delightful day, and with the restlessness characteristic of our men, some of them sallied out, *gunning;* they returned with several parrots, which they had killed, and "Pretty poll" was cried by every rascal in the command, during the whole of the night, until sleep was nearly out of the question.

December 19. We were on the march this morning at sunrise, our road skirting the base of a mountain, and our course east-southeast; marched very rapidly until we reached a stream of ice-cold water, which we waded with many a shiver and hard word; met a good many angry-looking Mexicans—real mountaineers they were, and not at all abashed by our presence; they had evidently heard of Santa Anna being on the war-path, and hoped to see him at Monte Morelos; we would have turned back if we had not been ordered forward, for a more reckless, daring body of men were never brigaded together than were now marching with Quitman through this foreign land.

One of the rumors circulating on the march to-day, coming from the head of the column, was that they never slept in the camp of the Baltimore Battalion; that when anybody wanted to sleep, he would go out in the chaparral. So much for *pretty poll.*

We made but eleven miles to-day, owing to the mountains we had to ascend, and the necessity of keeping well closed up. We halted and bivouacked with but little wood for fire, and passed a cheerless night.

December 20—Sunday. Got up from my bed on the hard earth at two o'clock this morning, being so cold that I could not sleep; found most of my company stirring about for wood to make fires with; cooked coffee long before daylight, and awaited the reveille; off at sunrise, and had a hard day's march over the spurs of the Sierra Madre. I suffered a good deal from my sore feet, the road being hilly and rocky hurt them; water scarce to-day, and for some reason impossible to explain, the men marched rapidly without any apparent cause. We saw wild turkeys and several deer running, the mountains being full of game. Toward night we descended into the valley of Linarez, and were once more among the cane-fields. We bivouacked in a thick chaparral among rocks on the banks of a rapid stream. Made eighteen miles to-day, and instead of rest I was detailed for guard, with instructions to be on the alert and to visit my posts continually during the night. No rest this Sabbath, so I sat by the camp-fires, and with their light made my notes of the day's march; very cold, and my eyes full of smoke.

December 21. After nine miles of pleasant marching, we halted on the banks of a rapid river called the San Fernando, *not* the San Juan, opposite the town of Linarez, one of the principal towns of the State of New Leon, distant forty leagues from Monterey, being about one-half the distance to Victoria. Linarez has a population of from six to ten thousand inhabitants, is a handsome town, and has more respectable-looking citizens than any town yet seen. The greatest novelty was the large number of its people on the streets, which made the contrast to the other towns we had passed through striking and agreeable. Among the ladies who were looking at us, I noticed several with parrots perched on their hands, and they seemed pleased with the fun our men made as they marched along. I saw here the first house I had seen in the country which had the appearance of an hotel; it had for a sign "Tienda de Abundancia." In fact, we all voted Linarez *muy buéno.*

On the nine miles of to-day's march we passed through thousands and thousands of acres—yes, miles—of cane-fields, luxuriant in their growth, and with large establishments for the manufacture of sugar scattered at intervals through this famous valley of Linarez. I think that we were the first American troops the inhabitants had seen, and although they were shy they seemed not to be afraid; it may be that they knew, what we as yet were ignorant of, that a force of their countrymen was close at hand.

December 22. Took an early start this morning, and confidently expected an attack, as our division picket, just in, had reported a body of Mexican Lancers to be in sight. We marched with loaded arms and in compact column; as we crossed the summit of a mountain, we caught a glimpse of the town of Linarez several miles in our rear, lighted up with the rising sun. I believe that every man in the division cast a look upon the charming picture that this town presented, in its nest among the mountains. Our road was bad, very bad, rocky and uneven, no water, and not a ranch to be seen. We halted at the first stream we came to, and in a very picturesque spot, but a very uncomfortable one; we pitched our tents in the midst of a thick wood with rocks piled up all around us. The men soon sallied out, despite Lancers, with their guns, to look for game, and they returned with wild hogs, turkeys, parrots, and armadillos. The parrots were excellent eating, but I had not the heart to eat the armadillos,—they looked so beseeching while alive.

December 23. It rained incessantly all last night; fortunately we had had time to pitch our tents, nevertheless we were very damp, and the mud was thick. We slept but little, as there was firing at intervals from tattoo to reveille, and several Mexicans are reported to have been shot; there was more or less of alarm all night. We delayed starting this morning, so as to have daylight to get out of the forest; the road was heavy, and my sore feet were much blistered from so frequently treading upon stones covered with mud, which I could not avoid; we passed but one ranch until four o'clock in the afternoon, when we reached a handsome house on the banks of a river, where we halted; here there was much consultation, as it was thought we had lost our road, so primeval and undisturbed was the appearance of the country. Large flocks of parrots were flying overhead in countless thousands, just as I have seen the wild pigeons in Maryland; deer, turkeys, wild boar, a bird like a pheasant, and another like a guinea-fowl, were numerous and unquestionably not much alarmed by man; the road looked as if it were not often travelled, and the few people about the ranch knew nothing, or would tell nothing. It was determined to pass the night here, and await a reconnaissance which was ordered.

December 24. A damp, drizzly morning; Captain Steuart's and my company were detailed for rear-guard, just as the brigade was about moving; halted until the division and its train had passed, when we fell in and marched. The wagons kept well closed up, but we had much difficulty keeping the mules and their arriéros up with the wagons. I pitied the mules and saved them all I could, yet they were heavily loaded and seemed to suffer. We crossed a river, and here the mules were disposed not to come out of the water; and as there were several hundred of them in the stream at the same time, some idea may be formed of what the rear-guard had to do, with the knowledge that every minute's delay increased the distance between our troops and us. We got them all over after awhile, and pushed on rapidly, overtaking our brigade at the town of Villa Grande; we received orders to let the mules go in advance, while we waited until a number of wagons were loaded with corn, purchased in the town from the Mexicans. We helped them to load, and then started after the troops. We marched rapidly, but did not get into camp until after dark, and bivouacked in the midst of a thicket of chaparral and thorns so dense that there was scarcely room to pile a stack of arms. We had one satisfaction, however, that if we did not know where we were, we were certain that the enemy would never find us. Here we spent our Christmas eve; around the camp-fire I told my officers that if they would find the *materials* for egg-nog, I would supply the means; volunteers were soon off in search, but it was midnight before they returned with a single bottle of muscal (a strong Mexican brandy), and a dozen eggs. A camp-kettle filled with water was boiling, and with plenty of sugar, we had a sweet but not very strong mess-pan full of egg-nog for ourselves, and a tin-cup full for each one of my men to drink *a happy Christmas to all at home.*

December 25. Christmas day, 1846. It rained last night, and having no shelter but the bushes our festivities were much dampened. To add to our hilarious feelings this morning, we were *credibly* informed that General Canales would commemorate the day by attacking the Yankees on the march.

We got out of the thicket about sunrise, ascended a high mountain; descending, we passed through an orchard of orange-trees, noticeable for their great size and quantity of fruit, then through a forest, when we came to a river running alongside the wood. We waded this river waist-deep, and took a cold bath by way of a Christmas drink, so as to enter the town of Hidalgo, now in sight, in proper trim for the festivities of the day. We had a hearty laugh before entering the town. A dense growth of timber was growing on the river bottom, the trees must have been of the famous banyan species of Hindostan; from the trunk, great arms spread out, from which descended *roots* or branches which entered the earth and gave birth to another tree, which in its turn threw out similar arms, and again reproduced itself in others. Astride one of these huge arms was a Tennessee volunteer with his musket at a support, evidently waiting for the Baltimore Battalion to come along; as soon as our men saw him they sent up a shout which made the woods ring. Some one asked him what he was doing up there on guard. He replied, "Stranger, I have *he'erd* tell of the elephant being on show in this *he'er* country, and seeing as how I've found him, why I am jist taking a ride."

If the Moors in the first century of their occupation of the Peninsula had built this Mexican town of Hidalgo, which we were now entering, it could not have presented a more striking picture of the "Dominacion de los Arabes en España" so graphically narrated by Condé. Its very church, now in ruins, was a mosque in all its features, and here in New Spain, the tramp of the followers of Mohammed was marked as distinctly as the heel of the Roman on the plains of Carthage.

Hidalgo, with its high-sounding name, has seen its best days; it was very dilapidated. We saw but few people, and no sign of Christmas; marched two miles beyond, and encamped on the road-side. Made fifteen miles to-day.

December 26. On guard again last night; took an early start this morning, and after two hours' march came to a deep and rapid stream; there was great difficulty in fording it, and much delay before our whole division had crossed. The First Brigade was in line when we got to the further bank, and we marched forward, letting it remain to cover the wagons and the mule train. At noon we halted and went into camp, all wondering why we had done so, as we had not made more than six miles. Before long we learned that the rear-guard of May's Dragoons had been attacked* and his whole baggage captured. Things looked squally, everybody on the alert, arms discharged, cleaned, and inspected. General Urrea, not Canales, was on our flank with a large body of good cavalry, and an attack was expected. I now admired the order of march of Quitman, and his excellent judgment in selecting camps so unfavorable for cavalry to act in with any hope of success against such troops as we had.

December 27—Sunday. March resumed, Baltimore Battalion in the advance. We marched this whole day with arms loaded and bayonets fixed; and as they say of horses sometimes in a race, you might have covered the whole division with a blanket, so closely did they keep their ranks. At 4 o'clock P.M. we reached a large ranch, at which there was a sugar-mill. The Mexicans had just left, intending, as they said, to fight us at Victoria. We went into camp, and here I took a lesson in the proper formation to resist a night-attack from cavalry. During the night firing was heard, and in a few minutes the division

* He lost eleven men, twelve horses, and all his baggage.

was under arms. An attack had been made upon the picket-guard lying in the road to Victoria, but the enemy finding it on the alert and the whole camp alarmed did not press the attack. We remained under arms until nearly daybreak, when we got a little sleep.

December 28. We are now at the corner where the three Mexican States of New Leon, San Luis Potosi, and Tamaulipas, join each other; close on our right, the main chain of the Sierra Madre uplifts its towering heights, and in the south-west may be seen the famous gap in the mountain, called the Tula Pass, through which the road from the Gulf of Mexico passes into the interior. The river which we crossed day before yesterday is named the Santander, which finds its sources among these ridges and flows north-eastwardly, emptying into the Gulf about the tropic of Cancer.

Again we marched slowly and cautiously, hugging the base of the mountain on our right flank, still under the impression that we would be attacked, until we reached a large sugar plantation named the Hacienda of Santa En Gracia, distant ten miles from Victoria.

Here we halted, and having to report in person to General Quitman for orders, I was instructed to march with my guard to a ford, a mile distant, and to prevent the passage of the river, should such be attempted by the Mexicans.

I marched with my guard, and during the night, whilst sitting on the river-bank, watching over the ford, I was startled by the report of a gun fired by one of my sentries. Hastening to his side, as I had seen no enemy, I found a Georgian coolly reloading his musket. I asked him how he dared to suffer his piece to be discharged, despite my instructions, as he knew the whole division would be aroused; and even whilst talking the roll of the drums beating the long-roll came drifting down with the wind. The sentry saw the scrape he had got himself in, and replied, "Captain, you see I was so tired and so sleepy that to keep myself awake I kept *pinting* my gun at a duck I saw on the river, and I thought how I would like to *whisper* to it,—and, dang it, I forgot the gun was cocked, and away she went." I had barely placed him under arrest, and another sentry on his post, when a staff officer came galloping from headquarters to ascertain the cause of alarm. I made the best excuse I could, that I would prefer charges against the sentinel, and said that I would report in person at headquarters as soon as relieved, to explain the needless alarm. I did so, and after telling the general the soldier's story, he sent for him and told him, that if ever he *whispered* again without orders, it would be his last. The general ordered his release, and giving me a bowl of hot coffee, we both left equally gratified, to take our places in the column then forming for the march.

December 29. We advanced on Victoria and entered the town at noon, the enemy retiring as we approached, which gave me a very good opinion of the military capacity of General Urrea. With a force of three thousand cavalry, he had been hanging on our line of march from Linarez to this place, without a single opportunity being offered him to make an attack with any hope of success, and he very wisely saved his command and withdrew it to the Tula Pass, among whose mountain fastnesses it was never our fortune to follow him.

I found here a Mexican chart which made the distance from Monterey seventy-nine leagues, which at two and a half miles to the league (that we learned to be the length of their league) gives the distance at one hundred and ninety-seven and a half miles; by my itinerary I estimated it at one hundred and ninety-two miles; if we call it two hundred miles in round numbers, it will be very near the correct distance by a pretty good road between the two capital cities of New Leon and Tamaulipas.

CHAPTER XVII.

VICTORIA.

General Quitman took formal possession of Victoria, the capital of the State of Tamaulipas, on the 29th day of December, 1846, and the flag of the "Baltimore Battalion," of his division, was hoisted on the flag-staff of the State House. The ceremonies attending the entry and occupation were formal and imposing; the infantry, preceded by Bragg's (now Thomas's) Battery, formed in close column of companies, marched with arms at a support and bayonets fixed around the main plaza, the artillery filing out of the column and massing in the centre; we then opened our column and wheeled into line facing inwards from each side of the square, officers to the front and arms presented, as the flag selected from our battalion was hoisted amid the music of all the instruments in our command, playing "Hail Columbia" and the "Star Spangled Banner." At this time, the Alcalde and municipal authorities came forward and made an address to General Quitman, when we marched out of the city and went into camp in a charming field near by, where, foot-sore and weary, I hoped to get some rest.

I was disappointed; at sunset, Major Buchanan was ordered into town with three companies of his battalion, as rumor was rife that an attempt would be made to recapture Victoria. We occupied the State House, and I was ordered to fortify it. In doing so I necessarily entered the legislative chambers, and found on the desks of the members written motions made on the preceding day, showing that they had only then determined to withdraw without a fight, trusting for an opportunity to take us at a disadvantage. So hasty had been their flight that their national flag, which had been flying that day, was left, and we found it in the Speaker's desk, which was upon a handsome rostrum on the south side of the hall. I took supper in General Urrea's quarters, and as he had breakfasted there and was likely to return, I ate a very hearty one.

It was a beautiful moonlight night, and we patrolled the town every half-hour, keeping up communications with the main body at camp. It was a melancholy sort of duty this wandering about an enemy's town, and it would have been a pleasant relief to have met with armed resistance. A great many of the citizens had witnessed the ceremonies attending the occupation, and I had looked at them carefully. They seemingly beheld the parade with that love for military display which is characteristic of the nation; but their countenances showed they felt that their country was being humiliated, and I must say that I really felt for them.

Now all was still as death, even the dogs did not bark; and, as tired as we all were, it was noticed that not a man of our guard even said he was sleepy,—so intense was the excitement.

December 30. On duty all day, patrolling the town and strengthening the defenses about the State House; the stores were generally closed, all business suspended, and but few people to be seen. Some few Indians gathered in the plaza to hold their accustomed market, but even they with all their stolid indifference were forced to yield to the general gloom, and soon left for their country ranches. At sundown we were relieved by four companies from the First Brigade, and gladly got under our blankets at camp after forty-eight hours' constant duty.

December 31. No news from General Taylor since he left us at Monte Morelos,—not even a rumor today. Our single division, with a light Battery, comprising the whole force (as far as we know), now confronting the Mexican army gathering in the mountains on our west. Where will they strike?

General Patterson is undoubtedly coming this way

with his volunteers from the Rio Grande, and whether we shall move toward San Luis Potosi, through the Tula Pass, or toward Tampico, is the question now upon the lips and in the thoughts of every one in Quitman's Division. There is a very general restlessness, indicative of uncertainty, and groups of officers discuss the question with more than usual earnestness. We all want to go to Tampico; this is the military judgment, that we should abandon the line of the Rio Grande for offensive purposes.

If Santa Anna had had the same judgment, he would not have sacrificed the best army Mexico ever put in the field at Buena Vista, but would have saved it for the defense of the capital. He made the same mistake that Ampudia did at Monterey; he mistook tactics for strategy. Anxious to fight, he fought the troops nearest at hand, without an idea that it might be possible he could be outgeneraled.

While he was now marshaling his army in the State of San Luis, the near road to the city of Mexico was left open; this was about to be seized by the superior genius of one of the greatest soldiers of the age—Major-General Winfield Scott.

We knew nothing as yet of the plan of campaign, but we were in the field, and wits become wonderfully brightened in the presence of danger. As before said, we were unanimous in the opinion that we should change our strategy; it was idle to talk of conquering a peace in the valley of the Sierra Madre. That we would have to *conquer* one, no one now doubted. Santa Anna, the recognized head of the State, had made known the sentiment of the nation, that not while a hostile soldier trod their soil would Mexico make peace.

This had been my opinion; its semi-official promulgation did not startle me. And thus closed upon the Baltimore Battalion, at Victoria de Tamaulipas, the year 1846.

CHAPTER XVIII.

THE ARMY OF OCCUPATION AT VICTORIA, AND THE ARRIVAL OF GENERAL TAYLOR.

January 1, 1847—New-Year's day. Off duty and on a visit to the city; no school-boy ever enjoyed a holiday more than I did this. True, there was not much to be seen, but I was free to go where I chose and from the cares belonging to a Captain of a company. I rambled over the town, visited the cathedral, in which divine service was being held, looked into the few shops that were open, gossiped with my brother officers of the division, many of whom—like myself—were wandering about as only Americans do wander, and finally brought up in the market, looking with interest at the vegetables, fruit, merchandise, and country produce offered for sale.

Victoria is on an elevated plain, close to the mountains on the west. This plain is of great extent, highly cultivated, and its chief products, corn and sugar, make the town an *entrepôt* and place of considerable trade with the adjoining mining States of San Luis and Zacatecas, the main road to which runs from this town through the mountains, by way of the gap in the Sierra previously spoken of. Its population does not exceed from three to five thousand, although the number of houses (many of which are unoccupied) would lead one to suppose that its population was much greater. The plaza is very large, the cathedral occupying one of its faces, and the buildings in this vicinity are respectable; as you leave the square and approach the suburbs, the houses decrease in size, and the outskirts are the reed huts of the poorer classes. It is by no means comparable to Monterey, either as a city or in extent of trade or population. There are many genteel-looking citizens, but they appear to be of a more peaceable disposition —milder than any before met. They were not indifferent to their situation, were not indolent or apathetic. I have given the only word by which I can express the opinion I formed of them,—mild, they seemed mild.

I learned that one of the officers who had retired, as we approached, was a Captain Augustine Iturbide, who had been a scholar at Saint Mary's College, Baltimore, and was now on the staff of General Urrea.*

I went out to camp at sunset, and was just in time to meet with the first *norther* I had ever seen or felt. The wind blew a hurricane, prostrating in a minute nearly every tent, and the air was filled with dust,

---

* He subsequently called to see me, and made himself known while I was at the National Bridge. He seemed much pleased to meet a Baltimorean who knew some of his former schoolmates.

sand-burs, ticks, and various flies and insects; while overhead clouds of parrots, disturbed in their roosts on the mountain sides, were flying, whirling, and screaming like mad. Two thousand men were turned out of house and home in the twinkling of an eye, and a scene of utter confusion prevailed in the darkness which fell like a pall over everything. For fully half an hour the storm-king was in command, and not a rag of canvas could be raised to shelter us from the fury of the gale; by midnight, the wind had abated and the thermometer must have been down to freezing; it was very cold, and the noise of driving tent-pins into the earth showed the activity with which our houses were being reconstructed, for even a canvas shelter is better than none, against cold.

One of the gravest objections to this climate is the violent alternation of heat and cold within twenty-four hours. I think there must be an average difference of thirty or forty degrees of Fahrenheit between noon and midnight. At mid-day, the sun is *hot;* by sundown, the weather is so cold that you want the heat of a fire; and at midnight, you are lucky if you have blankets enough to keep warm enough to sleep. This has been so to a greater or less extent since last September, and serious fears are expressed by our surgeons, that many of our troops will be unfit for service three months hence, on account of chills and fevers.

January 4. General Taylor arrived to-day with Twiggs's First Division, and we were very glad to know that they were again with us. They had had a useless and tiresome march back to Monterey from

Monte Morelos, merely to find that the troops at Saltillo had been stampeded. So they again set out to reach Victoria, and came to find Quitman in possession for five days. General Patterson also arrived today with his division of volunteers, having suffered a great deal from the scarcity of water on his march from Camargo.

We of Hamer's Brigade knew all about this last August, and it is very strange that these troops had not been forewarned to carry water with them.

The number of troops concentrated here is about five thousand men of all arms, and we have undoubted information that a force of the enemy equally large, under Generals Valencia and Urrea, is at Tula, one hundred miles west, while Santa Anna is at San Luis with an unknown force. General Taylor is awaiting instructions, as he is not disposed to abandon his movement upon Tampico to look after Valencia or his chief, the redoubtable Don Antonio Lopez de Santa Anna.

January 8. The weather here has been very disagreeable; we have had two more *northers*, and twice my tent has been blown down; cold and stormy weather is very bad for living in the open air. A very noticeable fact in these fierce blows of wind is the quantity of fine black dust that is carried along with the gale; it is so penetrating that my face has been covered with it when I awoke in the morning, notwithstanding the tent was tightly closed and my head well covered. I am not sure that the ticks (as we call them in Maryland) are also borne along by the wind; but that is the opinion in camp, and we are *more* annoyed by them than we were by the mosquitoes on the Rio Grande last summer. We have another annoyance, destined to persecute us until we left the country,—fleas; their number is legion.

January 9. I think I may safely say that *every* tent went down last night; the wind changed suddenly after dark last evening from the south to the north, and again we had a *norther* from the ice pole itself, which had gathered strength from every degree as it flew toward the equator; it is really impossible to paint or imagine the quantity of discomfort we have experienced in camp this month of January at Victoria.

CHAPTER XIX.

GENERAL SCOTT PLACED IN COMMAND—HIS ARRIVAL IN THE COUNTRY.

January 11. It was at Victoria that General Taylor first learned that General Scott was in the country, had arrived at the Brazos Santiago; and this was why his march on Tampico had been stopped, to await instructions, which it was to be supposed would follow the totally unexpected arrival of the Commander-in-chief.

These instructions came, and were of such a character, as now to merit the attention of every citizen, and to deserve the profound consideration of every lover of his country; for history cannot show a brighter example of patriotism, of military subordination, of high-toned integrity, than was presented in the conduct of General Taylor at this time.

On the 7th he had written the following letter:

"HEADQUARTERS ARMY OF OCCUPATION,
"CAMP NEAR VICTORIA, MEXICO, January 7, 1847.

"SIR,—I have the honor to advise you that on the 29th ult. Brigadier-General Quitman occupied, without resistance, the city of Victoria, capital of the State of Tamaulipas. The enemy had a body of some fifteen hundred cavalry in the town, with its advanced picket at Santa Engracia, but it fell back as General Quitman approached, and is understood to be now at Jaumave, in the direction of Tula. At Tula there is a strong division of observation, under the command of General Valencia. An examination of the mountain pass leading to Tula shows that it is entirely impracticable for artillery or wagons. Such is also believed to be the character of the Santa Barbara Pass, which opens in the direction of Tampico.

"I arrived here with the division of Brigadier-General Twiggs on the 4th inst., and was joined on the same day by the force which Major-General Patterson conducted from Matamoras. The force now collected here is over five thousand strong, and, I am happy to add, in excellent health and in good condition for service.

"I am unofficially advised that Major-General Scott is now in the country, under orders from the government. I propose to remain at this point until I can hear from him, and determine what disposition to make of the troops now here. I am constantly expecting dispatches from his headquarters.

* * * * * * *

"I am, sir, very respectfully, your obedient servant,

"(Signed) "Z. TAYLOR,
"Major-General commanding.

"TO THE ADJUTANT-GENERAL OF THE ARMY,
"Washington."

The above letter I did not see or know anything

about until the year 1850. On the 14th of January, 1847, I wrote from camp, at Victoria:

> "I have just returned from town; saw a train of wagons, escorted by Kentucky cavalry, arrive from Matamoras; it was loaded with supplies. I heard many rumors. There is evidently some grand move in contemplation, and I am inclined to think Vera Cruz will bring us up. I am just informed that General Scott is at Matamoras, and that General Taylor has received dispatches from him; if so, our movements may be changed. I am satisfied that we would not have remained here so long, but for the fact that General Scott was in the country, and General Taylor would do nothing until he heard from him."

From the above it will be perceived that on the 14th I had just learned what Taylor knew on the 7th, but had correctly surmised the cause of delay, although I, in a measure, ascribed it to the want of necessary supplies.

General Scott arrived at Matamoras on the 30th day of December, 1846, from the United States, having left New Orleans on the 23d of the same month.* General Taylor was then on the return march from Monterey to Victoria, and he was in the latter city when he first heard, unofficially, that Scott was in the country. It is well to bear these facts and dates in mind.

On the day of his arrival at Matamoras, General Scott sent the following to the Honorable Secretary of War, and the official heading shows that he was then in command:

---

* He had landed at the Brazos on the 28th, and immediately assumed command.

"HEADQUARTERS OF THE ARMY,
MATAMORAS, December 30, 1846.

"SIR,—I came here this morning, and found nothing but the same contradictory rumors which prevailed yesterday at the Brazos Santiago and the mouth of the river. But an officer has just arrived here (for additional subsistence) from Major-General Patterson, at San Fernando, who says, positively, that the latter had, on the morning of the 27th inst., official dispatches from Major-General Taylor, saying that he was about to return, with a part of his moveable column, to Monterey, in order to support Brevet Brigadier-General Worth, understood to be menaced at Saltillo by Santa Anna and a powerful army.

"This information has determined me to proceed up the river to Camargo, in order to meet dispatches from Major-General Taylor, and, if his outposts should be seriously menaced, to join him rapidly. Otherwise I shall, at Camargo, be within easy corresponding distance of him in respect to my ulterior destination.

"If the enemy be acting offensively, with a large force, which I yet somewhat doubt, we must first repulse and cripple him in time to proceed to the new and more distant theatre.

"No boat has come down the river in many days, on account of the heavy winds, which make descent and ascent extremely difficult. Hence, nothing, it is believed, has passed here from Major-General Taylor's headquarters of a later date than the 14th instant. The steamer in which I write is ready to depart.

"I have the honor to be, etc.,
"(Signed) "WINFIELD SCOTT.

"To Hon. W. L. MARCY,
"Secretary of War."

It was on the 11th day of January, 1847, that General Taylor received the following astounding and extraordinary communications, which I give entire, because of their interesting character and intimate connection with the thread of history; merely premising that it must be borne in mind that at this time Taylor had by the capture of and terms of capitulation at Monterey, driven the Mexicans beyond the Sierra Madre, and that the whole valley of the Rio Grande was clear of the enemy; that the campaign, inaugurated solely by him, had been successfully terminated, leaving him free to act, as he was about doing, from another base on a new theatre.

"NEW YORK, November 25, 1846.

"*Private and Confidential.*]

"MY DEAR GENERAL,—I left Washington late in the day yesterday, and expect to embark for New Orleans the 30th instant. By the 12th of December I may be in that city, at Point Isabel the 17th, and Camargo say the 23d, in order to be within easy corresponding distance from you. It is not probable that I may be able to visit Monterey, and circumstances may prevent your coming to me. I shall much regret not having an early opportunity of felicitating you in person upon your many brilliant achievements; but we may meet somewhere in the interior of Mexico.

"I am not coming, my dear General, to supersede you in the immediate command on the line of operations rendered illustrious by you and your gallant army. My proposed theatre is different. You may imagine it, and I wish very much that it were prudent at this distance to tell you all that I expect to attempt or hope to execute. I have been admonished that dispatches have been lost, and I have no special messenger at hand. Your imagination will be aided by the letters of the Secretary of War, conveyed by Mr. Armistead, Major Graham, and Mr. McLane.

"But, my dear General, I shall be obliged to take from you most of the gallant officers and men (regulars and volunteers), whom you have so long and so nobly commanded. I am afraid that I shall, by imperious necessity,—the approach of yellow fever on the Gulf-coast,—reduce you for a time to stand on the defensive. This will be infinitely painful to you, and for that reason distressing to me. But I rely on your patriotism to submit to the temporary sacrifice with cheerfulness. No man can better afford to do so. Recent victories place you on that high eminence, and I even flatter myself that any benefit that may result to me personally from the unequal division of troops alluded to will lessen the pain of your consequent inactivity.

"You will be aware of the recent call for nine regiments of new volunteers, including one of Texas horse. The President may soon ask for many more, and we are not without hope that Congress may add ten or twelve to the regular establishment. These, by the spring,—say April,—may, by the aid of large bounties, be in the field, should Mexico not earlier propose terms of accommodation; and long before the spring (March) it is probable you will be again in force to resume offensive operations.

"I am writing at a late hour of the night, and more than half sick of a cold. I may dispatch another note before I embark; but from New Orleans, Point Isabel, etc., you shall hear from me officially and fully.

"It was not possible for me to find time to write from Washington, as I much desired. I only received an intimation to hold myself in preparation for Mexico on the 18th instant. Much has been done towards that end, and more remains to be executed.

"Your detailed report of the operations at Monterey, and reply to the Secretary's dispatch, by Lieutenant Armistead, were both received two days after I was instructed to proceed south. In haste, I remain, my dear General,

"Yours, faithfully,

"(Signed) "WINFIELD SCOTT.

"To Major-General Z. TAYLOR,

"United States Army Commanding, etc."

On the 12th day of the preceding month of September, General Scott had written the following:

"HEADQUARTERS OF THE ARMY, WEST POINT,
"New York, September 12, 1846.

"SIR,—In the letter I had the honor to address you on the 27th of May last, I requested that I might be sent to take the immediate command of the principal army against Mexico, either '*to-day or at any better time he* (the President) *may be pleased to designate.*'

"The horse regiments (twelve months' volunteers) destined

for that army being, I suppose, now within fifteen or twenty marches of the Rio Grande, and the season for consecutive operations at hand, I respectfully ask to remind the President of that standing request. I do this without any hesitation in respect to Major-General Taylor, having reason to believe that my presence at the head of the army in the field, in accordance with my rank, is neither unexpected or undesired by that gallant and distinguished commander.

"A slight return of chills and fever may detain me here with my family long enough to receive your reply to this note. Should the President yield to my wishes, a few hours in New York and Philadelphia would enable me to make certain arrangements and save the necessity of a return to those cities from Washington. I suppose it would be easy for me to reach the Rio Grande by the end of this month.

"With high respect, I have the honor to be, sir, your most obedient servant.

"(Signed) "WINFIELD SCOTT.

"Hon. W. L. MARCY,
"Secretary of War."

It will thus be perceived that General Scott had done all that he could officially, to take command in Mexico, at the commencement of the war; and there is nothing to show that he ever, subsequent to this letter on the 12th September, directly or indirectly, contributed to deprive Taylor of his command.

To this note of General Scott, the Secretary replied:

"WAR DEPARTMENT,
"Washington, September 14, 1846.

"SIR,—I have received your letter of the 12th instant, and submitted it to the President. He requests me to inform you that it is not within the arrangements for conducting the campaign in Mexico to supersede General Taylor in his present command, by assigning you to it.

"I am, with great respect,
"Your obedient servant,
"(Signed) "W. L. MARCY.

"To Major-General W. SCOTT."

This curt answer of the Secretary settled the matter, for, as before said, Scott had written himself into disfavor with the administration.

But the terms of the capitulation of Monterey had been disapproved, and the following letter of the 23d of November speaks for itself:

"WAR DEPARTMENT,
"Washington, November 23, 1846.

"SIR,—The President several days since communicated in person to you his orders to repair to Mexico, to take command of the forces there assembled, and particularly to organize and set on foot an expedition to operate on the Gulf-coast, if on arriving at the theatre of action you shall deem it to be practicable. It is not proposed to control your operations by definite and positive instructions, but you are left to prosecute them as your judgment, under a full view of all the circumstances, shall dictate. The work is before you, and the means provided, or to be provided, for accomplishing it are committed to you, in the full confidence that you will use them to the best advantage.

"The objects which it is desirable to obtain have been indicated, and it is hoped you will have the requisite force to accomplish them. Of this you must be the judge when preparations are made, and the time for action has arrived.

"Very respectfully, your obedient servant,

"W. L. MARCY,
"Secretary of War.

"To Major-General WINFIELD SCOTT,
"Commanding the Army, Washington."

More ample powers or more absolute authority were never given to general-in-chief; and the high trust was nobly, faithfully, and successfully discharged. But the blow fell with crushing effect on the modest soldier who had done so much to exalt the character and the reputation of American valor.

Beside the disapprobation of the terms of capitulation, there was another disagreement between the War Department and General Taylor, owing to the Secretary having sent orders direct to Major-General Patterson on the Rio Grande, without transmitting them through Taylor's headquarters. This the latter took umbrage at, as it disposed of his troops without his knowledge: strictly speaking, General Taylor was in the right; but the reasons given by the Secretary, the chief of which were the necessity for prompt action, the uncertainty of Taylor's whereabouts in the enemy's country, and the danger of the orders being captured by the enemy on their way from the Rio Grande, would seem to justify him. General Taylor was very much hurt, as it induced him to think that the Department had grown unfriendly; but I believe there was no intention whatever to derogate from or interfere with the authority of Taylor as the commanding general at the time.

It was a mistake, however, on the part of the Secretary, beyond a doubt, and it is equally clear that the complaints of Taylor tended to hasten his removal.

The orders now received by Taylor from General Scott were to send his *whole command*, with the exception of two batteries of light artillery and a squadron of dragoons, to Tampico, where he, General Scott, would meet them in the latter part of this month, January, or the 1st of February. General Taylor was to return to Monterey and remain on the defensive. Orders had been dispatched already by Scott to General Worth, to move with all *the regulars*, except four batteries, to Point Isabel, and thus was the old hero stripped. It was a hard blow, but it was met with the firmness of a soldier and a patriot. Nothing I ever met with in Plutarch surpasses Taylor's behavior.

Before leaving Victoria he wrote on the 14th to Major-General Scott:

"Had you, General, relieved me at once from the whole command, and assigned me to duty under your order or allowed me to retire from the field, be assured that no complaint would have been heard from me; but while almost every man of the regular force and half the volunteers (now in respectable discipline) are withdrawn for distant service, it seems that I am expected, with less than a thousand regulars, and a volunteer force partly of new levies, to hold a defensive line while a large army of twenty thousand men is in my front. . . . . . .

"I cannot misunderstand the object of the arrangements indicated in your letters. I feel that I have lost the confidence of the government, or it would not have suffered me to remain up to this time ignorant of its intentions, with so vitally affecting interests committed to my charge. But however much I may feel personally mortified and outraged by the course pursued, unprecedented at least in our own history, I will carry out in good faith, while I may remain in Mexico, the views of my government, though I may be sacrificed in the effort."

General Scott replied on the 26th of January, from the Brazos:

"If I had been within easy reach of you at the time I called for troops from your line of operations, I should, as I had previously assured you, have consulted you fully on all points, and probably might have modified my call, both as to number and description of the forces to be taken from or to be left with you. As it was, I had to act promptly, and to a considerable extent in the dark. All this, I think, will be apparent to you when you shall review my letters.

"I hope I have left, or shall leave you, including the new volunteers who will soon be up, a competent force to defend the head of your line (Monterey) and its communications in the neighborhood. To enable you to do this more certainly, I must ask you to abandon Saltillo and to make no detachments, except for reconnaissances and immediate defense, much beyond Monterey. I know this to be the wish of the government, founded on reasons in which I concur; among them, that the enemy intends to operate against small detachments and posts."

General Taylor issued the following order the day he left Victoria:

" It is with deep sensibility that the commanding general finds himself separated from the troops he so long commanded. To those corps, regular and volunteer, who had shared with him the active services of the field, he feels the attachment due such associations; while to those making their first campaign, he must express his regret that he cannot participate with them in its eventful scenes. To all, both officers and men, he extends his heartfelt wishes for their continued success and happiness, confident that their achievements will redound to the credit of their country and its arms."

Many an eye was filled with tears when this order was read, for General Taylor possessed the affections of his soldiers. I called to see him and bid him good-by; he received me, and I parted from him not to see him again until I saw him on the eastern portico of the national capitol, being inaugurated President of the United States of America, as he deserved to be.

CHAPTER XX.

DEPARTURE FROM VICTORIA, AND MARCH TO TAMPICO.

January 16, 1847. General Taylor left this morning to return to Monterey, taking with him the dragoons, two batteries, and the Mississippi Rifles. The Baltimore Battalion struck its tents and marched out of the camp occupied by it since the 29th ultimo, to take its place in the column under orders to march to Tampico. We were still in Brigadier-General Quitman's Brigade, now consisting of the First Georgia, the Fourth Illinois, and our Battalion, of infantry, and one company of mounted Tennesseans. We constituted the Second Brigade of the Volunteer Division, commanded by Major-General Patterson; the other brigade is composed of the First and Second Tennessee and the Third Illinois regiments of infantry and the Tennessee regiment of cavalry, with one section of artillery, under Brigadier-General Gideon J. Pillow, which marched on yesterday.

On the preceding day, the 14th, Brigadier-General Twiggs marched with the First Division, consisting of the First, Third, Sixth, and Seventh regular regiments of infantry and two companies of rifles. We are now under the orders of Major-General Winfield Scott. We marched this day, through an arid and mountainous country, a south-east course; the road was very dusty and stony, and the heat *intense* at noon. Toward evening we reached the San Rosa River, and encamped.

On our march from Monterey, instead of hard ship-biscuit, flour was issued as the ration of bread; we had been told that we could get hard bread at Victoria, and such not being the case, there was a great deal of dissatisfaction. Three tin cupsful of flour was the issue for three days, which was carried on the person in the haversacks of the men; to cook this flour, except in one way, was next to impossible on the march: this way was to mix it with water, then pour it into a pan in which pork-fat was frying, replace it over the fire, and we had slap-jacks—the only bread I tasted for weeks. This mixture called bread, with the meat, which was from cattle on the hoof, driven with the column and slaughtered at the evening's halt, laid the foundation for the discharge of many soldiers from the army. It took a strong man to stand it.

January 17—Sunday. Last night, after I had laid down in my blanket, I was aroused by a report that an express had reached camp with a mail direct from the United States. I flew through the chaparral, scratching my hands and tearing my clothes, but was amply rewarded by receiving two letters from HOME, which I read over and over again before I turned in or closed my eyes. The reveille beat this morning before daylight, and we were on the tramp before sunrise; our march was a very dusty one, but the heat was not so oppressive as on yesterday; the Sierra Madre was close on our right and throwing off spurs or buttresses toward the east; we had to cross hill and dale, up one and over the other for miles, not passing a single ranch the whole day. The great object of interest on this Sunday's march was the President's message, which one of my men had received direct from his father, Colonel Nathaniel Hickman, of Baltimore. It was not the message that we cared so much about as the paper upon which it was printed; it was the first fresh thing we had seen for seven months. We had received letters, but they had a travel-stained look; this newspaper had yet the smell and the damp of the press. I think every man in my company had it in his hands and handled it with great circumspection and decorum. Sergeant Hickman was by long odds *the* man of the brigade on this day's march; the news flew like lightning that the President's message to Congress was in the Baltimore Battalion, and from headquarters down, applications came through staff officers for its loan.

From the top of a ridge we beheld our camping ground at El Pasto, and pushing on through the moschete bushes reached the pond, where we halted, and from the waters of which we made slap-jacks for this and the ensuing days' meals. It was a miserable place, we had passed over a miserable country, and we felt miserable.

January 18. We this morning buried one of Captain Piper's men; he was sick, too sick to be brought on this march, when we left Victoria, and had died in the wagon on the road. We were ordered off just as his remains were about being laid in their final resting place, and Captain Piper's company remained to pay the last sad duties to a brother soldier.

This has been the most disagreeable day's march we have had since we left the Brazos; the dust was more than ankle-deep, and the wind blowing hard covered us in clouds, rendering it impossible to see twenty yards ahead; eyes, mouth, and nostrils were nearly closed, and we were as black as negroes when we got to camp upon the Arroya Alhagilla, in whose gullies we found water enough for coffee. We passed to-day many isolated palm-trees, which, with their tufted tops of long green branches, were very refreshing to the sight when, emerging from the clouds of dust, we would strike a harder bed of earth not yet tramped into an impalpable powder.

January 19. Off before daylight, our road the whole day being through a *wilderness*, nothing more nor less. Cloudy, and not so dusty; passed through a deserted village, the picture of wretchedness, and crossed a stream called the Tamisee, where we encamped. We made eighteen miles to-day, and were pretty tired when we halted. Our beef contractor, Mr. Biglowe, while riding with his party ahead of the column, was attacked to-day by Mexican cavalry, shot through the leg, and his party dispersed; he had been warned not to keep out of sight, but with the rashness of his class rode ahead and fell into an ambush; he will lose his leg if not his life, for his temerity.

January 20. A long march to-day, but rather a pleasant one. My company, the advance guard, came up to the Tamisee River again about two miles from camp; waded through it, water very cold; passed through dense thickets of chaparral and forests of large palmetto-trees, and came to a ruinous hamlet called Panucho; here formerly was a mission of pious Catholic priests, named the *Mission del Refugio*, where the old Spaniards had labored for a century to Christianize the native Mexicans after the conquest. All gone, priest and peon, Spaniard and Mexican, before the Great Judge of the quick and the dead. He will render the proper judgment.

> "All in the grave as equals meet;
> And God, upon his judgment seat,
> Alike impartially will greet
> The mighty and the mean."

Being in the advance, and the weather not uncomfortable, we marched rapidly and enjoyed the scenery which the mountains presented. The sunset was grand, one lofty peak in the far distance being lighted up until it looked like a cone of fire; looking at it as we did from the natural amphitheatre in which we were, it required but little imagination to realize the "pillar of fire" before the Israelites in their journeyings to the promised land. This peak was formerly an active volcano, and is named Mount Bernal; rising three thousand feet straight up from the plain, its elevation is so great that it is a noted landmark to mariners in the Gulf of Mexico.

We encamped upon the banks of a stream among some large beech-trees; no sooner were arms stacked than the men hurried off to gather the fruit from the palms, called the cabbage-tree; we had been marching by them off and on all day, and fortunately halted near a number. This *cabbage* grows among the leaves at the top of the trunk, in the tuft which crowns the shaft of the tree, and when boiled is a good vegetable, very savory to those whose palate has been cloyed with slap-jacks and fried beef. I never learned who first told our men about this cabbage, but they prized them highly, and never passed a tree without expressing an opinion as to the *size* of the cabbage hid among the foliage.

January 21. We made a hard march of twenty-three miles to-day, nearly the whole of the Georgia regiment giving out, and many of our men threw themselves down, unable or unwilling to keep up with the column. From one of those inexplicable causes, the advance started off at such a gait that the left of the line had to nearly run to keep up; the consequence was the column became first straggling, finally broken up. It was fortunate that we had a division of troops in front of us, although I believe we would have done better had there been apprehension of attack. There is nothing which frets an officer more than a disorderly march, and this of to-day was as bad as I ever saw.

It was a cold and stormy day, the appearance of the country rough and rocky. We passed through the Hacienda Alamitas, one of the largest in the country. By *hacienda* is meant an estate, upon which the proprietor is surrounded with all the buildings and appurtenances necessary for successful cultivation of the soil, machinery for the manufacture of its products, houses for his tenants or quasi slaves, called peons, and a church for religious worship. The mansion of the owner was a large stone building, quite respectable in appearance; the church looked well, with a portico of columns recently yellow-washed, but the hovels of the peons were nothing like as comfortable looking as the quarters of the slaves throughout the Southern States of America. This was the largest country establishment I had seen, and in much the best condition; there were large droves of ponies running about, and such a surplus of corn that our quartermaster's department purchased and loaded many wagonsful. Our arrival caused an immediate suspension of all out-door and in-door labor, except that of sight-seeing and indulging in a little harmless conversation with our troops, through the only two phrases known to the brigade,—"Aguardiente?" "Mucho fandango."

Mount Bernal kept in view until night, and the chain of mountains on our left hand became more distinct as we neared the south, showing that we were in a valley between the Sierra Madre and a sierra lying between us and the Gulf.

Night came at last, but not until night did we cease marching, and I threw myself on the earth, nearly broken down from the fatigues of the day, and so helpless that I went to sleep without getting coffee or anything else for a supper.

January 22. Took an early start, although I was so stiff and sore that I could scarcely move; passed through the little village called, I believed, Atamas, and beheld the glorious vision of the lofty peak, lighted up with the rising sun, more beautiful than when its parting rays had fired its summit with a beacon for the night. Our road now lay across a prairie, upon which large numbers of horses were grazing; we could see around us for miles, and our road stretching far away in the distance. There was no straggling over this plain; apart from reports that we would be attacked, our infantry had had some experience, and they marched as compactly as if closing in mass prior to a deployment. At noon we unexpectedly closed upon the rear of General Pillow's Brigade, which, like our own, was marching slowly; we marched together over the prairie, keeping a bright lookout; we are evidently nearing the coast, although the mountains are still on either side of us. The cactus exceeds in size anything ever seen, and I am sure it would appear Munchausenish if I were to attempt to describe it. There are very large numbers of horses running wild over the plain, mustangs, jacks, also horned cattle innumerable. We met a party of Mexicans *en route* to Victoria; they said that the Mexican Congress had unanimously determined to continue the war "hasta la muerte."

Tired enough, we were glad to find water in a pond, around which the division was regularly encamped. After the fatigue of a march, the halt and movements prior to occupying the site designated to a regiment as its camp are trying beyond description; there is nothing a soldier dislikes more than this, except, after having got through with all this marching and countermarching before settling down for a rest, to be called on, as I was to-night, *to go on guard.*

I think that all infantry soldiers who have been thoroughly tired out with marching, entertain a great liking for the horse-arm of the service, cavalry. They want to ride. Is it to be wondered at? I had now walked one hundred and ten miles* in seven consecutive days, without counting the miles lost in manœuvring for camp, and, tired as I was and foot-sore, to have to be up all night, because a brother captain, whose tour of duty it was, played sick, made me a very angry man and *somewhat* disgusted with foot-soldiers. If I had anticipated it during the day's march, I would not have minded it, being in the natural order of things; but just as I had got my boots off to look at the condition of my soles previous to bathing them (the best of all remedies), to have to go on guard, be up all night, and march all the following day, was as well calculated to disturb one's equanimity as anything one can imagine, particularly as I knew the reason of the officer, whose name preceded mine on the roster for guard, being sick. The very anger, however, that I felt, "made me young again," and I marched off with my guard some eight hundred yards through the prickly branches of thorn, cactus, moschete, and chaparral generally, to spend the entire night waiting for the reveille. It came at last, and in such a way that it is worthy of being noted. It was what was called the *Texas*

* It is much more difficult to march with a body of troops than it is to walk singly; in other words, a man walking alone can make thirty miles a day, and be not more fatigued after a week's tramp, than he would be if he had made but one-half the distance in the same number of days marching with a brigade. One hundred men can march one hundred miles in less time and with less fatigue than if the same hundred men were marching with and forming a part of a division or an army corps. Every soldier understands this.

Reveille, and came from the camp of the Tennessee regiment of horse attached to Pillow's brigade.

It will be readily apprehended that there was not much music in the army of occupation. Outside of the regular regiments there were but few musical instruments, except fifes and drums, and of these there was a great scarcity among the volunteers. The Texas regiment of horse had no music of any kind, and, being disturbed in their morning naps at Monterey by the music of the troops encamped about them, had in revenge got up a reveille of their own. This was that, as soon as a Texan woke up in the morning and found he could not get to sleep again, he commenced yelling; this very naturally awoke his comrades, and as fast as each man got cleverly awake he united in the cry, and such a din was raised that, laughable as it was at first, it became a nuisance almost unbearable. Many a sleeper has cursed this Texan music, but now I hailed it with pleasure, coming from the Tennesseeans, as they heralded the new-born day with their shouts of welcome in the morning song of military undiscipline.

January 23. On returning to camp I was told that several of our men had been killed yesterday by the Lancers, who were still hanging about our march, and that one of them was Henry Forbush, a member of my company. He had fallen out of the ranks, and, failing to overtake us, I felt uneasy about him, as he was a quiet, obedient, and orderly soldier, and I knew would have come into camp if able to do so. He was one of my men that had been detailed to serve in Ridgely's Battery at Monterey, and Captain

Ridgely told me that his behavior was exemplary and he was loth to part with him. I regretted his loss very much, yet his manner of death was of great service in hindering the men from straggling, and made them more obedient to authority.

It is also said, that the Mexican merchants who passed us *en route* to Victoria were first plundered and then murdered by their countrymen for alleged complicity with us, of which they were as innocent as Santa Anna; and I presume by this time the idea that *he* was anything but a thorough Mexican has been entirely dissipated. What sheer nonsense to have supposed that a man of his distinguished nationality would have been anything else but a Mexican, in a war popular with the entire country. It was a folly unexampled in its magnitude, and was near proving fatal to our success.

After some five or six miles' march the plain fell off suddenly, and we came to a peculiar country, entirely dissimilar to any heretofore traversed; it appeared to be, or to have been, a marshy flat of rich black soil, and was heavily timbered. While the earth was still wet it must have been much trampled by cattle, for now it was in hard lumps, very uneven, making the marching laborious,—to tender feet, painful,—and the men suffered or seemed to labor more than usual. We made very slow progress. I was near giving out, but continued the march until we halted at a large lake, or, more properly, lagoon, upon an extensive flat. This lagoon empties into, or is supplied from,—I do not know which,—the Tamisee River. Our officers all think that if we had had rain we never would have been able to have reached this point on foot. The country evidently for miles is subject to overflow, and that to such a depth that men could not have marched through it. Our opinion is confirmed by that of the country people, who seem astonished that we should have dared to undertake a march to Tampico from Victoria, through the interior of Tamaulipas, at this season of the year.

There was but little wood near our camp, and there was difficulty between our men and some of the other volunteers about it, as, without wood to cook coffee with, there would be no peace in camp. The rule established by common law or custom, and well understood in our army, was that all the wood standing or felled in front of or in the rear of the space occupied by the regiment's front belonged to it.

In our order of march, the details for guard were made at roll-call in the morning; when we halted to go into camp, if possible always before dark, the brigade was formed in line of battle, with the proper intervals between regiments, the lines dressed and standing at attention. The sergeant-major of each regiment then marched off with his detail for grand guard to the parade, where it was turned off by the assistant adjutant-general to the field-officer of the day, who reported for instructions to the brigade commander. The regimental camp-guard, with its officer of the day and guard, were then turned off by the regimental adjutant and marched to its post; after these details, left the ranks, arms were stacked, and the accoutrements of each soldier were hung upon his stack, the non-commissioned officers having a separate stack to themselves. In a country scarce of fuel as this was, all the time these details were being got ready to march, the rest of the men were intently gazing before and behind them to see what the prospect was for wood.* This evening a large log, the trunk of a fallen tree, was lying opposite our right and the left of the regiment on our right. As soon as ranks were broken, which was nearly simultaneous, the men of both battalions rushed to the log, and a free fight sprung up immediately. It was very difficult to say to which regiment the log belonged; but our men were too quick with their fists for the others, and it was dragged, pulled, and rolled into our camp. The respective camp-guards were already formed, so that there was no difficulty in preventing a serious disturbance. If this had not been the case, I think we would have had a good deal of trouble to-night.

My tent is pitched near to and immediately facing the lagoon, upon the dry mud, over which thousands of cattle must have passed while it was wet, as I had to have men beat it down with axes to make a level to stretch my blanket for sleep. In the rear is a thicket, composed, it might be said, entirely of thorns, for no one would dare to enter through the prickly pear and other stickers, that grow so luxuriantly that some of these thorns, shaped like the horns of an ox,

---

* In my company it was not an unusual thing, for the men to commence picking up wood for the night's coffee, as soon as they left camp in the morning. This they would carry until the evening's halt.

and from four to five inches in length, are as formidable as knives.

Before dark I took a stroll along the shores of the lagoon; I found an old Mexican, living in a cane hut, from whom I learned that the name of the ranch was La Tuna, the people of which were principally engaged in drying hides, large numbers of which were spread upon the ground, with pegs driven through the edges into the earth to keep them extended; some hides were also kept stretched by poles running athwart them, and were used as sails for boats upon the lake.

The word *tuna*, which gave name to the ranch, or the ranch to the hamlet, means either the American fig, fig-tree, or *the idle life which vagabonds lead.* I could not ascertain which signification was adopted by its people, although I tried to learn from my aged friend, my Spanish not being quite equal to this case. During the night, however, I found it out; at least I could not help thinking so.

Our men had by some means discovered a large quantity of muscal (an intoxicating drink made from sugar-cane) in one of the houses near camp, and it was carried by the camp-kettleful through the guards into camp. I discovered it by the smell, as it was being brought into my company; and, notwithstanding every effort to destroy it, such large quantities were in camp that we had a night of drunkenness which, once seen, is not desired again. We had not had such trouble since we left the Brazos, and I accepted the latter as the proper meaning of La Tuna.

January 24. The Sierra Madre Mountains, it is not generally known,—because no thought is given to the subject,—are a prolongation of the Rocky Mountains of the United States into Mexico, which decreasing in size and elevation as they trend southward, are finally lost in the Central American States, to be reproduced south of the Isthmus of Panama, in the Andes of South America. The term Madre, or mother mountains, is synonymous with backbone or main chain, as used by Americans; and the crest of these mountains, as we marched southward, bounded our horizon on the west all the way down from Monterey. Their craggy summits were a never-ending variety of castle, cathedral, palace and spires, frequently reproduced by a mirage so wonderful, as to make us at times doubt whether we were not mistaken in our direction, so completely would they be transposed by the illusion. I never tired of looking at the varied beauties of these mountains, when the sun would first strike their tops in the early morning, and to-day they seemed so beautiful that I felt sorry to know we were soon to leave them for the uninteresting flats of the Gulf-coast.

This was Sunday, and it seemed as if we always had harder marching and more trouble on this than on other days. I was assigned to the command of the rear-guard of three companies of infantry, with special orders to leave nothing behind me. The road was very bad, several of the wagons broke down, a considerable number of the men were still drunk from last night's debauch, and had it not been for fear of the Mexicans, I do not think I could have got them all into camp. The main body, without regard to the rear, pushed on rapidly, so that when I was in a condition to move, we would frequently have to march so fast to keep within a reasonable distance, that the stragglers fell out from sheer exhaustion; these would beg me not to leave them, and I had a very trying day.

Towards evening I got up to camp with my charge, and grateful enough that there was no cause of complaint at headquarters.

The camp was on the shores of another large fresh-water lagoon, upon which was built the old town of Altamira, and with its fine large venerable cathedral, it looked very pretty rising from the waters. This town was the original settlement on the coast, Tampico having been founded at a much later period, and it continued to be for a long time the seat of the Spanish power on the Gulf. It was rather a melancholy sight to behold the signs of decay and the tumbling into ruin of this old Spanish settlement, and I thought I could see in the garb and mien of its inhabitants, the haughty pride and sombre dignity characteristic of the race that had won, by the sword, a new world for the sovereigns of Castile and Leon.

That we were now approaching the end of our march was clear from the arrival of a sutler in camp from Tampico. He brought with him cigars and potatoes. All who had money, bought; without money they were not to be had; no kind of promise or entreaty was of any avail; no claim of former acquaintance either with self or friend was recognized by that sutler. He charged just as much as he thought he could get, and he did get high prices. My purchase of potatoes was soon in a camp-kettle, and I ate the first vegetable that I had had since leaving the ship last July, with the exception of the cabbage-palm; and these potatoes, with a tin-cup of vinegar, of which we had had none for a month past, gave me a relish for the cigars known only to those who have been long deprived of these *necessaries* of life,—a soldier's life.

Our camp to-night was a scene of great noise and confusion, but not quite so bad as the past one. We were within sixteen or eighteen miles of Tampico, and could hear the roar made by the breakers tumbling in from the ocean; the approach to a town had raised the spirits of the men to the highest pitch, and liquors flowed from unknown sources through the swarming hive of the division. A town or city is to a *marching* soldier the fountain of life, so long and so fruitlessly sought by Ponce de Leon. To our battalion, the image presented was more attractive than that held up before the followers of Mohammed as their paradise of repose. A man raised in a city, a genuine cockney, is nowhere at home except in a crowd of people, traversing thoroughfares lighted up with shop-windows, and with resting places for the idle and thirsty, in drink-shops and billiard-saloons.

Our men were good soldiers, but they were all city-men, and their absence for nearly eight months from the United States had made them picture exaggerated pleasures from a visit to Tampico, which the sutler had told them was overflowing with attractions from New Orleans. They were sadly disappointed in the realization of their fancies; but it was enough for the present to know, that they were approaching a town that was in direct communication with home.

January 25. After a sultry march of five miles through a forest of live-oaks and a dense thicket of chaparral, over a sandy road, we were halted on the shore of a lagoon. After half an hour or so we were told that we were to make our camp here; if we had been ordered to march back to Monterey it would not have caused more vexation. Everybody wanted to go to Tampico, which was yet ten miles distant, and a sullen hum arose through the division, broken at intervals by anathemas upon the head of the commanding General. Into camp, however, we went, on a narrow strip of clear ground, which ran between the chaparral and the water; the ground was wet, and from it a hot steam engendered by the sun arose, noisome, stifling, and oppressive; the thicket in our rear was so dense that it was useless as a shelter, for no one dared to force his way through the thorns to find shade. It was a horrid, low, swampy place, and a large iguana, running from a tree which was being burned, gave notice of the kind of reptile by which it was peopled. This caused a great deal of amusement at the time; the men were just getting their coffee, when this huge lizard, several feet in length, heated by the fire, ran from the hollow log which was being used to cook with, and the men scattered and ran for some distance before they rallied and captured it. Many a story was subsequently told of the behavior of some of the men on this occasion.

January 26. Our blankets were reeking with moisture this morning, and the surgeon waited upon

General Quitman to inform him that the camp would prove highly injurious to the health of the command. The regimental commanders made a similar remonstrance, and General Quitman, accompanied by Major Buchanan, rode into the city to induce General Patterson to order us away from this place. In addition to mosquitoes and the usual insects we have been tormented with, we had for companions last night several varieties of pinching-bugs, large spiders, and what the men seemed to dread more than anything else,—scorpions; no doubt about this. I saw where one had bitten the leg of a servant; the bite caused a whitish swelling the size of a hickory nut, but being promptly treated by Dr. Miles with hartshorn, the swelling subsided, and the man suffered no very great inconvenience, except from fright; he was very much frightened.

We did nothing to-day except lounge about the shores of the lagoon, talk about scorpions, and catch and kill big spiders, which we were sure were the genuine, original tarantula, carried from here into Italy, for the dance of the people of that favored land.

January 27. I have been in some ugly places, but this is the worst camp I was ever in. Our clothes as well as blankets were all wet this morning from the moisture which permeated through all covering, and as soon as the sun struck us, we were steaming like kettles of boiling water; there was barely enough wood for cooking purposes, so we dried in the sun; one of my men said that if he stayed there much longer his friends would not recognize him, as he could feel the *moss* growing all over him.

In the afternoon we learned that the application had met with favor, as well it might, and we were ordered to hold ourselves in readiness to march to-morrow.

January 28. After a tiresome march—for it seemed as if we would never reach El Dorado—of eight miles, for part of the way through groves of lime- and lemon-trees, we reached some hills distant about three miles from Tampico, and went into camp on the left of General Twiggs's division.

We had marched one hundred and fifty-six miles from Victoria, making the whole distance from Monterey between three hundred and fifty and three hundred and sixty miles.

If we call it three hundred and fifty miles from Monterey to Tampico, it will be found to approximate very nearly to the correct distance.

The Baltimore Battalion has now marched upwards of six hundred miles from the Brazos Santiago, every foot of which I stepped.

CHAPTER XXI.

TAMPICO—GENERAL SCOTT MARSHALING HIS FORCES FOR CAPTURE OF VERA CRUZ.

TAMPICO, the ancient capital of the Aztec-Mexican province of Guasteca or Mechoacan, lies on the left bank of the Panuco River, five miles from its mouth, in the Gulf of Mexico, in north latitude 22 degrees 40 minutes, and 98 degrees 36 minutes west longitude from Greenwich.

It was a famed locality in the days of the Montezumas; and Viejo Tampico, on the opposite side of the river, was a bishop's see when Panuco was a department of Mexico, in the days of the Viceroys.*

Being the port of entry for the city of San Luis Potosi and the adjoining State of Quérétaro, it has long had very considerable commerce with England, France, and Spain; giving in return for their merchandise, the precious metals (especially silver in large quantities), hides and tallow.

Were it not for the bar at the mouth of the river, rendering access dangerous to vessels of heavy draught, this port would always be desirable, be the power what it might holding the government of Mexico, by reason of its geographical position.

I found it in the occupancy of the United States, having been taken possession of by Commodore Connor of the United States Navy.

The activity, the zeal, and the valuable services of the navy from the commencement of hostilities, had more than justified the high reputation it had won in previous wars; and its commanding officers in the Gulf and on the Pacific shore had shown as good judgment as zeal, in the conduct of their fleets.

---

* The site and remains of an ancient city have been discovered at but a few leagues from Tampico. Among its interesting features may be noted a wild fig-tree growing in the ruins, which reaches the gigantic height of more than a hundred feet; a large head beautifully cut in stone; a gigantic turtle, with the head of a man protruding from between its highly-wrought stone shells; fragments of obsidian and other curious relics of a people far advanced in the arts and habits of semi-civilized races.

General Scott was now about to have its powerful co-operation in the great enterprise for which he was marshaling his forces.

General Santa Anna had ordered the evacuation of Tampico, and this step was severely criticised in Mexico and the United States. He defended his action on military grounds, which are so conclusive to my mind that they need no argument in support. He undoubtedly saved its garrison, and by withdrawing it to Tula and subsequently to San Luis, had it within the field of his contemplated operations.

The army now being concentrated here was awaiting the arrival of General Scott.

On the 3d of this month (January, 1847), having learned that General Taylor had returned to Victoria upon finding that Worth's alarm was groundless, he wrote to Major-General Butler,* the second in command, at Monterey, as follows :

"Of the number of troops at Tampico and assembled at or in march for Victoria,—regulars and volunteers,—I can form only a very imperfect estimate, having seen no returns of a late date. I estimate, however, the whole force now under Major-General Taylor's orders to be about seventeen thousand,—seven of regulars and ten of volunteers. Two thousand regulars and five of volunteers I suppose—the whole standing on the defensive—to be necessary to hold Monterey, Seralvo, Camargo, Reynosa, Matamoras, Point Isabel, the Brazos, the mouth of the Rio Grande, and Tampico. I do not enumerate Saltillo and

---

* He also stated particularly to Butler, that it was his intention to embark troops from Tampico and Brazos for an attack upon Vera Cruz; that this was the object contemplated by his orders.

Victoria, because I suppose they may be abandoned or held without hurting or improving the line of defense I have indicated. . . . . . You will, therefore, without waiting to hear from Major-General Taylor, and without the least unnecessary delay, in order that they may be in time, as above, put in movement for the mouth of the Rio Grande the following troops:

"About five hundred regular cavalry of the First and Second Regiments of Dragoons, including Lieutenant Kearney's troop.

"About five hundred volunteer cavalry,—I rely upon you to select the best.

"Two field-batteries of light artillery, say Duncan's and Taylor's, and

"Four thousand regulars on foot, including artillery acting as infantry; the whole under Brevet Brigadier-General Worth.

"In addition, put in movement for the same point of embarkation, and to be there as above, four thousand volunteer infantry.

* * * * * * * *

"P.S.—I expect to be personally at Tampico to superintend that part of my expedition which is to embark there, towards the end of this month.

"The whole of the eight regiments of new foot volunteers will be up with the Brazos, I hope, by that time. Major-General Taylor may rely upon three, if not four of them, for his immediate command; and make your calculations now for him accordingly."

At the date of these interesting instructions, the premonitions which that very distinguished soldier General Worth had of being attacked, the fact that General Santa Anna was massing an army at San Luis, the fact that Taylor was to act on the defensive after Worth and his best troops were withdrawn, with an uncertain reinforcement of new regiments to replace them, seem to have been overlooked, ignored, or totally unknown, by General Scott.

General Taylor was instructed not only to act on

the defensive, but to enable him to do this, detached posts were to be held, scattered over a hostile territory with the Rio Grande as a base, whose navigation, as Scott well knew, was so uncertain that for days steamers could neither ascend nor descend it.

The game of cross purposes inaugurated by Ampudia at Monterey was being continued by the two chiefs of rival armies, both alike distinguished as skillful and experienced generals, while he who was to be shelved in the coming struggle, or else ignominiously driven off the fields he had won by his valor, was destined to reap additional laurels, and save the name, and the army of him who had, perhaps unwittingly, deprived him of his command.

Scott, intent upon Vera Cruz and the city of Mexico, looked but to this road. Santa Anna, intent upon crushing Taylor, never deigned a glance at the gathering hosts threatening his Capital.

Buena Vista was between San Luis and Monterey; General Taylor between Scott and the loss of fame and name.

The friends of Santa Anna say, that he was not ignorant of the danger he had exposed the Capital to by operating in the northern States, but that he had left the government to take care of the road from the Gulf. The friends of Scott say, that Taylor himself did not apprehend the advance from San Luis.

If Scott were ignorant of the strength of the army at San Luis, he is less blameable than Santa Anna; if the latter had reason to believe his government could protect its Capital, he is less obnoxious to censure than Scott; the whole truth is, however, that they were alike indifferent as to the other's purposes or means of accomplishing results, violating a maxim of war which tyros in the military art are familiar with.

January 29. Our camp is now on an elevated piece of land which separates the lagoons which flow, the one into the Gulf, the other into the Panuco. On our right, the Georgians are encamped; on our left, General Shields's brigade, consisting of the Third and Fourth Illinois regiments; * in front of us Twiggs's division is lying. The different beats and calls of each regiment are distinctly heard in our camp, and military music—drums, fifes, and bands—is sounding at all hours of the day. The main building of the hacienda or sugar estate upon which we are encamped is within a stone's throw of my tent, and I frequently visit it. The huts in which the peons live are like those I have heretofore spoken of, made of cane and reeds, with interstices through which the Indian-looking women may at all times be seen crushing or grinding the corn for their tortillas or corn-cakes, as we would call them; the men are at work in the adjacent fields, cutting the sugar-cane or grinding out the juice with the huge wooden rollers of the sugar-mill, or else drying and making jerked beef out of the long strips of meat, cut from the beeves just slaughtered.

The revenue of this estate, derived from the sale of hides, tallow, and sugar, is very large; and the owner, having fought with the famous Guarda Costa of Tampico, at Palo Alto and Resaca, is left at liberty

* The Third was commanded by Colonel Ferris Forman, and the Fourth by Colonel Edward D. Baker.

to reap some of the profits, as he had shared in the disasters, of the war.

Borrowing a horse from the adjutant, I rode into Tampico; a large number of troops were constructing elaborate fortifications landward, steam vessels of war in the river; a battery was drilling in the plaza, a heavy guard marching off with field music; well-dressed, business-looking citizens bustling over the side flagstones of paved streets, well-looking ladies flitting along, in and out of handsome stores, life and activity everywhere visible, and the hum of trade perceptible.

I visited the "Commercial Exchange" in the main plaza: a coffee-house with handsomely decorated apartments, billiard-rooms, private parlors, etc., which would be considered good in any capital city. I ate a meal here which, if not *couleur de rose*, gave that tinge to all I saw. Seven months without a decent meal is a good appetizer, and the prospect of visiting the theatre at night (which I did) was a dish fit to set before the king.

Riding homeward, General Persifer F. Smith overtook and joined me; the sand in the road was ankle-deep,—over the horses' fetlocks; as we rode along, I saw a silver dollar lying in the sand; to stop and pick it up was soon done; remounting, I told the General, and before going a half dozen yards I was off my horse again, and picked up another dollar; remounting, the General said we had better change sides so as to give him a chance, as we were certainly on the road to fortune. I agreed, and he took my side of the road; going on, we both kept our eyes on the sand, when I perceived the bright face of another dollar, which I secured. We were both now full of laugh, and I believe he was just going to dismount,—at least I charged him with it,—when I found half-buried in the sand the woolen sock of a soldier, in which there were thirty-four silver Mexican dollars, and one-half of a dollar, making with the three which I had picked up, a total of thirty-seven dollars and fifty cents.

The General claimed halves, and I agreed to give it, provided I did not find the right owner; we both concurring that it belonged to some soldier, who after having been paid off in town, had got drunk and lost his money on the way to camp.

I gave notice to the various camps, and many an applicant came for the money, and many and various were the schemes to get it from me. It was a source of a great deal of amusement, and finally the loser made his appearance, but not until several days after my finding it. His name was Abraham Murphy, of the Third United States Infantry, and his behavior was interesting; he wanted, evidently, to reward me for finding his money, to give me some of it; but he knew how improper that would be, for he was a disciplined soldier, with proper sensibilities, and his embarrassment was very expressive. He thanked me, left, and I never saw him again.

February 14—Sunday night. We have had more than a week of continuous bad weather; rain-storms daily. My dilapidated tent leaks; being a line officer there is no fly, and the earth is wet beneath my feet, no amount of ditching sufficing to keep it dry. I went out to listen to the music of the Second Infantry's band; the sergeants were calling the regular tattoo roll-call, the rain falling on the groups assembled on their company parades, as each answered quietly to his name. The night was intensely dark, and the total absence of all life or animation save the dull rolling of the drums beating tattoo gave a sombre cast to my feelings, in unison with the heavy gloom and silence of the camp. For two weeks we have been doing nothing; no drills, no news, nothing but rains and storms. The men are complaining; for nearly six months' pay is due them, they complain of their rations, and are ragged and nearly barefoot; we are without one scrap of news, knowing nothing of our probable movements, and the monotony has become so wearisome that even rumor has silenced its tongue for want of thought. But one question is now asked: "Has General Scott arrived?" and the same answer heard, "No; he is expected this evening." Everything revolves around this centre. He has been expected daily since our two divisions of Taylor's army arrived here; no one blames him, for each man knows that Vera Cruz and the plans for its capture are of more importance than a soldier's restlessness or a soldier's grumbling. None of the new troops of which we have heard so much have as yet arrived, except a volunteer regiment from New York, and they were scanned by our soldiers with much curiosity and interest. I met three Baltimoreans in town yesterday, Messrs. George Bradford, Robert Armstrong, and Richard Edes; they came to seek some position in the army, with no very definite idea, I think, of what was before them, and I know not what success they have met with. Such weather as this, if it does not dampen their ardor, will at least warn them what they may expect, and may determine their future action.

February 16. Our battalion has been paid to-day all arrearages due up to December 31, 1846, and the officers and men are as bright and as full of life as if the past eight months had been a season of uninterrupted happiness. With the promise of an issue to them of new clothing and new shoes, they are as gay as boys home for the Christmas holidays, and it is a pleasure to see them so happy.

February 19. The sound of heavy guns firing a salute announced to-day the long-looked-for arrival of General Scott; and I rode in to the city to see him, as I had never had that pleasure, and to learn the news.

The city was in a fever of excitement, the streets and the plaza thronged with soldiers and citizens, drums beating, cannon firing, troops marching, batteries hurrying along, and all the indescribable incidents to an army roused to action were in motion and replete with interest. The ladies crowded the streets, dressed in a style which astonished me. I never saw anywhere more fashionably dressed women, European in everything, except where Parisian modes fail; the head, adorned with their beautiful black hair, braided so as to expose a rare flower, was slightly covered with the rebosa*, of gaudy pattern, which fell

---

* A long, narrow shawl worn by all classes of the Tampicoans, as the only covering for the head.

gracefully over their shoulders. With their inimitable carriage, the birthright of a Spaniard, no one would suppose that aught but the blood of Castile or Aragon was coursing in their veins; they were Mexicans, yet they were women, and their curiosity to see General Scott subdued their repugnance to the *Llanquies*.* In the centre of the plaza, the fine band of one of the artillery regiments was playing, surrounded by a dense mass of soldiers of all arms, and sailors from the men-of-war in port. The adjacent coffee-houses were filled with officers, and rumor, her tongue now again free, filled Tampico with the buzz of her joy. Everybody talked, everybody knew what was just told him, everybody was delighted, and everybody made a night of it, except the town-guard, and it had a night of it, for there was the sound of revelry on the banks of the Panuco. Drunken soldiers and drunken sailors fraternized, and the long bitter oath of the western volunteer and teamster drowned the caramba of the Mexican. The full moon came up to lighten the scene, while the glowing fires and the fiery furnaces of the steamers in the river threw a lurid glare upon the heavy armaments bristling upon their decks. The sharp challenge of "Who comes there?" was answered, and "Boat ahoy!" was followed by the plunge of oars, deep into the morning watch. Everything was overflowing with enthusiasm and life on the eve of the descent upon Vera Cruz, for it was an-

* This is the way I saw the word *Yankees* spelled, written with chalk on a wall, and it was some time before I could make out what it meant.

nounced that this was the step now to be taken. In that mass of men, not one reckoned the cost, not one doubted the success, not one thought of the future.

I did not see General Scott, as he was closely engaged with the chiefs of divisions, preparing his orders and necessary details; and I returned to camp, where my arrival was awaited with anxiety, as it was supposed that I would be able to tell what were to be our orders.

February 25. The orders are out, and we are to remain. Colonel De Russey's Regiment of Louisiana Volunteers, the Baltimore Battalion, and Captain Wyse's Battery of Regular Artillery, are to constitute the garrison of Tampico, with Colonel William Gates, of the Third Artillery, U. S. Army, commanding.

The good name and reputation of the Baltimore Battalion were now unequivocally established, and its designation as a portion of the garrison of this important city was due as much to this, as to the signal ability and military appreciation of the worth of Major Robert C. Buchanan, our commanding officer, whose valuable services were thus secured to the support of Colonel Gates.

We marched in on the same day, and I was assigned to the command of a fort on the eastern defenses of the city, armed with four eighteen- and four thirty-two-pound guns, with a detail of sixty picked men from the battalion, to be drilled in the manual of heavy artillery, for service of the guns.

CHAPTER XXII.

TAMPICO.

On the 19th of February, 1847, Colonel J. G. Totten, Chief of the Corps of Engineers, made the following report to General Scott, at Tampico:

"Sir,—I have to report, for the information of the General, that I have this day examined with care the works lately thrown up for the defense of the two avenues into this town. These works are nearly complete, and it gives me great satisfaction to state my opinion that they have been planned with judgment and executed with skill; nothing less, however, was to have been expected from the officers who have been engaged thereon, namely: Captain Barnard and Lieutenant Beauregard, of the Engineers, assisted for the greater part of the time by Lieutenants Coppée, of the artillery, and Woods, of the infantry. Lieutenants McGilton, G. P. Andrews, and Sears, are reported to have rendered valuable aid, though for shorter periods.

"Although the defensive lines were designed to meet the case of a weak garrison, and much talent has been displayed in profiting by local circumstances to that end, still, the space to be covered is large, and even a minimum garrison must consist of a considerable body of men. I do not now take into account the value of the object covered. If its importance be such as to justify the leaving of a garrison at all, that garrison must be able to maintain itself for some time, *entirely independent of succor from without; any less garrison we might expect to lose.*

"Knowing how important it may be to other issues of the approaching campaign to take hence all the force that can be spared, I have looked at the subject with a sincere desire to reduce to the utmost my estimate of the numbers indispensable to an efficient defense; but I have not been able to reduce it below the following figures.

"Along the Allaneira front of the town, there are eight distinct works requiring garrisons, varying, according to magnitude or position, from twenty men to one hundred and twenty men each, at least,—provision being made for mounting thereon twenty-six pieces of artillery.

"The aggregate of these posts will be . .	540	men.
"Reserve of four companies	320	"
"Giving	860	"
"On the canal front; at the other extremity of the town, there will be needed in these posts	200	"
"Total	1060	"

"Making a total of, say, one thousand men.

"There should also be a reserve on the canal front of not less than two hundred men, making the whole force of that front four hundred men, and the total force twelve hundred men; but, in my desire to reduce the estimate, I have omitted this reserve, on the supposition that a body of at least two hundred volunteers may be raised at a moment of need among the residents of Tampico.

"Twenty-four pieces of artillery are actually mounted in the several works, which ordnance should be left in the hands of the regular artillery only. I have, therefore, in conclusion, to recommend to the General-in-Chief that there be left for the defense of Tampico a force of not less than one thousand effective men, with twenty-four pieces of artillery; of which force, one full company, at least, should be of regular artillery.

"I purpose leaving orders with Lieutenant Beauregard to complete the defenses at once, so that he may be in time to afford his aid in the contemplated operations at Vera Cruz.

"I have the honor to be, etc.,

"(Signed) "JOSEPH G. TOTTEN,
"Colonel and Chief Engineer."

On the same day, doubtless after the receipt of Colonel Totten's report, General Scott issued the following instructions to General Patterson:

"SIR,—I am desirous that, after designating a competent garrison for the defense of this place (Tampico), the strength and composition of which will be given below, the whole of the remaining forces under your command should be promptly embarked and dispatched to the harbor behind the island of Lobos, some sixty miles south of this place, there to await further orders. . . . . Should I have left that rendezvous before your arrival, you will please direct all vessels of the expedition you may find there to join me off Anton Lizardo, and follow yourself to that anchorage; but I shall exceedingly regret to leave Lobos before you are up with me.

"The garrison to be left for holding and defending this position may be one company of artillery, the Maryland and District of Columbia Battalion of Volunteers, and the Louisiana Regiment of Volunteers; the whole under the command of Colonel Gates, of the Third United States Artillery. You will please give him such instructions as the importance of the place evidently requires. His command will commence from the time he shall find himself the senior officer at that place. . . . . .

"Besides the troops mentioned above for the garrison of this place, there will no doubt be a number of men in hospital—invalids and convalescents left by other regiments found—available in emergency.

"I remain, sir, etc.,

"(Signed) "WINFIELD SCOTT."

It will be perceived, from Colonel Totten's report, that he knew that the moment the army left, the garrison of Tampico would have to maintain itself independent of any succor from without; and General Scott, while himself selecting the troops destined for the garrison, carefully avoided express instructions to General Patterson. He was well acquainted with De Russy and Buchanan; they were both graduates of West Point, and De Russy had been a captain of artillery in the regular army, so that compelled as he was to leave so small a force as one thousand men, he at least determined to leave good officers; yet he hesitated to direct by command, General Patterson to detail the garrison. Patterson avoided all responsibility, as he had a right to do, and adopted the recommendation of Scott, and the garrison of Tampico was thus constituted and organized. If the expedition to Vera Cruz should prove successful, this garrison could maintain itself; but should that expedition fail, we would have been badly situated, as the nearest help would have to be looked for from General Taylor, distant three hundred and fifty miles, at Monterey. The navy would have proved a powerful and ready ally in case of need, but I am only speaking of the military features incident to the defense; however, Colonel Gates was a very cautious commandant,—indeed, we thought that he kept us too much on the alert, for we were nearly all the time apprehensive of a real or imaginary attack.

We will now follow General Scott. On the 28th of February he wrote from the Massachusetts, off Lobos Island, to the Secretary of War:

"SIR,—I left the Brazos the 15th and Tampico the 20th instant, having done much official business at the latter place, in a delay of some thirty hours. . . Perhaps no expedition was ever so unaccountably delayed,—by no want of foresight, arrangement or energy on my part, as I dare affirm,—under circumstances the most critical to this entire army; for everybody relied upon knew from the first, as well as I knew, that it would be fatal to us to attempt military operations on the coast after probably the first week in April, and here we are at the end of February.

"Nevertheless, this army is *in heart;* and crippled as I am in the means required and promised, I shall go forward, and expect to take Vera Cruz and its castle in time to escape, by pursuing the enemy, the pestilence of the coast.

* * * * * * * *

"We find this harbor against *northers* even better than I had anticipated. One has now been blowing some forty hours, and has brought down all the vessels ready to sail that were outside of the bars at the Brazos and Tampico. The next will take the fleet to Anton Lizardo, whither I am sending off ships with surf-boats, in order that the latter may be launched under the care of the navy, and held ready for my arrival. . . . The island (Lobos) has afforded the volunteers means of healthy military exercises, and tolerable drinking-water. The few surf-boats landed are admirably fitted for the purposes intended."

In connection with this initial step,—the capture of Vera Cruz by Major-General Scott,—I find place for two letters from Commodore Connor, interesting for the matters embraced in them, but still more as showing the zealous co-operation and essential value of the services of the navy, in this first effort by our government to combine the power of the land and naval forces of the republic, in an attack upon a foreign port of any magnitude.

"*Commodore Connor to Major-General Scott.*

"U. S. FRIGATE RARITAN,
ANTON LIZARDO, January 11, 1847.

"SIR,—Your esteemed favor of the 23d ultimo was received two days since by the United States ship Albany, from Pensacola.

"I had received, some days previously, communications from the Navy Department, apprising me of your being about to take command of the army in Mexico, and of the joint operations contemplated against the enemy. In the prosecution of these measures, you may rely on the cordial co-operation of the naval forces under my command.

"In consequence of some apprehensions being entertained of an attack from Mexican privateers, supposed to be fitting out in the island of Cuba, I dispatched the St. Mary's some days since to the Brazos for the protection of the transports before that place. Commander Sanders is directed to perform any service you may require of him; and as I attach little credit to the report concerning the privateers, the St. Mary's might be withdrawn from the Brazos without much risk to the transports, to carry your dispatches to me or to Tampico, should you wish to communicate with that place. I would employ steamboats for the purpose of communicating with you; but, unfortunately, with the exception of the Princeton (and she is in very bad condition, and scarcely fit to keep the sea), I have no steamer that is capable of making the passage to the Brazos with certainty or safety at this season of the year.

"My information from the shore in regard to the movements of the enemy has not of late been either so full or so exact as could be desired. From a source, however, which I believe may be relied upon, I learn that there are now about one thousand men in the castle, and in the town, eighteen hundred effective men, independent of the town militia, who do not amount to one thousand men. The provisions in the town or castle seldom or never exceed a supply for three or four days. In this matter all accounts concur. I am not aware of there being any regular force of any consequence between Vera Cruz and Mexico. There possibly may be a regiment or more at Xalapa, and also at La Puebla and the city of Mexico; but this I think doubtful, as great exertions have been made by Santa Anna to assemble the whole regular force of the country at San Luis. The National Guards, or such numbers as can be armed, have in some instances garrisoned the towns from which the troops of the line have been withdrawn. Such it is believed has been the case in most if not all of those above mentioned. I am therefore of opinion little opposition is to be expected from anything like a regular army in your descent on the coast, or from any other force than that within the city of Vera Cruz. Nor do I believe it in the power of the Mexican government to assemble a force in a reasonable time in the neighborhood of the city sufficient for its protection.

"No neutral vessels are permited to enter or depart from the harbor of Vera Cruz, except the English steam packets that arrive on the 14th and sail on the 2d of every month. Your agents may either avail themselves of these vessels, which I will direct to be boarded at their departure, or be conveyed on board the vessels blockading the port, by means of the fishing boats, which are still allowed to pass out to sea for the purpose of fishing.

"The vessels of the squadron have all been withdrawn from Tampico; but I will send one to that place without delay, for the purpose of bringing any dispatch you may find it convenient to send to that place for me.

I am informed there is good shelter at the Isle of Lobos for any number of vessels; but no water is to be obtained there. Nevertheless, it is highly important the transports employed should be well found with *ground tackle,* to enable them even in the most sheltered positions to ride out in safety the sudden and violent gales from the north, so frequent at this season of the year. This anchorage is considered one of the best and safest on the coast, yet in the gale of the 24th of November three vessels either foundered or were driven on shore from their anchors in this road, and lost. A gale is now blowing, in which, during the last night, this ship parted one of her best cables, and was only saved from imminent danger of being wrecked by others which were down bringing her up.

"Some reduction has occurred lately in the naval force in the Gulf, by the withdrawal of the Cumberland and Mississippi. Still, it is probable I should be able to land upwards of six hundred seamen and marines.

"I have the honor, etc., etc.,

"D. Connor."

"U. S. Ship Raritan,
Anton Lizardo, January 18, 1847.

"Sir,—Your esteemed favor of the 26th ultimo, accompanied by a duplicate of your communication of December 23d, dated at New Orleans, was handed to me yesterday afternoon by Lieutenant Rains. My reply to the latter was dispatched some days since to Brazos Santiago, in a prize schooner, under charge of Lieutenant Commanding Smith. By this time it has probably reached its address.

"The present would be the most favorable time for the contemplated attack upon Vera Cruz. There is every reason to believe the information contained in my former communication, as to the force now in the castle and town, correct. Provisions for the garrison are obtained with the greatest difficulty, and in quantities sufficient only to last from day to day. The supplies at present in the castle may be perhaps enough for a week or ten days at the utmost, all accounts agreeing that there are no salt provisions in either. So far as I am able to judge, I am of opinion that if four or five thousand troops could be landed in the neighborhood of Vera Cruz by the end of this month or the beginning of the next, so as completely to invest the place, and cut off all communication with the country, its surrender, in less than ten days, with that of the castle, would be certain, and probably without the necessity of firing a gun.

"The best point for landing can readily be ascertained on your arrival, after an examination of the coast. Indeed, in my opinion, there are but two points at all eligible for this purpose—one on the beach, due west from Sacrificios; the other on the shores of this anchorage.

"I have already given you such information as I possessed in relation to the anchorage at Lobos. It is perfectly safe and easy of access. 'Blunt's Coast Pilot' contains full and exact directions for the entrance. Pilots can be procured, should they be deemed necessary, at Tampico.

"I would advise by all means that the transports which pass Lobos be directed to rendezvous at Anton Lizardo, instead of Sacrificios. The anchorage at the latter place, not already occupied by foreign men-of-war, is unsafe at this season of the year; that of Anton Lizardo, as I have before stated, the safest and best on the coast, and sufficiently extensive for two or three hundred sail. No apprehensions are as yet entertained at Vera Cruz of the design contemplated against the place. But it is to be feared that, before long, the movements of the army and other indications may excite suspicion. It would indeed be greatly to be regretted should so favorable an opportunity of making a successful attack on the town, as the present, pass without your being able to avail yourself of it.

"Accounts received here state that General Wool had joined General Worth at Monterey, about the 1st of January. The forces of Santa Anna had commenced their advance some days previously from San Luis to Saltillo. The return of General Taylor to Monterey, which from all accounts seems likely, will probably have the effect of retarding your movements some weeks.

"I have the honor to be your obedient servant,

"D. CONNOR,
"Commanding Home Squadron

"Major-General SCOTT."

As early as December 20, 1846, General Scott wrote to General Taylor, from New Orleans:

. . . . "The particular expedition I am to conduct is destined against Vera Cruz, and through it the Castle of San Juan d'Ulloa, so as to open, if we are successful, a new and shorter line of operations upon the capital of Mexico.

"The first great difficulty is to get together, in time, and afloat, off the Brazos, a sufficient force to give us a reasonable prospect of success before the usual period—say the end of March—for the return of the black vomit on the coast of Mexico.

"I have supposed fifteen thousand land troops, including five of regulars, and the co-operation of the blockading squadron, to be desirable, if not absolutely necessary, but am now inclined to move forward to the attack should I be able to assemble the five thousand regulars, and, say, three of volunteers. . . .

"To make up the force for the new expedition, I foresee that I shall, as I intimated in my letter, of which I enclose a copy, be obliged to reduce you to the defensive at the moment when it would be of the greatest importance to the success of my expedition that you should be in strength to manœuvre offensively upon San Luis de Potosi, etc." . . . . .

The elucidation of what I have meant by *cross-*

purposes, and the key to the approaching grand successes, is to be found in the concluding lines of the above extract.

On the 1st day of February, 1847, Santa Anna had the game in his own hands. Taylor was too weak to act offensively toward San Luis; Scott had, by no fault of his, lost precious time; yet, with the road open and the troops at command, Santa Anna elected to march away from his Capital to attack Taylor. Nothing but the *certainty*, the *absolute* certainty, of success, would have justified this movement.

Doubtless he thought that he could crush Taylor; but—he was mistaken, mainly because he did not properly appreciate the character of his antagonist. He estimated the number of troops he had to encounter, not the weight of the hero at their head.

We must advance a little in the order of time to see how thoroughly the government at Washington was alarmed at the status of the war, before information reached it of Taylor's success at Buena Vista, and necessarily of the result of Scott's expedition to Vera Cruz.

The subjoined letter, from the able pen of the distinguished Secretary of War, Hon. W. L. Marcy, to Major-General Winfield Scott, is a compendium of history in itself, and the best commentary ever written, on the conduct of the war in the Valley of the Rio Grande, subsequent to the withdrawal from Taylor of the army with which he had stormed and carried the city of Monterey:

"WAR DEPARTMENT, March 22, 1847.

"SIR,—The information which has just reached us, in the shape of rumors, as to the situation of General Taylor and the forces under his command, has excited the most painful apprehensions for their safety. It is almost certain that Santa Anna has precipitated the large army he had collected at San Luis de Potosi upon General Taylor; and it may be that the General has not been able to maintain the advanced position he had seen fit to take at Agua Nueva, but has been obliged to fall back on Monterey. It is equally certain that a Mexican force has been interposed between Monterey and the Rio Grande, and that it has interrupted the line of communication between the two places and seized large supplies which were on the way to General Taylor's army.

"If the hostile force between the Rio Grande and General Taylor's army is as large as reports represent it, our troops now on that river may not be able to re-establish the line, nor will it, perhaps, be possible to place a force there sufficient for the purpose in time to prevent disastrous consequences to our army, unless aid can be afforded from the troops under your immediate command.

"From one to two thousand of the new recruits for the ten regiments from this quarter will be on the way to the Brazos in the course of three or four days. All the other forces will be directed to that point, and every effort made to relieve General Taylor from his critical situation. You will have been fully apprised, before this can reach you, of the condition of things in the Valley of the Rio Grande and at the headquarters of General Taylor, and have taken, I trust, such measures as the importance of the subject requires. I need not urge upon you the fatal consequences which would result from any serious disaster which might befall the army under General Taylor, nor do I doubt that you will do what is in your power to avert such a calamity.

"A state of things may exist on the Rio Grande and at Monterey which will require that a part of your forces, after the capture of Vera Cruz and the reduction of the castle of San Juan d'Ulloa, should return to Tampico or the Brazos, to carry on operations from these points. It is here deemed of the utmost importance that the line of the Rio Grande should be maintained, and that Monterey should be held by our forces. You will be kept advised of all done here to sustain General Taylor and augment the forces under him. In ignorance of what may be your own situation, and what may be required for the relief of General Taylor, I can give no distinct indication of what is deemed proper for you to do, if anything, beyond what you may have already done, but must request that no assistance which you can render, without too much hazard to your own operations, and he may need, should be withheld.

"I herewith send you a copy of a letter addressed to General Brooke. You will learn, as soon as it can be known here, what action he will take under the authority therein given to him. I also enclose herewith a dispatch from the Secretary of the Navy to the commander of our squadron in the Gulf.

"Very respectfully, etc.,

"(Signed) "W. L. MARCY.

"To Major-General SCOTT, etc.

"P.S.—I have just received your letters of the 23d ult. and 1st instant."

If such was the alarm in Washington, then ours in Tampico may be readily imagined. We were at our guns night and day, for we knew not at what moment after the departure of Scott's army we would be attacked, it being generally rumored and credited, that Santa Anna had abandoned his forward movement from San Luis, and would debouch from the Tula Pass upon Tampico to strike Scott's base.

But let us return to the expedition on Vera Cruz; for, although its success was subsequent to Taylor's at Buena Vista, we will follow it so as to continue the thread of our narration.

At the time I paid a visit to General Taylor at Victoria, in January, 1847, I found him engaged reading a work on Vera Cruz and its castle. Several maps and charts were lying about him, and I was satisfied that the General at that time was deliberating upon an attack on Vera Cruz, or an advance on that line to the city of Mexico. It will be remembered that we were then on the march from Monterey to Tampico, and that in a few days thereafter General Taylor was superseded by General Scott as chief in command, and retired to Monterey.

Before General Scott left the United States, he had submitted several projects to the government for the capture of Vera Cruz, and he inaugurated his advent into Mexico by his preparations for that enterprise.

All that he did was planned according to military art, and was successfully executed.

Vera Cruz was defended on the land side by several redoubts, mounting seventy guns, and was garrisoned by three thousand men. The strength of the city as a military position, however, was, or was supposed to be, in the castle of San Juan d'Ulloa. This fortress, built upon a reef of coral rock at about the distance of one thousand yards north-east and immediately in front of the city, on the sea side, mounted upwards of a hundred guns, many of them new and of heavy calibre. Its garrison was weak for the capacity of the work and the weight of its armament; it was counted in round numbers at one thousand men.

On the morning of the 9th of March, General Scott landed Worth's Division on the Gulf shore three miles south of the city, by the boats of the navy, pulled by the seamen of the fleet. No enemy opposed the landing, and before the ensuing morning Scott's whole army of about ten thousand men was on shore. The investment commenced from the landing of the first troops, and was completed by noon of the 12th, making a line of six miles, stretching from Punta Hornos on the south to Vergara on the north.

The trenches were opened and batteries planted, including one manned exclusively by officers and seamen of the fleet, when, on the 22d, General Scott, having fruitlessly demanded the surrender of the city, gave the orders to commence firing.

For four days and nights shot and shell were poured into the city, and the fire rapidly returned by the guns of the city and castle. The suffering and loss of life in the city were great, and each hour that passed added strength and effect to the fire of the besieging force. On the night of the 25th, the foreign consuls in the city sent a flag to General Scott, asking permission for the foreigners and Mexican women and children to leave the city. Scott replied that as they had had full knowledge of the proposed investment, and had been furnished with safeguards which they had failed to take advantage of, they must now stand the consequences.

On the morning of the 26th, General Landero, who had succeeded Morales in chief command, sent proposals to General Scott, which were entertained. These led to a convention, by which Vera Cruz and the castle with all their guns and ordnance stores were unconditionally surrendered to the United States. On the 29th of March the garrisons of both marched out with the honors of war, saluted their flag, and then laid down their arms as prisoners of war, not to serve again unless regularly exchanged.

As a military achievement, this will rank as one of the most brilliant on record, for it was the result of calculation and combination, entirely the work of the commander-in-chief. From the number of men requisite, to the number of intrenching tools, the co-operation of the navy, and the structure of the surf-boats, the number and size of guns and mortars, the quantity and character of ordnance stores, all had been prearranged, all were aptly chosen, all systematically used, and all worked as planned.

The casualties on the side of the Americans did not exceed one hundred men, while that of the Mexicans, soldiers and civilians, was fully one thousand; the best port in the Gulf of Mexico was in our hands, and a sure base established for the conquest of Mexico.

The convention was agreed on by the commissioners on the night of the 28th, and approved by General Scott, Commodore Perry (who had succeeded Commodore Connor in command of the Gulf Squadron), and General Landero. The terms were, the surrender of the castle of San Juan d'Ulloa and the city of Vera Cruz, with all their guns and munitions of war; the troops to march out with the honors of war, and to surrender their arms, and the officers were to give their paroles for themselves and their men not to serve during the war until regularly exchanged. I give in full the three last articles:

"6. The sick and wounded Mexicans to be allowed to remain in the city, with such medical officers and attendants and officers of the army as may be necessary to their care and treatment.

"7. Absolute protection is solemnly guaranteed to persons in the city and to property, and it is clearly understood that no private building or property is to be taken or used by the forces of the United States, without previous arrangement with the owners, and for a fair equivalent.

"8. Absolute freedom of religious worship and ceremonies is solemnly guaranteed."

The 1st and 4th articles were as follows:

"1. The whole garrison or garrisons to be surrendered to the arms of the United States, as prisoners of war, the 29th instant, at 10 o'clock A.M.; the garrison to be permitted to march out with all the honors of war, and to lay down their arms to such officers as may be appointed by the General-in-Chief of the United States armies, and at a point to be agreed upon by the commissioners."

"4. The rank and file of the regular portion of the prisoners to be disposed of after surrender and parole, as their General-in-Chief may desire, and the irregular to be permitted to return to their homes. The officers, in respect to all arms and description of force, giving the usual parole that the said rank and file, as well as themselves, shall not serve again until duly exchanged."

Incidental to the fall of Vera Cruz was the capture of Alvarado, a town of some fifteen hundred inhabitants, distant two days' march from Vera Cruz. On the day after the surrender, General Quitman with his brigade was ordered there, and on his arrival found the place in the virtual occupancy of the navy; Commodore Perry had sent a vessel to watch the mouth of the river upon which the town is situated, and Lieutenant Hunter, its commander, had landed some sailors and taken possession before the arrival of General Quitman.

On the 5th of April General Scott wrote a very lengthy communication to the War Department, from which I make a few extracts:

"I am now organizing a movement of three or four brigades upon Jalapa. . . . .

"In the meantime, the city and camps remain free from signs of malignant fever, and we may hope will continue healthy for weeks longer. . . . . Being by default of others thrown upon this coast six weeks too late in respect to the *vomito,* I have been made to feel the deepest solicitude for the safety of the army. Tampico is not less unhealthy than Vera Cruz, and Tuspan is considered the worst of the three places. . . . . Our depots must of necessity be at this place (Vera Cruz). The harbor is the best on the coast, and hence to the capital is the best road in the country."

Leaving General Scott here, preparing to march into the interior, we will return to General Taylor and the army under his command.

And first, we must place Brigadier-General John E. Wool, which we can now do, and show how wonderfully he had turned up at the right time and in the right place, to render with his Division highly important and valuable service. At the outset of the war, an expedition had been organized by the government, in Texas, to march overland into the State of Chihuahua, the most northern of the Mexican republic, and seize the city of Chihuahua. The column named "Central Division, Army of Mexico," marched from San Antonio the latter part of September, and got as far as Monclova, in the State of Cohahuila, about the 1st of November, 1846. It was here that General Wool, in command of this Division, was enabled to learn that General Taylor had captured and was in possession of Monterey, the capital of the adjoining State of New Leon, and he determined to abandon his march after Chihuahua, and endeavor to form a junction with Taylor. He established himself at Parras, in the same State of Cohahuila, and when Worth was alarmed, whilst Taylor was on the march to Victoria, General Wool had by a rapid march reinforced Worth at Saltillo, and was now near that place in camp, on a ranch named Buena Vista, which had been selected by General Wool and his engineer officer, Captain George W. Hughes, of the Topographical Engineers, with especial reference to its suitableness for advantageous defense; a pass two miles in advance of this camp was the key to the position, and it was here that was fought the battle which gave *éclat* to the name of the ranch, and imperishable renown to American arms.

General Taylor returned to Monterey about the 1st of February, 1847, after having been superseded by General Scott, whilst at Victoria *en route* to Tampico, with the feeble (in point of numbers) escort of two companies of dragoons, two batteries, and one regiment of rifles. His arrival was greeted with the sad news of the capture of several parties of Americans, a general advance of Santa Anna with an overwhelming force, and a good deal of demoralization among the troops outside of Wool's Division, and not including the body-guard he had brought with him.

His heart must have been very heavy; he had been shamefully outraged, all his tried troops with the exception of a handful taken from him, and now the life of every American in the valley of the Rio Grande, the honor of our arms, the success of the war, his own laurels, were in jeopardy, and in his single keeping.

He had said that he would do his duty to his country, though he might be crushed in the effort; and he was about to illustrate that he shrank from no responsibilities which the duties of his office demanded.

Moving rapidly forward from Monterey, he was at Agua Nueva, sixty miles from Monterey, and eighteen miles south of Saltillo.* On the 5th of February, not liking this position, he fell back to the pass in front of Buena Vista, which had been observed by Wool and Hughes, and this ground meeting with his approval, he prepared to resist here the coming of Santa Anna and his army.

On the 8th Taylor had his whole army, including Wool's Division, concentrated here; it was composed of two companies of the First Dragoons, under Captain Enoch Steen; two companies of the Second Dragoons, under Lieutenant-Colonel Charles A. May; Bragg's, Sherman's and Washington's Batteries of the regular army; one regiment of Arkansas Cavalry, under Colonel Archibald Yell; one regiment of Kentucky Cavalry, under Colonel Humphrey Marshall; Second Kentucky Infantry, under Colonel William R. McKee; First Regiment Mississippi Rifles, under Colonel Jefferson Davis; Second Indiana Infantry,

---

* The town of Saltillo was defended by a field work in which our old friends of Monterey, two twenty-four-pound howitzers, and Captain Webster's and Lieutenant James L. Donaldson's company of regular artillery, were posted to guard the approaches, whilst some infantry were within the city.

The train was under the care of two companies of infantry, with Captain Wm. H. Shover's field pieces, U. S. Army.

under Colonel Bowles; Third Indiana Infantry, under Colonel James H. Lane; First Illinois Infantry, under Colonel John J. Hardin; Second Illinois Infantry, under Colonel William H. Bissel; two companies of Texas Volunteers, under Captains McCullough and Conner; making his whole force three hundred and thirty-four officers and four thousand four hundred and twenty-five men.

The army of Santa Anna, according to Mexican accounts, was composed and numbered as follows: sappers and artillerists, with nineteen guns and one howitzer, six hundred and fifty men; First, Third, Fourth, Fifth, Tenth, and Eleventh Regiments of the line, First and Third Light Troops, six thousand two hundred and forty men; Fourth Light Troops, mixed, of Santa Anna; First Active, of Calayo, of Guadalaxara, of Lagos, of Queretaro, and of Mexico, three thousand two hundred men; General Parrodi's command from Tula, one thousand men; artillery, two hundred and fifty men; Mejia's Division, four thousand men; with the cavalry of Miñon, estimated at two thousand men. General Santa Anna advanced from San Luis Potosi with about twenty thousand men of all arms, on the 29th day of January, the very day that our division marched into Tampico. He was going *north* with the *élite* of the Mexican army, while we were going *south* away from the great shock of battle. Certainly military annals may be searched in vain for a parallel campaign. The reader must look at a good map, to intelligently comprehend the situation and the movements of the armies in Mexico in this month of February, 1847.

On the 18th, Santa Anna reached the hacienda of Encarnacion, distant sixty miles south of Saltillo; on the 19th, his army was concentrated and he made his arrangements for battle; advancing on the 20th, he reached Encantada on the 22d, and immediately sent a flag by his Surgeon-General Lindenberger to Taylor's headquarters, with a summons, of which the following is a copy, translated:

"You are surrounded by twenty thousand men, and cannot in any human probability avoid suffering a rout and being cut to pieces by our troops; but as you deserve consideration and particular esteem, I wish to save you a catastrophe, and for that purpose give you this notice, in order that you may surrender at discretion, under the assurance that you will be treated with the consideration belonging to the Mexican character; to which end you will be granted an hour's time to make up your mind, to commence from the moment my flag of truce arrives in your camp.

"With this view, I assure you of my particular consideration.

"God and Liberty!

"(Signed) "ANTONIO LOPEZ DE SANTA ANNA.

"CAMP AT ENCANTADA, February 22, 1847.

"To General Z. TAYLOR, Commanding Forces of the U. S."

To this was sent the reply:

"HEADQUARTERS, ARMY OF OCCUPATION,
NEAR BUENA VISTA, February 22, 1847.

"SIR,—In reply to your note of this date, summoning me to surrender my forces at discretion, I beg leave to say that I decline acceding to your request.

"With high respect, I am, sir,

"Your obedient servant,

"(Signed) "Z. TAYLOR,
"Major-General U. S. A. Commanding.

"Señor General D. ANTONIO LOPEZ DE SANTA ANNA,
"Commander-in-Chief, La Encantada."

General Taylor, aware of Santa Anna's approach, had marched out of camp on the morning of the 21st, and had taken up his previously selected position for battle; it began immediately after the return of the flag with Taylor's answer, by an attempt to turn our left, but the decisive battle was not fought until the next day, the 23d February.

On this day the battle raged from right to left, with varying success, for eight hours. Again and again our line was broken, overwhelmed by the masses of the enemy. Repeatedly in rear of our broken yet unconquered troops, the Mexicans were again and again compelled to retire. While one portion of the field was apparently lost, another was tenaciously held by American valor. Cavalry charges alternated with the advance and repulse of infantry columns, and artillery hurled its missiles at pistol-shot range. Two hundred and sixty-seven of our dead were lying scattered among five hundred of the enemy, while the groans of four hundred and fifty-six Americans were mingled with those of fifteen hundred Mexicans. Among our killed were Colonels Hardin, McKee, and Yell; Lieutenant-Colonel Henry Clay, Jr., a son of Honorable Henry Clay of Kentucky; Captain George Lincoln, of Massachusetts, Assistant Adjutant-General U. S. Army; Captain Woodward, of Second Illinois; Captains Kinder and Walker, of Second Indiana; Captain Taggart, of Third Indiana; Captain Willis, of Second Kentucky; Captain Porter, of the Arkansas Cavalry; Lieutenants Moore and McNulty, of the Mississippi Rifles; Lieutenant Houghton, of First Illinois; Lieutenants Campbell and Leonard, of the

Texas Volunteers; and Lieutenants Roundtree, Fletcher, Ferguson, Robbins, Steele, Kelly, Bartleson, Atherton, and Price, of the Second Illinois. Of the little army of Americans, twenty-eight of its officers were killed and forty-one wounded, while two hundred and eighty-nine dead, and four hundred and fifteen wounded of the brave rank and file attested the tenacity and unflinching courage of the United States troops. General Taylor, in his official report of this battle, dated the 6th of March, 1847, after referring to the general good conduct of his army and its brilliant success, thus speaks of his Batteries: "The services of the light artillery, always conspicuous, were more than usually distinguished. Moving rapidly over the roughest ground, it was always in action at the right place and the right time, and its well-directed fire dealt destruction in the masses of the enemy." With such officers as Washington, Sherman, Bragg, Thomas, Kilburn, O'Brien, Reynolds, Bryan, and Whiting, the artillery arm of the service reflected an undying lustre on the Military Academy at West Point, and proudly displayed the standard of its training, before the admiring gaze of the American people.

I have read various reports of this great battle, in which five thousand American volunteers (only the dragoons and artillerists were regulars) successfully fought against four times their number; and I have conversed with officers and men of both armies who were in that battle, and my opinion is this, that the victory was due to the facts, that our right was inaccessible by reason of the deep gullies which ran athwart the plain; that our volunteers used their fire-arms with telling and fatal accuracy; that our light artillery was served with such fearful rapidity that the Mexican infantry could not bear up against its fire; that Santa Anna threw his columns against our light batteries, when he had heavier guns and of longer range without using them; that in broad daylight Santa Anna or Lombardini, his infantry commander, hurled his brave footmen by column in mass against artillery, which was capable of and was in fact being manœuvred as rapidly as infantry, precisely as if he were sending them against guns in fixed positions; and finally and chiefly was the victory due to the coolness and sagacity and personal courage of General Zachary Taylor. It is notable of this battle that all who were in it bear witness to the great courage displayed by both armies; it was a very sanguinary battle, and deeds of personal daring so numerous that they were not conspicuous. Its results were of untold importance, and are incalculable, except to those who know that from the Rio Grande to the base of the Sierra Madre mountains, from Tampico to Saltillo, the cavalry of Miñon and Urrea held undisputed sway, and that the enraged rancheros of the States of New Leon, Cohahuila, and Tamaulipas, would have sprung from the earth upon every North American, so luckless as to have been in the area described, had General Taylor been less the soldier, and less the man he was, at Buena Vista on the 22d and 23d days of February, 1847.

On the night of the 23d, the army of Santa Anna, shattered and disorganized, retreated toward San Luis, leaving the road as far as Encarnacion strewed with the dead, the dying, and débris of a routed army.

Scott was free to act from a new base; the laurels of Taylor imperishable; the campaign of the Rio Grande was ended.

CHAPTER XXIII.

TAMPICO—VISIT TO VERA CRUZ.

I HAD the honor to fire salutes at Tampico for the victories of Buena Vista and Vera Cruz, and we were now comparatively at rest; but I had been overworked, and a chronic disease contracted on the Rio Grande had become so aggravated, that I was forced into the military hospital. Here, at the coolest place in the building, the thermometer stood at 102 degrees, Fahrenheit, for several successive days, and the heat was so smothering and enfeebling that the surgeon in charge advised my leaving for the United States. I determined not to leave before my company's term of service had expired, and thinking that a trip to Vera Cruz would be beneficial, I readily obtained permission to go. On Saturday, the 10th of April, I went on board the government steamer New Orleans; two companies of the First Infantry, and two hundred and eighty mules, also destined for Vera Cruz, being embarked, we weighed anchor, and, after one or two bumps on the bar at the mouth of the Panuco, were rolling in a heavy sea on the Gulf of

Mexico. On Monday we cast anchor between the castle and the city, and I went ashore for a stroll through the city. On the ensuing day I wrote the following letter:

"CASTLE OF SAN JUAN DE ULLOA,
VERA CRUZ, April 13, 1847.

"MY DEAR PARENTS,—I expected to find on arriving here that all my friends would have been away, but how agreeably I have been disappointed! My old brigade commander, Colonel Henry Wilson, of the First Infantry, is the Governor of Vera Cruz, and my friend Major Bacchus is stationed at and in command of this castle; in fact, it so happens that the First Infantry, with whom we were so long a time brigaded, and which we served with at Monterey, constitutes the garrison, and I am surrounded with acquaintances and comrades. They have all been very kind, and have offered their quarters as a home during my stay, and I am now the guest of Major Bacchus.

"On approaching this castle from the sea, I was disappointed, it being so much smaller in appearance than I anticipated; but now I realize its immense strength and its power to resist, if well defended, the navies of the world.

"I have just returned from an exploration of its interior labyrinths, which remind me of my visit to, and recall the wonders of, the Mammoth Cave, Kentucky; through vaults, dungeons, casemates, passages, and covered ways, deep down beneath the terre-plein of the fort; across ditches, moats, bridges, under portcullis and over drawbridges; every side bristling with artillery. I wandered with my guide until I gave up, unable to visit much that was yet to be seen of its mysteries.

"Everything that man as a soldier would require is to be found within these walls, from the chapel for worship to the dungeon for punishment, from the foundry to the smith's shop, from the arsenal to the marine rope-walk, from the handsomely fitted-up apartments for the priests and officers to the more humble barracks of the soldiers, from the twenty-four-inch shell to the canisters of grape, from the beautiful bronze English guns to the long copper guns of old Spain, from the handsome English musket to the matchlock of the buccaneers: the labor of a hundred years to render this work impregnable, and the wealth of the Indies to complete the design, have made this a wonderful tower of human strength and skill.

"The quantity and *variety* of the munitions of war now piled and heaped up are, I should say, inexhaustible, and there are enough guns, pistols, swords, iron and copper shot lying beneath the water of the ditches, yet plainly visible, to arm at least a regiment of troops.

"Some of the bronze guns mounted en barbette on the upper terrace of the works are magnificent; the precision and accuracy of their fire you may judge of, when I tell you that the Mexican gunners put twenty-eight shot through the brick wall of the cemetery, over on the main land, behind which they supposed our infantry were, (as we had a mortar-battery next adjoining,) the wall being five feet high and about one hundred and fifty feet in length, and this at the distance of one and a half miles.

"When I looked at this perforated and shattered wall on yesterday, and was told that it had been done by guns at the castle, I felt a strong desire to see the guns that did such shooting; here they were, made at Deptford, England, but a few years ago; just lovely, they were so beautiful. I can't say whether they are twenty-four- or thirty-two-pounders; somewhere about that calibre, perhaps heavier.

"There are about one hundred and fifty pieces, of various calibre, mounted now in this work, but it is capable of showing twice as much artillery if needed; built of the coral rock upon which its walls stand, it crumbles, but it is not shattered, by projectiles fired against it. Seaward, its reefs project far into the Gulf, while toward the city a heavy water-battery adds weight to its upper guns. It is truly a formidable fortress.

"On entering the city, I was disappointed at not seeing as many houses in ruins as I had supposed would be the case; but as I continued my stroll, I soon saw the dreadful destruction which our shells occasioned, while solid shot from our batteries had passed entirely through the city, reaching in their flight the quay or mole running into the sea, upon which the affrighted citizens had fled for safety from the bombs. As I passed along, the poor women were cleaning up a house in which a thirteen-inch shell, after falling through three stories, had exploded in the cellar; among the plaster and bricks and stones were several fragments of the shell, and I took a piece to preserve as a curiosity and memorial; the poor creatures looked at me as if I were, or must be, a demon to rejoice at their griefs, for I judged from their looks that they supposed I was glorying at seeing the effect of our fire upon their homes. How much they were mistaken the Good Father knows. Many of the houses were completely demolished, and several bear the marks of fire occasioned by the explosion igniting the wood-work. I went into one of the churches, now converted into a hospital, in which there are upwards of five hundred patients; it was a curious sight thus to see the pallets of the sick placed in the chapels, and the various ornaments of the church, sacred to many eyes, made use of as need required. On looking up at the vaulted ceiling, behold there were several large holes through which the sky was visible; several thirteen-inch shells had dropped through the roofing as if it had been paper, exploding within the body of the church; all around, walls, paintings, and wood-work showed the terrified force of their bursting; the débris was still lying over the floor or swept into piles to make room for beds. It is owing to the effect that these shells produced in the city that the castle was surrendered, for *it* was very little damaged; it scarcely shows a scar, and I am told was but little injured by the French in their bombardment a few years ago. Our victory, in its present gain and future results, is very great indeed, and I doubt whether ever as great a one was obtained with less loss to the victors. Scott deserves immense praise.

"One of my company, Benjamin F. Nimocks, is on detached duty in the Pay Department, and was here during the siege; he came after me yesterday, and giving me a horse, guided me round our lines of investment and showed me the position of all our batteries and the enemy's line of works, fort by fort, so that I think I am quite conversant with the military operations which resulted in the fall of Vera Cruz. The cemetery, a beautiful burial-place, was an object of especial interest, for I never expect to see again a graveyard knocked to pieces—the chapel was in ruins, monuments shattered, the graves of the dead torn up, and the silent tenant of one coffin was *now* exposed to my sight by a solid shot having *unburied* it. I saw this sight.

"Vera Cruz reminds me of Havre in its commercial-looking houses and filthy streets; it is much larger than any Mexican town yet visited. Its mole is magnificent, running far out into the sea; here I have passed hours gazing at the throng, who find the sea-breeze so grateful, at the castle, the large fleet of vessels of war in the offing and the numbers of small boats plying between the shore and the vessels lying in the roads; there are one hundred and fifty transports lying here, besides our own,—and English, French, and Spanish war-ships.

"Will we have peace? This I cannot answer, nor can any-one else. I am in possession of much curious and important information direct from the city of Mexico, but I do not feel at liberty to communicate it, although I was not held to secrecy. My informant is Mr. Moses Y. Beach, of the New York *Sun*, who came down with me from Tampico. He is *direct* from the city of Mexico, and his conversation was highly interesting.

"An eminent and wealthy merchant, who has been eighteen years in the country, told me on yesterday that *he* could not tell what would be the result, etc.

"I believe that my health is nearly restored, and that I am now acclimated. I shall return to Tampico by the first steamer.

"Your affectionate son, JOHN."

I copy from "Chambers's Encyclopædia" its article upon Vera Cruz:

"Vera Cruz, or Villa Rica de la Vera Cruz (the Rich City of the Real Cross), an ancient city on the east coast of Mexico, about one hundred and eighty-five miles* east of the city of Mexico, with a population of about eight thousand, composed chiefly of

---

* Vera Cruz, by Mexican count, is ninety leagues from the city of Mexico, and I judged this to be correct, giving two and a half miles to the league. I made the distance two hundred and thirty miles.

a motley collection from many nations. The city is built in a semicircle, facing the sea, and is regularly laid out; the streets, which are wider than is usual in tropical countries, running east and west from the harbor, with others crossing them at right angles. The town is well defended by a strong wall* and other substantial works, as also by the castle of San Juan de Ulloa, which stands upon an island of the same name about half a mile from the shore. The principal buildings are the cathedral and fifteen other churches, generally built in the Moorish style, only six of which are in use; several monasteries, the court-house and prison, which stand on one side of the great square in the centre of the city. The houses and public buildings are generally built of rubble masonry, formed of small stones, interspersed with red tiles, the whole being afterwards covered with good durable plaster, and colored with a variety of tints; and as most of the houses are in the old Spanish style, with open arcades, balconies, galleries, etc., the city presents a very picturesque aspect. There are a few good hospitals. The drainage of the city flows down open channels in the centre of the streets, which are almost on a level with the sea. This combined with the wretched water which the inhabitants are compelled to use, the marshy and utterly barren nature of the surrounding country, and the pestilential nature of the climate, generally easily accounts for the frightful ravages of yellow and other fevers. Yellow fever is most prevalent from May to November. Although it is the chief port for all Mexico, Vera Cruz has no harbor, but only an open roadstead between the town and the castle. The anchorage is exceedingly bad, and when the north gales, the *nortes* (terrible hurricanes bearing along with them clouds of sand from the sand-hills behind the town), prevail, many vessels are wrecked on the adjacent shores.

"The chief exports are the precious metals, cochineal, sugar, flour, indigo, provisions, sarsaparilla, leather, vanilla, jalap, soap,

---

* It was much better defended by the prickly pear, which grew outside in an impenetrable jungle, than by the walls. Infantry could not, or would not, have forced their way through in some places at the time I examined the defenses.

logwood, and pimento; and the imports cotton goods, woolen, linen, and silk goods, brandy, iron, steel, wax, quicksilver, paper, hardware, and cutlery, earthenware, etc. The imports in 1856 were about £3,700,000, and the exports about £1,863,100, the latter consisting principally of the precious metals."

On the afternoon of the day of my arrival, the 12th of April, I saw General Scott, with his staff and head-quarters, leave Vera Cruz for his march on the city of Mexico,* and on the evening of the 15th I re-embarked on the steamer New Orleans to return to my post.

On the voyage we were overtaken by a *norther*, which exceeded in violence and power all that I had ever known or imagined the wind to have. Our steamer was put head-on to the gale, the full force of her steam used, and yet she was driven, stern foremost, before the storm. Fortunately we were enabled to get under the lee of Lobos, where the steamer's anchors held her securely until 2 o'clock P.M. the ensuing day, when we proceeded on our course, and reached my quarters at Tampico on the evening of the 17th.

---

* He entered the city of Mexico at the head of his army, September 14th, after his victories in the valley.

CHAPTER XXIV.

TAMPICO—DISCHARGE FROM THE SERVICE, ETC.

As the end of our term of service approached, various efforts were being made to induce the officers and men to re-enter for the war. My friends had written to me to come home, that a regiment for the war would be accepted from the District of Columbia and Maryland, and that Governor Thomas G. Pratt, of Maryland, would have the appointment of its Major, as soon as a battalion, then organizing in Baltimore, was ready for the field, and that he had said I should have the Majority. This determined my action, otherwise I might have united with Captain James Boyd, of our battalion, who was receiving the names of volunteers for a company to be raised at Tampico from our own and other sources.

Our battalion continued on duty until the 30th day of May, 1847, at Tampico, when and where we were mustered out and honorably discharged from the service by Major William W. Morris, of the United States Army, under orders of Colonel William Gates, commanding United States forces at Tampico. Thus, after twelve months of honorable service, the Battalion of Baltimore and Washington Volunteers completed, with fidelity, its obligations to the government and prepared to return to the United States.

On the 31st day of May I received my pay and

allowance for mileage from Major J. Y. Dashiell, paymaster United States Army. The distance from Tampico to Washington was computed by the Pay Department at eighteen hundred miles, and upon this estimate the calculation was made for the pay of the men.

They were generally satisfied to be discharged here, although some insisted that the government was bound to carry them back to the United States. I thought so; but the necessity of the case perhaps justified the retention of their services until the last hour of the term of enlistment.

On this night I gave a supper to my own company at the Italian Fonda. Our association had been pleasant, and our parting was painful. So long as life lasts will the recollection of their fidelity and attachment to me be a bright spot for memory to dwell upon. With every man in the company I parted in friendship and good-will.

I had to remain when they left. One of them, Henry P. Norris, of Baltimore, had, on the night of the 30th, unfortunately killed a man employed in the quartermaster's department. I could not leave him; Major Buchanan in the kindest manner volunteered to assist in his defense, and we defended him before a court and jury organized under general orders from the headquarters of the army. He was found guilty of murder in the second degree, and sentenced to be imprisoned in the prison of Tampico at hard labor during the war.

I was very sick at the time of the trial, suffering from a high fever and a return of my old complaint;

but, after the verdict was rendered, I fortified myself with such recommendations and evidence as induced the President of the United States, James K. Polk, promptly to order his unconditional release, when I laid the case before him on my return.

I am satisfied that Norris would not have been convicted if his witnesses had remained; but it was uncertain when his trial would take place, and they, not dreaming that he would be convicted, left within a few days after their discharge, for it was growing very sickly.

Captain James Boyd and Lieutenant James Taneyhill remained at Tampico, and accompanied me on the 12th of June on board the schooner Elvira, bound for Mobile, she being the only vessel then up for the United States. Bidding them an affectionate and final farewell,* I sailed from Mexico homeward. I suffered a good deal during the voyage from my disease and want of attention, for the little vessel in which I was sailing had no accommodations for passengers; the rain-squalls were frequent, and the cabin occupied by the master and I was small and far from dry. Still, I was homeward bound, and the light at the Balize revived and strengthened me. On the 18th I landed, at sundown, at Mobile, and on the 27th of June, 1847, reached home, after an absence of twelve months and twenty-three days.

I conclude this record of a year's service in the army of the United States with the general orders

* They were both killed in an engagement with the enemy at the river Calabozo, not far from Tampico, within less than a month after we parted.

issued by Colonel William Gates, Third Artillery, United States Army, commanding the Department of Tampico, dated at Tampico, Mexico, May 30th, 1847, which honorably discharged me from the service, and a letter from Brevet-Major Robert C. Buchanan, Fourth Infantry, United States Army, lately commanding the Baltimore Battalion, dated at Tampico, May 31st, 1847, to the Hon. Jacob G. Davies, Mayor of Baltimore, concerning the presentation of the Battalion flag to the corporation of the city of Baltimore.

"HEADQUARTERS DEPARTMENT OF TAMPICO,
TAMPICO, MEXICO, May 30, 1847.

"*Orders No.* 23.]

"It has been the earnest wish of the Colonel commanding that orders from the general headquarters of the army should have been received directing him when and where the Battalion of Baltimore and District of Columbia Volunteers should be honorably mustered out of service, but circumstances not within his control have obliged him to detain it at Tampico until the last day of its term of service.

"He cannot here refrain from expressing the satisfaction he has experienced in beholding this brave body at its post, where it is so much regarded, and where he would gladly retain it during the war. Nevertheless, as that period has arrived when the expiration of the relations so long amicably existing between that corps and their commander must cease, he here proclaims it HONORABLY DISCHARGED this day.

"His Excellency the President of the United States foreseeing these results, and desiring the continuance of the services of volunteers requisite for the prosecution of the plans in the event of the prolongation of hostilities with the enemy, the Colonel commanding would testify his desire that these well-drilled, experienced, and gallant companies would again promptly present themselves for enrollment, under the respective officers, determined to abide the issue of their country's struggle, whatever it may be, secure in their acknowledged prowess and capacity in asserting her rights.

"Major Buchanan, whose well-tried fidelity and judicious performance of service have won the entire confidence of your commander, who seizes this opportunity to make known his thanks, has been officially authorized to make terms with the officers and men of this battalion from the city of heroic monuments and patriotic associations, by which, if any of you think proper to re-enroll yourselves, leave of absence for sixty days will be given, and on your return to Mexico, the twelve dollars bounty paid; and highly pleased will the commandant be if even one company will raise their standard on the parade for this purpose; but if not, and he is left to see you pass away, he offers you his cordial good wishes that you may have a speedy passage, and find your families, relatives, and friends, ready and proud to greet you as your honorable services justly entitle you.

"(Signed) "WM. GATES,
"Colonel Third Artillery Commanding."

Letter from Major Buchanan to the Mayor of Baltimore.

"TAMPICO, May 31, 1847.

"DEAR SIR,—The term of service of the Baltimore Battalion having expired, it becomes necessary to make a suitable disposition of the flag under whose folds it so gallantly fought and so faithfully sustained the toils and privations incident to the last twelve months' campaign.

"The officers of the Battalion desire that it should be presented to the corporation of the city, to be kept in the City Hall as a memorial of their regard for Baltimore. In this arrangement I most heartily concur.

"It therefore becomes my agreeable duty to forward the flag to you, the Chief-Magistrate of the city, with the request that it may be disposed of in accordance with the wishes of the donors.

"By our fellow-citizens it may well be regarded with feelings of pride, as having been the standard of a body of their friends which, for good discipline, soldierly deportment, and efficiency for hard service, stood in a most enviable position. The Rio Grande,

Monterey, Victoria, and Tampico will all bear witness to the services of the Battalion.

"Sergeant-Major William T. Lennox, who carried the flag in the battle of Monterey, after Hart was wounded, and who has been the color-bearer since that time, will be intrusted with the duty of delivering it to you.

"I am, sir, with much respect,

"(Signed) "ROBERT C. BUCHANAN,

"Brevet-Major Fourth Infantry, commanding Battalion.

"To Hon. JACOB G. DAVIES,

"Mayor of Baltimore, Maryland."

CHAPTER XXV.

THE DISTRICT OF COLUMBIA AND MARYLAND REGIMENT; ITS ORGANIZATION, DEPARTURE FOR THE SEAT OF WAR, AND ARRIVAL AT VERA CRUZ.

BY an understanding between the War Department and the Governor of Maryland, a battalion (and in certain contingencies a regiment) of volunteers, to be enlisted for the war with Mexico, was to be raised in the District of Columbia and the State of Maryland, of which the President was to appoint the Lieutenant-Colonel, and the Governor of Maryland the Major.

Shortly after my arrival at home, I was unofficially informed by His Excellency, Thomas G. Pratt, that I should be appointed the Major of the battalion as soon as the three companies then being recruited at Baltimore should be accepted by the government.

Recruiting had been going on very slowly, and there was some difficulty between the several officers as to the command of the companies that were being organized. I lent my assistance to recruiting and reconciling differences, so that by the 20th of July a sufficient number of companies were accepted from the District and Maryland to authorize my appointment; on that day I was commissioned Major of the District of Columbia and Maryland Regiment of Volunteers by the Governor of Maryland, and entered on my duties at once.

At the time these companies of infantry were accepted, several gentlemen were engaged in raising volunteers for a company of artillery, to be attached to the battalion, it being understood that such would be accepted by the government. After much discussion, an amicable arrangement was made by which the artillery company was to be commanded by Captain Lloyd Tilghman, of Maryland, the other gentlemen from Baltimore yielding their claims in his favor.

There was much difficulty in the District of Columbia between Brevet-Major George W. Hughes, of the United States Army, and Charles Lee Jones, Esq., as to the command of the battalion about being jointly raised in the District and in Maryland; each gentleman claiming a right, based either upon personal services or a promise from the War Department to be appointed its commanding officer. Finally, Major Hughes was commissioned Lieutenant-Colonel of the District of Columbia and Maryland Regiment of Volunteers by the President of the United States, and immediately assumed command.

The Maryland companies were quartered at Fort McHenry; upon the receipt of my commission I took command of this detachment, and upon the 23d received the following order (the other three companies from the District having arrived at the fort):

"HEADQUARTERS BATTALION OF D. C. AND M'D VOL'S.,
"July 23, 1847.

"*Orders No.* .]

"I. The three companies heretofore indicated to sail on board the transport ship Alexandria will be in readiness to leave Fort McHenry to-morrow morning the 24th instant.

"II. The camp and garrison equipage, arm-chests, personal baggage, etc., will be deposited on the wharf at 9 o'clock A.M. by companies, in the following order, viz.: Captain Barry's, Captain Henrie's, and Captain Brown's; and the company property will be placed on board by the men of the company to which it belongs, quietly and orderly.

"III. Major Kenly, who takes command of the detachment, will assign the men to berths by companies.

"IV. The officers will select their berths according to rank.

"V. Dr. Campbell, of the Voltigeurs, accompanies the detachment as medical officer, under orders from the War Department.

"By order,
"GEORGE W. HUGHES,
"Lieutenant-Colonel, etc."

In obedience to the above orders I superintended the embarkation from Fort McHenry of the three companies designated, and put them on board the transport ship Alexandria on the 24th day of July, 1847. The detachment consisted of eleven officers and one hundred and ninety-eight enlisted men, with some half-dozen servants. With the experience I had encountered, I hesitated going to sea on a voyage to the tropics, in the months of July and August, with troops on a transport ship, unless I was assured of the attendance of a medical officer and a full supply of water; to write plainly, I refused to go until a medical officer was with the detachment; and then having made a personal examination as to the quantity of water on board, and being supplied by the quartermaster with a barrel of chloride of lime as a disinfectant, I announced myself as ready to sail. There was a great deal of preliminary work to do, looking to the casualties of a month's voyage, and I attended to it in person to see that it was done; and it *was* done.

My instructions were to go to Vera Cruz; being ready, as far as my judgment went, on the 26th, the steamer Relief, Captain Sprigg, made fast to the Alexandria, and towed us as far as Poplar Island, where, casting us off, we made sail down the bay.

Previous to leaving, the following was placed in my hands:

"BALTIMORE, 23d July, 1847.

"SIR,—Enclosed herewith is a charter-party for the ship Alexandria, under cover to the quartermaster at Vera Cruz, which I request you will seal and hand to him, after having placed the requisite certificate upon it,—the same as on that in the hands of the captain of the ship.

"Very respectfully, your obedient servant,

"(Signed) S. B. DUSENBERY,

"Quartermaster.

"Commanding officer troops on board transport ship Alexandria, off Fort McHenry, Md."

From the tenor of the charter-party I learned that the captain of the ship could not obtain his freight money unless my certificate was given, and I felt much greater security for my detachment when aware of this condition to the charter. No security however was needed as far as seamanship could go, for a better sailor never trod a ship's deck than Captain

Ordeman, of Baltimore, with whom from first to last my relations were harmonious and agreeable, although he was fretted because I would not consent to sail on the 24th.

The other detachment, consisting of Captains Degge's, Dolan's and Taylor's companies, were embarked on board the ship Napier; to this detachment was assigned the surgeon of the regiment, Dr. Stedman R. Tilghman, of Maryland, and the ship sailed for the same destination a day or two after the Alexandria.

We left the capes on the 27th, having had a favorable wind down the bay; soon the roughness of the sea was followed by its usual consequences, and I had a very sick detachment of troops; they were very sick. Notwithstanding this, I mounted a regular guard daily, held the officer of the day responsible for the discipline on board, and established a school of instruction for the officers. The medical officer with the detachment, Dr. A. B. Campbell, of the Voltigeurs, was efficient, and made daily reports of the condition between decks (where the men were quartered), and the general health of the command. We were not too much crowded, the bunks kept scrupulously clean, decks scraped every morning before guard-mount, and as soon as the men were able to stand, squad drills in the manual of arms were begun and continued until our arrival at Vera Cruz.

On the 9th of August we made the Caycos Islands, and on the next day were becalmed between Cuba and San Domingo, both islands in sight, Cape Nicola Mole twelve miles to the eastward.

It was now very warm, the heat between decks oppressive, the thermometer standing at 94 degrees of Fahrenheit; extraordinary precautions were necessary to preserve the health of my command. The hatches were kept open, rain or shine, wind-sails for the ventilation of the hold were rigged, lime liberally spread and scattered between decks, and the men made to leave their bunks in the day-time, unless excused by the surgeon. I established a system of *feet washing*, which I claim as an original idea, at least I had never read or heard of it when I put it in practice. Every evening at retreat the companies were paraded successively upon the ship's deck; every man with his shoes and stockings off and pantaloons rolled over and above his knees; details were made who hoisted and threw sea-water upon the legs and feet of the men as they stood in ranks, until each man had had one bucketful as his quota of the briny element. At first, the men were very restive, and it required command to enforce the order, both to distribute the water and submit to the bath, but after a few evenings' exercise they became fond of it, and the chief difficulty was to make them behave orderly while the douching was going on, each man desiring to give particular directions *how* and *where* the water should be thrown.

The experiment was very successful, and it was continued daily until the end of the voyage; it contributed to the preservation of our health, and I was enabled to land the detachment without the loss of a man.

I had with me an excellent set of officers; they not only assisted me, they did more, for they gave me their entire sympathy as well as their support. In the thirty days we were together on board the Alexandria, I am sure that a cross word was never heard between us; and I soon had occasion to test the strength of the discipline which should mark their character as soldiers. There were with me Captain Edmund Barry, First Lieutenant John M. Thornton, and Second Lieutenants John Carr, Acting Adjutant, and Benjamin R. West, of Company B; Captain Dan Drake Henrie, First Lieutenant Frederick A. Klopfer, and Second Lieutenant Richard P. Henry, of Company D; Captain George W. Brown, First Lieutenant Washington Hopper, and Second Lieutenants James O'Brien and John H. Gronewell, of Company E. The officers of Companies B and D were from Washington; Company E was raised in Baltimore.

On the 12th of August, while lying to the southward of Cuba, and in sight of the town of Santo Jago de Cuba, the pitch between the seams of the deck oozing up from the burning rays of the sun, Captain Ordeman informed me that a great deal of water was being consumed, that the ship was getting too light, and asked me to have the empty water-casks filled with sea-water; that he would have the pumps rigged, and he would like it done at once, as he feared that the great heat would be followed by a hurricane. I issued an order directing a detail to be made for the purpose indicated, and retired to my cabin to write. While thus engaged, the officer of the day came and reported that the men detailed refused to work; I paid but little attention to him, merely repeating the order, and continuing at my desk. In fifteen minutes he returned, and asked what he was to do, as the men flatly refused to obey his orders. I went on deck, saw that the pumps were rigged, the detail standing about them, the sailors grouped about the forecastle, and an ominous silence over all. I directed the detail to be aligned, then inquired why it was they refused to work; several of the men answered at the same time, "that it was the sailors' place to pump water into the ship; that they were soldiers, and would not do sailors' work." I saw that it was a matured plan to refuse this duty, and deeming it advisable to temporize, I replied that the work was necessary for the safety of all, that the captain of the ship was the judge as to what was expedient to be done for our common good, and that when he had told me the necessity of filling the empty casks, the reason was so palpable that I had not hesitated for an instant in giving the order which I had issued, and that they must obey it; that a good soldier always obeyed an order and discussed its propriety afterward. They all answered that they would not obey the order to pump water into the casks; one of them saying he had been a sailor and had done sailors' work; now that he was a soldier he would not be a sailor. Inquiring this man's name, and calling him by it, I ordered him to step two paces to the front; he did so. I directed the officer of the guard to procure several pairs of handcuffs; these were promptly brought. I ordered the man to hold out his hands; fortunately, he obeyed. I told the officer of the guard to iron him; it was done at once; the mutiny was quelled. The second man named in the detail was ordered to step to the front, extend his hands, and he was ironed; the third was called, and likewise ironed. As the fourth man stepped to the front, he said he would obey the order, as did all the others of the detail, and the pumps were soon going.

It was a touch-and-go piece of work.

I kept these men ironed and guarded by officers on the quarter-deck until a heavy storm came on; when they begged so hard to have the irons removed, that I released two of them, but kept the ringleader securely fastened.

I had no more trouble in maintaining discipline on board the ship; the drills were continued, and as the fresh water was consumed, sea-water was pumped from the ocean and the empty casks filled. We lay becalmed for several days to the southward of Cuba; the heat continued to increase, as did the consumption of water, and grave apprehensions of a want of the latter daily arose. On Sunday, the 15th of August, when off the island of Jamaica and out of sight of land, a bird flew toward the ship and alighted on my head. I did not move, and it then hopped on my shoulder. We took a good look at each other, then it flew away. It would be untrue for me to say that I did not consider this incident a fortunate augury.

On the 17th we made Cape San Antonio, the westernmost point of the island of Cuba; at 9.30 P.M., on the night of the 18th, saw a meteor, which like an immense globe of fire traversed at least one-fourth of the horizon. This was followed by a hurricane storm, which drove us rapidly on our course across the Gulf. On the 19th we were on the Banks of Campeche, off

Yucatan, in thirty-six fathom water, and on the 22d made the mainland of Mexico, forty miles to the north of Vera Cruz.

At 9 o'clock P.M., on the 23d, made the lighthouse on the castle of San Juan de Ulloa, and at the same time approached a large ship, which proved to be our consort, the "Napier" from Baltimore, with the other detachment of our regiment. I have heard louder but never more joyous cheers than those which went up from the decks of the two ships, when in response to our hail, it was learned that the two detachments had again met.

August 24. This day one month ago we embarked at Baltimore, and to-day at 10 A.M. we dropped anchor in the roads between the castle and the mole of Vera Cruz. Our whole ship's crew was well, our health excellent during the voyage, while the Napier buried in the sea one of its detachment, and brought along a good many sick. The first object that attracted our attention was the lowering of two dead bodies in coffins from the sea-wall of the castle into a boat, and the next a pile of empty coffins on the mole as we landed from the ship to report our arrival. Everything else was dead in the blazing, glistening sunlight; not a living object, not one moving thing could I see, as I walked along the mole to the governor's quarters, which I knew where to find. It needed nothing but the appearance of things, the absence of all life,—not a soldier, citizen, or sailor to be seen, not an animal, —to tell me that the yellow fever, the dread black vomit, was raging in this fiery oven of a plague-stricken city.

I found my old friend and former commander, Colonel Henry Wilson, of the United States Army, still Governor, and on his back with the yellow fever. After a brief consultation I left him, went to the quartermaster's office, and putting life into things generally,—I had every man from both transports landed on the beach by 4 o'clock in the afternoon. Before dark, my camp and garrison equipage, arms and stores, were all landed, and a regular camp established at a point called Vergara, distant three miles from Vera Cruz.

This night proved a rough beginning for young soldiers; our sentries (with one single exception) were driven in by the Mexicans, who fired into our camp from the adjacent sand-hills, while the torrents of rain which fell washed the sands upon which we lay and stood into the surf and ocean, tumbling up swelling waves on our parade ground, where I had had a dress parade the preceding evening.

There was much alarm at Vera Cruz; no tidings had been received from General Scott for weeks, as the road to the city of Mexico was closed except to strong bodies of troops. Rumors were rife that Scott's army was in great peril, and the whole country from the Gulf coast to the valley of Mexico was swarming with guerillas; to add to the demoralization, there was lying near my camp a detachment which had started to join Scott, but had met with a disastrous repulse at the National Bridge, and retreated to Vera Cruz. It was believed that the city itself was not safe from sudden attack, and Governor Wilson had obtained from the naval commander the presence of a vessel of war in the roads. On the day next succeeding my arrival, I received the following order:

"HEADQUARTERS, DEPARTMENT OF VERA CRUZ,
"Mexico, August 26, 1847.

"*Orders No.* 53.]

"Major John R. Kenly, Maryland Volunteers, will take the entire command at Vergara.* On the 31st inst., at half-past 7 o'clock A.M., he will muster the Maryland Volunteers; and Captain Sheppard, Eighth United States Infantry, will muster the rest of the troops encamped and on guard at that place, except that Captain Fairchild's troops of Louisiana Mounted Volunteers will be mustered by Lieutenant-Colonel Miles,† United States Army.

"By order of Colonel Wilson,
"(Signed) B. H. ARTHUR,
"Adjutant First U. S. Infantry, and A.A.A.G. Dep't. Vera Cruz."

Things looked very gloomy; I had never before seen anything like the depression and despondency which prevailed. The heat was literally intense, and the sun from its rising to its going down looked and felt like a huge globe of fire. At night the mosquitoes—and their name was legion—were worse than those I had known a year ago on the Rio Grande, and the fear of the fever was becoming very general. We

* The troops thus assigned to my command consisted of one company of the Eighth United States Infantry, Captain Sheppard; two companies of the Eleventh United States Infantry, Captains W. H. Taliaferro and McComas; one company of the Twelfth United States Infantry, Captain Wells, and Captain Fairchild's Louisiana Mounted Men; in all about eight hundred men. On the 27th I mounted a grand guard with details from the various detachments, which proved an excellent school of instruction, and in the several attacks which were nightly made upon our camp, displayed a creditable degree of discipline.

† Lieutenant-Colonel Miles was not with the detachment which had just been defeated at the National Bridge, nor was Captain W. H. Taliaferro.

had one relief, one source of great enjoyment: at night we rolled among the breakers of the Gulf without danger from undertow, and this luxury of a bath strengthened us to bear the heat of the day, by giving us the sweet sleep of repose.

At an interview with Colonel Wilson on the 29th of August, I told him that Colonel Hughes would shortly arrive, and begged him to permit us to proceed as soon as he came, to help General Scott, as I believed from all I could learn, he needed every man that could be raised. The Governor intimated that the force could not be spared from Vera Cruz, and was not sufficiently strong to force its way through the interior, but that he daily expected additional troops from the United States, and knowing the efforts I had made to hasten forward, he would give me orders to march as soon as he deemed it safe.

In coming out of town on my return to camp, I could not but laugh at the handbills staring one in the face at every corner: " *Zinc coffins of various sizes and patterns* were to be had *on sale*, No. so and so, Calle de etc. etc.;" and every man I met looked as if he were coming into town to get one of these identical coffins. I made this reflection as I rode along, that if I were a rich man or of much higher rank than that of Major, I would also be afraid of the yellow fever.

"HEADQUARTERS BATTALION D. C. AND M'D. VOL'S.,
CAMP, VERGARA, August 27, 1847.

"*Orders.*]

"The regular stated calls in this camp will be as follows:

"I. Reveille at 5 o'clock A.M.; sick-call at 6 A.M.; the first call for guard-mounting at 7½ A.M.; orderly call at 11 A.M.; retreat at 6½ P.M., and tattoo at 9 P.M.

"II. At reveille the men will be turned out, the roll called by the orderly sergeants, superintended by a commissioned officer of each company, and each company parade will be policed; the prisoners at the guard-house will at the same time be made to police the regimental parade; at the sick-call the sick of each company will be conducted by the orderly sergeants to the Surgeon's quarters, which will be hereafter designated; the first call for guard-mounting at 7½ o'clock, A.M., will be the signal for the men warned for duty to turn out on their company parades for inspection by the orderly sergeants superintended by a commissioned officer of each company; at the orderly call each orderly sergeant will repair to the Adjutant's office for orders; at retreat there will be a dress parade on the regimental parade ground, prior to which the commanding officers will make a minute inspection of the arms and ammunition of their companies; at tattoo the men will be ordered to their quarters, and half an hour afterward taps will be sounded, at which signal the patrol will be sent through the camp for the purpose of arresting those who, without a legitimate excuse, are found wandering about the camp.

"III. Guard-mounting will take place at 8 o'clock A.M., the orderly sergeants of each company conducting their respective details to the parade; and commanding officers will be held strictly responsible for the fitness of their details for guard duty.

"IV. A morning report from each company must be handed in to the Adjutant's office before guard-mounting, each report to be signed by the orderly sergeant and the commanding officer of the company.

"V. As it is of the most vital importance that the men should be instructed in the school of the soldier, the captains of companies are hereby strictly enjoined to drill and cause to be drilled at every seasonable opportunity, their respective commands. The efficiency or inefficiency of a company will rest alone upon its commanding officer.

"VI. No intoxicating drinks will be permitted to be sold, offered for sale, or kept by any sutler, storekeeper, or camp-follower, within the camp, or its immediate vicinity; any person violating this order will be most summarily dealt with and punished.

"VII. In case of an alarm or a night attack, each company will be rapidly formed and marched to the regimental parade, with the exception of those companies, the commanding officers of which have received separate instructions.

"By order

"JOHN R. KENLY,
"Major Battalion D. C. and M'd. Vol's.,
commanding the Forces at Vergara."

"*Muster Roll of the Field and Staff of the District of Columbia and Maryland Volunteers, on the 31st day of August,* 1847, *at Camp Vergara, near Vera Cruz.*

"COMMISSIONED STAFF.

"Lieutenant Colonel George W. Hughes, absent on duty.
"Major John R. Kenly, present for duty.
"Surgeon Stedman R. Tilghman, present for duty.
"Adjutant John Carr, present for duty.
"Assistant Commissary of Subsistence, Henry A. Addison,
"present for duty.

"NON-COMMISSIONED STAFF.

"William J. Gary, Sergeant Major, present for duty.
"John Purden, Quartermaster's Sergeant, present for duty.

"I certify on honor that this Muster Roll exhibits the true state of the Field and Staff of the Battalion of District of Columbia and Maryland Volunteers, called into the service of the United States by the President, under the Act of Congress approved May 13th, 1846, and that the remarks set opposite to each are correct and just.

"JOHN R. KENLY,
"Major Battalion D. C. and M'd. Vol's.,
Inspector and Mustering Officer.

"CAMP VERGARA, NEAR VERA CRUZ,
"August 31, 1847."

September 1. Colonel Hughes arrived last night from New Orleans, and about the same time we learned that General Scott had been victorious in a battle fought not far from the city of Mexico. The change that this news made in Vera Cruz was so great that one scarcely recognized his acquaintances of the preceding day. It was from darkness and gloom to sunshine and joy. I this day paraded the battalion, and felt great pride in its appearance when I turned over the command to my ranking and commanding officer. His praise of my conduct was very gratifying, and I had an honest pleasure in feeling that I deserved it, for I had made a handsome battalion out of the command. I had reason to believe, that the officers and men shared the pride they knew I felt on hearing Colonel Hughes's address.

The steamer that brought Colonel Hughes from New Orleans brought also five companies of the Second Illinois regiment of infantry, so that our force, with the co-operation of the sailors, was deemed sufficient by Governor Wilson to relieve all apprehensions for the safety of Scott's base, which would have been seriously endangered had his first battle in the valley resulted unfavorably.

On the 5th of September we received orders to prepare to advance; during the day the companies selected were notified, and soon the busy hum of men was heard through the camp. There was an unmistakeable reluctance to move on the part of those who had tried it once before, and the heat, the intense heat which prevailed, depressed the spirits of others, so that there was not the same enthusiasm I had always before noticed among troops ordered to march. We all wanted to get away from the fever, but some thought we might go further and fare worse.

CHAPTER XXVI.

MARCH INTO THE INTERIOR.

THE city of Mexico lies to the west and north of Vera Cruz, and is distant by my calculation two hundred and sixty-two miles from the latter city. To reach it from the Gulf, you pass literally through the torrid, temperate, and frigid zones, for although the valley of Mexico is but seven thousand five hundred feet above the level of the sea, you have to cross the mountains which hem it on its eastern border at an altitude of between ten and eleven thousand feet.

The State of Vera Cruz, into which we were now about to penetrate, lies under the burning sky of the tropics, between 17° and 22° of north latitude, and 96° and 101° degrees west longitude from Paris; it is bounded on the north by the State of Tamaulipas, on the east by the Gulf of Mexico, and on the south and west by the States of Tabasco and Puebla. On the Gulf coast and for several miles inland there is a belt of sandy desert and burning wastes; here from the month of May to November the black vomit rages uninterruptedly, and the city of Vera Cruz, in the centre of this arid plain, is the focus of the deadly scourge.* As you march to the west the country

* Mr. Brantz Mayer, in his valuable work, "Mexico: Aztec, Spanish, and Republican," says "that none but natives of the town, or acclimated foreigners, are free from its attacks, and the

rises gently to the Antigua, and from thence upward through the Cerro Gordo pass, toward and beyond Jalapa, until you meet with the spur of the grand Cordillera, called the Cofre of Perote, whose southern apex is the magnificent and unparalleled mountain peak of Orizaba.* Still farther to the west, as you enter upon the vast plateau or plain of Puebla in the State of the same name, you are in a temperate region, growing the cereals of an excellent quality and amazing productiveness, until finally you commence the ascent of the mountains which form the iron and icy barrier of the far-famed valley of Mexico. The State of Puebla lies west of Vera Cruz, and the State of

---

frightful inroads it made among our troops in the year 1847 will long be remembered in the history of our country. Time does not appear to have had any effect on this dreadful disease. Increase of population and sanitary precautions do not seem to abate its malignity; and the science of the ablest physicians is entirely at fault in dealing with it."

When I was in Vera Cruz last, an expedient had been adopted which was believed to be beneficial, that was, building huge fires in the streets of the town, which were kept burning night and day by fresh supplies of fuel.

* The Peak of Orizaba, in the Aztec tongue "mountain of the star," is an extinct volcano which rises to the enormous height of seventeen thousand nine hundred and seven feet, and is said to be the highest point on the continent of North America. Although one hundred miles from the coast in the interior, it is visible fifty miles at sea, and is a prominent landmark to all mariners who voyage in the Gulf of Mexico. It is covered with perpetual snow; no language can do justice to the beauty and unsurpassed loveliness of its majestic cone of silver, when glistening under the rays of the rising and setting sun. On two occasions while in the Tierra Caliente we thought we saw smoke issuing from its summit; we might have been mistaken.

Mexico, to which its capital gave the name, lies west of the State of Puebla. The State of Mexico lies between 16° and 21° of north latitude, and 100° and 105° of west longitude from Paris; it is bounded on the north by the State of Queretaro, on the east by the State of Puebla, on the west by the States of Guanajuato and Michoacan, and on the south-west lies the broad Pacific Ocean and its harbor of Acapulco.

Between the Gulf coast and the valley of Mexico, we have three distinct and diverse lands, with three several climates, and with three several names, viz.: the *Tierras Calientes*, or hot lands; the *Tierras Templadas*, or temperate lands; the *Tierras Frias*, or cold lands.

Humboldt says "that the climates succeed each other in *strata* or *layers* as we pass from Vera Cruz to the capital—beholding in our varied journey the whole scale of vegetable life. The wild abundance of vegetation on the shore of the Gulf—its beautiful palms whose stems are wreathed by a myriad of impenetrable parasites which grow with such rank luxuriance in the hot and humid air of the tropics—are exchanged, as we begin to rise from the level of the sea, for hardier forest trees. At Jalapa the air is milder, though the vapors from the Gulf, which concentrate and condense at this height on the sides of the mountains, sustain the perpetual freshness of the verdure. Farther on, the oak and the orange give place to the fir and the pine. Here the rarefied air becomes pure, thin and perfectly transparent; but as it lacks moisture, which condenses below this region, the vegetation is neither so luxuriant nor so constantly vigorous. Great plains or basins spread out in silent and melancholy vistas before the traveler—many of them cold, bleak, and lonely moors, whose dreary levels sadden the heart of the spectator. The sun which comes down through the cloudless medium of an atmosphere, unscreened by the usual curtain of vapor, parches and crisps the thirsty soil, whilst the winds, that sweep uninterruptedly over the unbroken expanse, fill the air during the dry season with sand and dust." Many of the fruits and flowers, the grains and vegetables, the forests and the trees, the birds and the animals of the torrid, the temperate, and the frigid zones are to be found in this narrow strip of less than three hundred miles, lying as above described, between the ocean and the mountains around the valley of Mexico. Among the plants and fruits and trees which grow luxuriantly may be mentioned tobacco, coffee, sugar, cotton, corn, barley, wheat, jalap, sarsaparilla, vanilla, pineapples, oranges, citrons, lemons, pomegranates, bananas, chirimóyas, pears, water-melons, peaches, apricots, grapes; among the trees, the mahogany, ebony, cedar, oak, tamarind, palm, fig, dye-woods, and near Jalapa, a mimosa, from which the pungent gum exudes to make the incense used in the Catholic church ceremonies. In one day's ride a traveler may pass through and experience every gradation of climate, from the torrid heat of the Gulf coast to the icy shiver of the frigid, from the equatorial to the polar circle; every zone marked by its own peculiar vegetation, the sugar-cane and the fir, the vanilla and the pine-cone, the cactus and the maguey.

The *Tierras Calientes* is the home of the orange,

the banana, the pineapple, and the innumerable variety of the cactus. Here swarm countless herds of cattle, whose hides, tallow, and horns constitute a large portion of the country's commerce. Here may be found the Bedouins of the New World, the rancheros,—herdsmen by name, but true children of the desert; nomadic, brave, faithful, and attached to their country, they furnish arriéros for trade and guerilléros for war.

The *Tierras Templadas* is the land of the cereals, and the human eye never beheld such fields of barley as we saw on the grand plateau of Anahuac and in the valley of San Martin. On its eastern borders the sugar-cane and the orange flourish luxuriantly, whilst the perennial vegetation in the vicinity of Jalapa makes it the garden spot of the world. Tobacco and coffee grow side by side with the pineapple and pomegranate, and the smoke of the sugar manufactories mingles with the perfume of the mimosa and vanilla. Countless numbers of orange groves are interspersed with orchards of pineapples; and the melon, and the unique chirimóya aid in making the Department of Jalapa the land so long sought by Ponce de Leon,—the land where the *dolce far niente* of life may be enjoyed in an unrivaled climate, and amid a people whose nature is peace and whose habits are Arcadian.

There is nothing to mark the *Tierras Frias* until, after ascending the eastern slopes of its rocky fastnesses, you perceive the valley of Mexico lying at your feet; here is the land of flowers and the maguey, both indigenous, both intimately connected with the habits and the history, the traditions and the character, of the Aztec Indian race. It was here in the lake lying at your feet, that the eagle seized the serpent upon the cactus, and marked the spot where the wanderings of their people should cease; and the beautiful flowers which decked the edges of these magnificent reservoirs of sweet water, and which their women plucked with girlish admiration, are still interwoven with the dark locks of their descendants at this day, as they come in their boats laden with roses to the market-places of the capital. The maguey was to the Aztec what the cocoa-palm is to the Hindoo and the Malay. From its fibres thread was made; from its bark paper, better than the papyrus of Egypt; their houses were covered with its leaves, sewn together by the needles in the shape of thorns shooting out from each edge; its fluid—pulque—was meat and drink, life, luxury, and the pursuit of happiness then to the Aztec, as it is now to the Mexican.

If, instead of the cactus, the maguey were blazoned upon the shield of Mexico, I think perhaps they might have better luck.

The three States of Vera Cruz, Puebla and Mexico contain about one-fourth of the whole population of the Republic, say one and a half millions of inhabitants. Some writers estimate the total population of Mexico at eight millions. I doubt this; for from appearances the population has been decreasing, and this estimate of eight millions was based upon an increase of ten per cent. over a former estimate.

I may as well give some data about Mexico, although I am only personally acquainted with the States of Tamaulipas, New Leon, Coahuila, Vera Cruz,

Puebla and Mexico. It lies between 17° and 32° of north latitude, and 95° and 115° west longitude, and comprises an area of about eight hundred and fifty thousand square miles. Its population has been before referred to, and I think does not exceed, if it equals, six millions of inhabitants. The States composing the federated republic are: Chiapas, Chihuahua, Durango, Guanajuato, Guerrero, Jalisco, Mexico, Michoacan, Nueva Leon, Oajaca, Puebla, Quérétaro, San Luis Potosi, Sinalao, Sonora, Tabasco, Tamaulipas, Tlascala, Vera Cruz, Zacatecas, and perhaps Yucatan may be included, but its relations with the central government have been more than equivocal for some years past.

This territory is occupied by three peoples, as distinct, as diverse, and as strongly marked in their difference as its physical and geographical divisions: the *Indian*, the *Spaniard* of old Spain, and the offspring of these two races, making a third, known as or which we should call, the *Mexican*. I include among the Spaniards the white creoles, that is, white people born in the country, and the whole number does not exceed one million; there are between three and four millions of pure-blood Indians, and the remainder of the population embraces all the castes and colors from the Mestizo, the offspring of the white father and Indian mother, to the Mulatto and Brown Mestizo or Zambo, which includes the small proportion of negro blood brought into the country from the neighboring West India Islands.

I may have occasion hereafter to speak of the characteristics of each of these races.

The religion of the country is Roman Catholic, but it seemed to me that as a people they were not devoted to the church; the Indians were docile and bittable, but it also seemed that the story told of one of them shortly after the conquest was still true. He was reproached for his inattention to the duties of mother church, when he replied that the gods given his people by the Spaniards were doubtless very good, but he thought that they might have left them a *few* of their own.

I make no reflection against the church or its clergy; they have done wonders, and wrought marvellous works in reclaiming an idolatrous people from image worship, and the sacrifice of human beings to hideous stones; yet the field remains seemingly but half-worked, and there is abundant room for Christian labor, yea, for all manner of labor looking to the welfare of our fellow-creatures.

CHAPTER XXVII.

CAPTURE AND OCCUPATION OF THE NATIONAL BRIDGE.

On the morning of the 6th of September, 1847, we bade farewell to the sea-breezes of the Gulf and its exhilarating surf-baths for nearly ten months. At 4 o'clock A.M. we broke camp at Vergara, and at 5 our command took up its line of march over the sands, with our backs to the blazing sun; for it is a strange fact that the sun is as hot a half hour after it rises as it is at mid-day, in this tropical region. Our backs were also *from home*, and many a long lingering look was turned to the east, as we plodded slowly through the desert which environs Vera Cruz. Our force consisted of five companies of our regiment, one company of the Eleventh Infantry, one company of the Twelfth Infantry, two squadrons of Louisiana mounted men, and one company of United States Artillery, with two guns, a six-pounder and a twelve-pound howitzer. It was a well organized and appointed force, the whole under the command of Lieutenant-Colonel George W. Hughes, of our regiment.

At noon we arrived at the village of Santa Fé, which had been burned at our approach, and we were warned by every indication that we would have to fight our way. We remained here for rest and reorganization until 5 P.M., when we resumed the march.

As we approached the river San Juan, firing was commenced against us on both flanks, but without doing us any damage, as the guerillas were away in the chaparral, and their aim was uncertain. We drove them back deeper into the thicket, and bivouacked immediately upon the stone bridge which spans the river, as its parapets were an excellent protection to the annoying fire continued at intervals during the night.

September 7. At daylight resumed our march; at 8 o'clock had a glorious view of the Peak of Orizaba, whose lofty silver cone was tinged by the sun to colors as beautiful as ever charmed the eye; it soon became overpoweringly oppressive and sultry, so that the men marched with great difficulty over the heavy sands; we had to halt for several hours to refresh the troops; at 5 P.M. resumed our march and discovered a considerable body of the enemy on the first heights we had seen since we left the coast; halted, made a reconnaissance, and I advanced with two companies of infantry, driving the enemy from the hills, which were taken possession of and held, while the cavalry was thrown forward toward the town which was to be seen at our feet. I saw the enemy leaving the town, and our cavalry returned and reported it as being entirely abandoned.

This was the famous "Robbers' Den," as it was called, a noted haunt of guerillas and robbers, but properly named, *El Paso de Ovejas*.

We marched into it very carefully, after crossing a beautiful bridge, and bivouacked in the plaza, occupying the market-house as a place d' armes. Our camp-fires lighted up the gloomy surroundings, and a more compact body of men I never before saw than was to be found that night in this little town. There was no attempt to pass beyond our line of sentries by either friend or foe, and the night passed quietly.

September 8. As we left the town we were fired upon with great rapidity, the firing seeming to come principally from the arches beneath the bridge; I was with the rear-guard at the time. It was at once about-faced and put to firing, and this soon checked the demonstration. At 9 A.M. our advance guard reported large bodies of the enemy ahead; we still advanced, the enemy slowly retiring, until we reached a range of hills distant some two miles from the Antigua, where we halted. The men could go no farther,—the heat was fearful. We *had* to stop, or we would have had no command, as the men were unable to march.

During the day, the enemy hovered around us, firing, and feeling us, at every step of our march, and after we halted they threw a volley into us, having approached to within less than fifty yards of our camp. Our escape was miraculous; not a man was struck. Several of the balls went through our only wagon, in which our colored servants were enjoying a lunch; their exit was so sudden that a general laugh followed their hasty flight to a place of greater security. Captain M. K. Taylor's company of rifles was thrown out, and the guerillas kept at a more respectful distance. About midnight, all lying on our arms, in the midst of a deluge of rain, we heard heavy firing in the direction of the National Bridge. Springing up, we were totally at a loss to account for the firing in that direction; the sharp challenge of our sentries soon brought to a halt the party upon whom the fire had been directed, and we learned that in trying to run the gauntlet of the bridge, the enemy had killed two of their party and two of their horses. All night long the firing was continued at intervals, and the Mexicans seemed to be in great exultation at the loss they had inflicted upon our cavalry. It might have proved a much more serious misadventure than it turned out. As it was, combined with the rainstorm which deluged our camp, and the fatigue and loss of sleep, our men were a good deal out of spirits.

On this very day, there was being fought in the valley of Mexico a bloody battle at Molino del Rey, between the armies of Scott and Santa Anna, the result of which caused great gloom among our little handful of braves; for although the Mexicans were driven from their defenses, it was at a frightful sacrifice of life, and without any corresponding equivalent or advantage. Of course we were entirely ignorant of this, but we all *felt* that duty demanded every effort on our part to carry and hold the pass which we were now approaching. There was an indescribable sense of isolation and of responsibility which was shared by each and every one of us.

September 9. We left our bivouac at sunrise, marched slowly and with flanking parties for a couple of hours, and came in sight of the large stone fort on the summit of the hill to the left of the road, and which overlooks the bridge and commands the road for a long distance on both sides of the river. We could see numbers of the enemy on the walls and parapets, waving their guns and swords by way of inviting an attack. This we came to do, and preparations were immediately made to take the fort, to drive the enemy from the surrounding heights and force the passage of the bridge, which was strongly barricaded and covered toward us by an earth-work.

Our guns were placed in position by Lieutenant Fields, United States Army, and opened fire upon the fort; the solid shot flew over it or were buried in its parapets, the shell exploded all about it, but owing to the elevation the artillery fire did nothing but make the Mexicans drop their heads below the walls as the missiles came towards them. Colonel Hughes now ordered two companies to move to the right of the road toward the river, and in person gave me orders to take three companies of our regiment, Captains Dolan, Barry and Brown, with fifty dismounted dragoons, to endeavor to ascend the hill and take the fort in reverse. At the same time he gave to me a Mexican who had promised, for the sum of fifty dollars, to guide my detachment to a pass, and by a way through which we could reach the fort. I doubted the trustworthiness of this fellow, but he was true to us and proved a trusty guide in this instance.

Dismounting from my horse, and ordering my men to throw off jackets and haversacks, I descended the slope on the left of the road, the guide at my side, with a full understanding that his position was a very delicate one; we were soon in a sedge-grass higher than our heads, which fortunately concealed us from the enemy, who could easily overlook us from the fort, but they were kept close by the shot which were flying above us, and which we could see burying themselves in the fort. The heat down here was smothering, but we toiled noiselessly and rapidly to the ridge and reached a break which looked as if formerly a rivulet of water had poured down at this point. Our guide said this was the place to ascend. There was no time for hesitation, though I believed that not one half my command could get to the top, which was at least fifty feet from where we stood. There was a stout grapevine running down this washed rut in the face of the cliff, and several bushes were growing with their roots in the earth between the foot and the crest of the height. I ordered the guide to mount, told him that I would follow, and rapidly gave my instructions to Captain

Dolan who was at my side. The guide hesitated, said it was not a part of his bargain,—that all he had promised to do he had complied with,—had shown us the way to get to the rear of the fort. If we were now discovered where we were, we were helpless, and my command would have been destroyed; and, still doubting the guide, I advanced arguments so forcible that he sprang to his work and I followed him to the top.

Captain Dolan was next after me. By posting several men who held on with one hand to the bushes and vine, leaving the other hand free, I passed the musket of each soldier after him as he progressed to the top, and as soon as I got one company up I felt more relieved than words can express. It was a very hazardous undertaking; we could hear the voices of the soldiers in the fort, and every thud made by the solid shot striking seemed to be felt by us, so close to the earth were we pressed whilst climbing up the face of the height. In much less time than I had anticipated my command was on the plateau in line, with the dismounted dragoons advancing as skirmishers. There was not width enough for the front of my three companies, the precipice on my left dropping down to the river at its base, and on my right, the hillside by which I had ascended fell nearly as abruptly but not to so great a distance. The spur rose rapidly toward the fort, which was built on its farther end, overhanging the main road to the city of Mexico, and looking down on the bridge which crossed the Antigua at this point. Beyond the river, on the opposite side of the road, was another and corresponding height, which was likewise occupied by the enemy but not fortified. My command formed in a column of companies, dashed forward with a yell, and was soon over a wall which I thought at first was belonging to the fort, but soon saw my mistake, for the main work yet loomed up fifty yards farther on.

The Mexicans were completely taken by surprise; our pace was rapid, we received one straggling fire and we were within the fort. I confess to this being the happiest moment of my life, for my anxiety had been intense. The enemy escaped by leaping over the walls which fronted toward the river and descended well-known paths, but concealed from us, to the jungle on its banks; while toiling up the height from the road came Major W. B. Taliaferro's companies of the Eleventh and Twelfth Infantry, firing as they advanced, fully believing that the Mexicans were still in the fort. Colonel Hughes had sent forward these companies as a diversion in my behalf, and it was their advance which doubtless saved me from a severe loss. I had but one man wounded in the assault, and one of the strongest natural passes in the country was in our possession; the road to Mexico through the Tierras Calientes was never afterward closed during the continuance of the war. The loss of this place was the death-blow to the guerilla system which had nigh been successful in paralyzing the efforts of our army. The view from the parapets of the fort was magnificent, and at our feet our men were destroying the barricades on the bridge, and the artillery passing with the troops. It was really a very interesting display, and to Colonel Hughes great praise is due for the admirable manner in which he had succeeded in the attack and capture of the National Bridge, which during the whole war had been a thorn in our flanks, and had never before been held by the American army.

In the course of a couple of hours orders were got up to me to descend with one of the companies; crossing the bridge I passed through the village and took up my quarters with Colonel Hughes in the mansion of Santa Anna, which fronted the highway some hundred yards west of the bridge.

In its marble-paved halls my hammock was slung, and side arms with horse accoutrements soon made things look comfortable, despite the absence of beds and chamber furniture.

CHAPTER XXVIII.

GUERILLEROS.

As early as the 6th of May, 1847, General Scott wrote to Secretary Marcy:

> "Our difficulties lie in gathering in subsistence from a country covered with exasperated guerillas and banditti, and maintaining with inadequate garrisons and escorts communications with the rear."

The following was published in the *Monitor* newspaper, in the city of Mexico:

"PROCLAMATION.

"*The citizen Mariana Salas, General of Brigade and Colonel of the Regiment Hidalgo, to my fellow-citizens.*

"MY FRIENDS: The present movement is the most proper to excite the public spirit, and form a nation of men truly free. When an enemy triumphs by his union to rob us of our dearest interests, there is nothing more sure and more certain than to vanquish him by valor and constancy. For this end I have obtained permission to raise a guerilla corps, with which to attack and destroy the invaders in every manner imaginable. The conduct of the enemy, contrary both to humanity and natural rights, authorizes us to pursue him without pity. *War without pity unto death!* will be the motto of the guerilla warfare of *vengeance.* Therefore I invite all my fellow-citizens, especially my brave subordinates, to unite at general headquarters to enrol themselves, from nine until three in the afternoon, so that it may be organized in the present week.

"JOSE MARIANA SALAS.

"MEXICO, April 21, 1847."

On the 4th of June, 1847, General Scott wrote:

"It is ascertained that any sick or wounded men left in the road, or in small villages, would be certainly murdered by guerilla parties, rancheros or banditti. And I am not absolutely certain that threats of punishment will render our hospitals safe, even in large cities. Explain, to all, the rules of war in such cases. Military hospitals are universally regarded by civilized enemies as sacred."

On the 19th of July, 1847, the Secretary of War wrote to General Scott:

"The difficulties to be encountered on the route to the interior have rendered it necessary to detain the successive detachments at Vera Cruz, until concentrated in sufficient force to take up the line of march for your headquarters. The breaking up of our post at Jalapa appears to have greatly increased the difficulties of our communications with the interior of the country. Efforts are making to raise several mounted companies of acclimated men at New Orleans and in that region, principally for the purpose of having them employed at Vera Cruz to protect the public property at that place, and to defend it, and to clear the route into the interior, of the guerillas who infest and obstruct it."

Again General Scott wrote:

"It is the universal opinion of well-informed persons in this country that troops may land at Vera Cruz, and by marching promptly reach the healthy region, with little or no loss from disease, as late as some time in June;* whereas even Mexicans of the upper country would suffer greatly in a week, by a visit to the Tierra Caliente. General Santa Anna is at present at Cordova or Orizaba, endeavoring to create a new army of irregulars. Other generals are also endeavoring to prepare for a guerilla war upon our detachments, trains and stragglers, and they may, without great precautions on our part, do much harm in the aggregate. Our dangers and difficulties are all in the rear, between this place (Jalapa) and Vera Cruz: 1st. The season of the year, heat; and, below Cerro Gordo, sand and disease. 2d. An impossibility (almost) of establishing any intermediate post, say at the National Bridge, or any other point, on account of disease, and the want of sufficient supplies within easy reach. 3d. The danger of having our trains cut and destroyed by the exasperated rancheros. And 4th. The consequent necessity of escorting trains.

"The yellow fever at Vera Cruz, and on the road fifty miles this way (Jalapa), may soon cut us off from our depot. Deep sand, disease, and bands of guerillas constitute difficulties.

"Within the distance of fifty miles from Vera Cruz I doubt whether I can hazard a depot or garrison (from fear of the fever)."

In a letter to Lieutenant Semmes, of the navy, General Scott wrote from Jalapa:

---

* We arrived in *August.*

"The difficulty of sending forward a flag of truce at this time with communications to the Mexican government, if there be a competent government anywhere, consists in the necessity of protecting the flag by a large escort against rancheros or banditti, who infest the road all the way to the capital, and who rob and murder even wounded Mexican officers returning on parole to their friends."

On the 1st of September, 1847, Secretary Marcy wrote to General Scott:

"The last communication received from you here is dated at Puebla, on the 4th of June. No doubt is entertained that the difficulties of communication with Vera Cruz have produced this long interruption in your correspondence with the department."

And on the 6th of October, 1847, the Secretary of War wrote to General Scott:

"The guerilla system which has been resorted to by the Mexicans is hardly recognized as a legitimate mode of warfare, and should be met with the utmost allowable severity. Not only those embodied for the purpose of carrying out that system, but those who at any time have been engaged in it, or who have sustained, sheltered, and protected them, are much less entitled to favorable consideration than the soldiers in the ranks of the regular Mexican army. They should be seized or held as prisoners of war, and sent to the United States if it is not convenient to hold them. Their haunts and places of rendezvous should be broken up and destroyed. Those implicated in the murder of non-combatants, or in robbery and plunder, should be subjected to a severer treatment."

The nature of the country in this Tierra Caliente greatly favored the guerilla system; for miles from the Gulf coast the road was over deep sands, through sand-hills and chaparral, and our men marched slowly, distressed by the intense heat which prevailed. The Antigua River, finding its sources in the

Cordilleras, which fringe the western border of the State of Vera Cruz, runs nearly an eastern course to the Gulf of Mexico, emptying into the latter about forty miles north of the city of Vera Cruz, at the old town of Antigua, founded by the companions of Cortez. Stretching out on either bank for some dozen miles, there is a district of strictly tropical vegetation, a dense jungle of nearly impenetrable forest foliage. The river and the noble stone bridge which spans it, with the surrounding heights, was a formidable military position; the jungle was a sure refuge in danger, and a still better lurking place from which to emerge for sudden attack. Thoroughly acquainted with all the by-ways among the sand-hills and the trails through the wilderness of cane and vine and cacti of the jungle, they would pounce upon our troops, discharge an unexpected volley of balls in their midst, and if successful in producing a stampede, would plunder and set fire to the wagon or mule-train of supplies. If unsuccessful in their first assault, they generally withdrew, being lost to view in a few minutes, and their vicinity only known by the dropping shots into our ranks, fired from a distance, but sufficient to harass and annoy the weary men toiling through the burning sands. Their chief haunts were at El Paso de Ovejas and the National Bridge, where they were in considerable force under three of their famous leaders, Chico (or little) Mendoza, Zenobio, and the Priest Padre Jarauta. It was these bands that attacked us, and that we drove from the occupancy of their strongholds.

CHAPTER XXIX.

VIEWS OF OUR GOVERNMENT AS TO THE CONDUCT OF THE WAR.

Up to the 6th day of October, 1847, the War Department was not in receipt of any later dispatches from General Scott than those dated at Puebla, June 4th. At this date, October 6th, however, the government had learned of the operations at Contreras and of the success of our arms in the battle at that place. It is interesting to know the views of the administration at this epoch, and we have the whole history in two letters from the War Department at Washington; the one dated September 1, 1847, written by the Honorable John Y. Mason, acting Secretary of War, the other dated October 6, 1847, and written by the Secretary himself. Both of these gentlemen were very able men, and this consideration gives additional weight to the fact that they were the accredited organs of our government and supposed to speak its views.

They were both addressed to General Scott, and the first is as follows:

"War Department, September 1, 1847.

"Sir,—In the temporary absence of the Secretary of War, caused by sickness, the President has requested me to take charge of this department.

"From information which has reached us, it is supposed that you commenced your forward movement on the city of Mexico on the 7th (of June), and it is confidently believed that you are now in possession of the enemy's capital.*

"The obstinate persistence of the Mexicans to treat, their utter disregard to the rules of civilized warfare, and the large expenditures we are compelled to make, have impressed on the President the firm conviction that those rights of exacting contribution from the enemy which are conferred on a belligerent by the acknowledged law of nations should be exercised. Your remarks in your dispatch, dated at Jalapa, May 20, 1847, have been carefully observed. Your circumstances are since materially changed; and if, as we doubt not, you have triumphantly entered the city of Mexico, the President directs me again to call your attention to the dispatch of the 3d of April last, a copy of which is here inclosed.

"The property-holders of Mexico have no claim to find in the market afforded by sales to our army an actual pecuniary benefit resulting from the war. They must be made to feel its evils; and it is earnestly hoped and expected that you will not find, in your present circumstances, a necessity to adhere to your opinion, that a resort to forced contributions will exasperate and ruin the inhabitants and starve the army. Contributions may be exacted from cities or states or wealthy individuals, and payment made for provisions and other supplies brought to the camp or collected in kind. It is not improbable that men of wealth and means may profess to belong mainly to the peace party; and it may be apprehended that they will be driven from their pacific position by coercive proceedings. But, however such an effect may be apprehended, it is more probable that their exertions to promote a termination of the war will be made more serious and efficient when they feel the oppressive evils of the state of war. Judging from the cruelties and atrocities which are reported in different parts of Mexico to have been inflicted by the Mexicans whenever an opportunity presents itself on a single soldier or a weaker party, there is no hope of their reciprocating kind, generous, or humane exercise of the rights of war

---

* This was far from the fact, and I am inclined to think that Mr. Mason only *hoped* so.

on our part; and, without retaliating such disgraceful atrocities in kind, every dictate of duty to ourselves requires that we shall not abstain from the exercise of our right of exaction from the enemy.

"The mode of exercising this right is, and must be, left to your discretion; but it is earnestly hoped that you will put the system into operation to the utmost practicable extent. The safety and subsistence of the troops under your command will, of course, not be placed in jeopardy by the desire to enforce this system if you find that in its exercise such a result will follow.

"Very respectfully, your obedient servant,

"JOHN Y. MASON,

"Acting Secretary of War."

Mr. Marcy's letter is as follows:

"WAR DEPARTMENT,
"WASHINGTON, October 6, 1847.

"SIR,—

* * * * * * *

"Accounts upon which reliance is placed have recently reached us that the negotiations for peace have terminated unsuccessfully, and that hostilities recommenced on the 8th or 9th ultimo (September). We have also the gratifying intelligence that you have succeeded in capturing the city of Mexico, and are waiting with deep anxiety for the particulars of your operations up to and including that important event.

"The terms insisted on by Mexico, on which only she will consent to conclude a peace (which also have been received here), are so extravagant and inadmissible that there is no alternative left but to prosecute the war.

"It is quite evident that the authorities of Mexico would not present and insist upon, as a basis for peace, terms which could not be entertained for a moment by us without national dishonor, were they not encouraged to continue the war by that portion of the population as well as others upon which the burdens of the war ought to fall, and upon which, in the further prosecution of it, they must be made to fall as the only means now left of bringing it to a close. We have hitherto been far more forbearing than is customary in exercising the extreme and even some of the ordinary rights of belligerents. It is now evident that our leniency has not been appreciated nor reciprocated, but, on the contrary, has been repaid with bad faith and barbarity, and it is only met by a blind obstinacy and a reckless determination to prolong the conflict.

"However unwilling we may be to modify our humane policy, a change now seems to be required even by the considerations of humanity. We must take the best measures within the clearly-admitted course of civilized warfare, to beget a disposition in the people of Mexico to come to an adjustment upon fair and honorable terms. It should be borne in mind that the people of Mexico, indulging, as it is evident they do, the most hostile feelings, are not less parties to the war than the Mexican army; and as a means of peace they must be made to feel its evils.

"The guerilla system which has been resorted to is hardly recognized as a legitimate mode of warfare, and should be met with the utmost allowable severity. Not only those embodied for the purpose of carrying out that system, but those who at any time have been engaged in it, or who have sustained, sheltered, and protected them, are much less entitled to favorable consideration than the soldiers in the ranks of the regular Mexican army. They should be seized and held as prisoners of war, and sent to the United States if it is not convenient to hold them. Their haunts and places of rendezvous should be broken up and destroyed. Those implicated in the murder of non-combatants, or in robbery and plunder, should be subjected to a severer treatment. Independent of restraints, etc., upon their persons, all their property and effects within our reach should be unhesitatingly seized and devoted to public use. In relation to other prisoners and officers I refer you to my dispatch of May 31st.

"Permit me to invite your attention to the dispatch from this department of the 1st ultimo (a copy of which is herewith sent), and urge the suggestions therein contained upon your particular consideration. The burden of sustaining our forces in Mexico must be thrown, to the utmost extent, upon the people of that country; its resources should be resorted to in every manner consistent with the usages of civilized war for that purpose, and it is hoped that your situation is such as will warrant you in making this resort, at least to the extent required for the support of our army. The men of means who have willingly contributed aid to support the Mexican army should be forced to contribute to the support of ours.

Without a particular knowledge of your situation, of the available force you now have at your command, or of the resistance the enemy are still capable of making, nothing more than suggestions, in regard to your future proceedings, will be submitted for your consideration.

"I need not urge upon you the adoption of all measures necessary for holding the city of Mexico and the principal places between that city and Vera Cruz. To open and keep open the way between these two cities would seem to be required for holding securely what is already conquered and for future operations. For this purpose a considerable increase of your force, it is presumed, will be indispensable. . . . .

. . . . . "With this augmentation of strength, it is hoped that you will be able to accomplish not only the objects before indicated (should you deem them preferable to others), but to carry on further aggressive operations, to achieve new conquests, to disperse the remaining army of the enemy in your vicinity, and prevent the organization of another. Left, as you are, to your own judgment as to your military operations, the fullest confidence is entertained that you will conduct them in the most effective way to bring about the main and ultimate object of the war, namely, to induce the rulers and people of Mexico to desire and consent to such terms of peace as we have a right to ask and expect.

"Should they offer through you terms of accommodation, or propose to enter on negotiations, the President directs that such propositions be forwarded without delay to him; but it is not expected that your movements or measures for carrying on hostilities will be thereby relaxed, or in anywise changed.

"I have the honor to be, very respectfully, your obedient servant,

"W. L. MARCY, Secretary of War.

"Major-General WINFIELD SCOTT,

"Commanding United States Army, Mexico."

CHAPTER XXX.

OPERATIONS AT AND ABOUT THE NATIONAL BRIDGE.

WE were in full occupancy of the pass, but our active foe gave us little rest; by day and by night the report of firearms was heard, accompanied by the ringing of metal through the air, and we were not less active. In fact, there was a busy time about the National Bridge, and the kind of warfare waged on both sides was entirely opposite to all my feelings. This was uncongenial work to me. The system inaugurated against us was the apology for our course; but it never met with the approval of my judgment, and at the earliest opportunity I made known my sentiments with regard to it. But I am anticipating.

To return to my journal.

September 13, 1847. We were under arms all last night, hearing, at intervals, heavy firing, which appeared not far from us, and not knowing which way to move, as we could not locate the whereabouts of the contest, the windings of the river and nature of the country carrying sound in varied reverberating echoes. We had to wait until we knew where to strike. At 10 A.M. to-day a train of thirty wagons arrived, escorted by about five hundred recruits, under Captain Heintzelman, Second Infantry, United States Army. He had been attacked where we had been, at El Paso de Ovejas, and, less fortunate than we, had lost one man killed and one wounded. This was the firing which we had heard. He had had a lively time on his way up. As his harassed troops threw themselves on the ground in front of our quarters, a musket was accidentally discharged, and two of the men severely wounded. I was struck with the absolute indifference with which this mishap was treated by the comrades of the wounded men. About sundown an odd-looking vehicle—an antique family carriage—hove in sight, drawn by any number of mules. It contained the family of the Señor Don Antonio de Maria Campos, which had the requisite permission to leave the country. We gave up to the ladies two of *our* rooms and made much of the children.

September 14. Señor Campos and family left this morning. One of our companies scouting to-day lost one man by drowning in crossing the Antigua River, and Lieutenant Thom, of the Eleventh Infantry, was wounded. The priest of the neighboring country came into camp, waving a white handkerchief. I admitted him, and learned from him his business, which was to procure the release of one of our prisoners.

September 16. A great many of our men are sick, and the duty upon all of us who are well is very heavy. We don't know what rest is. To-day Colonel Hughes issued an order turning over the command to me, as he was too sick to continue on duty; the heat and over-exertion had broken him down. Lieutenant Newby, of the Second Regiment of Illinois Volunteers, died at 9 o'clock P.M., from the yellow fever contracted at Vera Cruz; it was a case which, when once seen, would leave no doubt of what was meant by the black vomit.

September 17. I issued the following order:

"HEADQUARTERS U. S. TROOPS,
"PUENTE NACIONAL, September 17, 1847.

"*Orders.*]

"I. It becomes the painful duty of the commanding officer to announce the death of Lieutenant H. B. Newby, of the Second Regiment Illinois Volunteers, who died last night of vomito contracted at Vera Cruz. The deceased, though separated from his brother officers and friends, had every attention and medical aid furnished him which this post could supply, and by none will his death be more regretted than by his brother volunteer officers from the District of Columbia and State of Maryland.

"II. Captain Lawrence Dolan, of Company C, District of Columbia and Maryland Regiment of Volunteers, is hereby detailed to take charge of the funeral escort, and to cause to be paid to the remains of the deceased the usual military honors.

"By command JOHN R. KENLY, Major
"D. C. and M'd. Regt. Comd'g.
"JAMES STEELE, First Lieut. and Adj't."

His remains were interred in the north-east corner of the court-yard of Santa Anna's hacienda.

September 22. A train got through and reached us this morning, escorted by some sixteen hundred men under Brigadier-General Lane. It was attacked at El Paso de Ovejas, and, among others, Lieutenant Klein of the Louisiana mounted men was killed. His body was brought to my post and excited great interest; there was an unmistakable smile on his pallid countenance; there was something of fascination about it, so much so that you felt indisposed to leave the body. He was a large man, and had been shot through the head, the ball making but a small orifice in the forehead where he was hit; and his features were as regular, and his expression as pleasant, as if he were dreaming of home and of those whom he loved. Groups continued around the corpse until it was enveloped in a blanket and buried in the earth. He was buried by a detail from General Lane's command.

September 25. Before leaving, General Lane reviewed all the troops now concentrated at this point; the heat was blistering, and ill-health and ill-humor sat upon the countenances of many. In the evening immense flocks of parrots flew over our camp, going in a north-westerly direction. They invariably fly in pairs; among the tens of thousands that went screeching and palavering in the air each pair was noticeable; if there were an odd one, a bachelor or a spinster, it might be distinguished on the flanks of the main body of couples. After night-fall, the perfume of the vanilla is very observable in the miasma which rises like a fog from the rank vegetation. This fog is dense, humid, and unpleasant to all one's sensibilities; you feel that there is poison in its vapors; our sick list shows its power, and the mounds of upturned earth, its effects upon the troops. I would single out this place for its unhealthfulness, as the most to be dreaded, not excepting Chagres, on the Isthmus, in North America.

September 27. An express reached us to-night from above, bringing the extraordinary intelligence that General Santa Anna was in the vicinity of Puebla, the garrison of which had been driven into the citadel by the inhabitants, and that a general stampede existed among the American troops. We had noticed during the day that the firing had been more continuous than usual, and I had held back the scouting parties. Colonel Hughes was again in command, and at the urgent request of General Lane he sent to his assistance the commands of Major Taliaferro, McCoy, and Captain Simmonds,* which left us in the midst of all this excitement with but four companies of our regiment to hold the bridge, and but two companies occupying the fort on the heights. This was a very anxious night; I can safely say no one slept, and from the Colonel commanding to the cooks, the condition of affairs above and below was the sole subject of conversation.

September 28. An American and a young Mexican officer arrived to-day from above (Jalapa), bringing a confirmation of the report that Santa Anna was at Puebla, and the, to us, astounding intelligence, that General Scott had fought another bloody battle and had entered the city of Mexico. The reader will bear in mind that this was the first intimation *we* had that Scott was in the enemy's capital. *But what was Santa Anna doing at Puebla?* The solution of this question at this time was beyond my military genius, and I gave it up in despair, only after worrying myself nearly sick in the efforts I made to understand it.

September 29. If you ever saw a beehive overturned, an uncommon degree of activity moves the busy bee; imagine a half dozen hives rudely upset,

* McCoy and Simmonds had been left by General Lane to strengthen the post at the National Bridge.

and instead of bees, guerillas were the occupants; then you can picture the buzz that was now about our post from the swarms of exasperated Mexicans, who, maddened by the loss of their capital, threw themselves on the line of Scott's communications. Whilst at breakfast this morning, a bullet passed over our table and buried itself in the wall; it was not safe to venture from shelter, and serious apprehensions existed that we would be unable to get water without the sacrifice of life, as our only supply was from the Antigua River in rear of the hacienda. A system of signals was devised to communicate with the fort, and during the day I got up the six-pound cannon to the top of the building in which we were quartered, and planted the twelve-pound howitzer in the piazza which ran around it. We concentrated our force in and around the building, grenelled the walls, and if we could only get water and rations we were going to hold on for some time, at least.

A little before this time, there had reached us from Vera Cruz two young officers of the army, endeavoring to join their regiments with General Scott. Not being able to go farther, they joined our command temporarily; their names were Lieutenants Ambrose E. Burnside and John Gibbon.* These gentlemen were ot material assistance to us, cheerfully laboring to instruct and drill the troops, and upon all occasions showing such zeal and alacrity in the performance of duty, as to inspire in our officers a noble emulation,

* Major-Generals, both of them, in the war for the maintenance of the Union.

to equal the example which the Military Academy at West Point had thus placed as frontlets before their eyes.

October 1. The courier of the British Legation, Captain John Bernand, an old cavalry officer of the Peninsular army, who rides post between the capital and Vera Cruz, for his legation, came in last evening from above, and although very careful in what he said, told me he *had seen* Santa Anna at Puebla; that Scott's army was in the city of Mexico, and the whole country in his rear swarming with armed Mexicans, who had escaped the defeat of their armies in the valley.

We are still fortifying this building, raising the parapets on the roof with bags filled with sand, and strengthening the palisade fence which surrounds the hacienda with chevaux de frise; it is the opinion of the prisoners that we will soon be attacked in force and driven out or captured. *Verémos.*

We may be starved out, for we are now living upon ship-biscuit (hard-tack) and beans, this is all we have of any kind of food; it is healthy, if not savory. The news we have heard, and the rumors on the lips of all, are meat and drink; and the very uncertainty which prevails as to each and everything,—whether this be true, or that but a rumor,—keeps us on the *qui vive* and out of the hospital.

They say that Colonel Childs is having a rough time in Puebla, and as soon as he is routed our turn will come; that Scott hemmed in at Mexico is in worse plight than if he had been repulsed in his attack; and that the loss of the national capital has united all classes and factions to a prolonged war of resistance.*

October 8. There is no further intelligence from above; the guerillas have been quiet for the past few days, rumor saying that they are being concentrated on the Orizaba Road. We are in the most intense anxiety to hear from Puebla and the fate of General Lane's column, which moved to the support of Colonel Childs, beleaguered at that city. We have abandoned all ideas of peace unless it be made by our Congress. We can get no particulars of the last battles at the city of Mexico, nor of what is transpiring there or elsewhere; rumors reach us that Tilghman's battery is en route from Baltimore to join us. Would that it were here!

October 12. A Frenchman arrived to-night at our post from the city of Mexico. He says that General Scott's force in the city is considered in a precarious situation, being reduced by his losses in the late battles to six thousand effective men; that the Mexican Congress will disband; that he saw Santa Anna at Puebla, but he was without artillery and his troops dissipated; that General Lane had arrived and our people had now no apprehensions; that the whole country was in a dreadful condition, and that Jalapa had been entered by robbers and guerillas who plundered all those said to be friendly to the Americans, many of the same unfortunates having been heretofore punished by our troops for furnishing the guerillas

* These were the rumors current at the time, and serve to illustrate the actual condition of affairs.

with supplies and munitions of war; and finally that anarchy reigned supreme in the capital, there being not even the semblance of a government anywhere. I really felt sorry for the poor Mexicans; their condition is deplorable.

October 16. Scouting to-day, my horse fell, and I with him, into a pit which looked to me like the cellar of one of our city houses;* neither of us were much hurt, but it required a good deal of labor to get us up again. The heat in this chaparral I lack language to describe; it radiated from the sands and danced about in front of you, impalpable but visible, like hideous phantoms of a diseased brain. We were glad enough to get again under the shelter of our hacienda when night brought to a close the labors of the day.

October 29. The English minister, Mr. Bankhead, arrived to-night *en route* to embark at Vera Cruz for home; an escort had been furnished him in Jalapa by the Mexicans, as they were in full possession of that city; and as the cavalcade approached I had directed, in obedience to orders from Colonel Hughes, that a salute should be fired. Whether by accident or design (I judge the latter), the non-commissioned officer in charge of the squad had trained the gun† on the crest of the ridge over which the road dipped as it descended to the bridge. As soon as the cortége

* I read, after I had returned home, in Mr. Brantz Mayer's interesting book, that there were ruins of an ancient Aztec temple within a couple of leagues of the National Bridge, and I had no doubt that it was these ruins I had fallen among; how I regretted I was ignorant of this when at the Bridge!

† It was the gun which was mounted on the *top* of the hacienda.

appeared the gun was discharged, and that was the last of the escort; we had no very good name before this, but from one end of the Tierra Caliente to the other it was soon known that we had not hesitated to fire on the British flag. It was a very ludicrous affair, and no one enjoyed it more than Mr. Bankhead. He was accompanied by a considerable number of Mexican families who were fleeing from the country under the shelter of his official protection. Under instructions, Colonel Hughes provided him with an escort to the coast; Captains Fairchild and Biscoe, with their respective companies of Louisiana mounted men, doing that duty to the satisfaction of the minister. I will mention here, and have no reason to doubt the truth of the story, for I heard it from one of the party, that whilst at Jalapa, after his escort had been provided, the minister had to pay five hundred dollars to the chief of one of the guerilla bands for *permission* to reach our post through his district. I was glad to learn from Mr. Bankhead that our sick which had been unavoidably left at Jalapa had not been ill-treated by the guerillas, being only compelled to give their paroles not to serve again during the war or until duly exchanged.

It will be borne in mind that we were literally in a state of siege; it was only when the siege was raised by the arrival of a body of troops sufficiently strong to fight its way successfully through, or the departure and return of our own mounted men, that we had communication with the outside world. We were surrounded by the guerillas, who gave us but little quiet, yet whose desultory firing annoyed without doing us much harm; they were in sufficient numbers to render it necessary to organize a considerable force at Vera Cruz before marching into the interior, and to keep us on the alert to hold the bridge. This we had done successfully for nearly two months, and had swept the country from the Cerro Gordo Pass to the San Juan River, north and south of the main road. A period was approaching, when we were to be relieved from the unpleasant and dangerous field of duty in which I had been so unwillingly compelled to act, and no wearied sentry ever hailed the approach of a relief with more pleasure, than I did the prospect of leaving this post.

CHAPTER XXXI.

NEGOTIATIONS WITH EL PADRE JARAUTA.

Our sentries and outlying pickets were instructed to recognize the holding up or waving anything *white* as a token of peace, and under proper precautions to suffer the party to approach our lines for intercourse. Scarcely a day passed in which women were not permitted to come into camp to visit the prisoners, under the white flag, and I can say positively, that I never knew or never heard of a woman being treated rudely or unkindly by us, who came in under this flag.

On the 3d of November a woman was brought to our headquarters who had come into camp in this way: she said that what she had to say was important and confidential. She told us that the guerillas were tired of the war, and wanted to know if two of them were to approach our lines under a flag of truce, would we receive them and permit them to return "*free and unharmed.*"

My relations with Colonel Hughes were intimate and friendly from first to last; we were alone with the woman when I interpreted the substance of what she had said, and we both saw at once the importance of this overture, and the probable consequences which might flow from it. Our intimacy was such, and we shared each other's confidence so fully, that a few words between us sufficed to determine our plan.

We answered that she might assure any two unarmed Mexicans that they could enter our lines in the daytime, and depart when it pleased them, with the usual reservation not to communicate anything which might prove prejudicial to us; that we would send an officer with her to receive the flag at our picket-post, and escort the bearers to headquarters.

In the course of the afternoon of the same day, the flag came in, and with it two officers of Jarauta's band. They were both white men, well-looking, and well appareled in the uniform of Mexican officers of the line. One of them I think was a Frenchman, as it was in the French tongue we communicated, this language being more easy for me to speak than the Spanish. They told us that the guerillas were tired of the war, as there appeared to be no national resistance to our arms; that they had been fighting us for months without any result, and they could see none as long as we could continue to send additional troops into the field ; that the country was being devastated to no purpose, and that the capital having fallen, they could find nothing to encourage them in the future. They told us that they belonged to Jarauta's band, and named the chiefs of other bands with whom they federated for general purposes, but with whom they were not very closely allied, and they could not, nor were they authorized to say what might be their action hereafter; but they believed that if we could agree upon terms with the padre, that his voice would control their future course.

Colonel Hughes told them the terms upon which we would receive their submission, and as the officer said that the padre only understood Spanish, I sat down and framed the following communication, which I now copy from the original sent to Jarauta.

As I had no grammar with me, the Spanish scholar must not criticise it too closely.

"El Señor Jarauta habiéndo enviado una proposicion á saber sobre cuales terminos se le recibiria; este es para garantizar la seguridad completa de su persona y la de sus oficiales y soldados y sus propriédades, con la condicion que se rinden sujétos à la disposicion del General Scott.

"En cualquiera evénto, sus vidas y propriédades del señor Jarauta, los de sus oficiales y sus soldados estarán solemnamente respetados.

"Puente Nacional, 3d November 1847."

These terms were, that if Jarauta would surrender, together with his officers and men, they would be guaranteed the complete security of person and property, subject, however, to the orders of General Scott, as Hughes had no orders or instructions to make terms with the guerillas, but neither of us had the shadow of a doubt but that our action would be approved. For greater security, however, to those who might surrender under this pledge, I added the concluding paragraph, " That under any contingency (should they surrender) their lives and their property should be solemnly respected."

After the delivery of this paper, which they assured us would be accepted by the padre, and, with a smile, they said *by many others*, we parted in the best of humors, and full of hopes.

Our arrangement was, that at 3 o'clock the next afternoon, the 4th instant, we were to get an answer at the same picket where we had received their flag.

November 4. During the morning, we learned that a column of troops was approaching from Vera Cruz, and might be expected at any moment. Here was a dilemma; for the war might recommence along the entire line at any moment; and our honor was involved in the pledge given to Jarauta, which he might accept, and coming in under it, might—and it was quite possible—be attacked by our troops, ignorant of the terms granted. We felt very awkward and uneasy all the morning; at 3 P.M. our officer was at the picket, and punctually came the same Mexican officers; again conducted to our quarters, they brought us the gratifying intelligence that Padre Jarauta had agreed to and accepted our terms, and that he was at that moment but a short distance outside of our lines, awaiting their return to come in person into our camp.

It may be, and the chances are many against its probability, that no one will ever read these lines who is acquainted with the facts I have narrated and am about to write, yet I cannot resist the sense of right and justice which drives me *nolens volens* to speak.

We were in the full height of mutual congratulations, at the end of the guerilla war,—for this, if it had been consummated, would have ended it at least upon our line,—when an orderly announced the arrival of the commanding officer of the troops *en route.*

Colonel Hughes hurried to meet him at the gate of the hacienda, and soon he came into the hall where our staff was entertaining the Mexican officers. Hughes was explaining the business to the general when they entered, and I saw at a glance something was wrong.

The first words uttered in reply to my presentation were, "Tell them that if I catch Jarauta I will hang him to the highest tree in the Tierra Caliente." These words and this language are yet ringing in my ears; there is not a letter, much less a syllable, added to or taken from the sentence.

The language needed no interpretation; but it is a pleasure to say that those Mexicans left our lines in safety; and the warm grasp of the hand, the uplifted cap, bade a final adieu without the utterance of a word.

The Thirteenth Regiment of United States Infantry, Colonel Echols, having been ordered to relieve us, we left the post on the 5th of November, and marched to reinforce General Scott.

CHAPTER XXXII.

NEGOTIATIONS FOR PEACE.

It will be borne in mind that at the time of our arrival at Vera Cruz, on the 24th of August, all was suspense and anxiety about the fate of our army, as no authentic information had been received from General Scott for several weeks. It was not until the night of September 1st that we learned of his success in the first battle fought in the valley of Mexico, and we must now glance at things past and present essential to a proper understanding of the period.

Although the battle of Cerro Gordo was fought on the 17th of April, 1847, no battle was fought between the two armies of American and Mexican troops until the 19th day of August following, when Scott struck Santa Anna a powerful blow, at Contreras, in the valley of Mexico.

To explain this delay in the advance of our army less than two hundred miles toward the capital in four months, would be to write a very interesting history, and it would be as difficult to write as it would be interesting to read. There was ill-feeling between the general-in-chief and the government. Instructions had been given him to impose a tariff for revenue, and a schedule of articles of trade to be admitted at such ports or places as might be at any time in his military possession, was furnished him, with such rates of duty, as well also upon tonnage, as would produce the greatest amount of revenue. The enforcement of this tariff was not all that was imposed upon him. He was informed, that it was expected of him to exercise all the acknowledged rights of a belligerent, for the purpose of shifting the burden off from ourselves upon the Mexicans.

> "The right of an army operating in an enemy's country to seize supplies, to forage, and to occupy such buildings, private as well as public, as may be required for quarters, hospitals, storehouses, and other military purposes, without compensation therefor, cannot be questioned; and it is expected that you will not forego the exercise of this right to any extent compatible with the interest of the service upon which you are engaged."*

The general was sadly in want of money for present purposes, yet these imposed military contributions were foreign to his nature, habits, and military train of thought. He openly expressed a desire to be relieved from the command of the army, and on the 20th of May, 1847, wrote as follows to the Secretary of War:

> "If it is expected at Washington, as is now apprehended, that this army is to support itself by forced contributions levied upon the country, we may ruin and exasperate the inhabitants and starve ourselves; for it is certain they would sooner remove or destroy the products of their farms than allow them to fall into our hands without compensation. Not a ration for man or horse would be brought in except by the bayonet, which would oblige the troops to spread themselves out many leagues to the right and left in search of subsistence and to stop all military operations."

---

* Secretary of War to General Scott. Ex. Doc. No. 1, Senate, 1st Session, Thirtieth Congress.

These views of this eminent and distinguished soldier are worthy the deepest consideration of all who would make the profession of a soldier subordinate to the duty of a citizen, and the honor of mankind.

In point of fact, supplies for men and animals were bought in the country and paid for at fair prices, from the commencement to the end of the war, as far as my knowledge extends, both on the line of the Rio Grande and on Scott's line. The only revenue derived from the country was from duties collected under the tariff above referred to, at the ports in our possession from which the naval blockade had been raised.

There were some buildings occupied as quarters and as depots for supplies, and some churches and other edifices used for hospitals and public purposes, without compensation; but from the barley growing in the fields, gathered by our men, to the corn husked by the soldiers for daily food to themselves and animals, all was paid for in hard dollars; and I have seen sugar taken from manufactories *within our line of sentries,* paid for by the commissaries of our army in coin brought from the United States.

Surely the history of the world cannot produce a parallel to this conduct, which was owing in a great measure—it might be said with truth, *entirely*—to the thorough American character of Generals Taylor and Scott, whose magnanimity and nobility of sentiment outweighed the meaner attributes of less exalted characters, which would seek elevation and success by subserviency to base motives.

Well, the forced contributions were not levied, and the general-in-chief was master of the situation, but there came a blow from Washington which nearly overthrew his equanimity.

I desire to say here, in all truth, and I think I have heretofore said it, that from the outbreak of hostilities to the present time, I fully believe that the administration of President Polk was sincerely desirous of making an honorable peace with Mexico,—such a one as would satisfy our just demands, without compromising the honor or integrity of Mexico.

I repeat it, with as full an understanding of the matter as observation and personal knowledge can give one, that the above were the views of the American government up to the departure of General Scott from Puebla on the 10th of August, 1847.

The blow referred to was the arrival in Mexico, while Scott was at Jalapa, in May, of Mr. Nicholas P. Trist as a commissioner from Washington to accompany the headquarters of the army, for diplomatic purposes. His mission was peace, his powers were well defined and limited, yet all the pride of a soldier (and if Winfield Scott were not one, history may be searched in vain) revolted at the presence about his headquarters of a civilian, whom Scott regarded as an aide-de-camp of the President of the United States, sent to degrade him in the eyes of the army and the authorities of Mexico.

Fortunately for the interests of humanity and the glory of our country, these gentlemen became reconciled, and worked harmoniously for the attainment of great ends.

Let us look at the turn of affairs in the interior, beyond our lines, before we take up the negotiations between American and Mexican officials, to which we propose to refer.

Santa Anna had lost Buena Vista, yet had nobly struggled to regain his tarnished military fame: Cerro Gordo lost, any other than a general bred amid the internecine strife of Mexico would have been irretrievably ruined, when the flower of his army laid down its arms because taken in reverse and rendered powerless through sheer negligence of military art.

The pride of the Mexican soldiers of the line had not been lowered by Monterey or Buena Vista; but it could not stand the humiliation of Cerro Gordo. They had been defeated, when most willing to fight; they had grounded their arms, with their boxes full of cartridges, after repulsing one and awaiting another attack; there was no road for escape, nothing but surrender before them; all owing, as all knew, to the incapacity of their chiefs,—not Santa Anna especially, but some to whom had been confided high trusts and grave responsibilities.

The courage of Cæsar's tenth legion would have been shattered by three such disasters as the battles of Monterey, Buena Vista, and Cerro Gordo. Yet the Mexicans did not abandon their *grito* of war to the knife; and their semblance of a Congress—yet still a respectable assembly of deputies—declared every individual a traitor who should make peace with the United States. Such a resolution was passed after the news of the loss of the battle at Cerro Gordo had been received in the city of Mexico.

General Scott had said that he wanted to make his army "a self-sustaining machine," and he depended for this, not upon forced contributions, but upon the credit of the United States; to raise this credit, as well as his own, there is no doubt but that he was as desirous to make a peace and to conclude a treaty as he was to win a battle or to fight one when ready. He was always open to propositions, perhaps too much so, and when arrived at Puebla, in June, there commenced the celebrated negotiations which were also self-sustaining; for, dig as deep as you may, no foundation can be found, no beginning, as there was no ending, none whatever, to those entamées at Puebla to which I shall now refer.

We must know that despite the defiant attitude of the Congress, Mexico was cruelly divided by faction, and the capital a prey to the fierce and apparently irreconcilable strife between the Puros and the Moderados. The army proper was demoralized, and a considerable number of leading and influential men were opposed to making the city of Mexico the area within which the further march of Scott's army was to be opposed. These men, if not a party, were at least a power in the state, and they determined to try diplomacy to stay, if not to avert, the loss of their capital. There was one man eminently fitted to embrace and further their views, none other than Antonio Lopez de Santa Anna. The necessity for his services, for the aid of his powerful and unquestioned capacity for such business, saved him; for the elections having gone against him, as he learned, he got Congress to postpone counting the ballots from the 15th of June, when they ought to have done it, until January, 1848, and this restored him once more to power and to the head of affairs.

In Executive Document No. 60 may be found the following, on page 967, dated Puebla, May 19, 1847. I insert it, as it was undoubtedly the general opinion at its date.

"The elections came off in the States on the 15th. It is generally believed Herrera will succeed. Shots are being fired in the capital. A *pronunciamento* is hourly expected, and *this* is probably the secret of Santa Anna's march upon that point. He is *in extremis*. All agree that his day is passed."

PAS ENCORE.

Mr. Trist was anxious to begin negotiations, and hoped through the channel of the British embassy at Mexico to open his guns; a letter from our Secretary of State, Mr. Buchanan, was forwarded, and there came, in reply, a guarded answer which amounted to just exactly what it was intended to amount to,—nothing. There was nobody to treat with, but there was somebody to do that which no nation that ever existed could surpass the Mexican in doing, *writing letters*.

Along with the Mexican minister's letter, there were found communications in cipher (key furnished) from parties in the city of Mexico, declaring themselves to be but agents, not naming however their principal, in which extraordinary propositions were contained in reference to making peace between Mexico and the United States. These propositions were deemed worthy the notice of the commander-in-chief, and were considered by him entitled to serious consideration. A reply was sent through the diplomatic pouch of England in Mexico (acting in good faith I believe to both belligerents), the purport of which can only be surmised. Now came distinct and unequivocal terms as a basis of agreement addressed to the commander-in-chief and signed by the "agents" for whom?—this time it was mysteriously hinted that none other than Santa Anna was the primum mobile of the cipher correspondence, and was himself the key of the whole transaction.

There is no doubt whatever of what I am now about to write: General Scott convened a council of general officers at Puebla, and to them was made known that there had come from the city of Mexico propositions looking to making a treaty of peace; that for purposes, as yet undeveloped, *a million of dollars was asked for:* that said sum was not in the military chest, but a project was submitted of the ways and means by which it might be raised; and finally, that the sum of *ten thousand dollars* cash in hand was demanded to bind the bargain.

There was difference of opinion in that council: to the honor of the American name be it known that there were gentlemen present who protested against the whole scheme, if even the same had come from the authorities of Mexico or other legitimate source; they protested against all secret machinations, and especially against the bribery which was indisputably the aim, if not the acknowledged purpose, for which the money was to be used; they lifted their voices and proclaimed the whole thing anti-American, and unworthy the consideration of honorable men.

Nevertheless, strange as it may seem, ten thousand

dollars was paid, cash in hand, to somebody, out of the fund at the disposal of General Scott.

Notes in cipher now flew thickly, and the hum of secret intrigue, for the first (and may it be the last) time, was heard in the camp of an American army.

The *plan* was somewhat modified when the ten thousand dollars in money fell upon its platform; with a finesse worthy of the policy which has given éclat to Florence, queries were covertly embodied in other propositions, the plain English of which was: Our palms itch more than ever since the gentle tickling you gave them; how about the million of dollars? there are deputies in a certain Congress whose motions are slow, but whose principles are well known; *when* may we expect the million of dollars? its receipt will antedate but a few days a treaty of peace. Memorandum: *Congress* will meet next week.

Still no million of dollars was sent, but another modification of the basis for the purchase of peace came from the "agents;" it was now intimated as delicately as the faintest penciling, that General Santa Anna thought it indispensable *that Scott should advance and carry at least one outwork of the capital*, to give color to the terms of surrender, which he, Santa Anna, would then submit.

Will it be believed in this age that such infamy was ever written, much less seriously considered? It was both written and received consideration, but there is nothing to show that General Scott ever believed that Santa Anna would give him an outwork of the city of Mexico.

He may have been deceived in his hopes and expectations; he may have mistaken, as he undoubtedly did, the character of Santa Anna; he may have lent too much of his high official position to these secret negotiations: but his native integrity was so lofty and his patriotism so pure, that never for one moment did he do other than what he thought was right, and never ceased an instant in the preparations daily made for strengthening his army for future battle.

And this is the remarkable feature of these negotiations, that neither of the high contracting parties seemed to have the least idea of each other's character.

This is my opinion: that Scott thought Santa Anna venal, and that it would be to the interest of our country to buy him; Santa Anna thought he was deceiving Scott, *might* get a million of dollars, and was getting and gaining precious time to strengthen the defenses of his capital, in every cipher transmitted to Scott's headquarters.

Both were deceived; Santa Anna was ten thousand dollars ahead, and this payment tended to strengthen his blindness, for what *could* he think of a general who had suffered himself to be humbugged out of so much money? He thought Scott an old fool,—he was much mistaken.

Scott was outwitted in diplomacy, he failed to see through the astute mystification which the wily Mexican had placed him in, he utterly ignored the honesty of Santa Anna and his fidelity to country, he was grossly deceived; but his instinctive military genius was a clue by which he disentangled the maze of his enemy's subtle intrigue. Following the path of duty, it led him safely through the mire of political machinations to the fields where glory crowned his brow with undying fame.

Santa Anna never for an instant dreamed of betraying his country, much less selling for money the life's blood of the brave defenders of a post, his old companions in arms, to whom he had entrusted the identical outwork indicated as the one to be assaulted; but his cunning overleaped itself, when after receiving the ten thousand dollars, the latter proposition came from the "agents;" for there were officers in the American army not as good soldiers as General Scott, but who possessed infinitely more shrewdness, and they openly denounced the base proposition as too absurd for serious thought.

It was the monstrous perfidy of this proposition which destroyed "the plan for the purchase of peace," and was near involving in its destruction the character of more than one of those who interested themselves in its success.

Negotiations, open and secret, failed; the Mexican Congress, after passing a resolution on the 13th of July, "that it was the duty of the President to make treaties, and theirs to approve or disapprove them," quietly dispersed, leaving the responsibility with Santa Anna; he, alleging a constitutional incapacity, and quite likely remembering the council of the Texan generals on the banks of the Rio Grande, referred the question to his generals; they relieved themselves of diplomatic functions, by saying, their voice was still for war.

Both armies prepared for battle.

CHAPTER XXXIII.

SCOTT'S ADVANCE ON THE CITY OF MEXICO.

On the 10th day of August, 1847, General Scott left Puebla with an army of ten thousand men, to attack the enemy in the valley of Mexico, and to conquer a peace. It was a daring plan, a daring march; for he knew that General Santa Anna had gathered thirty-five thousand men to defend their capital, and that military skill of no ordinary character had strengthened the natural defenses of the city and its environs.

On page 175 of vol. ii., Major R. S. Ripley's War with Mexico, the author says:

> "Under these circumstances, the American advance is without parallel. In daring and in rashness the march of Cortez over the same route, centuries before, can hardly compare with it."

The strength of this army lay in its prestige of success, the genius of its leader, the material of which it was composed, and especially in its undaunted courage.

On the 18th day of August, there fell the first American soldier in the valley of Mexico. Strange, that he whose misfortune had been the commencement of the war should find the first soldier's grave thus far beyond the Rio Grande. So it was. Captain Thornton, of the Second Dragoons, was killed by a cannon ball as our reconnoitering parties approached San Antonio.

On the 20th of August was fought the battle of Contreras; General Valencia with his division of seven thousand men and twenty-two pieces of artillery had left the position assigned him, and, contrary to the advice and in the teeth of positive orders from Santa Anna, had taken up a position about Contreras. There was an immense field of broken lava lying in front of his camp and between it and San Antonio, which was deemed impassable for troops, but through and over which our engineer officers had found several trails which were soon made practicable for troops. This field was called the *Pedregal*, and was a great natural obstacle in an advance on the Acapulco road through San Antonio directly to the southern gate of Mexico. Valencia must have thought that our army having turned from the eastern defenses of the city, and finding the southern approaches so strongly guarded by the lines of San Antonio and Churubusco, would deflect still more to the left and approach the city from the west; it being generally known that the fortifications on this west side, the farthest from the approach of the Americans, were of much less strength than the others. A road ran through Contreras from the southwest to the city, and here he posted his division in an intrenched camp, without any regard to the dispositions of the commander-in-chief, or, as before said, to his positive orders.

Valencia was the rival of Santa Anna; he commanded a corps d'elite,—the army of the north, had criticised his line of defenses on the east, and, when Scott wisely avoided risking heavy losses, by attacking very strong points, and was now feeling his way, as if from the south, Valencia is said to have exulted and boasted that now *his* time had come to chastise the Yankees.

Santa Anna is a lucky man, for it was the disaster now about to befall his rival which once more saved his reputation among his fellow-countrymen; for to the willful disobedience of Valencia to his orders was attributed, by the whole army and population of the capital, the final and sad termination of their heroic sacrifices.

Scott had sent General Pillow's division, which was followed by General Twiggs's, across the Pedregal on the afternoon of the 19th. These troops, supported by Magruder's and Callender's batteries, had engaged the enemy in front without doing him much damage. During the night General Persifer F. Smith devised a plan, which was approved by General Scott, for taking the camp in reverse and dislodging the Mexicans. At sunrise, on the morning of the 20th, Colonel Riley, with Cadwalader's and Smith's brigades, were in the rear of Valencia, and in half an hour were in the possession of the intrenched camp. The division of Valencia was routed with an actual loss of some seven hundred killed, one thousand prisoners, and the demoralization of the whole corps, if not of the entire Mexican army. There were twenty-two pieces of artillery, some of heavy calibre, within the work, all of which were secured by our force, which did not exceed in the aggregate four thousand five hundred men, and did not lose more than sixty men killed and wounded in these successful operations.

Well might General Scott doubt whether a more brilliant or decisive victory be found on record. It was a brilliant feat of arms, and a glorious forerunner of subsequent grand achievements.

Santa Anna is blamed for not making greater efforts to support Valencia, and gravely censured for not compelling him to withdraw on the night of the 19th, as his engineer officers had pronounced the position untenable.

I regret very much that I have never met with the pamphlet which was published by Valencia in defense of his conduct at Contreras.

Exhilarated by the success, our victorious troops, being rapidly brought together, pushed on through San Angel to Coyacan, which was well beyond and to the left of San Antonio, in front of which General Worth was awaiting orders for the assault. General Bravo, in command at San Antonio, had been ordered to retreat as soon as the fall of the intrenched camp was known; his troops, marching toward the capital by the causeway, and closely followed by Worth's division, were intercepted and cut in two by Clark's Brigade and Lieutenant-Colonel C. F. Smith's Light Battalion, which General Worth had sent to turn Bravo's right by the Pedregal. Another utter rout here ensued, although General Bravo escaped, with numbers of his division, by leaving the causeway and crossing the marshes to the east of the road. Our troops pressed on toward the city, and soon the sanguinary battle of Churubusco was begun.

The enemy held a very strong position: in front ran in an easterly course the river Churubusco, and in the small village of the same name, a little to the south of the river and toward the advancing Americans, was a large stone building, called the Convent, which was strongly fortified. The bridge which crossed the river on the San Antonio causeway was protected by an elaborate fortification or *tête du pont*, and in and about these lines and works, the army of Santa Anna resolutely stood to their guns. But they were in a distressed condition from the disorganization created by the rout of the two divisions of Valencia and Bravo, and, to add to their discouragement, the artillery and the ammunition train sent forward by Bravo from San Antonio had not yet entered the *tête du pont*, with the exception of three guns, and were jammed up on the causeway in inextricable confusion, when the advance of the American troops opened fire upon the mass of fugitives and upon the horses of the artillery trains.

Santa Anna still held the left and centre of his army intact; they numbered at least twenty thousand men,—*outnumbered* more than two to one the army of Scott, and behind chosen lines he ought to have repulsed his attack.

The battle soon commenced in earnest, our troops rapidly coming up, and along the extended front and about the detached works of the Mexicans a fierce struggle ensued between nearly the entire strength of the two armies; it raged for several hours with intense fury. The desperate courage and skill of the Americans was never more signally shown, and out of not more than eight thousand five hundred men, there were one thousand killed or disabled in this bloody encounter; but the Mexicans were forced to retreat, after suffering great loss, and our cavalry pursued the fugitives to the very gates of the capital.

Our troops did justice to the bravery of their foe, and no language is too strong in admiration of the gallant army of Americans that gained the victory at Churubusco.

The estimated loss of the Mexicans in killed, wounded, and missing at Churubusco was seven thousand men; but the effect of this disaster in the city of Mexico cannot be measured by the number lost to the army. When night fell on this memorable day, the population of the city was panic-stricken; all were in fear of the immediate entrance of the American army. But General Scott had apparently other views, and never showed more judgment, in my opinion, than halting, as he did, outside the city on the night of the 20th of August.*

I cannot say as much for his conduct on the ensuing days, with reference to the armistice which was agreed upon.

When Santa Anna entered the city he assembled, at midnight, those of the ministry whom he could find and several leading citizens. He told them that

---

* The city of Mexico contained at this time nearly 200,000 inhabitants; its streets and quarters were entirely unknown to our army. If the streets were barricaded and the houses defended, as at Monterey, our army might have been sacrificed by the infuriated lepéros and soldiers of the beaten army, who could yet be numbered by thousands.

there must be a suspension of arms to enable him to reorganize his shattered army, that time must be gained, or else the city was lost, and that they must take steps to interview Scott at once for this purpose. Again the British embassy was looked to as a medium of communication, and the minister of Spain lent his friendly offices to aid the beleagured capital.

General Scott on the same night matured his plan, which was to summon the city to surrender (and it was now at his mercy), and only to agree to an armistice upon the pledge that negotiations should be entered upon for a treaty of peace.

If he had firmly stood to this plan, it is more than probable that months of future toil would have been spared him; but it is not my purpose to assail him, or endeavor to meet the powerful reasons which were successfully urged against the maintenance of his original determination.

The main reason which induced him, as I understood from competent authority, was that, if he persisted in either taking the city or driving Santa Anna away with his army, there would be no government to treat with, and that nothing would be left to be done but pursue a war of conquest until all Mexico was held by American troops.

An armistice for the suspension of arms and other purposes was agreed upon the 22d, ratified by Scott on the 23d, and finally ratified by Santa Anna on the 24th of August.

It met with but little favor in the American army, chiefly because it was thought that the recommendation of Major-General Worth, that the Mexicans should give up to our army the possession of the military castle and hill of Chapultepec as a guaranty for good faith on their part, should be a *sine qua non* in the negotiation for the armistice.

The Mexican commissioners stoutly and successfully resisted the introduction of this article into the project, which was ratified as above related *without* this article.

In one of the articles, it was agreed that our army might obtain supplies from the city; a train for this purpose was attacked by the lepéros, the worst class of the most vicious of Mexicans who swarmed in the alleys and faubourgs of the metropolis, and blood was shed in the streets of Mexico.

Recrimination followed the just complaints of the American general, and the armistice was terminated on the 6th of September with a loss to the Americans of prestige, character, and much of the fruits of hard won battles.

The negotiations for peace industriously plied during its continuance had miserably failed, Santa Anna had recuperated his army, whilst that of Scott's was mildewing away under the malaria of the valley. He had now but eight thousand five hundred effectives of all arms, but he was a host in himself, and the consciousness of having acted in good faith left him the invincible support of his honor and his conscience.

On the 8th were delivered the bloody and fruitless battles of Molino del Rey and the Casa Mata with a loss of one hundred and sixteen killed and six hundred and sixty-five wounded out of our little army;

a still further demand was to be made upon a resource which had never yet failed, American pluck, and the enemy's capital was to be stormed.

Worth wanted to push on, and so did Pillow, after our troops had gained with such a loss of life the mill or foundry (as some called it) del Rey, but Scott held them back, for *he* was not yet ready.

The frowning hill of Chapultepec was the key to the Mexican line of defenses on the south and west of the city. To carry this was now the immediate object of the commander-in-chief. A strong corps held the hill, and Santa Anna had gathered the remainder of his army about the garitas (gates) on the southern side of the city, posting them in well-made field-works designed for the protection of this front.

During the afternoon of the 8th, bold reconnaissances were made under the superintendence of Captain Robert E. Lee, of the Engineers, and that night General Scott was occupied in gaining further information and maturing his plan of operations.

On the morning of the 9th there were twelve thousand Mexicans at work throwing up a line of intrenchments between the garitas Belen and San Antonio, and they continued at their labors during the entire day without interruption. As this was the front Scott purposed to attack, he was notified of what was being done by the enemy; but our troops remained quiet.

On the 10th the engineer officers again made reconnaissances; they found eleven pieces of artillery in position at the garita San Antonio, the other works strong and occupied in force, the curtains finished and the ditches full of water.

On the 11th, continuing their reconnaissances, they found the works strengthened and nearly the whole southern front of the city inundated.

Scott in person examined the enemy's lines, then called a meeting of general officers; there were present Pillow, Quitman, Twiggs, Pierce, Cadwalader, and Riley. The result of this meeting was orders from General Scott for the attack upon Chapultepec.

On the morning of the 12th of September, the battle opened against Chapultepec, whilst a demonstration was made against the lines of San Antonio; a bombardment of the castle which crowned the hill, and a cannonade against the lines, continued during the day. Night fell without anything decisive being accomplished; scaling-ladders had been brought up, but no assault was ordered, and the troops were occupying the positions they held in the morning. All night long preparations were being made by both armies for the struggle of the ensuing day; it was a night of sleeplessness and anxiety to every human being in the valley of Mexico, for all knew that to-morrow would decide the fate of the capital.

At daybreak on the morning of the 13th day of September, 1847, the American batteries opened on the castle of Chapultepec and the lines of San Antonio; the Mexican guns replied, and for several hours the cannonading was very heavy; in the mean time storming parties were being organized and properly equipped for the assault. Bravo, seeing that it was his post that was threatened, sent for a reinforcement, which had been promised him; no attention was paid to his request. He ordered two brigade commanders to bring their troops to his support; they properly refused to move from the positions to which they had been assigned, without orders from their commander-in-chief. He had six thousand men within his lines, and these ought to have been sufficient for the defense of the castle and its outworks, but they were not. For onward and upward came the gallant heroes of the Republic of the North, sweeping from their front all who dared to oppose,—leaving behind in their bloody tracks the dead and the dying, then planting their ladders they scaled the walls of the castle. Chapultepec was in their possession, and the flag of our Republic was floating from its summit.

One cheer of victory rolled its volume of sound into the terror-stricken city, and then "*Forward!*" was again the word of command.

Worth's command took the road to the San Cosme garita on the north; Quitman followed the fugitives from Chapultepec by the aqueduct, which entered the city by the Belen garita at the south-west angle of the city. The enemy made continued resistance with artillery and small-arms from behind every available point between the base of the hill and the garita; finally Quitman carried this, but found a strong obstacle in the citadel within the walls, which was being rapidly filled with troops brought by Santa Anna from the eastern defenses. During the afternoon, a fierce struggle ensued between the reinforcements brought up and the wearied American soldiers who were in the works at the garita, which they still continued obstinately to hold against the several attempts made to recapture them.

Worth had met with the same resolute resistance, the same fierce struggle; and, finally, Santa Anna having checked Quitman's advance beyond the Belen gate had now come up to San Cosme to beat him, if possible; this he did not do, but eight hundred and sixty-three killed and wounded of our army, in to-day's fighting, attested the spirit of the Mexican resistance.

Night fell upon the combatants lying upon their arms at these two gates of the capital, General Worth being *within* the garita San Cosme and *in the city of Mexico.*

At 9 P.M. General Worth thought he would show where he was, and directed a mortar, which was planted in front of his quarters, to be fired in the direction of the main plaza. This completed the work. The city was evacuated during the night; the Mexican generals having determined to give up the city and withdraw their beaten army before the ensuing day, when it might be too late. They left by the northern road, carrying with them a considerable park of artillery.

Early on the morning of the 14th, the town council approached Scott's headquarters to make terms with the conqueror; this time there was no negotiating; he told them that the city of Mexico had been in his power since the afternoon of the preceding day, and that now he was going to take it; and he did take it. On the same day General Scott established his quarters in the Palace (halls of the Montezumas, in newspaper parlance), the American army was quartered in its vicinity; hospitals were organized, the lepéros thrashed, the inhabitants protected from the villains turned loose in their midst, order was restored, life and property made secure, religion respected, by the army which had marched from the distant north to plant its victorious banners in the valley of the Aztecs.

All honor to Winfield Scott! ever green be his laurels, and forever honored may be the companions-in-arms who shared the glory of his conquest! Honor to the memory of the dead, who fell before victory was won! and honor, ye American citizens, the rank and file of an army, that sullied not the hour of triumph with the stain of rapine or lust!

No days of ancient Rome ever beheld on its Appian or Flaminian Ways a nobler host than that which crossed the Cordilleras of Mexico; and the Capitol never witnessed honors more nobly won, than those which this army placed upon the brows of Scott.

CHAPTER XXXIV.

CONQUERING A PEACE.

THE American army was in the city of Mexico, the capital of the country in the occupancy of the invaders; and that which Scott foresaw, and which doubtless influenced him, as I have before said, to agree to an armistice, had now happened. *There was no government to treat with.* The armistice was a mistake; it had cost the lives of many brave men, was near losing everything previously gained by American valor, yet it was granted in pursuance of and in furtherance of the policy of our government, in the hope it might lead to a treaty.

It looked much like a stalemate now. Santa Anna resigned the Presidency; even *he* could not meet the overwhelming indignation of the country at the loss of its capital, so he said he would continue to serve his country in the field.

I believe the executive functions of the government devolved upon the Justices of the Supreme Court; be that as it may, Santa Anna sent a corps of three thousand men to Querétaro, and a decree from some source made that city the seat of government; but there was no government there, not even the semblance of one; nor was there any government anywhere else; nor was there any army, unless that be called one, which Santa Anna led to throw upon Scott's communications. I doubt whether the world's history can show a similar spectacle to that which Mexico presented at this period. It was not only distressing to its citizens, it was most embarrassing to its conquerors.

Scott could not press hostile operations even if such had been his wish, for up to the last of November no reinforcements had reached him. He had levied a contribution of one hundred and fifty thousand dollars upon the city, and had issued orders forbidding the exportation of coin or the precious metals, or the payment of rent for any buildings required as quarters or storehouses for the army. The troops *en route* to the valley were stretched from Vera Cruz to the Rio Frio. A government was being formed or attempted to be formed at Querétaro by Peña y Peña, President of the Supreme Court, and General Santa Anna, relieved from the command of his troops by order of the latter, signing himself "*Provisional President.*" General Paredes, a known and avowed monarchist, had come into the country, and General Bustamente reappeared and issued his *pronunciamento.* All the former factions and elements of strife, strengthened instead of diminished by the misfortunes of the country, rallied at Querétaro, to thwart the good intentions and paralyze the efforts of all who labored for the good of Mexico. On the 11th of November a number of deputies, assembled at Querétaro, elected General Anaya (who had been unconditionally released by Scott) as Provisional President. He made Peña y Peña his Chief Minister; Señor Rosa, Secretary of State; General Moray Villamil, Secretary of War; and appointed General Bustamente Commander-in-Chief of the Army. This administration was regarded at army headquarters as favoring negotiations, but it was only to last until the 8th of January ensuing; and Scott, now diplomatic agent, as Mr. Trist had been recalled, was compelled to rely more upon his "self-sustaining machine," his army, than upon hopes of a peaceable settlement of existing difficulties between the two nations.

On the 27th of November, 1847, he wrote to Mr. Marcy, our Secretary of War, a letter dated Headquarters of the Army, Mexico, of which the following extracts will give a correct idea of the then situation:

"I have now been waiting with anxiety, for nearly a month, the arrival of the reinforcements with Major-General Patterson, and others, coming up from Vera Cruz. That general in an official report, dated the 10th inst., informs me that he halted, with some twenty-six hundred men, for duty at Jalapa.

* * * * * * * * * * *

"He had received my instructions of the 13th and 28th ult., directing the re-garrisoning of Jalapa with some twelve hundred men, and the establishing of at least two new posts between that city and Vera Cruz.

* * * * * * * * * * *

"I am happy to learn that Major-General Butler was hourly expected at Vera Cruz early in this month. On his or Major-General Patterson's arrival here, with four thousand or more reinforcements, over and above the eastern garrisons, I shall dispatch that surplus, or a force equal to it, to occupy the mining districts within — miles of Zacatecas; and should the surplus be sufficient, I shall also occupy the mining district of San Luis de Potosi."

* * * * * * * * * * *

On the 4th of December he again wrote to Mr. Marcy, from the city of Mexico:

"The force here and at Chapultepec, 'fit for duty,' is only about six thousand rank and file; the 'number of sick,' exclusive of officers, being two thousand and forty-one.

* * * * * * * * * * *

"No proposition looking to a peace has been made to me by the federal government of this Republic, or its commissioners."

* * * * * * * * * * *

On the 2d of December General Scott wrote to Commodore William B. Shubrick, U. S. Navy, commanding Pacific Squadron:

"SIR,—I have the honor to receive your letter, dated at Mazatlan, the 16th ult., and I am happy to learn that our Pacific Squadron, under your command, has, among other important points, captured Mazatlan, Guayamas, and, I suppose, San Blas.

"I have been waiting here two months and a half to learn the views of the government at home, or at least for the arrival of reinforcements, before undertaking any new and distant operations.

* * * * * * * * * * *

"According to instructions from the War Department, which may be changed on receiving late dispatches from me, I shall, in proportion to the arrival of reinforcements, occupy, successively, the principal mining districts, of which Zacatecas and San Luis de Potosi are the respective centres; next, the State capitals within my reach and surplus means; all with a view to the internal trade and revenue that may be derived therefrom, to aid in the payment of the expenses of the occupation, that is, should the government decide upon covering the country in order to force this Republic to sue for peace; and we now have in Mexico no minister or commissioner (since the recall of Mr. Trist) to negotiate a treaty. To effect that object, by occupying the sources of trade and revenue, the mining districts and principal cities, including State capitals and ports of entry, at least fifty thousand men in the ranks, *not* on paper (the number I have asked for), will be indispensable. . . . . . The common service intrusted to us, respectively, is interested in frequent inter-communication. I shall avail myself of every opportunity to give you information of the movements and operations of this army.

"I have the honor to remain, with high respect, your most obedient servant,

"(Signed) "WINFIELD SCOTT."

The intelligent reader has before him a picture of the war with Mexico as it existed on the 2d day of December, 1847, drawn in such a masterly manner that no comment is necessary. I will add a single remark, that for months subsequent to this period our married officers seriously entertained the idea of sending to the United States for their families, looking to a permanent residence in Mexico.

Nearly cotemporaneous with General Scott's letter to Commodore Shubrick, instructions for General Scott were penned at Washington, which will show the views of our government; they were dated War Department, December 14th, 1847 :

"It is expected that you will use the force under your command to hold the city of Mexico, and other places now in your possession, and to keep open the communication between that place and Vera Cruz, so that supplies, munitions of war, and merchandise, can be safely conveyed along that line with only a small force to escort and protect them. Should robbers and guerilleros continue to obstruct the road, to plunder and murder as heretofore, the most vigorous measures should be pursued to punish them and prevent their depredations. It is desirable to open the country to the ingress of merchandise, from the ports in our possession, to the utmost practicable extent. In this way it is anticipated that considerable assistance will be derived toward meeting the expenses of the war.

"You will perceive that the government here contemplate that the resources of the country are, to a considerable extent, open to us, and that they are to be resorted to for the purpose of diminishing the burden of our expenses. It is also expected you will make them available for this purpose as far as practicable.

"The internal revenues, to the extent, at least, to which they were levied by the Mexican government, are to be kept up and paid over to the use of our army, so far as it is within our power to control them, with the exception of the departmental or transit duties mentioned in a former communication. For this purpose, and to deprive the enemy of the means of organizing further resistance to protract the war, it is expedient to subject to our arms other parts of his country. What those parts shall be is left to your judgment. Our object is to obtain acceptable terms of peace within the earliest practicable period, and it is apprehended that this object cannot be speedily obtained without making the enemy feel that he is to bear a considerable part of the burden of the war.

"Should there not be at this time a government in Mexico of sufficient stability to make peace, or should the authority which there exists be adverse to it, and yet a large and influential portion of the people really disposed to put an end to hostilities, it is desirable to know what prospect there is that the latter could, with the countenance and protection of our arms, organize a government which would be willing to make peace, and able to sustain relations of peace with us. . . .

"(Signed) "W. L. MARCY,
"Secretary of War.

"Major-General W. SCOTT,
"Commanding U. S. Army in Mexico."

There was as much, if not more, embarrassment in administration circles at Washington, than at army headquarters in the valley of Mexico. Politicians could with great unction preach, Conquer a peace, but far-seeing men had difficulty in the *savoir faire:* it was unmistakably a difficult problem, so we will step along with the column now about to march, and await its solution.

CHAPTER XXXV.

MARCH FROM THE NATIONAL BRIDGE.

November 5, 1847. We bade adieu to the bridge, marching with a column of two thousand five hundred men of all arms to reinforce General Scott, who was clamoring, we were told, for our advance. I was glad to leave this post, not because it was unhealthy and the duty arduous, but because the warfare we had been engaged in was exceedingly distasteful to me. The whole command was, I think, glad to get away; it was still hot, though the rainy season had set in, and our sick list was increasing at a rapid rate; the incessant watchfulness, the same monotonous stillness, broken only by the sound of fire-arms, the isolation of the post, the enervating and depressing atmosphere, the indescribable earthy smell of vegetation which arose as the shades of night fell, the sultry oppressiveness of the heat, all had tended to dispirit us. The most of those we were now thrown with were new troops, and as our men regarded themselves as veterans, the association was beneficial in restoring health and spirits, so that by the time we reached Cerro Gordo we were once more in pretty good trim. We had had no rest since leaving the transport, and the novelty of the march with enough support to forbid all anxiety, exhilarated our men, and they really were beginning to step and look like soldiers when we passed through the city of Jalapa, distant seventy miles from Vera Cruz.

We had marched some half dozen miles beyond Jalapa, when we went into camp at a village called Cedeño; we were brigaded with the Second Illinois and Colonel Withers's Rifle Battalion; the other brigade, commanded by General Cushing, was composed of the First Massachusetts and Second Ohio Regiments. We learned here that General Lane's command, which preceded us, had had a sharp affair at Huamantla, and that Captain Samuel Walker, of the Rifles, whose company was raised principally in Baltimore, had been killed, with a good many of his company. I knew

Walker on the Rio Grande, and he had a high reputation among the Texans as a skillful soldier. As well as I could learn, he charged into the town before the infantry supports were up, and was overwhelmed by superior numbers. We also learned that our turn would come next, as Santa Anna, having abandoned his attempt upon Puebla, was now devoting himself to the troops marching to Scott, and that it was his troops which had handled Lane so roughly.

This portion of Mexico is far superior to any have yet seen, more populous, and in a better state of cultivation; whilst the town of Jalapa will rank with any European city of its size and population in refinement and civilization. We are now in the Tierra Templada, and feel the comfort of a blanket at night, though at mid-day it is nearly as warm as it was at the National Bridge. The objection to the climate is its humidity; at night we are dripping wet in our tents, and already the recognized grumblers are wishing they were somewhere else.

November 11. I rode in from camp to pay my respects to my old brigade commander, Major-General John A. Quitman, who was on his way home from the city of Mexico. The meeting was most cordial, and I congratulated him sincerely upon his well-earned reputation; he could give me no news as to the probable results of the victories in the valley, and seemed to be as much at a loss concerning the future of the war as we were. A year had elapsed since I was in his brigade, and he told me it was very likely we would be together, if living, a year hence, as it looked as if we would hold the country.

We are still uncertain as to our movements, and for the life of me I cannot comprehend this delay in our march; the whole command is fretting and chafing in a camp seemingly selected for those who, tired with sand, must necessarily need wet earth, for a couch.

November 16. The Massachusetts Regiment left for Perote. This was the regiment originally commanded by Colonel Caleb Cushing, now a Brigadier-General; the rest of the troops are still in the marsh, gradually losing strength as well as spirits; the calculation is, that one month more of this service, and there will be little remaining except what may be found in the hospitals.

November 22. Our regiment has been ordered into Jalapa as a portion of its garrison, and Colonel George W. Hughes appointed Military Governor of the department; the Second Illinois Regiment and the Battalion of New Jersey Volunteers, Lieutenant-Colonel Woodruff, being likewise ordered in from camp to the city. We relieved the First Pennsylvania Regiment, Colonel Wynkoop, and a brigade previously stationed here.

November 23. Two American teamsters were hung, by sentence of a military commission, for a cold-blooded unprovoked murder of a Mexican boy.

November 24. Two Mexican officers, Lieutenant Ambrose Alcalde and Second Adjutant Antonio Garcia, were shot to-day by sentence of a military commission for breach of parole. They both admitted that they had broken their paroles, and plead in justification an order, which they produced, from Juan de Soto, Governor of the State of Vera Cruz, commanding them to take up arms again, or they would be reduced to the ranks. They both died like brave men, the words "Viva la Republica Méjicana,"* being the last that fell from their lips.

November 25. Large numbers of paroled Mexican officers came into the city to-day, and registered their names at the adjutant's office, as a pledge that they would not take up arms until regularly exchanged.

November 27. Upwards of one hundred officers have already registered their names as having been paroled by the American arms; they protest in the most indignant terms against the conduct of De Soto.

November 30. I was this day appointed by Colonel Hughes the Military Commandant of the garrison at Jalapa; Colonel Cheatam arrived with a regiment of Tennesseeans; our troops were paid up to the 31st of August, 1847; and Major-General William O. Butler, of Kentucky, arrived with a large number of troops from Tennessee, Ohio, and Kentucky.

December 4. My command was reviewed by Major-General Butler on the plain adjacent to the city; it was a charming day, the troops looked and behaved well, and large numbers of the population turned out to see the parade. Captain Lloyd Tilghman's battery of artillery from Baltimore has arrived, and is attached to our regiment. I have no hesitation in saying it is among the best volunteer organizations in the army; the material of which it is composed is excellent, and Captain Tilghman's ability cannot fail to make it very efficient; a company of cavalry recruited at Vera Cruz by my old comrade, Captain

---

* "Long live the Republic of Mexico."

Chatam R. Wheat, of Tennessee,* has been attached to our regiment, and the Twiggs Rifles, mounted by order of General Twiggs; so that our own command is now composed of the necessary arms to constitute it a legion, viz., infantry, cavalry, and artillery. This looks as if there were some truth in the rumors flying about, that, since the appointment of Lieutenant-Colonel William H. Emory, another topographical engineer, by the President, our regiment is destined for service on the Isthmus of Tehuantepec.

CHAPTER XXXVI.

THE CITY OF JALAPA.

JALAPA (pronounced Halápa) is a handsome city, with charming environs; the surrounding country fertile, the vegetation perennial; the lands are well cultivated, producing sugar-cane, coffee, and some few cereals, while groves of orange-trees and orchards of pineapple flourish in luxuriant abundance. The people are generally peaceful and well disposed; many of the wealthy families of the city and neighborhood are refined, well educated, and hospitable; we have already been the recipients of well-bred civilities, without any attempt on the part of our hosts to be anything other than Mexicans in character, habits, and sentiments. I was much pleased at

---

* I have been told that his family was originally from the city of Baltimore.

noticing one habit of the Mexican ladies, heads of families: whenever they received us, all the *children* were invariably brought into the parlor, and when we dined or breakfasted with them the children were seated at the table with the family and guests.

This portion of Mexico has a high reputation for its climate, and Jalapa is visited during the sickly seasons by the citizens of Vera Cruz, as our summer resorts are frequented by our people. It is, however, at this, the rainy season, far from being a comfortable residence to North Americans, there being a great deal of rain with cold nights; so cold that blankets are indispensable for warmth.

There are many pretty women here, some with fair hair and blue eyes; all the ladies are seemingly highly prized by the gentlemen, for a more jealous set cannot be found elsewhere. In the main plaza, where the market is daily held, the Indian women are to be seen with their hair braided with flowers, sitting near their heap of oranges, vegetables, and fruits, gently inviting by their modest glances the attention of the purchaser, and never by look, manner, or speech showing aught else than innocence and purity of character. It seems so strange to me that an opinion should have got among the people of the United States that the Mexican women were immoral in their conduct. It is as groundless an error as ever prevailed, and as gross a calumny as was ever uttered or thought. So far from it, I can speak from an experience of nearly two years' acquaintance, that the women of Mexico are as pure as those of any land, and that in the relations of wife and mother they are unsurpassed in the performance of domestic duties. One fact will demonstrate this assertion: nowhere on the face of the earth is the wife and mother more loved and respected than in Mexico. I challenge any one to contradict this who has had the same opportunity of knowing as myself.

There is one feature connected with these markets which is interesting: the pulque is brought in skins of hogs and goats securely sewed to prevent leakage, the beverage being drawn from one of the animal's legs. Over and over again I have seen a Mexican mother, surrounded by her little flock of half a dozen children, from the babe in arms to the child of ten or twelve years, approach a pulque seller, take the skin from his hands, and, applying the leg to the open and expectant mouth, suffer the delicious (to them) drink to flow down the greedy throat. It was very attractive to me to witness this treat of the little ones.

This Indian blood of Mexico, as far as I have seen, is certainly the gentlest of any that runs among the creatures of the Almighty's hands. Men, as well as women, are mild and docile; no one can see them without being struck with these traits. Fire-arms and whisky destroyed our North American Indians. They cannot effect the same result with these races; for, unlike ours, these *yield*. On the advance of Scott he found the road filled with rock and other obstacles placed by the enemy to impede his advance. A large force of Indians was brought from a neighboring village to remove the impediment. They were the same men who, by order of the Mexican military, had placed them there. They smilingly went to work and got them out of the way, looking upon the whole matter as a good joke, thus to undo for one, without compensation, that which they had laboriously wrought, for the other army.

I never saw a Mexican woman show what we call *temper*, except upon one occasion, and that was in this town of Jalapa. General Scott had employed a spy company for escort and scout duty, which was composed of the worst-looking scoundrels I ever saw. Robbers and banditti before the war, being renegades, their characters were not improved. They came down from the city with their captain—Colonel Dominguez—as an escort to a specie train. Stopping in front of my quarters, I was looking at them with interest, when I noticed one of them, quite a lad, drinking from the usual drinking-cup, a gourd, which a woman on the sidewalk had just handed him. He drank with his head averted, unmistakably ashamed of the company he was in. He returned the gourd to the woman, who, without a word, threw it on the ground and crushed it under her foot. The action was seen by several of the villains, whose savage looks might have been followed by blows; but I made a move which attracted their attention, and the woman slipped into her house.

The society of Jalapa would be considered good in any metropolitan city, and I hope I may be pardoned for mentioning the name of Mr. James Kennedy, an American gentleman intermarried with a Mexican lady, whose interesting family and hospitable mansion were always open to our visits, and whose continued civilities to us all will be long remembered. We were also under great obligations to Mr. Henry Hall, of Poughkeepsie, New York, the superintendent of a cotton factory in the vicinity of the town, whose long residence in the country, and familiarity with the Mexican language and character, rendered his society not only agreeable but at all times advantageous to the officers of our garrison. Neither of these gentlemen had lost any of their attachment to their native country, and both were highly respected by the inhabitants of Jalapa.

Several of the Mexican residents were owners of estates in the vicinity, to which we were frequently invited, and where we enjoyed the delicious fruit of the country freshly gathered from plant and tree, where the luscious chirimóya, the pomegranate, and the pineapple were piled upon tables already beautiful with the golden hue of the orange and the dark green of the lime, and where the perfume of the vanilla mingled with the aroma of the mimosa and the arbor vitæ.

On one of these haciendas, belonging to Señor G., lying five miles south-west of Jalapa, and called Apacho, there was one field of cane three leagues square, which produced twenty thousand pounds of sugar per week for eight months in the year. As the fortune of this gentleman was princely, his entertainment was magnificent. After the repast we accompanied him to the pineapple orchard, which was then in full fruit; the laborers were all clad in skins, each with a long knife, called a machete, very sharp on both edges, with which the bushes or trees are kept trimmed. These trees are not more than four or five feet high, and the peon (laborer), severing the fruit from the tree by a single touch, seizes the branch beneath the fruit, when, with two or three rapid and dexterous cuts, the apple is pared, and, dripping with its fragrant juice, is handed you on the end of the knife. I am sure in this way the pineapple as a tropical fruit is unsurpassed for flavor, except by the peach and cantaloupe of dear old Maryland, in the temperate regions of the north. The orange-groves on this estate were so large and the quantity so great that Señor G. said he knew not what to do with the fruit,—the beauty of the orchard when the fruit was ripe, as now, and the perfume of the blossoms earlier in the season, compensating for their care and expense.

CHAPTER XXXVII.

IN GARRISON.

The Ayuntamiento or Town Council of Jalapa was continued in its civil functions, working harmoniously with the military authorities of the United States. The town was quiet, except when the passage of a train with its escort left in its wake the worthless and dissolute, to molest the citizens and annoy the military; as a general thing, the relations between our soldiers and the townspeople were friendly, and it was not at all an uncommon sight to see an American soldier mending his boots alongside a Mexican shoemaker, or a carpenter in uniform working at the same bench with a Mexican mechanic. I saw a soldier looking with great interest at some native masons laying brick.* They were at work upon a platform, elevated some dozen or so feet from the earth, to which a man was carrying mortar upon his head on a square board instead of a hod. The masons stood immediately in front of the wall they were constructing, placed each brick separately on its bed, used a plumb line, square, etc., to see that *each* brick was correctly aligned, occupying as much time in laying a half-dozen bricks as an American mechanic would in laying one hundred. The soldier asked if he might show the Mexicans how to work. I replied, certainly, if he were a bricklayer. He said that he was. Mounting to the platform, one of the Mexicans gave to him his trowel, the ordinary steel tool of English manufacture, and the soldier went to work. It was really a pleasure to witness the gratification of the Mexicans as they saw the rapidity and skill with which the American mason did his work. I left him instructing his fellow-craftsmen; and, as the *genius* of the Mexican is in imitation, I have no doubt that hereafter Mexican bricklayers will work *secundum artem.*

There were twenty-one companies of troops and a battery of artillery distributed over the town; the

---

* Bricks are now burned in kilns set up recently by Americans in several parts of Mexico. They are made of good quality, and the contrast between these kiln-burned brick and the sun-dried *adobe* of ancient days is greatly in favor of the former.

daily duties were onerous upon the Military Commandant; it was his duty to approve all the requisitions and returns, to receive and revise the morning reports (which I regard as second in importance to no duty devolving upon an officer), to attend or be present when the grand guard was turned off, to receive the reports of the old officers of the guard and to give instructions to the new, to inspect the company drills, the company quarters, and the hospitals, to revise and sign the consolidated morning reports, then present himself in person at the Governor's quarters for orders and instructions. These were the invariable regular morning duties; the afternoons were employed in drilling the District of Columbia and Maryland Regiment or the several Battalions, in evolutions of the line. At night the town was thoroughly patrolled by details made from the mainguard, the commissioned officer in charge being required to report immediately to the Commandant any cause for danger or disturbance. Scouts were daily sent in various directions, the main road patrolled by mounted men, pickets and videttes established on prominent landmarks, everything which ability or experience could suggest for the proper maintenance of the post was successfully done.

One of our greatest sources of anxiety was the ill health of the command, especially the mortality in the Second Illinois Regiment, one company of which had lost twenty-six men, including the captain and first lieutenant, since reaching Jalapa; in all, the seeds of disease were planted in the Tierra Caliente, and the imprudence of the sick in eating *pineapple pies* did the rest. Notwithstanding the advice of the surgeons, despite the most stringent hospital regulations, the invalids would eat these pies, and they were almost as certain death as a bullet through the body. The desire of the sick, the morbid craving of these poor fellows for cheese and pineapple, was as wonderful as it was painful to witness; no amount of punishment inflicted upon the vendors could keep them from selling their pernicious articles to the sick.

In the month of December, Major-General Thomas Marshall, of Kentucky, arrived with troops, among which was a fine company from Washington, recruited and commanded by my lieutenant and friend, Captain Francis B. Schaeffer; it was a rifle company, handsomely dressed in dark blue jackets and pants, and attracted marked attention from our weather-beaten companies from the same city. It was permanently attached to our regiment.

December 11. General Marshall reviewed the garrison of Jalapa on the parade-ground, and the concourse of people to witness it was greater than on the previous review. I dined with the general, and had the pleasure of hearing from his lips an account of the "free fight" which took place in Louisville some years ago, and which gave an éclat to his name.

January 1, 1848. Last evening I visited by invitation the dwelling of a citizen to witness a *Natividad* or *Nacimiento*, illustrative of the nativity of our Saviour. It was a scenic and panoramic representation of the manger, the adoration of the shepherds, the worship of the Magi, the star in the east, the hills of Bethlehem, etc., which occupied the walls of two parlors and was an artistic and creditable piece of work. These representations take the place of our Christmas-trees, much time and money being expended on their construction and adornment, the old as well as the young manifesting much interest in the display and the fêtes to which they give rise. On this evening, the house was visited by a procession of young girls dressed in white with wreaths of flowers on their heads, who passed round the rooms singing a hymn in adoration of the blessed virgin and the infant Messiah. Music from a piano, harp, and guitars accompanied the singing, adding to the melody and sweetness of the voices and the measured cadence of the march. Altogether it was a pleasing and attractive entertainment.

To-day I attended high mass at the cathedral; the church was filled, and as the bells pealed twelve meridian, the crowd which filled the main plaza uncovered, and for a few seconds a silence still as death reigned over all. The solemn ritual of the Roman Catholic Church, impressive at all times, is particularly noticeable in its effects upon the Indian population of this country; no man who knows its character would ever doubt the good results flowing from these ceremonies, and the introduction of paintings and music, to lead their plastic minds to the worship of the only true God, and away from the deviltries and superstitions of their former priests, and altars smoking from the blood of human victims sacrificed to their hideous idols of stone. Civilization has done, and will do, much to modify church ceremonies, but you might as well expect a child to read without knowing letters, or to speak other languages than its mother-tongue, as to expect an idolater to give up his images and accept a spiritual worship before his understanding can grasp the lesson intended to be taught. All men have a spiritual worship within their souls; and to guide it and to lead it, whether such be on the plains of Mexico or in the streets of London, requires all the wisdom of man, enlightened with the grace of God. To teach an Indian the ten commandments, is quite feasible; to explain the religion of Christ to them, is another matter; if a painting will illustrate a half intelligible idea, and music elevate the soul, why not use these adjuncts to instruction? Object-teaching ever has been, and ever will be, the true and elementary means of instruction, in the infant schools of the world.

January 6. To-day I was awakened early with the information that a train coming up had been attacked by guerilleros, and reinforcements asked for from our garrison. I soon received orders from Colonel Hughes to march with our regiment, and was informed by him that he would follow with the mounted men and the New Jersey Battalion. I marched rapidly, reaching Cerro Gordo early next morning; Colonel Hughes coming up with the cavalry assumed command and pushed the cavalry forward to Plan del Rio. Holding Cerro Gordo Pass, we watched the approach of the train, which we could plainly do by reason of the cloud of dust which hung over and above the line of wagons and column of troops. During the morning couriers reached us from the commanding officer of the train, with news that everything was going on well, that he had repulsed the attack, with a loss of three men killed, and of two hundred pack mules with their cargoes, and that he anticipated no further danger. This gave us leisure to look over the battle-field, which will forever prove an interesting study to soldiers. I have before referred to it, but notice it again to say that the whole right of the Mexican army was in a perfect *cul-de-sac;* as long as the line of Mexican battle was intact, the right was formidable, as the action proved; but when the left was turned, as it was, the centre was powerless, and the right prisoners of war, without a chance of escape. The observation of this field I would recommend to all students of the military art; it would be worth months of study in books at college. The field was yet strewn with the débris of battle, American and Mexican bones, clothing, arms, belts, cartridge-boxes, and some half-dozen heavy guns lying with battered carriages about their silent embrasures. It is a solemn feeling to look on, in stillness, where the crash of battle has been heard, and see the earth encumbered with the harness of men who grappled in mortal conflict, a belt plate here, a tuft of hair there, with a few buttons and a broken gun; these tell of anything else than soldier's glory living in story. They tell, in the solitude of your heart, of the utter nothingness of all this trash, that the living reap what the dead perished to win, and that the peace of God, which passeth all understanding, is more to be desired than all this world can give of honor or of riches, of glory or of renown.

We returned to Jalapa on the evening of the 8th, the head of the train being well up with us when we marched into the city. There was a good deal of amusement occasioned by the plunder of the mule train, as the merchandise belonged to English merchants, who had been loudest in their professions of friendship to the guerilleros, and who had boasted of the security with which their goods could pass through the Tierra Caliente.

January 10, 11, 12. President of a court of inquiry, convened by order of Colonel Hughes, to inquire into the matter of an alleged robbery of the church at the village of San Andres, by Lieutenant ——— and a scouting party from the garrison. The court could find but little to sustain the charge, and the proceedings were abandoned.

January 15. In company with Colonel Hughes and a large number of officers, I went by invitation to the hacienda of Señor ——— to witness some of the sports of the country; a large number of Mexicans were present. The first performance was this: a bull was driven from the corral or cattle-pen, and after he had got into the open fields numbers of men on horseback pursued; the foremost seized the bull by the tail, then by wrapping it round the leg and giving the horse a spur so as to make him turn suddenly, letting go the tail of the bull at the same time, they generally succeeded in pitching the bull on its head, when it would lie stunned and motionless for some time. Several cattle were subsequently started out together, and as many as thirty horsemen pursued with the same result, the most skillful riders and tail-seizers being first to catch and throw the startled and disconcerted animals. I could not but be pleased with the admirable horsemanship displayed, but was disgusted with this *sport*, and still more when a man bestrode the neck of a bull, and made him run by spurring him in the face, the rider holding on to the horns of the poor beast. They then gave us displays of horse-racing and throwing the lasso, which were interesting and novel, but I had become so vexed at the wanton cruelty of the preceding entertainments that I paid but little attention to the feats of skill. My estimate of Mexican character was not much raised by the visit to this hacienda, and I concluded that I had seen my last bull-chase.

January 20. Information having reached here that an attack was to be made on a train under charge of Captain M. K. Taylor of our regiment, the New Jersey Battalion and a section of Tilghman's Battery were dispatched to Corral Falso; these troops returned on the 22d, bringing the train in safely.

January 23. A prisoner named ———, under sentence for killing a Mexican, made his escape early this morning from the guard-house; he was recaptured at Coatepec, brought back, and at evening parade he and an accomplice were tied to the wheels of a cannon and received, each, fifty lashes on their bare backs, as a portion of their sentence.

January 24. In obedience to orders from the headquarters of the army, the larger portion of the garrison was marched out of the city to Coatepec, five miles distant, so as not to interfere with the Mexicans, who were to hold an election. There being much aguardiente—Mexican brandy—in this village, some of the command got drunk, and we had considerable trouble; two of the stragglers were murdered, and their bodies shockingly mutilated.

January 27. Having received information that a considerable number of deserters from the American army were being secreted in a village fifteen miles distant, Captain Lloyd Tilghman was sent with one hundred mounted men to capture them and the parties who were keeping them. He returned on the 28th, bringing with him four deserters, and on the 29th three more were brought in by a portion of his command. It is alleged that these men were seduced from their duty by an organization now existing among Mexicans, whose object is to corrupt the rank and file of the American army by money and promises of promotion in their army. Among these so charged is a priest or curate of Naolinco, with whom some of these deserters were found by Captain Tilghman; he has been arrested, and will be tried by a military commission.

January 30—Sunday. Inspected the garrison, hospital, and company quarters; in the evening went to an American circus which had travelled here from the coast *en route* to the city of Mexico; the soldiers were delighted, and it reminded one of home to hear the familiar cries of boyhood uttered by them at the ring performances, the antics and the witty sayings of the clown; I am sure our men were as near happy as it is in the power of mortals to be.

February 3. More rumors from Cerro Gordo; sent Captains Brown and Schaeffer's companies, which brought in safely the train said to have been threatened.

February 5. A Mexican named Bustamente was shot to-day by sentence of a court-martial, for being a guerilla, and for numerous acts of villainy. Having been solicited to act as counsel for the priest Rafael Ignacio Cortez, charged with seducing American soldiers to desert and harboring them in his house at Naolinco, I appeared to-day before the military commission in his behalf. I continued to act in his defense daily, until the 8th, when the proceedings against him were suspended.

February 9. A deputation of the citizens of Naolinco waited upon me to thank me for my services in behalf of their curate, the priest Cortez. They knew my services had been voluntary, and they behaved very well; no gentlemen anywhere could have shown more propriety of conduct.

February 15. To-day, for the tenth time at least, we have *certain* news from the city of Mexico that a treaty of peace has been signed by commissioners; a *certain* gentleman of high standing heard Mr. So-and-so, brother-in-law of the minister of foreign relations, say—these are the kind of rumors that occupy much of the conversation of this garrison.

February 16. To-day, Major C. and Herr ———, a magician, *en route* to the city, dined with us; after dinner, Herr ——— amused us with a variety of tricks, which suspended during their performance all military and domestic duties about my headquarters. I cannot say which were the most interested, the soldiers or the Mexican servants; this was inside the house, while outside the crowd was so great that the patrol had difficulty in dispersing it Before the guests left, I had inwardly resolved never to have a *magician* at headquarters, it not being conducive to military discipline.

February 20—Sunday. Having been officially informed that a bull-fight was to take place to-day at the amphitheatre for such purposes in the town, and further, that it was expected I would be present as commandant of the garrison, I went with all ceremony, and was ushered into a room or *box* of state, over the main entrance, and opposite to where the matadors entered. These soon came in, gaudily dressed, preceded by a clown, holding a baton, which he flourished as they approached, and made obeisance with oriental dignity. When the bull came in, the fight commenced by goading him with lances in the hands of the picadors, and shaking red flags by the bańderillos before his eyes; finally, blazing fireworks were attached to the flanks, shoulders, and *forehead* of the agonized beast, until, maddened to desperation, he received the fatal blow from the chief killer, who was honored by an enthusiastic round of vivas by the large audience which was present.

I saw several bulls killed, several horses ripped up, and was very much in hopes that I would see some of the Mexican performers killed or nicely gored, for the effect of the whole exhibition was to make me side with the bull, and it was as much as I could do to keep quiet. Nothing but what I deemed official etiquette kept me in my seat to the close of the performance. I permitted another one to take place on the 23d, and suspended the drills so as to enable the men to witness a bull-fight, but none other were ever allowed whilst I was in command.

February 29. Brigadier-General N. Towson, Paymaster-General, arrived to-day from Vera Cruz, escorted by Captains White and Besançon of the Louisiana Mounted Men. I gave him a review, and drilled the brigade in evolutions of the line; it was a beautiful day, the troops looked splendidly, and manœuvred so well that I was much pleased.

March 1. To-day the following order was issued at the headquarters of the army:

"HEADQUARTERS, ARMY OF MEXICO,
"MEXICO, March 1, 1848.

"*Orders No.* 16.]

"I. The troops of this army are organized into divisions as follows:

"REGULAR TROOPS—OLD AND NEW REGIMENTS.

"1. BREVET-MAJOR-GENERAL WORTH'S DIVISION. Brevet-Captain George Deas, Assistant Adjutant-General.—Light Company A, Second Artillery; the Second and Third Artillery; Fourth, Fifth, Sixth and Eighth Infantry.

"2. BREVET-BRIGADIER-GENERAL SMITH'S DIVISION. Brevet-Captain J. Hooker, Assistant Adjutant-General.—Light Company K, First Artillery; Regiment of Mounted Fourth Artillery; First, Second, Third and Seventh Infantry, and Marine Corps.

"3. BRIGADIER-GENERAL CADWALADER'S DIVISION. Brevet-Captain F. N. Page, Assistant Adjutant-General.—Field Battery under the command of Captain Steptoe; Third Artillery; Ninth, Eleventh, Twelfth, Thirteenth, Fourteenth and Fifteenth Infantry, and Voltigeurs.

"VOLUNTEER TROOPS.

"1. MAJOR-GENERAL PATTERSON'S DIVISION. Brevet-Captain

W. W. Mackall, Assistant Adjutant-General.—Battalion Georgia Horse, three companies Illinois Horse; Massachusetts, First and Second Pennsylvania, New York, District of Columbia and Maryland, South Carolina, Second and Fourth Ohio, Second Illinois, Regiments of Foot; New Jersey and Georgia Battalions of Foot, and one company of Florida Foot.

"2. BRIGADIER-GENERAL MARSHALL'S DIVISION. Brevet-Captain E. R. S. Canby, Assistant Adjutant-General.—Seven companies Louisiana Horse, Battalion Texas Horse, Lawler's Company of Horse; Third and Fourth Kentucky, Fourth and Fifth Indiana, Third, Fourth, and Fifth Tennessee; Louisiana Regiment of Foot; Mississippi and Louisiana Battalions of Foot.

"II. The field-batteries under the command of Lieutenants W. H. French, First Artillery, and M. Lovell, Fourth Artillery, are assigned to the First and Second Divisions of Volunteers, respectively.

"III. Commanders of Divisions will organize the troops under them into brigades; the Regulars into two and the Volunteers into three brigades.

"IV. The Fourteenth Infantry and Voltigeurs, under the senior officer, will proceed to Toluca, and there relieve the Sixth and Eighth Infantry, which latter regiments will then proceed to the city of Mexico.

"V. Colonel Bonham with the Twelfth Infantry will proceed to Cuernavaca, and relieve the First Infantry, which regiment will then proceed to the city of Mexico. Colonel Bonham is assigned to the command of the department of Cuernavaca, and will relieve Colonel Clarke, Sixth Infantry, who, on being relieved, will join his regiment.

"VI. The chiefs of the several departments will avail themselves of the change of troops to send supplies, should any be required, to Toluca and Cuernavaca, as well as receive stores from those posts.

"By order of Major-General Butler,

"(Signed) "L. THOMAS,
"A. A.-G."

This was the first official order we had seen not

issued by Major-General Winfield Scott; we knew he had been superseded, or suspended from command, but it pained me to see that, though in the country, another general officer was in command.

It will be perceived that we were in the First Division of Volunteers, and I was officially informed that unless peace was soon made our regiment would be relieved and ordered to the city of Mexico, that I might expect orders to march at any moment.

March 2. General Towson and staff left for Puebla and Mexico.

March 6. On court of inquiry in ——— case.

March 7. Visited the cotton factory under the superintendence of Mr. Hall.

March 8. Brigade drill and evolutions of the line; a train arrived from the city of Mexico, bringing me copies of an armistice which had been agreed upon; sent copies of the armistice to my father, to Hon. Reverdy Johnson, Hon. John Glenn, Mr. Thomas Hollingsworth Morris, and to Mr. A. S. Abell, of the *Baltimore Sun* newspaper.

March 10. The Illinois Volunteers left for Puebla; we are expecting daily our orders to march; peace-stock low to-day.

March 16. A train came down from the city escorted by the First Pennsylvania Regiment, under command of Lieutenant-Colonel Samuel Black, an old friend; Brigadier-General Joseph Lane was with the escort, *en route* for home; he seemed much pleased to meet me once more, and gave a full account of his fight at Huamantla and other incidents of the campaign. Captain Walker's company fought very bravely at Huamantla and lost heavily, which I have before stated, but mention again, as General Lane gave me the information. The general also said that General Butler had told him there would be a peace negotiated beyond a doubt, and that he thought the troops would be leaving the country about the middle of May; peace-stock up again to-day. After leaving General Lane, I met several of my old companions-in-arms, who agreed that the prospects of a peace were not encouraging, and the general opinion of army officers in the city of Mexico was that it was *doubtful* whether the *Mexicans* would make peace. I visited at night the principal hotel in Jalapa, the Vera Cruzano, which was thronged with officers of our army from above and below, a considerable number of paroled Mexican officers, and many citizens; there was but one subject of conversation,—the probabilities of peace. I knew nearly every gentleman in the hotel, and after hearing and observing all I could, arrived at the conclusions that a peace was doubtful, that the minds of both Americans and Mexicans were in doubt as to what was best to be done, and that neither cared much whether the armistice would end in peace or war.

March 21. Captain Marcellus K. Taylor, of the Twiggs Mounted Rifles, with his company, came up from Vera Cruz, bringing a mail-bag found by one of his men lying in the chaparral near the National Bridge. It had contained a mail sent from this post, and all the letters which were recovered had been torn open, presenting a muddy and very sorry appearance. I caused notice to be given to the garrison, and soon a very animated and amusing scene was witnessed. The officers were first permitted to approach the pile of soiled and crumpled letters, from which any written by themselves might be reclaimed. Next the non-commissioned officers came; then the privates. There were several hundred—perhaps five hundred—letters, and there were at least one thousand soldiers, many of whom had never written a letter in their lives, all desirous of a personal examination of the pile, to find a letter. There were, perhaps, fifty of these letters upon which the address could not be made out, nor the names of the writers. These were, however, claimed by one or other of the soldiers, and formed the reading matter of the entire garrison for several weeks. The shouts of laughter which at times were heard from the barracks indicated that one of these letters, containing *news from the army*, was being read to the great delight of the audience.

March 23. Visited to-day Coatepec, the Rancho de los Manueles, the Hacienda of Orduña, and a famous pineapple orchard near Coatepec.

March 25. A mail arrived to-day from the United States, bringing the intelligence that our Congress was expected to reject the project of a treaty of peace which had been received from the city of Mexico. The leading inhabitants of Jalapa were soon in possession of the information, and it created an immense excitement. The news took the Mexicans completely by surprise, as no one in this country thought that *we* would reject any treaty of peace. It will have a good effect.

CHAPTER XXXVIII.

GENERAL SANTA ANNA, AND HIS RECEPTION, BY THE DISTRICT OF COLUMBIA AND MARYLAND REGIMENT, AT JALAPA.

AFTER Santa Anna left the city of Mexico, on the morning of the 14th of September, he went to Guadalupe, where he resigned the Presidency to Peña y Peña, dispatched General Herrera to Querétaro, which, by decree, he made the seat of government, and then with his command marched eastward to Puebla. He had a double purpose in view: he was in rear of Scott and on his line of communications; and if he could get possession of Puebla, he was in a strong position, as a point d'appui for his friends and partisans. Puebla was near falling; but Colonel Childs heroically held out, until the approach of General Lane's column relieved him, by withdrawing Santa Anna and his troops to meet the latter at Huamantla. It was evidently the purpose of Santa Anna to fall upon the column of Americans, while on the march to the relief of Puebla. If he could have severed this, General Rea would have sallied out from Puebla, and thus Lane's troops would have been between the two bodies of Mexicans. Captain Walker brought on the combat before either general was ready; but the attack coming from the Americans disarranged Santa Anna's plans, and gave the victory to Lane. There were thirteen killed and eleven wounded, nearly all of which fell upon Walker's mounted rifles and the volunteer cavalry. The result of this engagement was, the relief of Puebla by the retreat of the Mexicans, and General Lane entered the city. This was on the 13th of October, and Huamantla was Santa Anna's last battle. He had fought his last fight for a country which requited his services by depriving him of command. Peña y Peña directed him to turn over his troops to General Rincon, and the greatest of all the generals of Mexico was an outcast and a fugitive.

There is nothing connected with the history of the war with Mexico so unintelligible as the permission given by our government, in May, 1846, to permit General Santa Anna to enter Mexico. He was at the time in Havana, and instructions were given Commodore Conner to let him pass, should he desire to return to Mexico. He did return, by means of having his agents and emissaries, thoroughly to blind and deceive those, who thought that through his agency peace might be made with the United States.

No fair man who was in the war from the beginning, but must admit, that Santa Anna was true to his country from first to last. But he never recovered from this act of our government, for it made the Mexicans distrust him. It was beyond even *their* statecraft, to imagine, that the United States would suffer their ablest man to return to Mexico, unless he had been bought.

It will be remembered that Buena Vista was his first battle, and a Mexican officer told me, at Tampico, that Santa Anna had designedly suffered his troops to be cut to pieces, and in that battle he had heard soldiers say "*they were sold by Santa Anna,*" as they were falling beneath the fire of the Americans. Such language as this was the result of our policy, unintentionally sowing distrust among the soldiers of Mexico; yet Santa Anna led the survivors from that field to meet the Americans again and again, until Valencia's conduct at Contreras crushed his fortunes and his military prestige. When the city of Mexico fell, the star of Santa Anna sunk beneath the horizon of his country; yet he continued to struggle, while there was the semblance of a hope, or the shadow of armed resistance to the American troops.

No man who claims to be a soldier can deny to Santa Anna military genius, courage, and fidelity to his country, in the war with the United States.

Some time in January, 1848, he made application to the Querétaro government for permission to leave Mexico. After some delay passports were granted, and, having opened a correspondence with Colonel Hughes, through two of his friends in Jalapa, he informed Colonel Hughes that he proposed to take up his residence at an estate belonging to him near Jalapa, called Encerro, until a vessel was ready to receive him at Antigua, when he would sail for foreign parts. He desired to know whether Hughes would give him a safeguard, concluding his letter with complimentary allusions to Colonel Hughes and this garrison. Hughes replied that he would receive his Excellency with all honors, and furnish him with the necessary safeguard and an escort when he wished to leave the country.

At 8 o'clock on the morning of the 28th of March Colonel Hughes and staff left the main plaza with the intended escort for Santa Anna of three companies of mounted men, which I had the honor to command. We marched on the Perote road six miles to the village of San Miguel, and halted at the residence of General Durand, who had command of the castle of San Juan de Ulloa at the time of its surrender to Scott. The general had a collation prepared for us of bananas, oranges, frijoles, cheese, wine, etc., which we heartily enjoyed. After lunch our videttes announced the approach of the distinguished Mexican leader. My command was formed to receive him. The first of the cavalcade was a small body of well-equipped and well-appointed lancers; next followed the General's carriage drawn by eight mules, close behind which another company of lancers followed. As the carriage was nearly up to my right, I gave the command, "*Present sabres!*" saluting at the same time. The General, who was sitting on the rear seat, arose and returned the salute, and I noticed, sitting at his side, his wife, "el flor de Méjico." The carriage halted at General Durand's house, and the ex-President, wife, and daughter alighted. We were presented formally, and I had an opportunity of looking at this extraordinary man. My first thought was, How like my father he is! and, whilst this first impression was dwelling in my mind, Captain Lloyd Tilghman remarked, "How much he is like Major Kenly's father!"

General Santa Anna is a little over the middle height in stature, rather stout, with a quiet, sedate air, and a countenance expressive of great firmness; it was now shaded with that cast which trouble and sorrow always give. He was dressed in a dark olive suit, the coat being large and long, like what we call a surtout, with large brass buttons. When he received me, he was standing up with his cork leg extended slightly out from his body, and his left side he was supporting with a cane. I begged him to be seated, but he declined, saying that although he was lame he was not fatigued, as he was accustomed to standing. I told him that to a soldier the honor of losing a leg in battle compensated for the inconvenience occasioned by its loss. He seemed pleased with the remark, and I stepped aside to permit others to be presented. I sat down by the daughter, who is a child of his first wife, and looked with interest at his present wife of whom I had heard so much. I judged her to be about eighteen or twenty years old, medium height, a beautiful figure, and with as lovely a face as I had ever seen—nothing at all Mexican in it, entirely Anglo-Saxon, fair skin, hazel eyes, dark hair, sweet mouth, and a set of teeth rivaling ivory in beauty. I readily understood why she was called *the flower of Mexico.* Her manner was ladylike and pleasing, but as cool as if she were dining in the President's house at Mexico, surrounded by the body-guard of her husband. How different the demeanor and conduct of the daughter, a girl about fourteen years of age! her features were literally pinched sharp with the most evident anxiety and trouble, her manner so nervous and uneasy that I pitied her very much. I asked her if she had ever studied the English language; she replied, No, that she was *siempre caminando*, that is, always on the move or traveling; it is difficult to give the full force of this sentence, accompanied as it was by a look of much sadness. Knowing as I did that her father had been hunted for months, narrowly escaping with his life, I could not doubt that she had been *siempre caminando.* Dinner was announced at two and a half o'clock P.M., and we sat down. Madame Santa Anna sat at the head of the table, the General on her right, with Colonel Hughes on her left. After dinner the General asked me if I would smoke, at the same time handing a case containing about a dozen cigars. I declined receiving them, when he inquired if I did not smoke; I replied that I did; he then asked me why I did not take one, to which I replied, that they were all such great smokers at my end of the table, that if they once got hold of his case he would never see his cigars again. He laughed very heartily and made me take them; they were soon distributed, except two, which I kept for my father, and subsequently sent home to him.

I was getting very uneasy; a few days before this there had arrived a regiment of Texas Rangers, who were encamped between San Miguel and Jalapa on both sides of the main road along which we had to pass. I was well acquainted with its commander, Colonel Jack Hays, a famous partisan, with whom I had served at Monterey and on the Rio Grande. Having heard that threats were made, that Santa Anna should not pass alive through their camp, I had spoken to Colonel Hays on the subject. He told me he thought there was no danger, but I was not satisfied, and now among the crowd which thronged at the door of the dining-room I noticed Colonel Hays. I rose from the table, and approaching the colonel, who was dressed as usual, with a round jacket, Mexican hat, and no badge of rank other than a silk sash tied round his waist after the fashion of the Mexicans, said to him, "Suppose you let me present you to General Santa Anna;" he said, "Well," and we walked toward the head of the table. As we approached him there was general suspension of conversation, a movement of alarm was perceptible among the Mexican officers of the escort, and a silence very painful to me pervaded the hall. Santa Anna as yet was eating fruit. I said, "General, permit me to present to you"—when I had got thus far, he turned his face toward us and was in the act of rising—"Colonel Jack Hays." When I pronounced this name, his whole appearance and demeanor changed, and if a loaded bombshell, with fuse burning and sputtering, had fallen on that dinner-table, a greater sensation would not have been caused. The Mexican officers arose from their seats; standing and motionless, they looked at me. Mrs. Santa Anna turned very pale; the General resumed eating fruit, with his gaze on the table; Colonel Hays, gentleman as he was, bowed politely and withdrew from the room. Almost immediately after his withdrawal the Mexicans surmised what had been my object, and, headed by the General, came pleasantly toward me and said they were ready to march. I had time to speak to Hays, and then mounted. Placing a company on either side of the carriage (which was resisted by the Mexican escort commander until I made him give way), with Sergeant David G. Murray, of Tilghman's Battery, and Sergeant William U. Stuart, of the Twiggs Rifles, each carrying a United States flag and riding at the head of each company, opposite the carriage-doors, I gave the command "Trot, march!" and we started at a swinging gait to Jalapa. The escort of Mexicans was next, the carriage and my remaining company closed the column. As we approached the camp of the Texans, they were seen on the stone fences on either side which separated their camp from the road. There were several hundred of them, and apparently as quiet as if at a camp-meeting listening to a sermon; with one of these companies I was on very friendly terms, as they had served with me; and, knowing this, I galloped to the head of the column, placing myself in the middle of the road just in front of the leading mules' heads. The Mexicans had now taken the alarm, and pressed forward; the drivers, there were two of them, whistled and cried their *upas, upas,* vociferously, the mules took the alarm, and away we came at a killing pace. We were now among the Texans; not a sound to be heard; not a motion perceptible; there they were in all manner of postures on and about the stone fences. At this moment I saw coming toward us a mounted Texan riding in the middle of the road. I made right at him, struck the right side of his horse's head with the flat of my sabre, he swerved, and we were past horse and rider before either I am sure was aware of what was the matter. There was no time for exclamation or explanation; we were going at full speed, and I drew one long breath when I saw the steeples of Jalapa. The Texans had behaved with great propriety, the well-disposed among them checking even an utterance of what might have been deemed disrespectful, to one under the safeguard and honor of our flag.*

When we got to the garita, the General halted, and, expressing a wish not to pass through the city, Captain Tilghman's company was detailed to escort him to Encerro, distant eight miles from Jalapa, and bidding us adieu, with a regret for having incommoded us, the carriage, with its escort, proceeded to its destination by the road outside the city.

March 30. In company with Colonel Hughes and most of our officers, we went by invitation to breakfast at 12 with General Santa Anna at his hacienda of Encerro. The General received us kindly, and we sat down to a sumptuous *déjeûner à la fourchette.* The ex-President spoke with much feeling of the conduct of the Mexican people toward him, and said that he would never return until recalled by the nation. He seemed in good spirits to-day, and said it was his in-

* It gives me pleasure to record an instance of the chivalric character of this regiment of Texans, with which I was unacquainted at the time of the occurrences I have just related. Just previous to his application for passports, Santa Anna had been surprised by a body of cavalry in his hiding-place near Puebla, and narrowly escaped with his life, leaving everything in his rapid flight. All his personal effects, carriage, writing-desk, money-chest, were captured, and the wardrobe of his wife. Among these troops was the regiment of Texans led by Colonel Jack Hays, who, without disturbing an article of the lady's apparel, sent the whole of it, under charge of some Mexicans, to be delivered to Mrs. Santa Anna.

tention to embark from Antigua for Jamaica, thence to England.

After breakfast I accompanied him to an adjoining room, where some half-dozen or more of his suite were engaged writing; at the head of the table, on an elevated seat, sat a fine-looking man, who was dressed in a blue coat with brass buttons, white vest and pants. He was a native of Belgium; the others were Mexicans, some in uniform, some in civilians' dress. After a few words between the Belgian and the General, the writers took fresh paper, Santa Anna com menced walking slowly about the room, and I soon understood him to be dictating his farewell address to the Mexican people. He spoke slowly and sententiously, the Belgian making occasional notes, the others writing rapidly. I left whilst the work was going on, and I much regret not having seen this address, if it were ever published.

After several hours pleasantly spent with the ladies of the family, and several other guests, friends of Santa Anna, we gave good-by to all, and in a few days Santa Anna had left Mexico, we giving him an escort to the ship's side in which he sailed for Antigua.

CHAPTER XXXIX.

VISIT TO THE CITY OF MEXICO.

April 3, 1848. Colonel Hughes having official business with the headquarters of the army, I accompanied him and Surgeon Stedman R. Tilghman of our regiment, to the city of Mexico. With a mounted escort, we left Jalapa in the morning, and reached Perote, distant thirty-two miles, in the afternoon. Jalapa being situated on the eastern edge of the first plain or terrace which lies at the base of the Cordilleras, at an elevation of four thousand three hundred feet above the sea-level, the road rises gradually, passing through the villages of San Miguel, La Hoya, and Las Vigas, until we turn the northern end of the mountain chain at Cruz Blanca, which is at an elevation of seven thousand and forty-eight feet. The famous landmark, El Cofre de Perote, which rises to an altitude of twelve thousand feet, is on our left as we follow the road at its base, which leads into Perote, three leagues from Cruz Blanca. I visited the castle, (now in the command of Lieutenant-Colonel Seymour, of the Georgia Battalion,) which is a mile or so from the town, and was less amazed at its strength than at its location. Why the Spaniard expended several millions of hard dollars on this immense fortress is a mystery; it commands nothing, being built on a plain of several miles in extent, and if it was intended, as some assert, for an arsenal, why locate it on an arid plain nearly destitute of water, and one hundred miles from Vera Cruz, at which post the castle of San Juan de Ulloa was of sufficient capacity to hold all the war material of Spain. It was called by our people the graveyard of Mexico, its reputation for unhealthfulness surpassing that of any other place in the country.* At sunrise the next morning we left, and after passing through several large haciendas,† reached the town of Tepeyahualco, a miserable place, nearly deserted, seven leagues from Perote; our ride now was over a sandy desert, with columns of sand moving and whirled by the wind over the plain, like huge water-spouts; for a distance of twenty miles not a vestige of vegetation was apparent, except the *Agave Americana*, the maguey, from which the pulque is made. We halted at the corral of Ojo de Agua, which means literally, "eye of water;" this was a beautiful spring of water gushing from the earth, around which the corral had been erected. Distance from Perote forty-two miles, and in a south-westerly course.

April 5. Left Ojo de Agua at 5 o'clock A.M., just as the peons (laborers) were going forth to their daily toil; there were several hundred of them, men, women, and children, moving in gangs, as I have seen slaves on the cotton plantations of the south; and these poor creatures were, in all but the name, held

---

* Except Camargo and the National Bridge.

† A *hacienda* is a large estate; a *rancho* or *ranch*, a small farm; a *corral* signifies what the word caravansary does in the east, a place of shelter for man and beast, within walls; it also means a pen or pound for horses and cattle, and also, an inclosure formed by an army or wagon-train for safety from attack.

to the same servitude. They were chanting, not singing, a kind of hymn, which was as melodious as it was melancholy; its tone was that of subdued grief, of passive obedience to a fate beyond their power to change, and a helpless submission to a tyranny it was impossible to be freed from. It made a strong impression upon me. I looked at the faces of many of them as they passed; each countenance was indicative of a soul's sadness, each lineament portrayed the sentiments I have endeavored to express above.

At 8 A.M. we got to Nopaluca, a small town or pueblo, situated at the crossing of the main road by a road which leads from Orizaba to a more northern route to the capital. Here we found my friend Colonel Willis A. Gorman, with his Indiana Regiment and some dragoons: our road, still going south-west, passed the base of *El Cerro del Pinar*, whose summit is nearly eight thousand feet above the sea-level, then on to Amazourka, famous over the whole of Mexico and Central America for its manufacture of steel spurs, bridle-bits, and horse-ornaments; we went through several of the manufactories, and were pleased and astonished at the skill and beauty of their workmanship.

We pushed on, and, considerably after nightfall, reached the City of the Angels, known more generally by the name of Puebla, where, after much difficulty, we found lodgings at a meson.* Distance, forty-five miles from Ojo de Agua, and still in a southwesterly course.

* The words *Meson*, *Venta* and *Fonda*, all mean hotel, or rather, what we used to call in English, a tavern.

26

Puebla is at an altitude of six thousand seven hundred and fifty-six feet above the level of the sea, nearly two thousand five hundred feet higher than Jalapa. It is really a beautiful city, and the day I passed here was one of enjoyment. Situated in a fertile plain, with a population of seventy thousand inhabitants, with wide, well-paved streets, a large cathedral, many imposing public edifices, and many of its dwelling houses ornamented in front with glazed tiles representing scriptural and allegorical subjects, it is no wonder that the Mexicans regard it with so much pride, and boast of it as being the City of the Angels. This name, however, was given it, I believe, because of its numerous churches, and the numberless sweet-toned bells, which, even yet, attract the population and the stranger to the portals of the convents, churches, and missions, with which the city abounds. The cathedral is very rich in its property, as well as in the gorgeous decorations of its interior—its altars, shrines and chapels; a chandelier, celebrated for its magnificent workmanship, hangs in the church, weighing several tons, and which is said to be mainly wrought from gold and silver metal. The Carmen convent, the San Franciscan, and the Bishop's palace, are large piles of masonry, which yet attest the power and wealth of a church that, in the days of the Viceroys, swayed the destinies of the Indias. We dined with Colonel Childs of the U. S. Army, the commandant, who showed us the defenses, made by him in his successful resistance against the populace of the city and the army of Santa Anna, when besieged by them; and we visited with him the other memorable places in the city and vicinity. I regretted not being able to go to Huamantla, which is in the adjoining district of Tlascala, so well known for the brave race of Indians who fought side by side with Cortez in the first conquest of Mexico. This race is nearly extinct, though I have seen some of its caste.

April 7. Left Puebla and marched a due northwest course to the pretty village of San Martin, twenty-one miles from Puebla. We breakfasted at the hacienda San Christobal, by the polite invitation of the proprietor, Señor Saviñon, who gave us an entertainment as abundant as it was in good taste. There was *butter* on the table, the first I had seen which had been made in the country; by a North American this luxury was highly prized, and, being deprived for so long a time of its use, we made fearful inroads upon the dairy product of San Christobal. A league from the town we were at the corral Buena Vista, whose name indicates the lovely view of a valley unsurpassed in beauty—the famed Valley of San Martin; it reminded me of a valley which one day will become celebrated, the Middletown Valley, between Frederick and Hagerstown, Maryland. This Valley of San Martin, though seven thousand two hundred feet above the sea, is luxuriant beyond description, producing not only the corn, wheat, and barley of the temperate zone, but pepper (chile), beans (frijoles), banana, tobacco, coffee, and maguey of the tropics; its wheat flour makes the bread which rivals the Parisian baker's loaf, and its pulque is as prized as the Lachryma Christi of Vesuvius.

Rising rapidly from the valley, we commence the

ascent of the Sierra Madre, crowned by the once-seen, never-to-be-forgotten mountains, Popocatapetl (the smoking mountain) and Iztaccihuatl (the white woman), the one seventeen thousand eight hundred and eighty-four feet, the other sixteen thousand feet, above the sea. We were now surrounded by mountains covered with eternal snow, but they were as pigmies by the side of these two colossi of the Sierra Madre; the crater of one receiving the first kiss of the rising sun, and the summit of the other its parting rays, as it sinks in the west. Called by the natives *husband and wife*, the traditions of the country are full of the poetry of an imaginative people about these two mountains: the one a volcano, of once frightful eruptions, the other forever at rest in the gorgeous grandeur of nature's dressing. There is a sublimity and mystery round and about them which impresses a traveller from their first view, and the charm increases as you lessen the distance; crossing the Sierra at an elevation of ten thousand feet, the summit of the White Woman on your left is so far and high up in the heavens above you, with her robe of spotless white and her diadem of gilded sunset, that you continue to gaze, for her beauties continue to increase, until dimness of sight—or is it the darkness?—conceals her in its embrace.

Before reaching Rio Frio (the cold river) we passed through an immense pine forest, and came to the little hamlet which takes its name from the river. It was a miserable place, the night cold and dark, but while shivering in the unaccustomed temperature of the frigid zone, we received an invitation to accept the hospitality of Colonel Wm. Irvin, whose Ohio Regiment of Volunteers was stationed here. Distance from Puebla forty-two miles, north-west course.

April 8. We got an early start; at daylight we saw a gang of rough-looking, armed Mexicans approaching, which caused us some uneasiness, as I am quite confident there was not a soldier in our party who could have used either sabre or pistol, we were so benumbed with cold. Both parties halted; after a reconnaissance, we saw a train of pack-mules and another gang of these ruffians escorting it; we learned, after a brief parley, that they had been hired to guard a specie train from the city to Puebla. We passed each other, and hailed the warmth of the rising sun with unalloyed pleasure, as it restored to us the use of our limbs. At 8.30 A.M. we caught our first view of the far-famed valley of Mexico, and, halting for breakfast at the *Venta de Cordova*, twenty miles from the city, we spent an hour in looking at the unrivaled view spread out before and beyond us. Passing by Lake Chalco and through the town of Ayotla, at 2 o'clock P.M. we were up with the Peñon mountain, an isolated mass of rock several hundred feet in height, rising up from the plain, at the base of which the road runs toward the city. Here was the first exterior line of Mexican defenses to guard the approach by the causeway, over which we rode for eight miles, and entered the capital city of Mexico at 4 o'clock in the afternoon. Distance from Rio Frio thirty miles. Course, west to Lake Chalco, then north-west to the city. Distance by my calculation, from Jalapa, one hundred and ninety-one miles.

CHAPTER XL.

THE CITY OF MEXICO.

Soon after our arrival we called to see Major-General Scott, though etiquette required that our first visit should be to Major-General Butler; our first duty, as it was our pleasure, was to call on General Scott, though he was not in command, and neither Colonel Hughes or I hesitated a moment in telling General Butler, when we called on the sàme evening, that we had been to see Scott.

Hughes was an old acquaintance and friend, so that our reception was cordial and pleasant; telling him our purpose to call on Major-General Butler, the Commander-in-chief, he invited us to come after our visit to sup with him at 10 o'clock. We returned, sat down to the first supper of the kind I had seen in Mexico, cold roast fowl and champagne wine, and spent one of the most agreeable evenings of my life. The General was in excellent humor; jested about his being superseded in command, said he was an old, broken-down soldier, in disgrace, etc., and, observing me looking at an object in the corner of the room which had attracted my attention, he changed his discourse, inquiring what I saw. Without waiting for a reply, he said, "Bring it to me." Leaving my seat, I went over to the corner, and took up what appeared to be a stick of round wood, capped with brass at either end; noticing a brass plate, with an inscription, attached to the middle of the log, I was about reading it, when he arose suddenly from his chair, and took it from me, saying, "What do you think this is?" I made no reply, for I did not know what it was, or what I should say. Holding the log at arm's length from him, so that the light fell upon the plate, he said, "This is my spy-glass; read," and I read that this was a portion of the "flag-staff of *Chapultepec*," captured by the American Army, and presented by General Scott to the United States Military Academy at West Point.* This is about the substance of what was engraved on the plate, and which I read with every nerve thrilling with a creeping sensation impossible to describe. When he saw that I had read the inscription, he rapidly reversed the stick, and placing one end, as if it were an elongated spy-glass, toward my eye, asked me "what I saw?" Without a thought, I replied, "*Glory!*" From that moment General Scott and I were friends. I was a young man, very fond of the profession of arms, and this notice from so distinguished a soldier was inexpressibly gratifying.

During the evening a gentleman came in hurriedly, and told the General that a courier from Vera Cruz had brought the astounding intelligence to the British Legation that Louis Philippe, King of France, had been driven from his throne, by a revolution in Paris. This news became the theme of conversation, General Scott saying that he was personally acquainted with the king, etc.

---

* As I was never at West Point, and never inquired, I do not know whether this is there or not.

That night the French residents in the city paraded in the main plaza, singing the Marseillaise, and I rarely ever witnessed a scene of wilder riot and confusion; there were twenty or thirty of these half-crazy Frenchmen, who entered the different gambling saloons, singing their songs and brandishing bottles from which they were drinking without stint. As the players did not like the interruption, I thought once or twice that there would be a serious ending to the frolic; finally, the party was induced to withdraw, but they kept the main-guard busy until morning.

April 9—Sunday. Major Osborne Cross (of Maryland), Quartermaster U. S. Army, had kindly invited us to share his quarters while in the city. These were in the principal street, the *Calle de Plateros* (Street of the Silversmiths), not far from the grand square or main plaza. As the cathedral fronted this square, our first visit was there, but before speaking of it, I will try to give a general description of the city.

The mean elevation of the great valley of Mexico is seven thousand five hundred feet, while the mountain barrier which encloses it will average ten thousand feet above the sea-level, on the east, south, and west sides. Its area is eighteen leagues, or forty-five miles, in length, and twelve leagues, or thirty miles, in width, or two hundred and forty-five square leagues.

There are five lakes in the valley, which cover an area of a hundred square miles, with a depth of from eight feet to several inches of water. When Cortez arrived in 1520, these lakes were surrounded with numerous populous villages, communicating with each other by canals supplied from these lakes, and in the centre of the largest lake, Tezcuco, was built the capital city of the Aztecs, called Tenochtitlan. The city was reached from the shores of the lake by well-constructed causeways, which were intersected by canals for the passage of boats; by which also the neighboring populations approached the capital for commerce or religious duty.

The present city of Mexico was built upon the site of the ancient Tenochtitlan, and amidst its ruins; but the lake no longer surrounds the city, it has been filled by the destruction of the old city, and the gradual evaporation of its waters has diminished its size, so that, unlike Venice, the water no longer occupies the place, nor is used for thoroughfares in the city. Nevertheless, as in the days of Cortez, the Indians come to the capital of the conquerors as their ancestors, in boats, from the neighboring shores of Chalco, Xochimilco, and San Christobal, the waters of whose lakes communicate with those of Tezcuco. The causeway by which we entered the city is the same that was in existence at the time of the conquest, but instead of passing through and over a lake, there are dry patches of earth and edifices where there was formerly water, except at intervals, which are fringed with the waters of Chalco and Tezcuco. The Lake of Tezcuco, being the lowest and the most southerly, receives the waters of the northern lakes, and, there being no outlet, it occasionally overflows its banks when flooded in the rainy season, inundating the city of Mexico to the depth of several feet Were it not for the rapid evaporation, owing to the great altitude of these waters, there would yet be serious cause for alarm, that the modern, like the ancient city, would be in the midst of the waters. There have been several attempts to provide against such a fate by constructing a *desagua,* and it is related that upon several occasions, when the valley was in danger of being submerged, the earth was split open by earthquakes, and the waters escaped through the fissures.

The modern city of Mexico is as regularly laid out as Philadelphia, with blocks or squares of large stately-looking stone houses, capacious streets, showy and attractive shops, and, were it not for the flat level upon which it is built, would be a handsome city. There is always a large concourse of people moving through its main streets and grand square; and its alaméda, or public square, and its paséos, or public walks, are thronged during the day and evening, with a motley crowd of all classes sauntering in shade or sunshine, in light or darkness, as the humor or taste suggests.

The great centre of the city is the grand square, upon which fronts the cathedral, the President's palace, the public buildings, and the richest shops of the metropolis. It is a large open space worthy of a large city; nothing contracted about it; paved with square flag-stones, regularly and artistically disposed, and radiating from the outer limits to a circular space in the middle, where it is designed to erect a monument commemorative of the independence of the country from Spain.

The cathedral occupies the site of the temple so famous in the history of the conquest; its chief attraction to me was the *Calendario Azteca,* or Mexican calendar, which has been placed in its western wall near the angle formed by that and the main front of the edifice. This stone, or basaltic rock, exquisitely and elaborately carved, is the most interesting object of antiquity on the North American continent; in size it is thirteen and a half feet by thirteen and a half feet, weighs forty-eight thousand two hundred and seventy-five pounds, and upon its face is sculptured the sun in its four seasons, *movimientos,* represented by the god Tonatiuh, with open mouth and extended tongue to picture the flight of time. This huge face of the sun, or god, is surrounded by several circles filled with hieroglyphics, expressive of the division of the days and nights by the revolution of the earth on its axis; of the days of the month; of the signs of the zodiac, and the number of days in the year. Upon the stone is also delineated the great feasts celebrated at the solstices and equinoxes, as, like the Egyptians, and subsequently the Israelites, the feasts were celebrated at the time of these celestial phenomena by the Toltecs and the Aztecs. The stone was found some feet below the surface of the main plaza in front of the cathedral in the year 1790, and was most judiciously preserved by being built in the existing wall of the church. There were observed upon its face on the outer edge several small holes. The Mexican savants judged the use of these; by placing wooden pegs in them and stretching strings over and above the surface of the calendar, the meridian was accurately marked upon the face at noon, and other most interesting astronomical observations made upon the stone. They reached the conclusion, that a people who regulated their religious festivals by the movements of the heavenly bodies, and sculptured their historic deeds upon a public monument such as this, had attained a high degree of civilization, and showed by their art and knowledge of astronomy a close analogy between the peoples of Asia and America. By placing this stone vertically on a horizontal plane, with the face to the south and fronting a line drawn due east and west, it was demonstrated that the artificers, or those who superintended its construction, were well acquainted with all the principal celestial movements, and had added to their division of the year into days even the number of intercalary days, to preserve the equation of time.

The cathedral church, outside and inside, is worthy the metropolitan see of the first city of the Hispano-Americans; you may measure its wealth of interior church adornments by its exterior size, four hundred feet front by five hundred feet in depth. We wandered through its maze of columns and chapels, through its atmosphere of incense and amid its altars and paintings, its gold and silver vessels and figures, with uncertain steps and undefined impressions. While all was gorgeous and rich, you trod upon uneven or sliding planks beneath you, which alone separated your feet from the dust and ashes of the graves beneath, which smelled of earth, earthy.

That which most excited my attention in the cathedral was a railing several hundred feet in length, the rails of which were at least three feet high, all of which, rails and balusters, top and bottom, inside and outside, were made of gold and silver metal; within this railing approach was had to the sanctuary, within which was an image of the Virgin Mary, dressed with brilliants, whose value is estimated by millions of dollars.

What a commentary this wealth was upon the character of our army! nothing whatever between it and sequestration, but the honor of a nation, which waged this war, not for pillage, but for a peace which would redress the wrongs done our citizens and give us compensation for losses occasioned thereby.

The eastern front of the square is flanked by the National Palace, a long line of not very showy buildings, yet imposing from their great length and uniformity of appearance. These were, when Mexico was a province of Spain, the residence of the Viceroys, and in republican days the Executive Mansion and halls of Congress; now, they are the headquarters of the American army, and the barracks of the main-guard of the city. Here is now sitting the court of inquiry, convened by order of the President of the United States, to inquire into the differences which unfortunately arose between Major-Generals Scott, Worth, and Pillow, after the fall of the city, and the publication of the official reports in relation thereto.

I have never witnessed a court whose proceedings were marked by more dignity and decorum than characterized this high military tribunal. I attended several of its sittings, which were deeply interesting, from the eminence of those who participated in the events which were the subject of the evidence adduced, and whose presence at the trial table, with their respective staffs, added weight to the prominence of the grave questions under discussion.

Military law and usage found able exponents among the experienced soldiers present, and when such officers as Major-General Worth gave their testimony as to the strategy or tactics of certain movements the evidence was listened to with profound attention. Large numbers of officers of the army occupied the court-room and galleries, groups of Mexican officials were noticeable, while numbers of Mexican officers, prisoners of war, passed away their time quietly listening to the proceedings, which they could not understand, but closely scanning the appearance and demeanor of the *dramatis personæ.*

The south side of the square was the building devoted to municipal purposes, and on the west the old palace of Cortez, still belonging to his family, now in its lower stories filled with shops, before which a portico forms, I think, the most attractive part of the city. This portico is ten or fifteen feet wide, arched, and covered with the second story of the long pile of buildings. It opens on the grand square, toward which the front windows of the shops expose their wares, and is the select promenade of the ladies, who manage to do a little shopping even in war times. There were large crowds of well-dressed people circulating along this portico for several hours of mid-day, and this, with looking in the shop windows, made the place a favorite resort of mine. It was much larger and more unique in its appearance and in the character of its merchandise exposed for sale, than the *galerie d' Orleans* in the old Palais Royal at Paris.

I was chiefly to be found, however, at the National Museum, in the university building, not far from the Plaza Mayor. It will repay any archæologist or antiquarian to visit the city of Mexico, by an examination of the interesting relics of an age and a people now unknown, which may be found about this building, in its galleries, courtyards, cellars, and garrets, for all is in confusion, as all is wonderful and strangely attractive to the imagination and the senses.

Here is the sacrificial stone as when it was thrown down by the Spaniards from the summit of the Teocalli, while the red blood of their countrymen, sacrificed a few nights previously, still added its stain to the countless rivulets which had flowed down the side, until the whole place smelt like a slaughter-house, as described by Bernal Diaz. Here is the stone yoke which was placed over the neck whilst the villains tore the heart out from the breast of the murdered victim; here the groove down which the blood ran, and here the obsidian knives with which the priests made the incision between the ribs. Here are idols, and there the huge basaltic block carved into the grotesque and yet grand image of Huitzilopuxtli, the god of war. Here the face of the mysterious Quetzalcoatl, the god of the air, which you will not pass without its attracting more than a casual glance; there is something in its expression that rivets your attention. Here a painting of a Mexican emperor in the council of kings, and there the coronation of Yxtlixochitl by the high-priest Taratzint in 1415. Here a painting of the army of Cortez, painted by the envoys sent by Montezuma for this purpose, and showing the effect produced upon them at first hearing a discharge of firearms; and here is another, painted by the same artists, of the tent in which, and the appearance of, Cortez when he received the presents sent him by Montezuma. Battles between the naked Indians, armed with sword, spear, and shield, are graphically represented, as the iron-plated, half-centaur warrior of old Spain slaughtered them, with the destructive and unseen missiles sent by heaven from the mouths of fiery serpents. Here are hundreds of square feet of hieroglyphic writing on maguey paper, as plain as when written hundreds of years ago, to record the daily marches of the Aztecs in their long pilgrimage. Here is a hieroglyphic delineation of the deluge and the confusion of languages, and here a genealogical tree of the Aztec family, mounting to the first couple (they go back to our first parents); here are the musical instruments, curiously wrought, mingled with the bow and the arrow, the sword and shield of the warrior; here a portrait of Zitlalpopoca, a senator of Tlascala; there the sad and handsome face of Montezuma; here the armor of Cortez, there the portrait of Don Diego de Almagro; here Pedro de Alvarado, there Diego de Ordaz; here Fr. Bartolomê de las Casas, there Fr. Bernardino de Sahagun. In the courtyard is the very fine equestrian statue of Charles IV. of Spain, by Tolsa, a Mexican artist; here are also several huge idols and feathered serpents grotesquely carved in stone, which will give a better idea of idolatrous worship than tomes of description.

The museum contains numberless little things which the curiosity-hunter loves more than gold; and to such I say, you have a pleasure in store, if you have not seen the museum in the city of Mexico. Read and read again the charming history of the conquest by William H. Prescott; then read the explanation of the ancient history of Mexico, by Isidro R. Gondra, it being the introduction to Prescott's history translated into Spanish, by Ignacio Cumplido.

As in all Spanish cities, there are public walks, or *paseos*, and an alameda, which corresponds with the English parks or the public squares of the American cities. The Paseo Nuevo is at the western, the Paseo de la Viga at the eastern, end of the city. Both are alike broad avenues for equestrians, with narrower ones for pedestrians,—planted with stately trees, adorned with fountains, plentifully supplied with seats comfortably located. The Mexican population of all ranks and conditions frequent these airy and picturesque walks to indulge in the luxuries of idleness and sight-seeing. It is delightful to sit and look at the handsome equipages, the tastefully-dressed ladies, the excellent horsemanship of the caballéros, the proud Don in his mantle and the poor lepero in his blanket, passing in crowds, like a spectacle on theatrical boards; but nothing charmed me so much as to see the Indian girls, crowned with wreaths of roses, as they danced in their boats, returning from the city to their homes on the shores of Lake Chalco, by the canal which runs for a long distance alongside the Paseo de la Viga. This sight, as historic as romantic, brought to memory the same scenes, related with so much pleasure by the companions of Cortez as so attractive when seen by them on their first entrance into the valley of Mexico. I have no doubt that the songs the girls were now singing, and to which the dance kept cadence, were the same which allured the soldiers of Spain, and which kept the hardy warriors in these Elysian fields of the New World. There was but little gold, plenty of hard blows; and a soldier must think that there were other attractions, besides the destruction of idols and the elevation of the cross, to the bold adventurers who climbed the sierras of this far-distant land and who planted the banner of Castile and Leon amid the ruins of the Aztec dynasty. Boat-load after boat-load of girls passed along this canal, as happy in their innocent merriment as if their parents had never known sorrow and the future would prove a dream of the present. Differing from all other Mexican songs I had heard, there was no melancholy whatever in the music, as there was none in the manner or tone of the singers. Coming from a district, Xochimilco, known in their language as *the land of flowers,* these artless children of nature mingled with the perfume of roses their melodious voices, in unconscious thanksgiving to the Almighty Creator of heaven and earth, as the bird warbles its praise, as the flower sends forth its fragrance.

There was one other place in the city of Mexico I liked to visit, and this was the *Monte de Piédad,* or pawnbroker's shop. Here were gathered the most bizarre articles, from the time of the conquest to the present day. Next to the museum, here were to be seen such curiosities as could be found nowhere else,—no, not in the broad world. It would not be saying too much that there are articles in this pawnbroker's establishment, that look as if they had been pledged by the companions of the Cid or the followers of Cortez. The offerings of all ages and all countries, of all sexes and conditions, seem to have been promiscuously heaped about this grand altar to the penury of mankind. Here, in this mountain-locked region, thousands of miles from the great world, have drifted and lodged the fragments of wreck scattered o'er the ocean of distress by the storms of life, until, mouldering away, their dust repeats the language of Solomon, "Vanity of vanities,—all is vanity!"

There was, indeed, pride as well as vanity in a pair of earrings which excited my admiration: they represented a pair of pea-fowl; the bodies, half an inch long, were formed of pure brilliants, the necks of small rose diamonds, topaz, and emerald, the tail-feathers, a little more than half an inch in length, of sapphires, rubies, and emeralds, all exquisitely set, and glistening with the unrivaled colors of these precious stones. I had the temerity to price them. Eight hundred dollars, and *muy barato* (very cheap), was the reply.

We called to see Major-Generals Worth and Patterson, and Brigadier-General Persifer F. Smith, the military commandant of the city, by each of whom we were kindly received and hospitably entertained. We attended guard-mount in the grand square, and were present at several drills of the division of regulars. We promenaded the portales, the paseos, the alameda, visited the mint, the aqueducts (which bring fresh water from the hills into the city), the citadel, the convent of La Merced, and the quarters of the *canaille* of Mexico,—the leperos, as bad a looking class of men as one would wish to avoid. We also visited the church of the Virgin of Guadalupe, in the village of Guadalupe Hidalgo, three miles north of the city. It was here, that the well-known picture of the Virgin of Guadalupe is said to have been miraculously painted on the blanket of an Indian, and which has given to its cathedral church a high reputation for sanctity over all Mexico. The name of Guadalupe is so entirely Mexican that it was a pleasure to be at the home of its nativity, and I visited the church with respect, if not with faith, to look upon the miracle as it is now shown to the public. There is a fountain adjoining the church, and carefully guarded, whose bubbling and muddy waters deposit a sediment, which, collected in a matrix at the bottom, gives a representation of the picture of the Virgin on the blanket, as seen by the Indian on this hill-top, the site of the church. I witnessed the manner of formation, and possessed myself of one of these casts as a memorial of a visit long to be remembered.

Honored by an invitation from General Worth, we accompanied him over the battle-fields of the valley. Leaving the city by the garita of San Antonio, we followed the causeway through Churubusco and San Antonio to San Augustin. Crossing the Pedregal by the route over which our troops marched on the 19th of August, we reached the point at which Captains John B. Magruder and Franklin D. Callender planted their guns and received the fire of the twenty-two pieces of Mexican artillery from Valencia's intrenched camp. We admired the daring and skill of our artillerists, and wondered that anything had been left of men, horses, or material in this unequal contest. The courage which brought the American guns here amounted to rashness; yet its result tended to increase the self-sufficiency of Valencia and keep him within the lines he had been twice ordered to leave. Crossing the ravine to Contreras, we next followed the road to San Angel, passing the fields within which Santa Anna unaccountably (to us) held his reserves on the 19th and came up to the lines of Churubusco. These must be seen to appreciate the obstacles that were overcome by the gallantry and steadiness of the American troops. The convent is a fortress, the *tête du pont* an elaborate fortification, and the river a natural defense, from which troops should not have been driven.

I listened and looked, and was silent; for the whole success of these operations was mysterious.

Out of eight thousand four hundred and ninety-seven Americans engaged, one thousand and fourteen fell killed and wounded here and at Contreras: this will give an idea that the Mexicans fought well; but how and why fifteen thousand armed men fled from such a position *is* mysterious.

We next went from Piedad, through Tacubaya, to Molino del Rey. There was not much said, but a great deal was noticed, on this field. Fronting the mill, and looking over my left shoulder, there was the lone fortress, forever memorable as the *Casa Mata;* in its front the dry ditch and maguey bushes from which the stream of fatal fire was poured upon the front and flanks of the Americans;* and here on this narrow field the blood of the flower of our army moistened the Mexican soil. General Worth led his division three thousand two hundred and fifty-one strong into this battle; he left seven hundred and eighty-one of these killed and wounded, to mark the victory won by the individual gallantry of the officers and men of the regular army of the United States.

It was the most desperately contested battle of the war, and was the proximate cause of much ill feeling among officers of high rank.

Going through the mill-building and adjacent grounds, we approached and entered the cypress-grove at the base of Chapultepec. This grove of trees—so old that the memory of man and the traditions of a race run not to the contrary—seems to have grown, for a Druidical order of priesthood. There is solemnity and priestcraft in every trunk, mystery in every rustle of a branch, dark and hidden ways in the sombre gloom of its shade. High up, isolated and grand, the rock of Chapultepec shoots

---

* Brevet-Major Daniel H. McPhail, a native of the city of Baltimore, and a gallant officer of the United States Army, commanded a company of the 5th U. S. Infantry in the attack upon the Casa Mata. His uniform coat evidenced and illustrated the character of the fire to which the troops were exposed: one bullet passed through it from the front, and another, striking near the right shoulder of the coat, passed entirely across the back and made its exit at the left shoulder. He providentially escaped without a wound

into the heavens: made by nature for a temple, idolaters may be excused for using it as such, soldiers pardoned for making it a fortress. It is now a fortress; and as the military college of the Republic of Mexico, it witnessed a brave defense made by professors and cadets, with the best Division of its army, on the 13th of September, 1847; but it fell, and with it the last hope of patriotic Mexicans. Yet they fought; and, descending the hillside, we continued along the line of their retreat, by the aqueduct, to the San Cosmé garita, and halted at the building occupied by General Worth, when he entered the city, on the night of the 13th of September, 1847.

Going from here by the way of the alameda and the citadel, we were at the Belen garita, where General Quitman so heroically held the position he had gained after his hard fighting on the Tacubaya causeway, and where, fortifying himself on the night of the 13th, he first learned that the Mexicans were evacuating the city.

Under no more favorable circumstances could we have gone over these fields, and we felt under great obligations to General Worth for the knowledge and instruction it had been our good fortune this day to receive.

While in the city there was an earthquake felt, which was so alarming that large numbers of the people rushed through the streets to the main plaza, where on their knees some gave vent to paroxysms of prayer and terror. It was an exciting time, and we went into the square, as it was considered the safest place. I noticed that there was no disposition on the part of any one to smile at the terror of others. There were two distinct shocks, one of them sufficiently strong to make a mantel-clock in our room lean forward considerably from its original perpendicular position. During the day I was shown a church-tower, in which a fissure twenty or thirty feet long, and from half an inch to an inch in width, had been caused by the second shock of the morning, and it was said that a little more heaving of the earth would have toppled over every steeple of the capital. It was a very unpleasant sensation while it lasted, and I had no desire to experience another.

We also had a horse-race, which was attended by every officer and soldier that could get to the grounds, outside the city. There were many Mexicans present, and the occasion which caused such an assemblage, presided over as it was by the Commander-in-chief of the army, was celebrated with all the *éclat* of a Derby or a St. Leger.

The captain of our escort had brought with him a horse which had won the money of both Mexican and American horse-fanciers at Jalapa. The captain had had much experience in racing in Texas, as well as Mexico; he was a natural born horse-jockey, and boasted of having learned horse-taming from the Comanches. Warily he had been making inquiry, and had gotten up a match between his horse and a fast horse of one of the Valley officers; we were confidentially advised that we could safely bet upon *our* horse. As the time for the starting approached, our excitement increased, and every man of our party wagered money on the result. We took so much interest in the race that the judges upon the stand invited several of us into that august presence. The time was blown from a bugle, the horses were brought to the starting-pole, the word was given, and away they went, the Jalapa horse ahead. Alas! and alas! he broke down, and was distanced, shamefully beaten. Unused to exertion at this great altitude, the extreme rarity of the air had exhausted his powers before the race was fairly begun, and our captain, looking upon the distressed and heaving flanks of his poor beast, exclaimed, "As big a fool as I ought not to own so good a horse." We lost our money, but we gained its value in experience,—never to depend upon a horse's bottom when the horse has not been trained to the climate, in which it is to be tested.*

We heard but little from our Captain on the homeward march about his experience in horse matters in Texas and the Tierra Caliente. He had been completely whipped.

A few words about peace. As near as we were to headquarters, we could learn but little more than we knew at Jalapa. The senior officers of the army believed that we would have peace before long; this was the opinion of a majority of the officers; there

---

* We had all suffered more or less from difficulty of breathing, sore throat, and dizziness, yet not one of us had had the judgment to think of the horse: though *we* found it difficult to make undue exertion, as to ascend a flight of stairs, without several halts to recover breath, we had permitted our horse to run a race without a thought of *his* powers of endurance. All this was so well known, that in more instances than one those who had won tendered the money back to the losers of our party.

were others who thought differently. My own opinion was, from all I could hear, read, and see, that there would be no treaty made before the end of the armistice, which would terminate June 2, and then, if nothing favorable turned up for the Mexicans, their Congress would seriously look to the ratification of a treaty of peace; not before.

We all feared that it would be impossible to leave the country before October or November.

On the 18th I dined at the *Gran Sociedad* with my old friend of the Tierra Caliente, Captain John Bernand, courier of the British Embassy; he was thoroughly *au courant* with the news and gossip of the capital, and it is quite likely the above views were chiefly drawn from him. We parted with mutual regrets, and indulged the hope of meeting again at London or Washington, to talk over our incidents at the National Bridge and along the Antigua.

On the 19th our party dined with General Worth; and now, after a stay of twelve days, having exhausted our leave, and, I much feared, the patience of our hosts, we prepared to leave the city of Mexico on the morrow, to return to our own post and our own duties.

We left the city of Mexico at noon on the 20th of April, and rode to the Venta de Cordova, where we remained all night. With a beautiful moonlight we left next morning, crossed the sierra six miles beyond, and, descending rapidly, for it was very cold, we got to Rio Frio at 8 A.M.; by 3 P.M. we were at San Martin, and halted for the night at the hacienda or corral of San Bartolo, distant from Cordova thirty-three miles.

April 22. Before daylight we were on our march,

and still in this lovely Valley of San Martin. On reaching the Casa de Diligencias, called *Prieto*, we procured a guide and started to visit the pyramid of Cholula, some three leagues distant. At ten o'clock we were in the village of Cholula, a pueblo of a few thousand inhabitants. At the time when Cortez was here, in 1520, there was a city on the present site, of the same name, which, in a letter written to the Emperor Charles V., he described as being as large as any city of Spain, and with as large a population. It was at that time regarded as a sacred city, and on these plains there existed a mighty population. On the pyramid, now in sight, was the chief temple of a nation whose mythology is believed to be more ancient than that of Greece, and in this temple was the altar to Quetzalcoatl (god of the wind, or air), whose history belongs to the golden age of the Indian race of America. This word Quetzalcoatl signifies a "serpent with green plumage;" yet so mysterious is all connected with the god, that he was represented with a white face and with a beard. He was the great high-priest of Tula; he founded colonies; would tolerate no sacrifices but those of fruits and flowers; established religious orders; was so great a friend of peace that he stopped his ears when they talked of war, and finally disappeared, to the great grief of his worshipers, who yet await his return, and who, it is said, secretly worship the god of their fathers, in the present temple of Christian worship which has replaced the temple of the lost Quetzalcoatl.

I ascended this pyramid, whose sides face lines running due north and south, east and west; it is upwards of two hundred feet high, rising by four successive terraces from a base of more than a thousand feet square; built mainly of sun-dried brick-adobes, and covered apparently with earth, giving support to the seed, wafted hither by the winds or brought by birds. The bushes and the trees growing in its soil hinder and obstruct a clear view of its shape and beauty. The platform on the summit of this pyramid is about two hundred feet square, and here Baron Humboldt made many astronomical observations. The temple of the Indian has given place to the church of the Christian, and the chapel, surrounded by cypress growing luxuriantly on this high terrace, is dedicated to the Señora de los Remedios, our Lady of Remedies.

I do not wonder that Humboldt wrote so enthusiastically of the view from this spot. He says "that you can enjoy the sight, at the same time, of three mountains, each higher than Mont Blanc, viz.: Popocatepetl, Iztaccihuatl, and the Peak of Orizaba (two of which are known to be volcanoes), without counting the Sierra of Tlascala, around whose summit the hurricanes are now forming."

It is a grand view; and when this plain of Cholula was filled with four hundred villages, each teeming with population, and the sacred city at its base a living swarm of priests and attendants, those who stood on this apex must have been bewildered with the multitude of objects that passed before the vision.

There is no tradition, much less history, that gives the slightest clue when, or by whom, this pyramid was constructed, and there are no ruins on the American continent at all comparable to it or more worthy the research of the historian or the examination of the archæologist and antiquary.

Some Mexican writers have drawn very cleverly an analogy between this construction and the remains on the plain of Babylon in Assyria. They have noticed that while this is a truncated pyramid, rising by terraces, so were those of Babel and Nineveh; that this, with half the elevation of the great pyramid of Cheops in Egypt, has double its extent of base. I have read also a costly and interesting work written by an English gentleman named Jones (whose Christian name I regret to have forgotten), on the ruins of Central America, who made the discovery that all these constructions were totally unlike those of Egypt, in their being terraces and not pyramids, yet of pyramidal form: his opinion was that the ruins of Yucatan were of Phœnician origin, that the ships of Tyre and Sidon had brought hither colonists, as they had landed them at Carthage, at Marseilles, in Britain, and elsewhere.

My own opinion is that whoever finds the key to the history of the people who built the pyramid of Cholula, and who dwelt on its plains, will find the history of the race that built Palenque, Uxmal, and the other cities of Central America. I do not at all agree with the general current of opinion that the Toltecs, the Aztecs, and other races of which we know a little, came from the north: far from it; there is not a trait in common between their descendants and those from known northern hives. It has been a subject of reflection with me, the present configuration of the two continents; and, as I have never met with the idea, I throw this out for the investigation of geographers and the curious. Look at the map of the world on Mercator's projection. See Cape San Roque, an extreme western projection of Brazil, in South America, throwing out its promontory toward the African coast; look at the comparatively narrow Atlantic Ocean between these two lands, the one of the western, the other of the eastern continent, and then look northward and southward at the immensity of the volume of water; the conclusion is irresistible to my mind that the two continents were one, that here the waters of the one or the other pole had cleft in twain the earth from some unwonted disturbance of its equilibrium, and that the inhabitants of Mexico, the races of whom we have been speaking, are of Asiatic origin; that the Aztec hieroglyphics depict the deluge recorded in the Bible, and their genealogy their descent from Adam.

After gathering a few small idols* of baked clay, by digging among the débris, we rode over the plain to Puebla, whose spires were in sight, distant eight miles due east.

April 23. This being Sunday, we remained at Puebla, entered once more the cathedral, and my recent visit to Cholula seemed to impart additional interest to my observation of the people who thronged its aisles and who worshiped at its altars. After

---

* All through the pyramid, as far as excavations have been made, these idols are found, having been evidently thrown in during its erection.

dining with Colonel Childs, we rode with him over the paseo, and again enjoyed the pleasure of viewing this gay and handsome capital in its holiday dress and favorite promenade.

We left Puebla on the morning of the 24th, and arrived at Jalapa the night of the 26th, after an absence of twenty-three days.

During our absence, Lieutenant-Colonel William H. Emory, of the Topographical Engineers, joined our regiment, having been appointed by President Polk. This gallant and accomplished officer gave to the regiment the benefit of his skill and experience by zealous efforts in its drill and instruction. He was successful in adding increased efficiency to the command and in winning the confidence and esteem of us all. From first to last, my relations with him, as they had been with Colonel Hughes, were intimate and friendly. He remained with the regiment until its final discharge at Pittsburg, Pennsylvania.

CHAPTER XLI.

THE COURT OF INQUIRY.

WHILE a nominal government was struggling into existence over distracted Mexico, a serious misunderstanding had arisen between Generals Scott, Worth, and Pillow, at the city of Mexico. The trouble had its origin in the several official reports of the Valley campaign, made by the General-in-chief and his Lieutenants. There were alleged errors and mistakes in detail and in substance, in essential and non-essential particulars, in these reports of the operations of the American army in the series of battles which led to the capture of the enemy's capital, which provoked a correspondence between the generals above named, and the issue of General Order "No. 349" by General Scott, that reflected severely upon several of the most distinguished soldiers, and caused intense feeling throughout the entire army.

The immediate cause of the promulgation of this memorable "Order No. 349" was the publication of a letter, signed *Leonidas*, in the New Orleans papers, and subsequently published at Tampico and Mexico. This led to the arrest of several officers, and personal quarrels between those highest in rank, and would have, in any other than the American army, shattered it into bloody fragments. I sometimes thought that the picture which was presented to our eyes by the condition of Mexico, mainly the result of the quarrels of its generals, helped to steady our devotion to country and government by elevating our patriotism above the fortunes of individuals. These disputes between the commanding generals of our army culminated in charges being preferred by General Scott against Generals Pillow and Worth and Lieutenant-Colonel Duncan, the latter having avowed the authorship of the *Leonidas* letter, at the same time expressly exonerating Pillow and Worth from all knowledge of or connection with it. General Worth also preferred charges against General Scott, and appealed to the President of the United States. General Scott was recalled, his recall being based on two grounds: first, his own request, and, secondly, for having placed General Worth in arrest, because the latter had appealed, from and through General Scott, to the War Department.

The order of recall was received on the 18th day of February, 1848, and on that day General Scott issued the following noteworthy order, formally transferring the command to Major-General Butler, in a vein that will never be forgotten by those who received the first notice of his recall through these orders:

"HEADQUARTERS OF THE ARMY,
MEXICO, February 18, 1848.

"*General Orders No.* 59]

"By instructions from the President of the United States, just received, Major-General Scott turns over the command of this army to Major-General Butler, who will immediately enter upon duty accordingly.

"In taking leave officially of the troops he has so long had the honor personally to command in an arduous campaign,—a small part of whose glory has been, from position, reflected on the senior officer,—Major-General Scott is happy to be relieved by a General of established merit and distinction in the service of his country.

"By command of Major-General Scott.

"(Signed) "H. L. SCOTT, A. A. A.-G."

Major-General Butler on assuming command issued the following order, characterized by good sense and good taste:

"HEADQUARTERS ARMY OF MEXICO,
MEXICO, February 19, 1848.

"*Orders No.* 1.]

"Pursuant to the orders of the President of the United States, and the instructions of Major-General Scott, communicated in his General Order No. 59, of yesterday's date, Major-General Butler hereby assumes command of the army of Mexico.

"In entering upon the duties assigned him, General Butler cannot be unmindful that he succeeds a General familiar alike with the science and the art of war, and who has but recently brought to a glorious termination one of the boldest campaigns to be found in its annals. He, however, feels less diffidence in assuming the important and responsible command assigned him, from the conviction that he is aided and sustained by many of the talented and experienced officers who contributed nobly to our recent success in arms, and by a gallant army who have learned too well the road to victory easily to mistake it.

"The orders and instructions issued by Major-General Scott for the government of this army will be continued in force.

"By order of Major-General Butler.

"(Signed) "L. THOMAS, A. A.-G."

When the news of these disputes reached Washington, they caused painful anxiety to the Cabinet, and it was not until after full deliberation that the government acted. On the 13th day of January, 1848, the orders of the War Department were issued: these embraced the recall of Scott, and the appointment, by direction of the President, of a Court of Inquiry, to consist of Brevet Brigadier-General N. Towson, Paymaster-General, Brigadier-General Caleb Cushing, and Colonel E. G. W. Butler, Third Dragoons (the above order was modified by detailing Brevet Colonel Wm. G. Belknap, of the Fifth Infantry, a member, in the place of Colonel Butler) members, to assemble in Mexico, to inquire and examine into the charges and allegations preferred by Major-General Winfield Scott against Major-General Gideon J. Pillow and Brevet Lieutenant-Colonel James Duncan, Captain of the Second Regiment of Artillery, and the charges or matters of complaint presented by way of appeal by Brevet Major-General William J. Worth, Colonel of the

Eighth Regiment of Infantry, against Major-General Winfield Scott; and also into any other matters connected with the same, as well as such other transactions as may be submitted to the consideration of the court; and, after duly investigating the same, the court will report the facts in each case, together with its opinion thereon, for the information of the President.

In a letter of the same date with these orders, the Secretary of War wrote to General Scott, giving him the reasons why the President had determined upon a court of inquiry rather than a court martial, and said: "Desirous to secure a full examination into all the matters embraced in the several charges which you have presented against Major-General Pillow and Brevet Lieutenant-Colonel Duncan, as well as the charges or grounds of complaint presented against you by Brevet Major-General Worth, and deeming your presence before the court of inquiry which has been organized to investigate these matters indispensably necessary for this purpose, you are directed by the President to attend the said court of inquiry, wherever it may hold its sittings; and when your presence before or attendance upon the court shall no longer be required, and you are notified of that fact by the court, you will report in person at this Department for further orders."

There were various and sincere efforts made in Mexico to settle these difficulties before the meeting of the court, in order to prevent the injury to the service likely to arise therefrom. They were mainly successful: the fiery spirit of Worth was appeased; for he had been released from arrest, and restored to command, until his appeal had been disposed of; he withdrew his charges against General Scott, although it is well known it was against the wishes of the latter. General Scott refused to prosecute his charges against General Worth, and withdrew those against Lieutenant-Colonel Duncan. In the case of General Pillow, the proceedings went on; they were interesting and lengthy, involving not alone the operations of the army in the Valley, but, incidentally, much of the history of the entire war.

The opinion of the court put an end at once and forever to these troubles. It concluded thus: "The court is of opinion that no further proceedings against General Pillow in the case are called for by the interest of the public service."

During the investigation there were offered in evidence several letters written by Mexicans in the city to parties outside, which were intercepted and captured by the American guard at Tacubaya. Their authenticity has never been questioned. I give them, with the testimony of several of our officers, as matters of interest, interwoven with the thread of my history.

THE INTERCEPTED LETTERS.

(WRITTEN BY MEXICANS.)

"SAN ANTONIO, August 19.

"Yesterday we commenced firing upon the enemy with our cannon, and killed some men and horses. To-day, up to 12 M., we have fired but few shots, and the enemy are retreating, with the object, I suppose, of going to Tacubaya by the way of Pedregal (Contreras). They have a long distance to march, and I do not know what will become of them in their unfortunate situation. Every day is a loss to them and a gain to us. The struggle will be severe, but favorable to us, as the measures we have taken are very good, and they will not laugh this time in their beard, as they have on former occasions.

"DN. P. I."

The following letter is from a member of the Mexican Congress, and is marked *private*.

"MEXICO, August 21, 1847.

"MY DEAR FRIEND,—I have before me your welcome letter of the 10th instant, in which, among other things, you are pleased to point out to me the reasons why you had suspended our correspondence. The idea you present to me, that I ought not to leave this place before having arranged everything relative to that ———, is a good one, but cannot be realized at present, owing to the afflicting circumstances which overwhelm us, everything being in the greatest disorder, and there being in fact no Congress, and government occupying itself only with matters of the war, and absolutely no other business can be attended to. In truth, this war is going to cease, as I suppose, because, on the 19th and 20th, at the gates of Mexico, our nation has covered itself with mourning and dishonor, and our generals and chiefs, in particular, with opprobrium. There is not even left to us the glory to say, with that French personage well known in history, that 'All is lost but our honor,' as our army has long since lost both honor and shame, which is not necessary to prove, when this capital groans with sorrow and anger against those who call themselves its defenders. The enemy has as yet not soiled with his tread the palaces of the Montezumas, but that is because a suspension of hostilities has caused him to pause in his triumphant march. This suspension, which has no other object than to collect the wounded and to bury the dead, as some say, has also another purpose, and that is to see the propositions of peace from the Government of Washington, of which Mr. Nicholas Trist is the bearer. The actual government, that is to say, the President, who finds himself compromised before the nation, has sent a message to Congress, which I take to be a matter of mere form, that upon hearing the above-mentioned propositions he would use only the powers belonging to him by the constitution. The Congress, besides the fact that it does not exist, there being assembled to-day but twenty-five deputies, as yet has nothing to do with the matter, so that the message of the President seems to me to be untimely; nevertheless, being so or not, Congress, as I said before, as it does not exist, can do nothing. From this I deduce, with other friends of the same opinion, the following results: that the case being an urgent one, the enemy waiting an answer at the gates of the city, a meeting of Congress being impossible in order to review treaties which must be concluded at the latest next week, the executive is necessarily obliged to assume powers not conceded to it by the constitution,—to wit, that of approving treaties after having made them. In a normal state of the country, this would be an assumption and against law, so that the executive, in order to exercise this power, finds it necessary to use revolutionary means. Hence the necessity for a dictatorship, which is already announced to us, and I think that but a few days will elapse before this will be realized. Be on the lookout. If I learn anything more I will inform you of it. It is true that if our army had been successful we should have fallen under a dictatorship, about which our military chiefs have so much occupied themselves, and perhaps they were dreaming of that when they were all beaten; but, being beaten, the same hope remains, with this difference, that as they must have something to lean upon, that support I suppose will now be the Yankees. Be that as it may, I will soon ascertain and tell you. I will not occupy myself in giving you a minute description of how the action was brought on and how lost, nor will I give you a formal opinion of the motives of the parties: however, I will tell you what I hear from rational and well-informed people. General Valencia, the rival of Santa Anna, wished the glory of defeating the enemy; but he needed assistance, which should have been sent him. Well, the battle once commenced, whether right or wrong, Santa Anna looked upon the rout of Valencia as a cold spectator, sending him no assistance, after which everything was rout and disorder on our part. You can make such commentaries as you please, but bear in mind, in order to make no mistakes, that our army was composed of twenty-four or twenty-five thousand men, and that of the enemy of only twelve thousand men, and that after the actions of the 19th and 20th our forces do not amount to over eleven thousand men, all of whom are frightened to death. Among the misfortunes which have befallen us, we have in the hands of the enemy many hundreds of prisoners, including the battalion of Independence and Bravo, the loss of Perdigan, Blanco, and Frontera, and other generals, and a great many killed. The ex-President Anaya and many others are prisoners, all our artillery lost, and our regular troops dispersed or cut to pieces.

"My friend, in all our misfortunes I do not note, as some people will have it, that there has been any treason or secret understanding, but I must say that there is great weakness and ignorance, and very little honor shown on the part of our generals-in-chief. We must only look to God for the salvation of our country. I am pleased that you intend to enter into relationship with the ministers and with his excellency the President; but I must recommend that you be very respectful in your letters, that you touch their pride without adulation. The minister of T—— says he will answer your note.

"No one knew of the intentions Valencia had; but after his rout it was said that had he gained the victory he would have overpowered Santa Anna and made himself dictator; for which purpose he had already named his ministers, and had promised the rank of general to several of his friends. Others say that Valencia was in league with the enemy; but this, to speak the truth, I cannot and shall never believe. However, the man (Valencia) who has been ordered to be shot by Santa Anna has escaped through the State of Mexico, which government has received him well, which I do not understand.

"Should there be a dictatorship or not, you must be very vigilant and take care of our interests; that is to say, should our territory not be benefited, that we shall not lose. I have heard it announced that the States of Jalisco, Guanajuato, and Zacatecas, etc, wish to make a separate republic, but I do not know what to think, Colina; on which account it would be necessary for them to think us instruments (tools) to be cheated. Others say that those States which are against the army will annex themselves, together with other States of the North, to the United States of America.

"August 21, 1847.

"OLD MAN,—Although I am a regidor (a civil officer), still I resolved to go to the fight, as I could no longer remain in the city taking care of disorderly women and drunkards. I determined to see the fate of my unfortunate country; consequently, on Tuesday last, I received an order from the Minister of War and government, directing me to join General Alcorta, as his aide-de-camp; and on Wednesday morning I went to the Peñon, resolved to endure all the privations of a campaign and to see in what I could serve my country. The enemy presented himself on Thursday morning before us, in order to allow their engineers to make a reconnaissance of our position, but he did not like the *patato*, and on Sunday night Santa Anna heard that the enemy had certainly taken the route towards Tlalpan (San Augustin). On Monday morning at nine o'clock we commenced our march towards the same place (by the city), and on Tuesday, after an examination of the place, we saw that we could not make resistance there, and it was resolved that we should take up our position at San Antonio. That same afternoon the Yankees arrived at San Augustin at 2 P.M. We proceeded with the greatest activity to make preparations for resistance, and ordered the heaviest pieces of ordnance to be brought from Peñon to San Antonio, and we protected our right flank as much as possible, fearing that the enemy might take advantage of us in that quarter. We made ditches and redoubts, and General Perez's brigade, composed of four thousand infantry, and seven hundred horse, of the hussars, who were at Jalapa, was ordered to go around by Coyoacan (near San Angel) The Fifth Brigade, composed of Victoria, Independence, Hidalgo, and Bravos, were ordered to march to Churubusco; this brigade was composed of two thousand men, and generally called Polkas. On Wednesday the Yankees presented themselves at the hacienda of Coapa, about the fourth of a league from San Antonio. There must have been seven or eight hundred men; and we fired several shots at them with our twenty-four-pound piece, and some shells, with a good result. In the mean time I took a nap at general headquarters, about half a league this side of San Antonio, where Bravo commanded. Day before yesterday (Thursday) we continued firing cannon on the enemy, and at one o'clock we observed that Valencia, who was posted at Magdalena to impede the enemy that way, commenced firing cannon. The fire was heavy, when an aide of Valencia's arrived, saying that he was being surrounded, and we sent an aid to Perez, and another to Mexico to Lombardini (Minister of War), in order that he might tell Rangel to march with his two thousand men, together with Perez's brigade, to the support of Valencia. At about half-past three o'clock in the afternoon we found ourselves in front of the enemy, who were taking a position on the left flank of Valencia, who, the enemy, on seeing five thousand men who came to reinforce Valencia, commenced covering themselves in the bushes and behind the church of San Geronimo. However, the enemy's forces in front of Valencia continued to fire upon him, and he, Valencia, returned their fire with twenty-one pieces of cannon. A little before dark we received three light pieces we had sent for, and we fired six times with good result. I had proposed not to ask where we were going, and what was my astonishment when, at night, we were ordered to retire to San Angel, two and a half leagues distance from Valencia's camp! We there met Rangel's division; and ours, together with his, amounted to twelve thousand men.

"Well, old gentleman, instead of marching early the next morning to the beautiful position we left on the 19th, we did not start till after six o'clock, merely, as it were, to see the destruction of Valencia, and we had not arrived at the position of the preceding day when we met two flying soldiers, at about seven o'clock, who brought the fatal news of the complete rout of Valencia. Then Don Antonio (Santa Anna) gave orders for our return to Mexico, as it was to be made another Troy. Rangel's brigade was ordered to take possession of the citadel, and Santa Anna gave Perez and Bravo orders to retire from San Antonio, as, San Angel being taken, we were cut off by the enemy; and you can imagine the confusion and the destruction of the morale of our army which ensued. In moving our artillery and ammunition we were put to much inconvenience and delay; for, as it had rained the night previous, the wheels stuck in the mud, and the mules, fatigued, could not haul them. The result was that, when the Yankee observed our movements, and saw us withdraw our pieces from the embrasures at San Antonio, he detached two columns, one by the Pedregal (rough, volcanic ground), and the other down the main road, and consequently took San Antonio; and most of Alvarez's troops, brought from the south, were made prisoners. Whilst this was going on at San Antonio, the same troops which had routed Valencia were detached in two columns, one of which attacked Churubusco, where, after a small resistance, the companies of Independence and Bravo were taken prisoners, as also other companies that were cut off in their retreat. The other column came down the main road and attacked the bridge by the same name, where our wagons (returning from San Antonio and fast in the mud) served them as trenches, and, after an attack of infantry alone, they took our position, which appeared impregnable, putting us shamefully to flight, and, had the enemy been any other, they would have gone directly into Mexico, for our cursed soldiers, frightened to death, were bellowing in the streets, 'Here come the Yankees!' Finally Santa Anna resolved to defend the city at the first line; and, if our soldiers would not run, we had a sufficient number left to defend this unfortunate city.

"But now they speak of a capitulation, or I know not what. The result is that the Yankees can march directly into Mexico at any hour they please, owing to the cowardice and ——— of our generals-in-chief. Bassadra, Mora Villamil, and Aranjois started at daybreak this morning, with orders from Pacheco, to ask Scott for thirty hours' armistice, in order to bury the dead and collect the wounded. Santa Anna became very angry, and said, This cursed Pacheco has made a fool of himself and compromised me, which remark having come to the ears of Pacheco he resigned. Some say it was a preconcerted affair. I will now give you, my old man, my opinion of all this. Valencia wished to be the hero, but had not the elements to make him so. Santa Anna wished to destroy him, and, by not sending him reinforcements day before yesterday, he has lost the nation. Keep this to yourself. Valencia received positive orders not to engage in fight; but, notwithstanding these orders, and the order to spike his artillery and retire if necessary, he remained, and replied that he considered himself strong enough to beat the enemy, and that his army from the north (it was from San Luis Potosi) could not be overcome, much less would it retreat before the enemy. From all I have said, you will judge the future destiny of our unhappy country.

"JUAN."

From a young lawyer to his father.

"MEXICO, August 21, 1847.

"DEAR FATHER,—The end has proved, in the most unequivocal manner, the correctness of our prophecies. The brigade under Valencia was completely routed between seven and eight o'clock yesterday morning, and, in continuation, the same fate befell the brigade of Perez, stationed at Coyoacan, and the troops at Churubusco.

"Who is to be punished for these disasters? The public voice accuses Santa Anna of having been a cold and impassive spectator of the rout of Valencia, whilst his assistance might possibly have decided the battle in our favor. The Yankees surrounded Valencia, and some of them placed themselves between him and Santa Anna, without any interruption from the latter. Some say that Valencia disobeyed the orders of Santa Anna, and Santa Anna was piqued by the disobedience; but this does not lessen the culpability of the rascal who gratifies a private feeling and thereby jeopardizes the most sacred interests of his country.

"The fact is that everything is lost, and the Yankees will be here to-morrow.

"J. W."

From a member of Congress.

"MEXICO, August 21, 1847.

"LOVED FRIEND,—The 19th and 20th of August have been to Mexico days of mourning and ignominy, as we have lost a great many valiant Mexicans, and our immense army has been routed by a handful of adventurers. We are all choking with grief at such a catastrophe, and we fear the sad consequences of the triumph of the enemy. The enemy has not yet entered the city, but they are at our very gates, awaiting the answer of our government, which has already entered into negotiations for peace. What will follow this negotiation, God knows. What does the United States want? Who knows? Congress cannot assemble, nor will it assemble; therefore I shall go to you in a few days, as I am anxious to see you and my family. Work for your country. Do not cease your labor. Do what you can to protect the public institutions, the arts, sciences, etc.

"L. B."

The first sheet of the original of this letter was lost.

"Scott, a man of superior talents in the art of war, as it appears, considering the position of Valencia very advantageous, established a small portion of his troops in a ravine very near our batteries, from whence he could use his muskets to advantage without injury from us, he, Scott, having no artillery. Afterwards he sent a column, with three light pieces of artillery, to take a position on the heights on the right of Valencia's camp, and another body of troops on the left of Valencia, in order to flank this general. At about six o'clock in the morning of the 20th of August he obtained his object, having troops concealed on both flanks of Valencia, and a very few in front, with a number of wagons, to call the attention of Valencia that way.

"The column which on the previous afternoon had taken position on the right of Valencia, Scott ordered should get in the rear during the night, and the body of troops that were in front of Valencia the same afternoon were divided, one part of which took the right of Valencia; and in the mean time he had sent reinforcements to the body stationed on the left, obliging his soldiers to cross a river half-body deep. In this manner Valencia during the night was entirely cut off, and at six o'clock the next morning he was attacked at the same time in the front, in the rear, and on both flanks. The engagement lasted about two hours, the result of which was that all our artillery was lost, with the entire train, ammunition and all, a great many killed and wounded, and those who were not made prisoners were entirely dispersed. On the afternoon of the day previous, Valencia, seeing that he was in danger of being flanked, asked assistance of Santa Anna, who ordered him to retire immediately; but he, Valencia, did not retire, probably because he considered victory possible. Valencia did not send for reinforcements once, but several times, on all which occasions he was refused by Santa Anna, and the order to retire was repeated, on account of which, after the unfortunate result of the engagement, Santa Anna ordered this general to be shot for disobedience. Some assure us there is foundation for this order; for Valencia was very obstinate, and thereby caused the loss of the whole army. Still, others do not think so, as having behaved with valor saves him from all discreditable imputation.

"My opinion is that Santa Anna should have sent Valencia reinforcements, and should have procured a victory by any means, and after that chastised him for his disobedience of orders. In this manner he would have rendered an important service to the nation, and it would have been a salutary example for generals-in-chief in future. Scott, having destroyed our best troops, the flower of the army, then proceeded with his forces and attacked the main army immediately afterwards, that is to say, those stationed at San Antonio and Churubusco and Mexicalcingo, thereby effecting in one single day the destruction of an army of more than thirty thousand men. The North American general, in a strange country, has fought us in detail and destroyed our large army, a thing which our general should have done with respect to his army.

"It is now five o'clock in the afternoon, and the enemy has sent in an intimation allowing forty-eight hours for the evacuation of this city, so that their troops may occupy it. Our troops, which with great difficulty have been brought together, do not exceed eight or nine thousand men, with which we can do nothing, as they have lost their morale.

"The companies of Bravo and Independence, with the exception of a few killed, are prisoners. Generals Salas and Gorostiza are prisoners, as also others, whose names I do not recollect.

As yet I hear only of the death of Generals Méjia and Frontera, colonel of cavalry. It is also said, but not certainly, that Perdigan was killed. I have just been told that Bravo is a prisoner, and also Anaya."

TESTIMONY BEFORE THE COURT OF INQUIRY AT THE CITY OF MEXICO.

"Brigadier-General Persifer F. Smith, duly sworn.

"Question by prosecution.—By whose orders did the witness pass the Pedregal, near the enemy, on the afternoon of August 19th last; about what hour did he reach the hamlet called San Geronimo, that afternoon; what does the witness know of any plan or order of battle respecting an attack by the American forces on the enemy's left flank, rear, or intrenched camp, coming from Major-General Pillow, and by whom was the plan actually executed upon that camp, conceived, laid down, and executed, on the morning of the 20th of August?

"Answer.—My brigade was in General Twiggs's Division. That division, by General Scott's order, communicated through General Twiggs to me, passed through San Augustin, and in front of General Pillow's Division, to cover that division in making a road by which the army might reach the San Angel road to turn the position at San Antonio. That was the explanation that accompanied the order for our movement through San Augustin and to the front of General Pillow. After passing a hill or mound to the right, we got under the fire of the enemy's position at Contreras. General Twiggs then ordered the advance, composed of two companies of riflemen, to drive the skirmishers of the enemy, which were in the corn in front, and cover the engineers in their reconnaissance. While that was doing, Magruder's Battery came to the front. On the report of the engineers, the battery was ordered to advance, and I was ordered with my brigade to support it. General Twiggs at the same time turned Taylor's Battery and Riley's Brigade off to the right, and they soon disappeared around the corn-field and into the Pedregal; one of the pieces of Magruder's Battery got fast in a stone wall, through which it was passing, which delayed us a few minutes. Just as we started again, General Pillow rode up. He asked me where General Twiggs was. I told him he had gone in that direction, pointing to the right, and he turned and went after him; at that very moment, as he turned off, I entered the corn-field, and could see no more of him.

"The next I saw of either of these general officers—General Twiggs or General Pillow—was after the action, next morning. General Twiggs joined the division just as its head was marching out of the village of San Geronimo. General Pillow came up to the head of the column where I was, just before entering San Angel, near some ruined arches of an aqueduct, on the left-hand side going in.

"The only orders I had received up to the time of General Pillow's turning off to the right, to follow General Twiggs, was the first order of General Scott in relation to the movement on to the San Angel road. The order of General Twiggs to move to the front and support Magruder's Battery, with some orders of detail, in the mean time, from General Twiggs. General Pillow gave me no order at all. Magruder's Battery moved forward and occupied a position pointed out by the engineers, and I moved my brigade to the left, and in a position to support the battery. There was a very heavy fire from the enemy's artillery, and the attack directly in front would have occasioned a very great loss. To turn their position by our left would not cut their line of retreat; and, seeing the church of the village between their position and the city, I determined to move round by our right into that village and take possession of it. I called the officers of the battalion together to explain my object, and that I should execute it in a few minutes if no orders came up to the contrary. After waiting probably fifteen minutes longer, to see if any order should come from the rear, I directed Captain Magruder to open again his fire, which had been pretty much silenced by the enemy, in order to cover my movement to the right. I then moved off by the right flank, filing round and then toward the village. I happened to come out from the Pedregal along with the rear of a regiment that was under the command of General Cadwalader. I do not know what regiment it was, but think from other circumstances that it was

Morgan's regiment. It was more than an hour before sunset when we got on the open field on the right of the village. As we started from the position of Magruder's Battery, we saw reinforcements coming out from the city. When we came out from the Pedregal, they were formed in considerable force between the village and San Angel, their left on a wood, their line perpendicular to the San Angel road. As my brigade was forming after getting to the village, these reinforcements filed round by their right flank and formed in two lines parallel to the road. At this moment General Cadwalader came up and reported to me. I inquired, first, if Colonel Riley's Brigade was over there, but could get no information about it. I then, in order to make force against the new line of the enemy, ordered General Cadwalader to form his brigade, or four regiments, by a movement by his flank in a line parallel to the enemy. I put Major Dimick's regiment of artillery in the orchard on the main road leading from Contreras to San Angel, and formed the third regiment and the rifles on the right flank of the village in column. I directed a company from Lieutenant-Colonel Graham's regiment, and Lieutenant Smith's engineer company, to take possession of the church in the centre of the village. Shortly after, an officer reported that he had met Lieutenant Porter, of the Fourth Artillery, who had informed him that Riley's Brigade was then at the farther end of the village, or beyond it, and Colonel Riley soon after reported to me that his brigade was there. The enemy in front were commanded by Santa Anna, those in camp by General Valencia, though then we did not know who commanded them. After examining Santa Anna's position, I ordered an attack upon it; Riley to attack towards his left, Cadwalader about one hundred and fifty yards to the right of Riley, and retire in echelon, both in column, by division, left in front. Riley was to pierce the right of the enemy's line about two battalions from the right, and then retreat to the right and take the enemy in flank; Cadwalader to form to the front. This was just about sunset, when the order was given. General Cadwalader had examined the ravine in his front, and reported that, though difficult, it could be passed. Riley soon returned, and reported his brigade ready to march out. In a few minutes afterwards General Cadwalader came up for some explanation of the order, and reported that the ground occupied by his brigade was so difficult, from ditches, walls, and bushes, that it would be some time before he could get his regiments out, as the staff-officers had to make great circuits on account of the obstructions, in order to convey orders for the movement to the different regiments.

"By this time it had got so dark that you could scarcely perceive the enemy's lines as he stood under the brow of the hill; and, as it would be, evidently, quite dark before we crossed the ravine, the order to attack was countermanded.

"Colonel Riley mentioned that while he had been to the upper end of the village, and outside of it towards the enemy, Captain Canby and Lieutenant Tower, engineers, had reconnoitered the ground towards Valencia's position, and had found that the ravine in front of the village led up entirely in rear of Valencia's camp, and that infantry could move up it. I then determined to attack before day, in that direction, and, upon my saying that I should be very glad to communicate my position and intentions to General Scott, Captain Lee volunteered to go to him. I desired him to go over and report that we should march out at 3 o'clock, attack Valencia's position in the rear, and requested that such diversion as could be made might be made on the front of said position. I then sent Lieutenants Brooks and Tower to examine again this ravine after dark, in order that we might be sure to find it before daylight in the morning. I then disposed of the troops to defend the place if attacked in the night, and to march out with most facility before day. After the return of Lieutenants Brooks and Tower, I sent for General Cadwalader, Colonel Riley, and Major Dimick, the commanders of the three brigades, and gave to each detailed instructions what he was to do in the attack in the morning, providing particularly for the case of an attack on us by Santa Anna while we were marching out to attack Valencia. About 10 o'clock, General Shields's Aide, Lieutenant Hammond, came up and reported to me that the general, with two regiments, had got through the Pedregal, and was lying between, I think, one of the ravines, at the edge of the Pedregal, and the road. Being

29

under the impression that I ranked General Shields, I directed that his two regiments should occupy the position that Major Dimick had occupied when we first got over,—that was the orchard in the road,—directing that the whole of my own brigade should then join the column that was moving out to the attack. About 12 o'clock General Shields came himself. I repeated the instructions to him, still under the impression that I ranked him; and he, with great delicacy, as well as with great magnanimity, did not even hint at his actual position, which was that of my senior. He went and joined his brigade, which was then in the orchard. He was to occupy the village after we marched out. A few minutes before 3 o'clock, Riley's Brigade marched out; two of Cadwalader's regiments followed; the other two, which were at the further end of the village, and in very difficult ground, not being ready. General Cadwalader undertook to remain and bring them up in time; Major Dimick followed the two leading regiments of Cadwalader with my brigade, and then the two other regiments of Cadwalader followed. Owing to the extreme difficulty of the path, it took us three hours until Riley's Brigade got into position in the rear of the enemy's works. It had been broad daylight for some time before he arrived there. As the enemy had a great deal of cavalry about their position, Riley was ordered to attack in two columns, and to deploy when the nature of the ground would permit him. Cadwalader's Brigade had been intended to make face against Santa Anna, if he moved to the assistance of Valencia, and Dimick to have assisted in either the one or the other attack, as circumstances might require. But Santa Anna, during the night, had withdrawn his infantry to some houses at the upper end of San Angel, so that, when it got to be broad day, we could only see Santa Anna's cavalry in its position, and the head of his infantry a great distance off, returning to its position. He was so far off that it was evident we had nothing to fear from any movement he could make. Just as Riley's column was formed for attack, cavalry were seen moving out from Valencia's position up towards the mountains. As they might by that way turn Riley's right flank, and as it was not necessary to pay any further attention to Santa Anna's force, I directed that Cadwalader's Brigade should also form in two columns, one to move round on Riley's right flank and rear, and the other on his left flank. This order was communicated to the senior officer of the two first regiments that had marched out; and at this moment General Cadwalader came up with the other two, and immediately the attack commenced. Seeing that there was no necessity for reserving any troops to meet the force under Santa Anna, Dimick was ordered to face to the left, and advance in line across the ravine, against the flank of Valencia's work, at the same time. I forgot to mention that the Engineer company and Rifles had been thrown on Riley's left and front, under the brow of the hill, to clear his front of the skirmishers.

"The whole of the enemy's works and position were carried at one sweep. A good many of the fugitives were intercepted by General Shields, at his position. After directing the artillery, prisoners, pack-mules, etc., to be secured, I directed the column to be formed to advance in pursuit of the enemy. I sent an order to the rear that Major Gardner's regiment of artillery should take charge of the captured artillery and ammunition; and another regiment of infantry, Colonel Trousdale's I think, to take charge of the other captured property; and General Shields's Brigade to take charge of the prisoners. I moved on, however, towards San Angel before these dispositions were completed; and I believe they were altered afterwards by other officers who came up. As the Rifles and Third Infantry moved out from among the incumbrances which were strewn along the road, General Twiggs came up; he directed the pursuit to be continued, making occasional short halts, until the other regiments could get into their positions in the column. We continued until, on approaching San Angel, General Pillow came to the head of the column and assumed command."

"MEXICO, April 16, 1848.

"Colonel Bennet Riley,* U.S.A., duly sworn for the defense.

---

* This gallant old soldier was born in Saint Mary's County, Maryland. He entered the army as an ensign in the Rifle Regi-

"Question by defense.—Was witness upon the battle-field of Contreras, on the 19th of August? if so, he will please state his movements upon that field upon that day.

"Answer.—I was upon the battle-field of Contreras on the 19th of August last. After Twiggs's Division joined General Pillow on the hills in front of the works, General Pillow rode up to my brigade and gave me two or three orders to move a little further to the right, or a little to the left, and, finally, to move forward. After halting a short time, General Pillow gave me an order to cross the Pedregal. I asked him if General Twiggs knew of the order. He said he did, and that he had sent the order to him. I think the direction was, as well as I can recollect, to cross the Pedregal, turn the enemy's left, and he would support me. He had scarcely done speaking, when Lieutenant Brooks, the acting Adjutant-General of the Division, came up and gave me a similar order. I executed the movement, and did not see General Pillow again that day.

"Question by defense.—Where was witness when the order spoken of by General Pillow was delivered? was he at or near the base of the hill? and where was witness's command when Brooks delivered the order?

"Answer.—I was on the left flank, I think, of the brigade, near some trees, and the brigade was in the same position, when I received the order through Lieutenant Brooks; as it was when General Pillow gave the order, I was near the Pedregal.

"Question by defense.—When witness asked General Pillow if General Twiggs knew of the order then given him (witness),

---

ment, in the year 1813; served through the war with Great Britain, and through the Florida and Black Hawk Indian wars. Brevetted Colonel U.S.A., for gallantry at the battle of Chokachatta, Florida; Brigadier-General U.S.A. for gallantry at Cerro Gordo, and Major-General U.S.A. for gallantry at Contreras. He was the first Military Governor of the newly-acquired Territory of California, and transferred the military to the civil powers, upon the inauguration of Peter H. Burnet, the first Governor, on the 20th day of December, 1849, at San José, the then capital of the new State of California.

did or did not General Pillow say to witness that he had given Twiggs the same order, and told witness he would probably meet Twiggs, who would deliver him the same order, and if he did not meet Twiggs, that he (witness) would go forward and execute the movement without further order?

"Answer.—He did not say that he had given the order to General Twiggs; he did tell me to go forward and I would probably meet General Twiggs, who would give me the same order about the cornfield, but if I did not meet him to go forward and execute the movement.

"Question by defense.—Did witness see and understand from the movement of General Smith's Brigade and the explanation and the orders given him (witness), that General Smith had then moved off to attack the enemy's works in front? and did witness understand that he was to turn the enemy's left and gain his rear? and if so, for what purpose?

"Answer.—General Smith's Brigade had moved off as I understood, to support Magruder's Battery; I never heard anything of the attack on Contreras, how it was to be made, or anything of the kind at that time. I supposed that the attack was to be made in front, and that I was sent across the Pedregal to cut off the retreat of the enemy, and check reinforcements coming from the city. This was, however, only my supposition at the time; I never had any explanation given to me.

"Question by defense.—Where was Magruder's Battery placed in position? was it in front of the entrenched camp, or in some other position?

"Answer.—I thought it was in front or nearly so; I judged so from the firing; I did not go near the battery.

"Question by defense.—Did witness pass the Pedregal, pass through the village, and engage the enemy's Lancers in the rear of the enemy's position in several conflicts? if so, was he or not endeavoring to gain the rear of the enemy's entrenched camp, with the view of assaulting that work? if not, why did he pass so far to the rear and beyond the road leading from the city to the camp?

"Answer.—I did pass the Pedregal and the village; I engaged the enemy in the first instance, in front of the village, between the village and the city. I passed the village and drove the enemy's Lancers from their position, which was on our right, but not exactly in rear of the entrenched camp. I passed through the village with the view of reconnoitering the rear of the enemy's works, and kept the enemy busy to cover my reconnaissance. I was not endeavoring to gain the rear with a view of assaulting the work; I passed so far beyond the village in chase of the enemy.

"Question by defense.—What was the object of making a reconnaissance? was it with the view of ascertaining the practicability of an assault from the rear, or with what view?

"Answer.—It was my object to get as much information of the practicability of an assault upon the rear as I could, to give my commanding officer, without knowing where or when he was going to make the general attack.

"Question by defense.—If witness had ascertained that an assault from the rear was *practicable*, and he had been *supported*, would he have assaulted that work on the 19th of August?

"Answer.—I should.

"Question by defense.—Did witness or not ascertain from the reconnaissance that an assault in the rear was practicable? and did he report that fact to Brigadier-General Smith?

"Answer.—I did discover that the assault in rear was practicable, and that it was the best possible place to attack the entrenched camp of Contreras; and I caused it to be reported to General Smith by Lieutenant Tower, engineer, that same evening about sundown.

"Question by defense.—Did witness on the 19th have a knowledge that General Cadwalader was sent to his support with four regiments; and that he was in the village of Ensalda that evening, shortly after witness left it, but was prevented from supporting witness by the large body of the enemy's reinforcements?

"Answer.—I never knew that there was a soul in the village belonging to the army, until I was returning to make a camp for the night; consequently, I did not know that he was stopped by a large force of the enemy. If I had known it I should have attacked the entrenched camp of Contreras on my own responsibility that evening.

"Question by prosecution.—Had or not any written or oral order been communicated to the witness on the said 19th of August last, either directly from general headquarters, or through Brigadier-General Twiggs, respecting the operations against the enemy?

"Answer.—Order No. 258 was read to me and brigade and regimental commanders at San Augustin, before I started, either by a staff-officer of General Scott or General Twiggs, I don't remember which; and he, the staff-officer, said that he had not time to copy it.

"Question by prosecution.—Had or had not the order, witness so heard read, any bearing or not upon the operations that followed against Ensalda and the enemy who might be found in that direction?

"Answer.—The order was to get everything ready, the tools and so forth; and that General Twiggs's Division should support General Pillow's; and that the army should gain the San Angel road; all of which I think bore upon the operations against the enemy—every part of it. General Pillow never gave me any instructions at all concerning the attack of the camp. I have always believed myself that any and every order from headquarters has a bearing upon the movements of the army. I knew of no instructions from headquarters further than the general order I have already stated.

"Question by prosecution.—On meeting Major-General Pillow at or near the captured camp on the 20th of August, did he then in conversation or remark claim to have given the plan of attack which had been so successfully executed?

"Answer.—He did not.

"Question by prosecution.—By whose order was the brigade of witness put in march from the captured camp, and again from Coyoacan, to support Twiggs, Smith, and Taylor, in the attack upon the convent?

"Answer.—By General Scott in person."

"Captain Joseph Hooker, Assistant Adjutant-General, for the defense, duly sworn.

"Question by defense.—Was witness present at a conference

of officers on the 11th of September last, at Piedad? If so, state what were the views of Major-Generals Scott and Pillow in reference to an early attack upon the enemy, in the direction of San Antonio (garita) and Chapultepec.

"Answer.—I was present during the greater part of that conference. I am confident, from the views expressed by General Scott, that he was decidedly in favor of attacking Chapultepec. He called on a number of officers present to express their views in regard to the proper point of attack, whether Piedad or Chapultepec. Several of the officers present, General Pillow among the number, evinced a great desire for more information than they possessed on the subject. They appeared to be anxious to know what position we should occupy in regard to the city and the interior defenses, after we gained possession of either one of those points. The difficulty appeared to be a want of knowledge of what was behind these two positions. General Pillow suggested or asked for information with regard to the citadel. Other officers present inquired as to the same fact, and suggested other difficulties on the Chapultepec route. There was one officer present, of whose views I could speak with more certainty, which was Captain Lee, who preferred the attack on Piedad.

"Question by defense.—What does witness mean by the Piedad works?

"Answer.—I mean the work at the San Antonio garita.

"Question by the defense.—Does witness chance to remember any prominent reasons advanced by General Scott in favor of attacking Chapultepec?

"Answer.—I know that General Scott said that he would have more elbow-room if he had Chapultepec; and also that he had reason to believe, or words to that effect, that he would be met by a white flag on taking it. I would also state that, during that conference, General Scott said to one of the engineers present that Captain Huger said he thought he could reduce Chapultepec with his batteries in one day. This was stated in form of a question when the engineer said he had his doubts.

"Question by defense.—At what hour of the night of the 11th of September did General Pillow move with his command from Piedad to Tacubaya, preparatory to the operations upon Chapultepec?

"Answer.—I think we moved between nine and ten o'clock at night.

"Question by defense.—What knowledge has witness of General Pillow having continued to direct the operations of the forces (after he was wounded) which made the successful assault upon Chapultepec on the 13th of September? state also what forces carried that work; was it those under his command, or other forces? if other forces, state what forces they were.

"Answer.—On the morning of the 13th, three regiments from General Pillow's Division, with a storming party from General Worth's Division, were ordered to move to the assault of Chapultepec. Four companies of the Voltigeur Regiment, under Lieutenant-Colonel Johnston, followed by the storming party under Captain Mackenzie, were the first troops put in motion. The balance of the Voltigeur Regiment, under Colonel Andrews, were the next to move to the attack. Colonel Johnston moved outside of the wall surrounding the grounds at the base of the hill at Chapultepec, the others passed through the Molino del Rey into the inside of the walls. The Ninth Infantry followed the Voltigeurs, and formed line of battle directly after passing through the gate into this field, at the base of Chapultepec. The Fifteenth Regiment of Infantry followed the Ninth, and formed line on the Ninth. In that order they moved forward to the attack. With slight interruptions they progressed until they reached the ditch inclosing part of the work on the summit of Chapultepec, at which place the Fifteenth, the Ninth, and a part of the Voltigeur Regiment, and the head of the storming party under Captain Mackenzie, were stopped by the wall inclosing the summit of the hill. Many of these men entered the ditch, and many of them concealed themselves behind rocks which lay upon the surface of the ground. The Voltigeurs that I refer to were particularly a part of Colonel Andrew's party; appeared at this time to be under the command of Major Caldwell. Colonel Johnston's command was more to the right. The hill prevented me from seeing the main body of the command. While these troops were occupying this position, the fire from the crest of the work directly in our front ceased. I saw several pieces discharged in the air behind the breastwork, but the

Mexicans appeared to be afraid to expose even their hands above the crest of the work. A fire, however, was delivered by the Mexicans from the roofs of the houses and from the windows, and at that time their right flank was occupied by the enemy. The fire did but little execution, as the shots were most of them high. The troops I have named, or the main body of them, were kept in this position I should think at least fifteen minutes —it seemed to me much longer—waiting for the ladders to come up. When the assaulting column was put in motion, these ladders were in rear of the storming party. After waiting some time with the troops at the top of the hill, I went after the ladders.

"In descending the hill, and nearly at the redan, about half-way up the hill, I saw the head of the Second Pennsylvania Regiment, the head of the South Carolina Regiment, and what I took to be the New York Regiment, for the colors were with that party, but which I have since been told were only two companies of the New York Regiment under Lieutenant Reid. The last named party were a little in the advance of the others, but they were all moving up the hill, and moving by a flank. These troops as I stood near the redan and facing down the hill were on my left; on my right was the head of Colonel Clark's Brigade. On reaching the foot of the hill, I found General Pillow wounded; I asked him where the ladders were, and said to him that we had more troops than were necessary at the top of the hill. I asked him for authority to take a regiment to attack the right flank of the enemy. He told me to take any regiment, and as the Eighth was on its way up the hill, I took the Sixth, which was directly in rear of the Eighth. On reaching the point on which the attack was intended to be made, we found that the ascent was very difficult. There was no cover, and that flank was occupied by the enemy, and they were firing very rapidly. I then directed Captain Hoffman to halt and move to the rear of Chapultepec with his command around the hill. I then returned to the troops who had been in advance, and reached the summit of the hill in time to see the first ladder planted to enter the work. It was planted in the bottom of the ditch, with one or two others; the others were laid across the ditch. The first man that I saw enter the work—and I think I saw the first one—was a private, I took to be of the Voltigeur Regiment; following him were officers and men rushing over the work in great rapidity. I think that the greater part of them belonged to General Pillow's Division, and to the regiments of his division I have before named. I think that the first officer that went into the work belonged to the Voltigeur Regiment,* and I know that the first colors that entered the work were those of the Voltigeur Regiment. When I entered the work—and I was not among the foremost—the terreplein was clear of our troops, except those that had entered on the side of which I speak. We had a number of men shot belonging to our party, by the cadets—they appeared to be—who were occupying the upper terreplein, the ground on the side of the work opposite to the point of our attack. They would not have fired upon us had an enemy been nearer to them than we were. I have said that the Voltigeurs, Ninth, Fifteenth Regiments, with a portion of the storming party, were the first as a body to enter Chapultepec; there may have been individuals of other regiments, but the regiments I have named were started in advance, and they kept it until they reached the summit of the hill, where they were so densely crowded together that it was impossible for any large body of men to pass through them."

CHAPTER XLII.

NEGOTIATIONS FOR PEACE.

ALTHOUGH Mr. Trist had been recalled, he had not yet left the country, and, acting in harmony and conjunction with General Scott, continuous efforts were made, through the channels heretofore referred to,

---

* Captain John E. Howard, of Baltimore, of the Voltigeur Regiment, grandson of Colonel John E. Howard, of the Maryland Line, in the war of the Revolution.

the British embassy and consulate at the city of Mexico, to make a treaty between the United States and the acting government at Querétaro.

On the 27th of November General Scott wrote to Mr. Marcy, informing him that commissioners had been appointed to negotiate for peace, but that, although they were in the city, they had not called on him, nor had they submitted to him any propositions whatever, although the government at Querétaro had been informed that he was at all times ready to send home any communication looking to a renewal of negotiations. He concluded by saying that it was doubtful whether the Mexican government or its commissioners would adopt that course.

On the 2d of February, 1848, General Scott wrote to the Honorable Secretary of War this important communication:

* * * * * * *

"I write, in haste, by the express who carries the *project* of a treaty, that Mr. Trist has, at the moment, signed with Mexican commissioners. If accepted, I hope to receive, as early as practicable, instructions respecting the evacuation of this country, the disposition to be made of wagons, teams, cavalry and artillery horses, the points in the United States to which I shall direct the troops, respectively, etc. (I have not yet read the treaty, except in small part.) In the same contingency, if not earlier recalled (and I understand my recall has been demanded by two of my juniors!), I hope to receive instructions to allow me to return to the United States as soon as I may deem the public service will permit, charging some other general officer with completing the evacuation, which ought, if practicable, to be finished before the return of the vomito, say early in May.

"In about forty days I may receive an acknowledgment of this report. By that time, if the treaty be not accepted, I hope to be sufficiently reinforced to open the commercial line between

Zacatecas and Tampico. The occupation of Querétaro, Guanajuato, and Guadalajara would be next in importance, and some of the ports of the Pacific the third. Meanwhile the collection of internal dues on the precious metals and the direct assessments shall be continued."

The dangers of a foreign war waged by a republic, no matter how justifiable the cause, need not be searched for in the speeches of Cicero, the doings of proconsuls, the history of Rome, or in the annals of later times. American citizens will reflect upon the subject-matter of the following letter and memoranda, and inquire *if General Scott had not been the pure man he was, what might he not have done, or any other general similarly situated, waging a war thousands of miles from the seat of our government?*

"HEADQUARTERS OF THE ARMY,
"MEXICO, February 6, 1848.

"SIR,—I have not reported on the subject of secret disbursements since I left Jalapa. First, because of the uncertainty of our communications with Vera Cruz, and, second, the necessity of certain explanations which, on account of others, ought not to be reduced to writing. I may, however, briefly add that I have never tempted the honor, conscience, or patriotism of any man, but have held it as lawful in morals as in war to purchase valuable information, or services voluntarily tendered me.

"Charging myself with the money received at Washington for the purposes indicated, the $150,000 levied upon this city for the immediate benefit of this army, in lieu of pillage, the proceeds of captured tobacco taken from the Mexican government, and with some other small sums, all of which I shall strictly account for, I have, on the other hand, expended $63,745.57 in blankets and shoes gratuitously distributed to enlisted men; $10,000 extra on account of hospitals, allowing $10 each to every crippled man discharged or furloughed; some $60,000, I think, for secret services, including a native spy company, whose pay, commencing in July, I did not wish to bring into account with the treasury, and I enclose herewith a draft for $100,000, making up according to the *memorandum*, also enclosed. I hope you will allow the draft to go to the credit of the Army Asylum, and make the subject known in the way you may deem best to the military committees of Congress. That sum is in small part the price of the American blood so gallantly shed in this vicinity, and, considering that the army receives no *prize money*, I repeat the hope that its proposed destination may be approved and carried into effect.

"Number one, of the same set of bills, is this day transmitted direct to the Bank of America.

"The remainder of the money in my hands, as well as that expended, I shall be ready to account for at the proper time and in the proper manner, merely offering this imperfect report to explain, in the mean time, the character of the $100,000 draft.

"I have the honor to remain, with high respect, sir, your obedient servant,

"WINFIELD SCOTT.

"The Honorable Secretary of War.

"Memorandum of account between Major-General Winfield Scott and Paymaster E. Kirby, at the city of Mexico, in the matter of the Asylum Fund.

"1848, January 19. By amount of gambling license, money received from Brigadier-General P. F. Smith	$9,000.00
"February 3. By the check of General Scott on Manning and Mackintosh	26,000.00
"February 3. By proceeds of tobacco sales received from Captain Lowry, account of late Captain Irwin	49,569.44
"February 5. By the check of Captain Grayson in favor of Surgeon Satterlee	2,650.40
"February 5. By the check of General Scott on Manning and Mackintosh	12,780.16
	$100,000.00

"Balance by my bill of exchange No. 18, in triplicate, in favor of Major-General Winfield Scott, upon the Paymaster-General, at ten days, at Bank of America, $100,000.

"[No. 18.] Pay of the army, $100,000.

"CITY OF MEXICO, January 21, 1848.

"At ten days' sight, for value received, please pay this my second of exchange (the first and third being unpaid) to the order of Major-General Winfield Scott, one hundred thousand dollars, on account of the pay of the army, for which I am accountable to the treasury. Payable at the Bank of America, city of New York, without further advice.

"E. KIRBY,

"Acting chief of the Pay Department at the headquarters of the army.

Brigadier-General N. TOWSON,

Paymaster-General United States Army,

City of Washington."

[Endorsed]

"The Bank of America, city of New York, will place the within amount to the credit of the Army Asylum, subject to the order of Congress.

"WINFIELD SCOTT,

"Major-General, etc."

Here was one hundred thousand dollars, the proceeds of gambling licenses, sales of captured tobacco, a levy upon a captured city, assigned for the benefit of an army under the immediate command of one who had distributed money to his soldiers without the shadow of other law than his own will. What might not a bad man do under similar circumstances, is the query I wish my countrymen to consider when war is suggested or advised.

I have said that General Scott was a pure man. He was, and so was General Taylor; and fortunate for our infant republic was the sterling integrity and genuine patriotism of its two chiefs in the war with Mexico.

Peña y Peña was again provisional President of Mexico, by virtue of his office as Chief Justice of the

Supreme Court, succeeding Anaya, whose term of office expired by limitation on the 8th of January, 1848, and who accepted the office of Secretary of War under Peña y Peña. Señor Rosa was the Secretary of State, with whom the chief responsibility of the new government rested. Its difficulties were innumerable, its dangers great and imminent. Protecting itself against the unfounded charge of bartering the national honor, it was at the same time resisting the pronunciamentos of Parédes and the insurrectionary movements of Alvarez; combating the friends of monarchy, and maintaining the army of Bustamente at Querétaro; struggling with honest zeal to keep alive and intact the government of their country, these officials, with Riva Palacios, the Minister of Justice, had to meet the stormy opposition of the majority of their countrymen and the vindictive machinations of disappointed generals, while endeavoring to heal the wounds of Mexico by an honorable peace with its invaders.

In an able address to the nation, Señor Rosa said truly

"That the existing government was that which had been formed when the country was without a head, and all the elements of strength and order were in utter confusion, and that one of the principal causes of the inability of the government to carry on the war was owing to the action of the generals in dispersing the army when discouraged by the results of the battles in the environs of the capital. The statements and insinuations that an ignominious treaty of peace had been concluded were calumnies. It is a calumny to assert that the national government has humbled itself to send propositions of peace to the cabinet at Washington, or that it has offered, in order to terminate the war, advantages which the same cabinet did not exact. His Excellency the President authorizes me to give the lie to these calumnies, and to assure you that, in the midst of the misfortunes of the country, the national honor has not been tarnished, and will not be under the present government, even should the condition of the republic become worse than it is. But it is also resolved to make peace, if the end of putting a stop to the calamities of a bloody and disastrous contest, which has been so long continued, can be accomplished."

This bold defense of the government, and its avowal of a determination to make peace, preceded a circular from the same minister, dated February 6, 1848, in which he announced to the Governors of States that the treaty of Guadalupe Hidalgo had been concluded. The main and chief difficulty of the administration of Peña y Peña was to secure its ratification by a Congress not *in esse*. An armistice had been wisely agreed upon by commissioners of the Mexican government, Generals Mora y Villamil and Quijano, and Generals Worth and Smith on the part of the Americans, in pursuance of an article in the treaty. One of the articles of this armistice is so notable, and its being announced in General Orders No. 18, March 6, 1848, the occasion of its being obeyed by the troops of our garrison at Jalapa, that I give it entire:

"ARTICLE 6. Whenever an election is to be held in any town or place occupied by the American troops, upon due notice thereof being given to the commanding officer, he shall march the whole of his force out of the limits of such town or place, and there remain with them until after the hour at which such elections should be concluded, leaving within the town or place only the force necessary for the security of his barracks, hospitals, stores, and quarters. And no person belonging to the American army shall by any means, or on any consideration, attempt to obstruct or interfere with any elections, in order that they may be conducted according to Mexican laws. In Vera Cruz the troops shall retire within the walls of the fortifications, and there remain until the election is concluded."

This article was introduced by the Mexican commissioners doubtless to save the government from the charge of the Congressmen to be elected being the choice of the American army. At any rate the article met with great disfavor in our army, though I believe it was the result of wise counsel, as was proved in the end.

It had leaked out that New Mexico and California had been ceded to us; and though it was likewise known we were to give Mexico fifteen millions of dollars, yet there was violent opposition to the cession of any territory, and members elect to Congress were afraid to assemble to assume the responsibility of severing the national domain. New elections were ordered, the government vigorously prosecuting its measures looking to the ratification of the treaty it had made, many wealthy citizens lending the aid of money and their influence, and finally the clergy seconding its efforts to assemble a congress at Querétaro.

The treaty had been sent to the United States, as the Secretary of War had been advised by General Scott, on the 2d of February, and early in March it was ratified by the Senate of the United States, to whom it had been transmitted by President Polk for its action. There were but slight modifications to the original articles, and to consummate the treaty

Messrs. Sevier, of the Senate, and Attorney-General Clifford, having previously resigned their respective offices, were sent as commissioners to the seat of the Mexican government.

Between the 5th of March and the 2d of June, 1848, the beginning and the end of the armistice agreed upon as a condition of the treaty, the fate of Mexico for a long series of years was to be settled.

In this period the elections took place, and the choice for President was General Don José Joaquin de Herrera, a native of Jalapa, of whose good name and character I have heretofore spoken. A Congress met, but there was no quorum until the 3d of May, though the election of Herrera had just shown that a change for the better had been effected, and the folly of continuing a war while Mexico was in such a distracted condition had been seen and felt by the good men of all parties.

Peña y Peña, still at the helm, as the time for the inauguration of Herrera had not yet arrived, strongly urged upon Congress the ratification of the treaty; the seasonable arrival of the American commissioners at Querétaro closed up the business so long, so anxiously, so earnestly labored for and desired, in the ratification of the treaty by the Mexican Congress on the 24th day of May, 1848.

The main features of this treaty were that Mexico gave to the United States the territories of New Mexico and California, and relinquished all claim to Texas and the country between the Nueces and the Rio Grande. In consideration of these grants, the United States were to pay to Mexico the sum of fifteen millions of dollars, and to assume the debts due by Mexico, estimated at three millions of dollars, to American citizens.

Thus I lived to see the war ended, and the objects for which I had taken up arms successfully vindicated. I sincerely hoped that a peace, lasting and honorable, between the two republics would continue, and that those who had fought against each other would henceforth and for ever be friends and allies.

CHAPTER XLIII.

END OF THE WAR—WE LEAVE MEXICO.

On the 29th day of May, 1848, at the city of Mexico, Major-General Butler announced in general orders that *the war was ended*, and that the object of it, a treaty of peace, just and honorable to both nations, had been duly ratified.

On the 12th of June the American flag was lowered from the National Palace, under a salute from Mexican batteries in the grand square, the Mexican flag hoisted with the same compliment, and Worth's Division, the rear of our army, marched out of the city of Mexico.

On the afternoon of the 15th we received orders to get ready to leave, and I copy from my journal:

June 16. At sunrise our regiment was formed in the plaza, and shortly after we took up our line of march for HOME. We halted for a short time at the garita of Vera Cruz, and I turned to take a last look at Jalapa, the garden of Mexico, and never had it seemed more beautiful. I really regretted to leave it, and our whole command seemed to feel with me.

We had abundant evidence of the good-will of many of its citizens, and I can unhesitatingly say that our departure was looked upon with sincere regret by a large portion of its people.

We halted and encamped at Encerro, where the whole of the volunteers were lying, except the Massachusetts and Pennsylvania regiments, which had moved off that morning.

June 17. The reveille was beat at 2 o'clock A.M., and with a bright moonlight we marched to Plan del Rio; we halted for the day at our old post, the National Bridge, and as soon as the ranks were broken, the men ran like boys out of school to visit the well-remembered haunts of former days.

June 18—Sunday. In the midst of heavy rain we left this morning at 3 o'clock and marched to the San Juan, where we halted to dry our blankets and wet clothing in the sun. At 8 o'clock P.M. we resumed our march, and at 1 o'clock A.M., the morning of the 19th, we arrived at Vergara; as soon as the guns were stacked, one rush was made, and the regiment was bathing in the waters of the Gulf. Oh, the luxury of this bath!

June 19. There being no vessels ready for us to embark in, and the Massachusetts and Pennsylvania regiments awaiting their turn ahead of us, I pitched my tent on the sands, in the identical place where I had put it when we landed last August.

June 20. This morning, with colors flying and music sounding, the Second Pennsylvania Regiment marched along the beach past our camp to embark from the mole at Vera Cruz; several vessels are to be seen in the offing, and we are in great hopes our turn will come in a few days.

June 21. This morning the Fourth Ohio Regiment marched past and embarked on a large ship lying off the castle.

June 22—Thursday. Happy day, and adieu to Mexico. At sunrise we struck our tents, and, marching through the city to the mole, we got on board a small steamer and were transferred to the decks of the steamer James L. Day, bound for New Orleans. As the steamer's capacity was not sufficient for our whole regiment, Companies A and F were embarked on the transport schooner Velasco, for the same destination. At noon we got under way, and, passing under the frowning walls of San Juan de Ulloa, before night the shores of Mexico had disappeared from our view. We watched its receding land, full of emotion; all eyes were turned toward it, and as it faded from the sight men looked at each other as if they were parting from home and from friends, so many had been the incidents and associations of ten months' service in that country. Soon there arose the favorite song of the regiment, "Columbia, the Gem of the Ocean;" and the voices of five hundred men swelled the anthem, "To the shrine of each patriot's devotion."

June 26. At noon we were in sight of the cupola of the St. Charles Hotel, and in the Mississippi, abreast of General Jackson's lines, so memorable in the history of the war with Great Britain. In an hour we were abreast of the levee in New Orleans, when Colonel Hughes went ashore for orders. We were ordered to proceed up the river to the Carrollton race-course, distant eight miles, and go into camp there.

Our surgeon, Dr. Stedman R. Tilghman, was sent on shore for medical treatment; he had been gradually sinking for the past four or five months, but none of us had serious apprehensions about his condition. He was much worse than we thought; going to see him on the ensuing day, I told him that if he wished me to remain I could easily get permission to do so. He rose from his cot, and replied, that I should go with the regiment, and that if it were his last request, he begged me to leave. Poor Tilghman! this was my last interview with him; we had been inseparable friends and companions since our first night on the beach together at Vera Cruz. The climate had been too trying on his constitution, and he succumbed to its influence. Descended from a Maryland family distinguished for its services to the country, he had abandoned the practice of his profession in the civil walks of life, to enter the army; an enthusiast in the science of medicine and surgery, he gave the whole of his energies and his superior natural and acquired abilities to their study and practice. No more faithful officer in the line of his duty could be found, no more honorable gentleman, than Surgeon Tilghman, of the District of Columbia and Maryland Regiment of Volunteers. He died at New Orleans, surrounded by sorrowing relatives and friends, on the 28th of July, 1848.

June 27. It being rumored that we were to be sent by sea from here to Baltimore, and the men being very averse to another sea-voyage in a transport ship, I went into the city of New Orleans, and returned with orders that we should go home by the way of the river.

June 28. Embarked on board the steamer John Hancock, and ascended the Mississippi. We spent the Fourth of July, the steamer halting for the purpose of accommodating us, at a noted place on the Ohio River, called "Cave in the Rock." A large concourse of the neighboring people had gathered here to attend a barbecue, which was largely attended by our regiment, and I think that the celebration of the Fourth of July at that barbecue will long be remembered at the "Cave in the Rock."

July 7. Arrived at Cincinnati; on the 9th—Sunday—the steamer Taglioni, on board which were some Pennsylvania troops, came alongside and commenced racing; for several hours, while under full speed, we were locked together, the men from either boat jumping on to the other; a scene of confusion and dangerous excitement ensued, which the officers of both regiments found it impossible to subdue or suppress. We expected every moment an explosion or the boats being set on fire from the fuel which was being put on the fires to increase the steam. We were finally separated, a volley of oaths being fired by the crews of the two steamers, whose animosity against each other seemed fierce and unrelenting.

July 10. At 9 o'clock A.M. we neared Pittsburg, the Taglioni close behind us. A steamer came down to us from the city with a committee of reception on board; we were to be received with all honors by the authorities. The Committee's steamer and the Taglioni made fast to the John Hancock, and the three approached the levee, where thousands had assembled to greet our arrival. We landed amid vociferous cheering, firing of cannon, ringing of steamboat bells, etc. Our reception was enthusiastic and highly gratifying; we paraded through the city, and from all hands and quarters the evidences of a hearty welcome were showered upon us.

July 12 When we landed, we were met with a telegraphic dispatch from the Adjutant-General U. S. Army, giving the regiment the option of being discharged at Pittsburg or Baltimore After many consultations and much difference of opinion, the regiment elected to be discharged here, and receive allowance for travel to Baltimore.

July 15. This evening the Pennsylvania officers gave a handsome entertainment to the officers of our regiment, at which I was present, and we parted as we had served,—as friends and comrades.

The First Pennsylvania Regiment arrived to-day, and many of its officers participated in the festivities of the evening.

July 20. Our companies having all been discharged and my duties ended, I left Pittsburg for Brownsville by the Monongahela River. Reaching here, I had come by steam direct from Vera Cruz well up into the interior of Pennsylvania, and was tired of steamboat navigation. I felt delighted to ride in a stage-coach, which I did to Cumberland, Maryland,

and thence by rail to Baltimore and my home, the home of my parents.

On the 24th day of July, 1848, I was honorably discharged from the service at Fort McHenry; and, closing these memoirs of two years in the armies of the United States, I bid you, my comrades, friends, and companions of the Battalion of Baltimore and Washington Volunteers, and the District of Columbia and Maryland Regiment, an affectionate good-by. I know you well; and the memory of the fidelity, the readiness, and the good nature with which you performed all the duties required of an American soldier in the field, will forever be associated with the proud recollection of your continuous acts of kindness done to me while serving with you in the War with Mexico. Once more—GOOD-BY.

CHAPTER XLIV.

CONCLUSION.

THE army and navy of the United States had co-operated zealously and had served harmoniously together in the prosecution of the war. In the far west and on the shores of the Pacific, Commodores Sloat, Stockton, Shubrick, Samuel F. Dupont, with Commanders Selfridge and Lavellette, had fought the seamen and marines side by side with the soldiers of Generals John C. Fremont, Kearney, Wm. H. Emory, Price, and Mason; at San José, the life of a gallant young officer of the navy, Midshipman Tenant McClenahan, of Baltimore, was lost in one of the many combats fought on that distant shore, and the possession of all the ports on the Pacific from San Francisco to Guayamas marked the successful career of the two arms of the service. In the Gulf, the blockading and capture of all the ports of Mexico displayed the zeal and arduous services of the navy, and the capture of Vera Cruz and the castle of San Juan de Ulloa was in a great degree successful, by reason of the powerfully efficient fleet of Commodores Connor and Perry, and the courage and skill of its seamen and marines; so that at the end of the war the whole nation looked with pride upon its army and navy, and everywhere was heard exultation at the victories won by their valor.

The government of the United States had waged a foreign war upon a distant theatre; it had raised and transported troops to that country; its generals had fought battles and gained them; it had dictated terms of peace and they were granted; its armies had been brought home and were disbanded; and now the Republic, scarce half a century old, could contemplate with the pride of a veteran the results of the battles it had fought.

Look at the map; all the territory between the 32° 50′ and 40° north latitude, and 106° and 124° west longitude, had been acquired by the United States: all of New Mexico and Arizona, California, Utah, and Nevada, with the gold fields lying unknown in the lap of the new acquisition. The area of this district of country is greater than that covered by the States of Maine, New Hampshire, Vermont, Massachusetts, Rhode Island, Connecticut, New York, Pennsylvania, Ohio, Indiana, Illinois, Michigan, Iowa, and Wisconsin. But this land and this gold in its bosom are as nothing to the power gained by the Republic in having its grasp upon the waters of the ocean, that bathes the Indias and the islands of the South Seas.

The human mind is not broad enough to compass the torrent of traffic and travel that is destined to flow through this western gate of the Republic; if we held the Isthmus of Panama, the keys to the world's commerce would be at Washington; *holding as we do* the harbor of San Francisco, the merchants command the trade of the East, which will bring wealth and prosperity along with its teas and its silks.

If we were to try, we could not lose the advantages gained by the war with Mexico: they are incalculable—the future alone will raise the veil.

May the same future be propitious to Mexico and all classes of its people! the causes of its internecine strife and destructive political action are plain to our mind—these result from attempting to settle their differences of opinion by a resort to arms. Mexicans! believe one who wishes you well; bury in the earth for ten years every fire-arm; pledge each other, simply upon the honor of men, not to take them up again for that length of time; and my word for it, you will regain confidence in each other; and that will establish a government of your choice, a government that will be unstained with the curse of Mexican blood shed by Mexican hands. Bury your fire-arms, and remember that the women of your land are struck by every bullet fired into a brother's breast.

APPENDIX

TO THE

MEMOIRS OF A MARYLAND VOLUNTEER:

WAR WITH MEXICO IN THE YEARS 1846-7-8.

APPENDIX.

A.

List of the Officers of the First Battalion of Baltimore and Washington Volunteers.

FIELD AND STAFF.

Lieutenant-Colonel William H. Watson, commanding: commissioned June, 1846; killed at Monterey, Mexico, September 21, 1846. Robert C. Buchanan, commanding, Brevet-Major U.S.A.* Assistant Surgeon George M. Dove, resigned August 8, 1846. Assistant-Surgeon Smythe M. Miles, mustered out May 30, 1847. Adjutant F. B. Schaeffer, mustered out of service as captain May 30, 1847. Adjutant William E. Aisquith, mustered out of service May 30, 1847.

COMPANY OFFICERS.

COMPANY.	RANK.	NAME.	WHEN COMM'D.	REMARKS.
A. Baltimore company.	Captain.	James E. Steuart.	1846. May 30.	Mustered out of service at Tampico, May 30, 1847.
	1st Lieut.	F. B. Owen.	"	Resigned at Tampico.
	2d Lieut.	Samuel Wilks.	"	Mustered out of service at Tampico, May 30, 1847.
	2d Lieut.	David P. Chapman.		Elected at Camargo, Sept. 1, 1846. Mustered out May 30, 1847.
B. Baltimore company.	Captain.	James Piper.	May 30.	Mustered out May 30, 1847.
	1st Lieut.	Lawrence Dolan.	"	Resigned after battle of Monterey. Service second time as Captain in Second Battalion.

* Brevet-Major-General U.S. Army. He commanded a Brigade of Regulars in the Peninsula campaign and at the battle of Antietam; subsequently he was in command of the District of Louisiana, 1861–5.

COMPANY.	RANK.	NAME.	WHEN COMM'D.	REMARKS.
B Co.—*Cont.*	2d Lieut.	M. K. Taylor.	1846. May 30.	Mustered out May 30, 1847, whilst detached. Service second time as Captain in Second Battalion.
	2d Lieut.	J. H. Marrows.		Elected at Camargo. Mustered out May 30, 1847. Second time as Lieutenant in Second Battalion.
C. Washington company.	Captain.	Robert Bronaugh.	May 30.	Resigned at Tampico, 1847, afterwards killed by the enemy near Puebla, Mexico.
	1st Lieut.	Phineas B. Bell.	"	Resigned. Service second time as private.
	2d Lieut.	William O'Brien.	"	Resigned.
	2d Lieut.	Thomas M. Gleason.		Com'd by the President. Appointed A. A. C. S. Mustered out May 30, 1847.
	2d Lieut.	Jacob Hemmick.		Elected after battle of Monterey, Oct. 20, 1846. Mustered out May 30, 1847. Service second time as Sergeant in Capt. Schaeffer's Company.
D. Washington company.	Captain.	John Waters.	May 30.	Resigned.
	1st Lieut.	William J. Parham.	"	Resigned at the Brazos Santiago, July, 1846.
	2d Lieut.	Eugene Boyle.	"	Resigned after battle of Monterey on account of ill health, and died on his way to the United States.
	2d Lieut.	Edward Murphy.		Elected Sept. 27, 1846. Mustered out May 30, 1847.
E. Baltimore company.	Captain.	John R. Kenly.	June 4.	Mustered out at Tampico, May 30, 1847. Service second time as Major of Second Battalion.
	1st Lieut.	F. B. Schaeffer.	"	Adjutant of Battalion. Mustered out May 30, 1847. Service second time as Captain.
	2d Lieut.	Oden Bowie.*	"	Resigned at Tampico by reason of promotion to the U. S. Army, and appointed Captain U. S. Army.
	2d Lieut.	William E. Aisquith.		Elected at Camargo, Sept. 1, 1846. Adjutant of Battalion, and mustered out May 30, 1847.
F. Baltimore company.	Captain.	James Boyd.	June 8.	Mustered out May 30, 1847. Remained in Tampico, raised a company of dragoons, and was killed by the enemy July, 1847.
	1st Lieut.	Jos. H. Ruddach.†	"	Resigned at Tampico.

* Governor of the State of Maryland from 1868 to 1872.

† Resigned at Tampico on account of ill health, March 1847.

COMPANY.	RANK.	NAME.	WHEN COMM'D.	REMARKS.
F Co.—*Cont.*	2d Lieut.	Robert E. Haslett.	1846. June 8.	Resigned at Tampico. Service second time as Lieutenant of Dragoons, U. S. Army.
	2d Lieut.	James Taneyhill.	"	Elected Sept. 1, 1846. Mustered out May 30, 1847. Remained with Captain Boyd as Lieutenant of his company, and shared his fate, being mortally wounded in the same action.

NON-COMMISSIONED STAFF.

Sergeant-Major William S. Reed, discharged from the service September 1, 1846. Quartermaster Sergeant John Hooper, discharged from the service December 3, 1846; service second time as Lieutenant in Second Battalion. Sergeant-Major Alfred Day, appointed Sergeant-Major September 1, 1846; discharged on surgeon's certificate November 12, 1846. Sergeant-Major Richard W. Reaney, appointed Sergeant-Major September 14, 1846; reduced to the ranks by order of Major Buchanan. Sergeant-Major William G. Lennox, appointed Sergeant-Major by Major Buchanan February 18, 1847; mustered out May 30, 1847; service second time as Sergeant in Captain Schaeffer's Company. Quartermaster Sergeant William S. Hyde, mustered out May 30, 1847.

B.

List of Officers of the District of Columbia and Maryland Regiment of Volunteers, enlisted for service during the war with Mexico, June and July, 1847. *Honorably discharged from the service July* 24, 1848, *at the end of the war.*

COLONEL.

George W. Hughes* (Captain and Brevet-Lieutenant-Colonel Topographical Engineers).

---

* Colonel Hughes was a graduate of the military academy of West Point, and a captain in the corps of Topographical Engineers, United States Army. He was brevetted major "for gallant and meritorious conduct at the battle of Cerro Gordo," and lieutenant-colonel "for meritorious conduct while serving in enemy's country" during the war with Mexico. He resigned from the army in 1851, and was elected to the Congress of the

LIEUTENANT-COLONEL.

William H. Emory* (First Lieutenant and Brevet-Major Topographical Engineers)

MAJOR.

John R. Kenly† (Captain in Watson's Baltimore Battalion).

SURGEON.

Stedman R. Tilghman.

ASSISTANT-SURGEON.

Wakeman Bryarly.

ADJUTANT.

James Steele (Second Lieutenant).

CAPTAINS.

William H. Degges.
Edmund Barry.
Lawrence Dolan (Lieutenant in Watson's Battalion).
Dan Drake Henrie (Texan Ranger).
Marcellus K. Taylor (Lieutenant in Watson's Battalion).
Francis B. Schaeffer (Lieutenant in Watson's Battalion).
George W. Brown.
Lloyd Tilghman (Light Artillery Company).

FIRST LIEUTENANTS.

Frederick A. Klopfer (commanding Company D).
Henry S. Addison.

United States as a member of the House of Representatives Abandoning the political arena, he devoted himself to agricultural pursuits, and died at his estate on West River, Maryland, in the year 1871, greatly regretted by family and friends.

* Brevet-Major-General U.S. Army. He commanded the Nineteenth Army Corps in Louisiana and Texas, and subsequently in the Army of Virginia to the end of the war, 1861–5.

† Colonel First Maryland Infantry and Brevet-Major-General U.S. Volunteers, 1861–5.

John M. Thornton.
Frisby Tilghman.
Washington Hopper.
Isaac H. Morrow (Lieutenant in Watson's Battalion).
Jacob S. Klassen.
William J. Corcoran.
John Hooper (Regimental Quartermaster; Quartermaster Sergeant Watson's Battalion).

SECOND LIEUTENANTS.

John Carr (Acting Adjutant).
Benjamin R. West.
James O'Brien.
David A. Griffith.
William H. Baker.
Richard P. Henry.
John H. Ballman.
Arnold Teusfield.
John H. Gronewell.
William J. Garey.
Henry M. Milnor.
Ira Mabbett.
Robert C. Bell.

List of Officers of Companies attached to the Regiment.

Chatam R. Wheat, Captain. Charles McDonald, First Lieutenant. Francis E. Smith, Second Lieutenant. Abner C. Steele, Second Lieutenant.	Company of Mounted Volunteers; served from July, 1847, to July, 1848.
Thomas A. Rowley, Captain. Andrew McClure, First Lieutenant. James McLean, Second Lieutenant. Alexander Scott, Second Lieutenant.	Company of Infantry from Pittsburg, Pennsylvania; served from October, 1847, to July 24, 1848.

James Boyd,* Captain (Captain in Watson's Battalion); killed, July 12, 1847. Joseph R. West, Captain after death of Captain Boyd. James Taneyhill, First Lieutenant (Lieutenant in Watson's Battalion); killed, July 12, 1847. Franklin B. Nimocks, Second Lieutenant (Private in Captain Kenly's Company, Watson's Battalion). George De Groote, Second Lieutenant. John A. Letten, Second Lieutenant.	Company of Mounted Volunteers; served from June, 1847, to July, 1848.

C.

Letter from Colonel George W. Hughes, U. S. Army.

West River, Maryland, January 25, 1851.

My Dear Kenly,—I have been directed to prepare an official report in reference to our operations in Mexico, and wish you to assist me, especially in regard to facts and dates. I kept no memoranda, and must therefore trust to recollection, assisted by my letter-book. I will thank you to state the days of sailing from Baltimore, the names of the transports (and captains), companies, etc., respective times of arrival at Vera Cruz, time of departure from Vera Cruz, and incidents of campaign, more particularly till the capture of the National Bridge; also, the designation of the troops, not of our battalion, that accompanied us. What is Taliaferro's Christian name, and to what regiment

* Captain Boyd's company was raised at Tampico upon the muster-out of the Baltimore Battalion. It served honorably until the end of the war, losing heavily at the battle of Rio Calabaso, fought by Colonel de Russey, of the Louisiana Volunteers, against the Mexican General Garay.

was he promoted as Major? Have you the Regimental Order Book? Write me as fully as you can.

I am glad of the opportunity of doing justice (however tardy) to my companions-in-arms, and especially to yourself.

Most truly your friend,

GEORGE W. HUGHES.

Major JOHN R. KENLY, Baltimore.

NOTE.—Colonel Hughes left the army before he had completed his report, and it was never sent to the Adjutant-General's office.

Notification of Membership of the Association of the Soldiers of the Mexican War.

WASHINGTON, August 9, 1854.

SIR,—I have the honor to inform you that, at the regular monthly meeting of the "Association of the Soldiers of the Mexican War," you were unanimously elected an honorary member of the Association.

Very respectfully, your obedient servant,

(Signed) JOSEPH P. SHILLENN,
Cor. Sec'y Association, etc.

Major JOHN R. KENLY, Baltimore, Md.

Letter from Major-General Wm. H. Emory, U. S. Army.

HEADQUARTERS DEPARTMENT OF THE GULF,
New Orleans, September 30, 1872.

MY DEAR GENERAL KENLY,—Your letter of the 16th September, and that preceding, followed me as far as Syracuse, N. Y., and back to this place, where they only reached me to-day.

I hasten to reply, and take great pleasure in stating that the Maryland Regiment, for the time it was under my command, during and toward the close of the war with Mexico, acted uniformly with great gallantry, steadiness, and good conduct.

When I took command of the regiment as Lieutenant-Colonel I had just returned from the expedition engaged in the conquest of New Mexico and California, under the lamented General James W. Kearney. There I served with what was then considered one of the *crack* regiments of the army, the old First Dragoons, and of course my ideas of discipline and efficiency were pitched pretty high, yet I was not disappointed in either the discipline or the efficiency of the gallant Maryland Regiment, with which your name is so honorably identified.

Excuse the shortness of this note, and believe me very faithfully yours,

(Signed) W. H. EMORY,
Brevet-Major-General U. S. Army.

General JOHN R. KENLY, Baltimore, Md.

Resolutions and Acts of the General Assembly of Maryland.

I.

Resolved, by the General Assembly of Maryland, That the thanks of the General Assembly of Maryland are justly due and are hereby tendered to the rank and file of the Baltimore and District of Columbia Battalion, also to the Maryland Battalion, and all other officers and citizens of Maryland, serving in the army and navy of the United States, for gallant and meritorious conduct during the late war with Mexico.

Resolved, That the Governor be requested to make the above resolution known in General Orders.—*Passed* January 29, 1850.

II.

Resolved, by the General Assembly of Maryland, That His Excellency the Governor be respectfully requested to make application to the proper department at Washington, to obtain a certified copy of all the muster and pay rolls, or other evidence of the services of the commissioned and non-commissioned officers, musicians, or privates of the State of Maryland, who were in the service of the United States in the war with Mexico; and upon application of any of those whose names appear upon said rolls, or of the nearest relative of any deceased soldier therein named, to furnish such person a copy of the same, duly authenticated with seal and signature.—*Passed* May 14, 1853.

III.

An Act authorizing the Governor to grant duplicate discharges to the Maryland Volunteers and certain citizens thereof, who enlisted in the Mexican war.

Section I. Be it enacted by the General Assembly of Maryland, That the Governor be and he is hereby empowered and directed, upon the application in writing of any volunteer officer or soldier who served in the First or Second Battalions of Maryland Volunteers in the Mexican war, or any citizen of Maryland who enlisted in any company composing a portion of the ten additional regiments called into service by Act of Congress during the said war, and served therein; and upon such proof as he may deem necessary to establish such service and an honorable discharge or muster-out from the same, to issue to such volunteer or enlisted officer and soldier a copy or duplicate of the discharge received by him when so discharged or mustered out of service, the said copy or duplicate to be printed upon parchment and signed by the Governor, the Secretary of State, and Adjutant-General of Maryland, and attested by the great seal of the State.

Sec. 2. And be it enacted, That the sum of five hundred dollars, or so much thereof as may be necessary, be and the same is hereby appropriated out of any unappropriated money now in the Treasury, to defray the expenses of carrying into effect the provisions of the first section of this act.

Sec. 3. And be it enacted, That this act shall take effect from the day of its passage.—*Passed* March 10, 1854.

D.

TREATY

BETWEEN

THE UNITED STATES AND MEXICO.

Treaty of peace, friendship, limits, and settlement between the United States of America and the Mexican republic. Dated at Guadalupe Hidalgo, February 2, 1848; *ratified by the President of the United States, March* 16, 1848; *exchanged at Querétaro, May* 30, 1848; *proclaimed by the President of the United States, July* 4, 1848.

In the name of Almighty God:

The United States of America and the United Mexican States, animated by a sincere desire to put an end to the calamities of the war which unhappily exists between the two republics, and to establish upon a solid basis relations of peace and friendship, which shall confer reciprocal benefits upon the citizens of both, and assure the concord, harmony, and mutual confidence wherein the two people should live, as good neighbors, have for that purpose appointed their respective plenipotentiaries, that is to say, the President of the United States has appointed Nicholas

En el nombre de Dios Todo-Poderoso:

Los Estados Unidos Mexicanos y los Estados Unidos de América, animados de un sincero deseo de poner término á las calamidades de la guerra que desgraciadamente existe entre ambas repúblicas, y de establecer sobre báses sólidas relaciones de paz y buena amistad, que procuren reciprocas ventajas á los ciudadanos de uno y otro pais, y afianzen la concordia, armonia y mútua seguridad en que deben vivir, como buenos vecinos, los dos pueblos han nombrado á este efecto sus respectivos plenipotenciarios; á saber, el Presidente de la república Mexicana á Don Bernardo

P. Trist, a citizen of the United States, and the President of the Mexican republic has appointed Don Luis Gonzaga Cuevas, Don Bernardo Couto and Don Miguel Atristain, citizens of the said republic, who, after a reciprocal communication of their respective full powers, have, under the protection of Almighty God, the author of peace, arranged, agreed upon, and signed the following

Treaty of peace, friendship, limits, and settlement between the United States of America and the Mexican republic.

ARTICLE I.

There shall be firm and universal peace between the United States of America and the Mexican republic, and between their respective countries, territories, cities, towns, and people, without exception of places or persons.

ARTICLE II.

Immediately upon the signature of this treaty, a convention shall be entered into between a commissioner or commissioners appointed by the general-in-chief of the forces of the United States, and such as may be appointed by the Mexican government, to the end that a pro-

Couto, Don Miguel Atristain, y Don Luis Gonzaga Cuevas, ciudadanos de la misma república; y el Presidente de los Estados Unidos de América á Don Nicolas P. Trist, ciudadano de dichos Estados; quienes despues de haberse comunicado sus plenos poderes, bajo la proteccion del Senor Dios Todo-Poderoso, autor de la paz, han ajustado, convenido, y firmado el siguiente

Tratado de paz, amistad, limites y arreglo definitivo entre la república Mexicana y los Estados Unidos de Amêrica.

ARTICULO I.

Habrá paz firme y universal entre la república Mexicana y los Estados Unidos de America, y entre sus respectivos paises, territorios, ciudades, villas, y pueblos, sin escepcion de lugares ó persones.

ARTICULO II.

Luego que se firme el presente tratado, habrá un convenio entre el comisionado ú comisionados del gobierno Mexicano, y el ó los que nombre el general-en-gefe de las fuerzas de los Estados Unidos, para que cesen provisionalmente las hostilidades, y se restablezca

visional suspension of hostilities shall take place, and that, in the places occupied by the said forces, constitutional order may be re-established, as regards the political, administrative, and judicial branches, so far as this shall be permitted by the circumstances of military occupation.

en los lugares ocupados por las mismas fuerzas el orden constitucional en lo politico, administrativo, y judicial, en cuanto lo permitan las circunstancias de ocupacion militar.

ARTICLE III.

Immediately upon the ratification of the present treaty by the government of the United States, orders shall be transmitted to the commanders of their land and naval forces, requiring the latter (provided this treaty shall then have been ratified by the government of the Mexican republic, and the ratifications exchanged) immediately to desist from blockading any Mexican ports; and requiring the former (under the same condition) to commence, at the earliest moment practicable, withdrawing all troops of the United States then in the interior of the Mexican republic, to the points that shall be selected by common agreement, at a distance from the seaports not exceeding thirty leagues; and such evacuation of the interior of the republic shall be completed with the least possible delay; the Mexican govern-

ARTICULO III.

Luego que este tratado sea ratificado por el gobierno de los Estados Unidos, se expediran órdenes á sus comandantes de tierra y mar previniendo á estos segundos (siempre que el tratado haya sido ya ratificado por el gobierno de la república Mexicana, y cangeadas las ratificaciones) que inmediatamente alcen el bloqueo de todos los puertos Mexicanos, y mandando á los primeros (bajo la misma condicion) que á la mayor posible brevedad comiencen á retirar todas las tropas de los Estados Unidos que se halláren entonces en el interior de la república Mexicana, á puntos que se elegirán de comun acuerdo, y que no distarán de los puertos mas de treinta leguas; esta evacuacion del interior de la república se consumerá con la menor dilacion posible, comprometiéndose á la vez el gobierno Mexicano á facilitar,

ment hereby binding itself to afford every facility in its power for rendering the same convenient to the troops, on their march and in their new positions, and for promoting a good understanding between them and the inhabitants. In like manner, orders shall be dispatched to the persons in charge of the custom-houses at all ports occupied by the forces of the United States, requiring them (under the same condition) immediately to deliver possession of the same to the persons authorized by the Mexican government to receive it, together with all bonds and evidences of debts for duties on importations and on exportations, not yet fallen due. Moreover, a faithful and exact account shall be made out, showing the entire amount of all duties on imports and on exports collected at such custom-houses, or elsewhere in Mexico, by authority of the United States, from and after the day of the ratification of this treaty by the government of the Mexican republic; and also an account of the cost of collection; and such entire amount, deducting only the cost of collection, shall be delivered to the Mexican government, at the City of Mexico, within three months

cuanto queda en su arbitrio, la evacuacion de las tropas Americanas; á hacer cómodas su marcha y su permanencia en los nuevos puntos que se elijan; y á promover una buena inteligencia entre ellas y los habitantes. Igualmente se libraran órdenes á las personas encargadas de las aduanas maritimas en todos los puertos ocupados por las fuerzas de los Estados Unidos, previniendoles (bajo la misma condicion) que pongan inmediatamente en posesion de dichas aduanas á las personas autorizadas por el gobierno Mexicano para recibirilas, entregandoles al mismo tiempo todas las obligaciones y constancias de deudas pendientes por derechos de importacion y exportacion, cuyos plazos no estén vencidos. Ademas se formará una cuenta fiel y exacta que manifieste el total monto de los derechos de importacion y exportacion, recaudados en las mismas aduanas maritimas ó en cualquiera otro lugar de México por autoridad de los Estados Unidos desde el dia de la ratificacion de este tratado por el gobierno de la república Mexicana; y tambien una cuenta de los gastos de recaudacion; y la total suma de los derechos cobrados, deducidos

after the exchange of the ratifications.

solamente los gastos de recaudacion, se entregará al gobierno Mexicano en la ciudad de México á los tres mesas del cange de las ratificaciones.

The evacuation of the capital of the Mexican republic by the troops of the United States, in virtue of the above stipulations, shall be completed in one month after the orders there stipulated for shall have been received by the commander of said troops, or sooner, if possible.

La evacuacion de la capital de la república Mexicana por las tropas de los Estados Unidos, en consecuencia de lo que queda estipulado, se completará al mes de recibirse por el comandante de dichas tropas las órdenes convenidas en el presente artículo ó antes si fuere posible.

Article IV.

Immediately after the exchange of ratifications of the present treaty, all castles, forts, territories, places, and possessions, which have been taken or occupied by the forces of the United States during the present war, within the limits of the Mexican republic, as about to be established by the following article, shall be definitively restored to the said republic, together with all the artillery, arms, apparatus of war, munitions, and other public property, which were in the said castles and forts when captured, and which shall remain there at the time when this treaty shall be duly ratified by the government of the Mexican republic.

Articulo IV.

Luego que se verifique el cange de las ratificaciones del presente tratado, todos los castillos, fortalezas, territorios, lugares, y posesiones que hayan tomado ú ocupado las fuerzas de los Estados Unidos, en la presente guerra, dentro de los limites que por el siguiente artículo van á fijarse á la república Mexicana, se devolverán definitivamente á la misma república, con toda la artilleria, armas, aparejos de guerra, municiones, y cualquiera otra propiedad pública existentes en dichos castillos y fortalezas, cuando fueron tomados, y que se conserve en ellos al tiempo de ratificarse por el gobierno de la república Mexicana el

To this end, immediately upon the signature of this treaty, orders shall be dispatched to the American officers commanding such castles and forts, securing against the removal or destruction of any such artillery, arms, apparatus of war, munitions, or other public property. The City of Mexico, within the inner line of intrenchments surrounding the said city, is comprehended in the above stipulations, as regards the restoration of artillery, apparatus of war, etc.

presente tratado. A este efecto, inmediatamente despues que se firme, se expedirán órdenes á los oficiales Americanos que mandan dichos castillos y fortalezas para asegurar toda la artilleria, armas, aparejos de guerra, municiones, y cualquiera otra propiedad pública, la cual no podrá en adelante removerse de donde se halla, ni destruirse. La ciudad de México dentro de la linea interior de atrincheramientos que la circundan queda comprendida en la precedente estipulacion en lo que toca á la devolucion de artilleria, aparejos de guerra, etc.

The final evacuation of the territory of the Mexican republic, by the forces of the United States, shall be completed in three months from the said exchange of ratifications, or sooner, if possible; the Mexican government hereby engaging, as in the foregoing article, to use all means in its power for facilitating such evacuation, and rendering it convenient to the troops, and for promoting a good understanding between them and the inhabitants.

La final evacuacion del territorio de la república Mexicana por las fuerzas de los Estados Unidos quedará consumada á los tres meses del cange de las ratificaciones, ó antes si fuére posible, comprometiendose á la vez el gobierno Mexicano, como en el artículo anterior, á usar de todos los medios que estén en su poder para facilitar la tal evacuacion, hacerla cómoda á las tropas Americanas, y promover entre ellas y los habitantes una buena inteligencia.

If, however, the ratification of this treaty by both parties should not take place in time

Sin embargo, si la ratificacion del presente tratado por ambas partes no tuviéra efecto en

to allow the embarkation of the troops of the United States to be completed before the commencement of the sickly season, at the Mexican ports on the Gulf of Mexico, in such case a friendly arrangement shall be entered into between the general-in-chief of the said troops and the Mexican government, whereby healthy and otherwise suitable places, at a distance from the ports not exceeding thirty leagues, shall be designated for the residence of such troops as may not yet have embarked, until the return of the healthy season. And the space of time here referred to as comprehending the sickly season, shall be understood to extend from the first day of May to the first day of November.

All prisoners of war taken on either side, on land or on sea, shall be restored as soon as practicable after the exchange of ratifications of this treaty. It is also agreed, that if any Mexicans should now be held as captives by any savage tribe within the limits of the United States, as about to be established by the following article, the government of the United States will exact the release of such captives, and cause

tiempo que permita que el embarque de las tropas de los Estados Unidos se complete, ántes de que comience la estacion malsana en los puertos Mexicanos del golfo de México; en tal caso, se hará un arréglo amistoso entre el gobierno Mexicano y el general-en-gefe de dichas tropas, y por medio de este arreglo se señalarán lugares salubres y convenientes (que no disten de los puertos mas de treinta leguas) para que residan en ellos hasta la vuelta de la estacion sana las tropas que aun no se hayan embarcado. Y queda entendido que el espacio de tiempo de que aquí se habla, como comprensivo de la estacion malsana, se extiende desde el dia primero de Mayo hasta el dia primero de Noviembre.

Todos los prisioneros de guerra tomados en mar ó tierra por ambas partes, se restituirán á la mayor brevedad posible despues del cange de las ratificaciones del presente tratado. Queda tambien convenido que si algunos Mexicanos estuviéren ahora cautivos en poder de alguna tribu salvage dentro de los limites que por el siguiente articulo van á fijarse á los Estados Unidos, el gobierno de los mismos Estados Unidos

them to be restored to their country.

ARTICLE V.

The boundary line between the two republics shall commence in the Gulf of Mexico, three leagues from land, opposite the mouth of the Rio Grande, otherwise called Rio Bravo del Norte, or opposite the mouth of its deepest branch, if it should have more than one branch emptying directly into the sea; from thence up the middle of that river, following the deepest channel, where it has more than one, to the point where it strikes the southern boundary of New Mexico; thence westwardly, along the whole southern boundary of New Mexico (which runs north of the town called *Paso*) to its western termination; thence northward, along the western line of New Mexico, until it intersects the first branch of the river Gila (or if it should not intersect any branch of that river, then to the point on the said line nearest to such branch, and thence in a direct line to the same); thence down the middle of the said branch and of the said river, until it empties into the Rio Colorado; thence across the Rio Colorado,

exigirá su libertad y los hará restituir á su pais.

ARTICULO V.

La linea divisoria entre las dos repúblicas comenzará en el golfo de México, tres leguas fuera de tierra frente á la desembocadura del rio Grande, llamado por otro nombre rio Bravo del Norte, ó del mas profundo de sus brazos, si en la desembocadura tuviere varios brazos; correrá por mitad de dicho rio, siguiendo el canal mas profundo, donde tenga mas de un canal, hasta el punto en que dicho rio corta el lindero meridional de Nuevo México; continuará luego hácia occidente por todo este lindero meridional (que corre al norte del pueblo llamado *Paso*) hasta su término por el lado de occidente; desde allí subirá la linea divisoria hácia el norte por el lindero occidental de Nuevo México, hasta donde este lindero está cortado por el primer brazo del rio Gila (y si no está cortado por ningun brazo del rio Gila, entonces hasta el punto del mismo lindero occidental mas cercano al tal brazo, y de allí en una línea recta al mismo brazo); continuará despues por mitad de este brazo y del rio Gila hasta su confluencia con el

following the division line between Upper and Lower California, to the Pacific Ocean.

rio Colorado; y desde la confluencia de ambos rios la linea divisoria, cortando el Colorado, seguira el límite que separa la Alta de la Baja California hasta el mar Pacifico.

The southern and western limits of New Mexico, mentioned in this article, are those laid down in the map, entitled "*Map of the United Mexican States, as organized and defined by various acts of the Congress of said republic, and constructed according to the best authorities. Revised edition. Published at New York, in* 1847, *by J. Disturnell.*" Of which map a copy is added to this treaty, bearing the signatures and seals of the undersigned plenipotentiaries. And, in order to preclude all difficulty in tracing upon the ground the limit separating Upper from Lower California, it is agreed that the said limit shall consist of a straight line drawn from the middle of the Rio Gila, where it unites with the Colorado, to a point on the coast of the Pacific Ocean distant one marine league due south of the southernmost point of the port of San Diego, according to the plan of said port made in the year 1782 by Don Juan Pantoja, second sailing-master of the

Los linderos meridional y occidental de Nuevo México, de que habla este artículo, son los que se marcan en la carta titulada: "*Mapa de los Estados Unidos de México segun lo organizado y definido por las varias actas del Congreso de dicha república, y construido por las mejores autoridades. Edicion revisada que publicó en Nueva York en* 1847, *J. Disturnell;*" de la cual se agrega un ejemplar al presente tratado, firmado y sellado por los plenipotenciarios infrascriptos. Y para evitar toda dificultad al trazar sobre la tierra el límite que separa la Alta de la Baja California, queda convenido que dicho límite consistirá en una linea recta tirada desde la mitad del rio Gila en el punto donde se une con el Colorado, hasta un punto en la costa del mar Pacifico, distante una legua marina al sur del punto mas meridional del puerto de San Diego, segun este puerto está dibujado en el plano que levantó el año de 1782 el segundo piloto de la armada Española Don

Spanish fleet, and published at Madrid in the year 1802, in the atlas to the voyage of the schooners *Sutil* and *Mexicana*, of which plan a copy is hereunto added, signed and sealed by the respective plenipotentiaries.

In order to designate the boundary line with due precision, upon authoritative maps, and to establish upon the ground landmarks which shall show the limits of both republics, as described in the present article, the two governments shall each appoint a commissioner and a surveyor, who, before the expiration of one year from the date of the exchange of ratifications of this treaty, shall meet at the port of San Diego, and proceed to run and mark the said boundary in its whole course to the mouth of the Rio Bravo del Norte. They shall keep journals and make out plans of their operations; and the result agreed upon by them shall be deemed a part of this treaty, and shall have the same force as if it were inserted therein. The two governments will amicably agree regarding what may be necessary to these persons, and also as to their respective escorts, should such be necessary.

Juan Pantoja, y se publicó en Madrid el de 1802, en el atlas para el viage de las goletas Sutil y Mexicana; del cual plano se agrega copia firmada y sellada por los plenipotenciarios respectivos.

Para consiguar la línea divisoria con la precision debida en mapas fehacientes, y para establecer sobre la tierra mojones que pongan á la vista los limites de ambas repúblicas, segun quedan descritos en el presente artículo, nombrará cada uno de los dos gobiernos un comisario y un agrimensor que se juntarán ántes del término de un año contado desde la fecha del cange de las ratificaciones de este tratado, en el puerto de San Diego, y procederán á señalar y demarcar la expresada línea divisoria en todo su curso hasta la desembocadura del rio Bravo del Norte. Llevarán diarios y llevantarán planos de sus operaciones: y el resultado convenido por ellos se tendrá por parte de este tratado, y tendrá la misma fuerza que si estuviése inserto en él; debiendo convenir amistosamente los dos gobiernos en el arreglo de cuanto necesiten estos individuos, y en la escolta respectiva que deban llevar, siempre que se crea necesario.

The boundary line established by this article shall be religiously respected by each of the two republics, and no change shall ever be made therein, except by the express and free consent of both nations, lawfully given by the general government of each, in conformity with its own constitution.

La linea divisoria que se establece por este artículo será religiosamente respetada por cada una de las dos repúblicas, y ninguna variacion se hará jamás en ella, sino de expreso y libre consentimiento de ambas naciones, otorgado legalmente por el gobierno general de cada una de ellas, con arreglo á su propia constitucion.

ARTICLE VI.

The vessels and citizens of the United States shall, in all time, have a free and uninterrupted passage by the Gulf of California, and by the river Colorado below its confluence with the Gila, to and from their possessions situated north of the boundary line defined in the preceding article; it being understood that this passage is to be by navigating the Gulf of California and the river Colorado, and not by land, without the express consent of the Mexican government.

If, by the examinations which may be made, it should be ascertained to be practicable and advantageous to construct a road, canal, or railway, which should in whole or in part run upon the river Gila, or upon its right or its left bank, within the space of one marine league from

ARTICULO VI.

Los buques y ciudadanos de los Estados Unidos tendrán en todo tiempo un libre y no interrumpido tránsito por el golfo de California y por el rio Colorado desde su confluencia con el Gila, para sus posesiones y desde sus posesiones sitas al norte de la línea divisoria que queda marcada en el artículo precedente; entendiéndose que este tránsito se ha de hacer navegando por el golfo de California y por el rio Colorado, y no por tierra, sin expreso consentimiento del gobierno Mexicano.

Si por reconocimientos que se practiquen, se comprobare la posibilidad y conveniencia de construir un camino, canal, ó ferro-carril, que en todo ó en parte corra sobre el rio Gila ó sobre alguna de sus márgenes derecha ó izquierda en la latitud de una legua marina de uno ó

either margin of the river, the governments of both republics will form an agreement regarding its construction, in order that it may serve equally for the use and advantage of both countries.

ARTICLE VII.

The river Gila, and the part of the Rio Bravo del Norte lying below the southern boundary of New Mexico, being, agreeably to the fifth article, divided in the middle between the two republics, the navigation of the Gila and of the Bravo below said boundary shall be free and common to the vessels and citizens of both countries; and neither shall, without the consent of the other, construct any work that may impede or interrupt, in whole or in part, the exercise of this right; not even for the purpose of favoring new methods of navigation. Nor shall any tax or contribution, under any denomination or title, be levied upon vessels, or persons navigating the same, or upon merchandise or effects transported thereon, except in the case of landing upon one of their shores. If, for the purpose of making the said rivers navigable, or for maintaining them in such state, it should be necessary or

de otro lado del rio, los gobiernos de ambas repúblicas se pondrán de acuerdo sobre su construccion á fin de que sirva igualmente para el uso y provecho de ambos paises.

ARTICULO VII.

Como el rio Gila y la parte del rio Bravo del Norte que corre bajo el lindero meridional de Nuevo México se dividen por mitad entre las dos repúblicas, segun lo establecido en el artículo quinto, la navegacion en el Gila y en la parte que queda indicada del Bravo, será libre y comun á los buques y ciudadanos de ambos paises, sin que por alguno de ellos pueda hacerse (sin consentimiento del otro) ninguna obra que impido ó interrumpa en todo ó en parte el ejercicio de este derecho, ni aun con motivo de favorecer nuevos métodos de navegacion. Tampoco se podrá cobrar (sino en el caso de desembarco en alguna de sus riberas) ningun impuesto ó contribucion bajo ninguna denominacion ó título á los buques, efectos, mercancías ó personas que naveguen en dichos rios. Si para hacerlos ó mantenerlos navegables fuere necesario ó conveniente establecer alguna contribucion

advantageous to establish any tax or contribution, this shall not be done without the consent of both governments.

The stipulations contained in the present article shall not impair the territorial rights of either republic within its established limits.

ó impuesto, no podrá esto hacerse sin el consentimiento de los dos gobiernos.

Las estipulaciones contenidas en el presente artículo dejan ilesos los derechos territoriales de una y otra república dentro de los límites que les quedan marcados.

Article VIII.

Mexicans now established in territories previously belonging to Mexico, and which remain for the future within the limits of the United States, as defined by the present treaty, shall be free to continue where they now reside, or to remove at any time to the Mexican republic, retaining the property which they possess in the said territories, or disposing thereof, and removing the proceeds wherever they please, without their being subjected, on this account, to any contribution, tax, or charge whatever.

Those who shall prefer to remain in the said territories may either retain the title and rights of Mexican citizens, or acquire those of citizens of the United States. But they shall be under the obligation to make their election within one year from the date of the exchange

Articulo VIII.

Los Mexicanos establecidos hoy en territorios pertenecientes ántes á México, y que quedan para lo futuro dentro de los límites señalados por el presente tratado á los Estados Unidos, podrán permanecer en donde ahora habitan, ó trasladarse en cualquier tiempo á la república Mexicana, conservando en los indicados territorios los bienes que poseen, ó enagenandolos y pasando su valor á donde les convenga, sin que por esto pueda exigirseles ningun género de contribucion, gravámen ó impuesto.

Los que prefieran permanecer en los indicados territorios, podrán conservar el título y derechos de ciudadanos Mexicanos, ó adquirir el título y derechos de ciudadanos de los Estados Unidos. Mas la eleccion entre una y otra ciudadania deberan hacerla dentro de un año contado desde

of ratifications of this treaty; and those who shall remain in the said territories after the expiration of that year, without having declared their intention to retain the character of Mexicans, shall be considered to have elected to become citizens of the United States.

la fecha del cange de las ratificaciones de este tratado. Y los que permanecieren en los indicados territorios despues de transcurrido el año, sin haber declarado su intencion de retener el carácter de Mexicanos, se considerará que han elegido ser ciudadanos de los Estados Unidos.

In the said territories, property of every kind, now belonging to Mexicans not established there, shall be inviolably respected. The present owners, the heirs of these, and all Mexicans who may hereafter acquire said property by contract, shall enjoy with respect to it guaranties equally ample as if the same belonged to citizens of the United States.

Las propiedades de todo género existentes en los expresados territorios, y que pertenecen ahora á Mexicanos no establecidos en ellos, serán respetadas inviolablemente. Sus actuales dueños, los herederos de estos, y los Mexicanos que en lo venidero puedan adquirir por contrato las indicadas propiedades, disfrutarán respecto de ellas tan amplia garantia, como si perteneciesen á ciudadanos de los Estados Unidos.

Article IX.

The Mexicans who, in the territories aforesaid, shall not preserve the character of citizens of the Mexican republic, conformably with what is stipulated in the preceding article, shall be incorporated into the union of the United States and be admitted at the proper time (to be judged of by the Congress of the United States) to the enjoyment of all the rights

Articulo IX.

Los Mexicanos que, en los territorios antedichos, no conserven el carácter de ciudadanos de la república Mexicana, segun lo estipulado en el artículo precedente, serán incorporados en la union de los Estados Unidos, y se admitirán en tiempo oportuno (á juicio del Congreso de los Estados Unidos) al goce de todos los derechos de ciudadanos de los

of citizens of the United States, according to the principles of the Constitution; and in the mean time shall be maintained and protected in the free enjoyment of their liberty and property, and secured in the free exercise of their religion without restriction.

Estados Unidos conforme á los principios de la constitucion; y entretanto serán mantenidos y protegidos en el goce de su libertad y propiedad, y asegurados en el libre ejercicio de su religion sin restriccion alguna.

Article X.

[Stricken out.]

Articulo X.

[Suprimido.]

Article XI.

Considering that a great part of the territories which, by the present treaty, are to be comprehended for the future within the limits of the United States, is now occupied by savage tribes, who will hereafter be under the exclusive control of the government of the United States, and whose incursions within the territory of Mexico would be prejudicial in the extreme, it is solemnly agreed that all such incursions shall be forcibly restrained by the government of the United States whensoever this may be necessary; and that when they cannot be prevented they shall be punished by the said government, and satisfaction for the same shall be exacted—all in the same way, and with equal diligence and energy, as if the

Articulo XI.

En atencion á que una gran parte de los territorios que por el presente tratado van á quedar para lo futuro dentro de los límites de los Estados Unidos, se halla actualmente ocupada por tríbas salvages, que han de estar en adelante bajo la exclusiva autoridad del gobierno de los Estados Unidos, y cuyas incursiones sobre los distritos Mexicanos serian en extremo perjudiciales; está solemnemente convenido que el mismo gobierno de los Estados Unidos contendra las indicadas incursiones por medio de la fuerza siempre que así sea necesario; y cuando no pudiére prevenirlas, castigará y escarmentará á los invasores, exigiéndoles ademas la debida reparacion: todo del mismo modo, y con la misma diligencia y

same incursions were meditated or committed within its own territory, against its own citizens.

energia con que obraria, si las incursiones se hubiesen meditado ó ejecutado sobre territorios suyos ó contra sus propios ciudadanos.

It shall not be lawful, under any pretext whatever, for any inhabitant of the United States to purchase or acquire any Mexican, or any foreigner residing in Mexico, who may have been captured by Indians inhabiting the territory of either of the two republics, nor to purchase or acquire horses, mules, cattle, or property of any kind, stolen within Mexican territory by such Indians.

A ningun habitante de los Estados Unidos será lícito, bajo ningun pretesto, comprar ó adquirir cautivo alguno, Mexicano ó extrangero residente en México, apresado por los Indios habitantes en territorio de cualquiera de las dos repúblicas, ni los caballos, mulas, ganados, ó cualquiera otro género de cosas que hayan robado dentro del territorio Mexicano.

And in the event of any person or persons, captured within Mexican territory by Indians, being carried into the territory of the United States, the government of the latter engages and binds itself, in the most solemn manner, so soon as it shall know of such captives being within its territory, and shall be able so to do, through the faithful exercise of its influence and power, to rescue them and return them to their country, or deliver them to the agent or representative of the Mexican government. The Mexican authorities will, as far as practicable, give to the gov-

Y en caso de que cualquier persona ó personas cautivadas por los Indios dentro del territorio Mexicano sean llevadas al territorio de los Estados Unidos, el gobierno de dichos Estados Unidos se compromete y liga de la manera mas solemne, en cuanto le sea posible, á rescatarlas, y á restituirlas á su pais, ó entregarlas al agente ó representante del gobierno Mexicano; haciendo todo esto, tan luego como sepa que los dichos cautivos se hallan dentro de su territorio, y empleando al efecto el leal ejercicio de su influencia y poder. Las autoridades Mexicanas darán á las de los

ernment of the United States notice of such captures; and its agent shall pay the expenses incurred in the maintenance and transmission of the rescued captives; who, in the mean time, shall be treated with the utmost hospitality by the American authorities at the place where they may be. But if the government of the United States, before receiving such notice from Mexico, should obtain intelligence, through any other channel, of the existence of Mexican captives within its territory, it will proceed forthwith to effect their release and delivery to the Mexican agent as above stipulated.

For the purpose of giving to these stipulations the fullest possible efficacy, thereby affording the security and redress demanded by their true spirit and intent, the government of the United States will now and hereafter pass, without unnecessary delay, and always vigilantly enforce, such laws as the nature of the subject may require. And finally, the sacredness of this obligation shall never be lost sight of by the said government when providing for the removal of the Indians from any portion of the said territories, or for

Estados Unidos, segun sea practicable, una noticia de tales cautivos; y el agente Mexicano pagará los gastos erogados en el mantenimiento y remision de los que se rescaten, los cuales entre tanto serán tratados con la mayor hospitalidad por las autoridades Americanas del lugar en que se encuentren. Mas si el gobierno de los Estados Unidos, ántes de recibir aviso de México, tuviéra noticia por cualquiera otro conducto de existir en su territorio cautivos Mexicanos, procederá desde luego á verificar su rescate y entrega al agente Mexicano, segun queda convenido.

Con el objeto de dar á estas estipulaciones la mayor fuerza posible, y afianzar al mismo tiempo la seguridad y las reparaciones que exige el verdadero espíritu é intencion con que se han ajustado, el gobierno de los Estados Unidos dictará sin inútiles delaciones, ahora y en lo de adelante, las leyes que requiera la naturaleza del asunto, y vigilará siempre sobre su ejecucion. Finalmente, el gobierno de los mismos Estados Unidos tendrá muy presente la santidad de esta obligacion siempre que tenga que desalojar á los Indios de cualquier punto

its being settled by citizens of the United States; but, on the contrary, special care shall be taken not to place its Indian occupants under the necessity of seeking new homes, by committing those invasions which the United States have solemnly obliged themselves to restrain.

de los indicados territorios ó que establecer en él á ciudadanos suyos: y cuidará muy especialmente de que no se ponga á los Indios que habitaban ántes aquel punto, en necesidad de buscar nuevos hogares por medio de las incursiones sobre los distritos Mexicanos, que el gobierno de los Estados Unidos se ha comprometido solemnemente á reprimir.

Article XII.

In consideration of the extension acquired by the boundaries of the United States, as defined in the fifth article of the present treaty, the government of the United States engages to pay to that of the Mexican republic the sum of fifteen millions of dollars.

Immediately after this treaty shall have been duly ratified by the government of the Mexican republic, the sum of three millions of dollars shall be paid to the said government by that of the United States, at the City of Mexico, in the gold or silver coin of Mexico. The remaining twelve millions of dollars shall be paid at the same place, and in the same coin, in annual instalments of three millions of

Articulo XII.

En consideracion á la estension que adquieren los límites de los Estados Unidos, segun quedan descritos en el artículo quinto del presente tratado, el gobierno de los mismos Estados Unidos se compromete á pagar al de la república Mexicana la suma de quince millones de pesos.

Inmediatamente despues que este tratado haya sido ratificado por el gobierno de la república Mexicana, se entregará al mismo gobierno por él de los Estados Unidos, en la ciudad de México, y en moneda de plata ú oro del cuño Mexicano, la suma de tres millones de pesos. Los doce millones de pesos restantes se pagarán en México, en moneda de plata ú oro del cuño Mexicano, en abonos de

dollars each, together with interest on the same at the rate of six per centum per annum. This interest shall begin to run upon the whole sum of twelve millions from the day of the ratification of the present treaty by the Mexican government, and the first of the instalments shall be paid at the expiration of one year from the same day. Together with each annual instalment, as it falls due, the whole interest accruing on such instalment from the beginning shall also be paid.

tres millones de pesos cada año, con un rédito de seis por ciento anual: este rédito comienzará á correr para toda la suma de los doce millones el dia de la ratificacion del presente tratado por el gobierno Mexicano, y con cada abono anual de capital se pagará el rédito que corresponda á la suma abonada. Los plazos para los abonos de capital corren desde el mismo dia que empiezan á causarse los réditos.

Article XIII.

The United States engage, moreover, to assume and pay to the claimants all the amounts now due them, and those hereafter to become due, by reason of the claims already liquidated and decided against the Mexican republic, under the conventions between the two republics severally concluded on the eleventh day of April, eighteen hundred and thirty-nine, and on the thirtieth day of January, eighteen hundred and forty-three; so that the Mexican republic shall be absolutely exempt, for the future, from all expense whatever on account of the said claims.

Articulo XIII.

Se obliga ademas el gobierno de los Estados Unidos á tomar sobre sí, y satisfacer cumplidamente á los reclamantes, todas las cantidades que hasta aquí se les deben y cuantas se venzan en adelante por razon de las reclamaciones ya liquidadas y sentenciadas contra la república Mexicana conforme á los convenios ajustados entre ambas repúblicas el once de Abril de mil ochocientos treinta y nueve, y el treinta de Enero de mil ochocientos cuarenta y tres; de manera que la república Mexicana nada absolutamente tendrá que lasta en lo venidero, por razon de los indicados reclamos.

Article XIV.

The United States do furthermore discharge the Mexican republic from all claims of citizens of the United States, not heretofore decided against the Mexican government, which may have arisen previously to the date of the signature of this treaty; which discharge shall be final and perpetual, whether the said claims be rejected or be allowed by the board of commissioners provided for in the following article, and whatever shall be the total amount of those allowed.

Articulo XIV.

Tambien exoneran los Estados Unidos á la república Mexicana de todas las reclamaciones de ciudadanos de los Estados Unidos no decididas aun contra el gobierno Mexicano, y que puedan haberse originado ántes de la fecha de la firma del presente tratado: esta exoneracion es definitiva y perpetua, bien sea que las dichas reclamaciones se admitan, bien sea que se desechen por el tribunal de comisarios de que hábla el artículo siguiente y cualquiera que pueda ser el monto total de las que queden admitidas.

Article XV.

The United States, exonerating Mexico from all demands on account of the claims of their citizens mentioned in the preceding article, and considering them entirely and forever cancelled, whatever their amount may be, undertake to make satisfaction for the same, to an amount not exceeding three and one quarter millions of dollars. To ascertain the validity and amount of those claims, a board of commissioners shall be established by the government of the United States, whose awards shall be final and conclusive: *Pro-*

Articulo XV.

Los Estados Unidos, exonerando á México de toda responsabilidad por las reclamaciones de sus ciudadanos mencionadas en el artículo precedente, y considerandolas completamente canceladas para siempre, sea cual fuere su monto, toman á su cargo satisfacerlas hasta una cantidad que no exceda de tres millones doscientos cincuenta mil pesos. Para fijar el monto y validez de estas reclamaciones, se establecerá por el gobierno de los Estados Unidos un tribunal de comisarios, cuyos fallos serán definitivos y concluyentes, con tal que al decidir sobre la

vided, That, in deciding upon the validity of each claim, the board shall be guided and governed by the principles and rules of decision prescribed by the first and fifth articles of the unratified convention, concluded at the City of Mexico on the twentieth day of November, one thousand eight hundred and forty-three; and in no case shall an award be made in favor of any claim not embraced by these principles and rules.

If, in the opinion of the said board of commissioners, or of the claimants, any books, records, or documents in the possession or power of the government of the Mexican republic, shall be deemed necessary to the just decision of any claim, the commissioners, or the claimants through them, shall, within such period as Congress may designate, make an application in writing for the same, addressed to the Mexican minister for foreign affairs, to be transmitted by the Secretary of State of the United States; and the Mexican government engages, at the earliest possible moment after the receipt of such demand, to cause any of the books, records, or documents, so specified, which shall be in their possession or power (or

validez de dichas reclamaciones, el tribunal se haya guiado y gobernado por los principios y reglas de decision establecidos en los artículos primero y quinto de la convencion, no ratificada, que se ajustó en la ciudad de México el veinte de Noviembre de mil ochocientos cuarenta y tres; y en ningun caso se dará fallo en favor de ninguna reclamacion que no esté comprendida en las reglas y principios indicados.

Si en juicio del dicho tribunal de comisarios, ó en el de los reclamantes se necesitáren para la justa decision de cualquier reclamacion algunos libros, papeles de archivo ó documentos que posea el gobierno Mexicano, ó que esten en su poder; los comisarios, ó los reclamantes por conducto de ellos, los pedirán por escrito (dentro del plazo que designe el Congreso), dirigiéndose al ministro Mexicano de relaciones exteriores, á quien transmitirá las peticiones de esta clase el Secretario de Estado de los Estados Unidos; y el gobierno Mexicano se compromete á entregar á la mayor brevedad posible, despues de recibida cada demanda, los libros, papeles de archivo ó documentos, así especificados,

authenticated copies or extracts of the same), to be transmitted to the said Secretary of State, who shall immediately deliver them over to the said board of commissioners: *Provided*, That no such application shall be made by, or at the instance of, any claimant, until the facts, which it is expected to prove by such books, records, or documents, shall have been stated under oath or affirmation.

que posea ó estén en su poder, ó copias ó extractos auténticos de los mismos, con el objeto de que sean transmitidos al Secretario de Estado, quien los pasará inmediatamente al expresado tribunal de comisarios. Y no se hará peticion alguna de los enunciados libros, papeles ó documentos, por ó á instancia de ningun reclamante, sin que ántes se haya aseverado bajo juramento ó con afirmacion solemne la verdad de los héchos que con ellos se pretende probar.

Article XVI.

Each of the contracting parties reserves to itself the entire right to fortify whatever point within its territory it may judge proper so to fortify, for its security.

Articulo XVI.

Cada una de las dos repúblicas se reserva la completa facultad de fortificar todos los puntos que para su seguridad estime convenientes en su propio territorio.

Article XVII.

The treaty of amity, commerce, and navigation, concluded at the City of Mexico on the fifth day of April, A.D. 1831, between the United States of America and the United Mexican States, except the additional article, and except so far as the stipulations of the said treaty may be incompatible with any stipulation contained in the present treaty, is hereby revived for the period

Articulo XVII.

El tratado de amistad, comercio y navegacion, concluido en la ciudad de México el cinco de Abril, del año del Señor 1831, entre la república Mexicana y los Estados Unidos de América, esceptuandose el artículo adicional y cuanto pueda haber en sus estipulaciones incompatible con alguna de las contenidas en el presente tratado, queda restablecido por el periodo de ocho años desde el dia del cange de

of eight years from the day of the exchange of ratifications of this treaty, with the same force and virtue as if incorporated therein; it being understood that each of the contracting parties reserves to itself the right, at any time after the said period of eight years shall have expired, to terminate the same by giving one year's notice of such intention to the other party.

las ratificaciones del mismo presente tratado, con igual fuerza y valor que si estuviese inserto en él; debiendo entenderse que cada una de las partes contratantes se reserva el derecho de poner término al dicho tratado de comercio y navegacion en cualquier tiempo luego que haya expirado el periodo de los ocho años, comunicando su intencion á la otra parte con un año de anticipacion.

Article XVIII.

All supplies whatever for troops of the United States in Mexico, arriving at ports in the occupation of such troops previous to the final evacuation thereof, although subsequently to the restoration of the custom-houses at such ports, shall be entirely exempt from duties and charges of any kind; the government of the United States hereby engaging and pledging its faith to establish, and vigilantly to enforce, all possible guards for securing the revenue of Mexico, by preventing the importation, under cover of this stipulation, of any articles other than such, both in kind and in quantity, as shall really be wanted for the use and consumption of the forces of the United States during the time

Articulo XVIII.

No se exigirán derechos ni gravámen de ninguna clase á los artículos todos que lleguen para las tropas de los Estados Unidos á los puertos Mexicanos ocupados por ellas, ántes de la evacuacion final de los mismos puertos, y despues de la devolucion á México de las aduanas situadas en ellos. El gobierno de los Estados Unidos se compromete á la vez, y sobre esto empeña su fé, á establecer y mantener con vigilancia cuantos guardas sean posibles para asegurar las rentas de México, precaviendo la importacion, á la sombra de esta estipulacion, de cualesquiera artículos que realmente no sean necesarios, ó que excedan en cantidad de los que se necesiten para el uso y consumo de las fuerzas de los Es-

they may remain in Mexico. To this end, it shall be the duty of all officers and agents of the United States to denounce to the Mexican authorities at the respective ports any attempt at a fraudulent abuse of this stipulation which they may know of or may have reason to suspect, and to give to such authorities all the aid in their power with regard thereto; and every such attempt, when duly proved and established by sentence of a competent tribunal, shall be punished by the confiscation of the property so attempted to be fraudulently introduced.

tados Unidos mientras ellas permanezcan en México. A este efecto, todos los oficiales y agentes de los Estados Unidos tendrán obligacion de denunciar á las autoridades Mexicanas en los mismos puertos, cualquier conato de fraudulento abuso de esta estipulacion que pudiéren conocer ó tuvieren motivo de sospechar; así como de impartir á las mismas autoridades todo el auxilio que pudiéren con este objeto; y cualquier conato de esta clase, que fuére legalmente probado, y declarado por sentencia de tribunal competente, sera castigado con el comiso de la cosa que se haya intentado introducir fraudulentamente.

Article XIX.

With respect to all merchandise, effects, and property whatsoever imported into ports of Mexico whilst in the occupation of the forces of the United States, whether by citizens of either republic, or by citizens or subjects of any neutral nation, the following rules shall be observed:

1. All such merchandise, effects, and property, if imported previously to the restoration of the custom-houses to the Mexi-

Articulo XIX.

Respecto de los efectos, mercancías y propiedades importados en los puertos Mexicanos durante el tiempo que han estado ocupados por las fuerzas de los Estados Unidos, sea por ciudadanos de cualquiera de las dos repúblicas, sea por ciudadanos ó subditos de alguna nacion neutral, se observarán las reglas siguientes:

1. Los dichos efectos, mercancías y propiedades, siempre que se hayan importado ántes de la devolucion de las aduanas

can authorities, as stipulated for in the third article of this treaty, shall be exempt from confiscation, although the importation of the same be prohibited by the Mexican tariff.

2. The same perfect exemption shall be enjoyed by all such merchandise, effects, and property, imported subsequently to the restoration of the custom-houses, and previously to the sixty days fixed in the following article for the coming into force of the Mexican tariff at such ports respectively; the said merchandise, effects, and property being, however, at the time of their importation, subject to the payment of duties, as provided for in the said following article.

3. All merchandise, effects, and property described in the two rules foregoing shall, during their continuance at the place of importation, and upon their leaving such place for the interior, be exempt from all duty, tax, or impost of every kind, under whatsoever title or denomination. Nor shall they be there subjected to any charge whatsoever upon the sale thereof.

4. All merchandise, effects, and property described in the

á las autoridades Mexicanas conforme á lo estipulado en el artículo tercero de este tratado, quedarán libres de la pena de comiso, aun cuando sean de los prohibidos en el arancél Mexicano.

2. La misma exencion gozarán los efectos, mercancías y propiedades que lleguen á los puertos Mexicanos, despues de la devolucion á México de las aduanas marítimas, y ántes de que expiren los sesenta dias que van á fijarse en el artículo siguiente para que empieze á regir el arancél Mexicano en los puertos; debiendo al tiempo de su importacion sujetarse los tales efectos, mercancías y propiedades, en cuanto al pago de derechos, á lo que en el indicado siguiente artículo se establece.

3. Los efectos, mercancías y propiedades designados en las dos reglas anteriores quedarán exentos de todo derecho, alcabala ó impuesto, sea bajo el título de internacion, sea bajo cualquiera otro, mientras permanezcan en los puntos donde se hayan importado, y á su salida para el interior; y en los mismos puntos no podrá jamas exigirse impuesto alguno sobre su venta.

4. Los efectos, mercancías y propiedades designados en las

first and second rules, which shall have been removed to any place in the interior whilst such place was in the occupation of the forces of the United States, shall, during their continuance therein, be exempt from all tax upon the sale or consumption thereof, and from every kind of impost or contribution, under whatsoever title or denomination.

reglas primera y segunda que hayan sido internados á cualquier lugar ocupado por las fuerzas de los Estados Unidos, quedarán exentos de todo derecho sobre su venta ó consumo, y de todo impuesto ó contribucion, bajo cualquier título ó denominacion, mientras permanezcan en el mismo lugar.

5. But if any merchandise, effects, or property described in the first and second rules shall be removed to any place not occupied at the time by the forces of the United States, they shall, upon their introduction into such place, or upon their sale or consumption there, be subject to the same duties which, under the Mexican laws, they would be required to pay in such cases if they had been imported in time of peace through the maritime custom-houses, and had there paid the duties conformably with the Mexican tariff.

5. Mas si algunos efectos, mercancías ó propiedades de los designados en las reglas primera y segunda se trasladaren á algun lugar no ocupado á la sazon por las fuerzas de los Estados Unidos, al introducirse á tal lugar, ó al venderse ó consumirse en él, quedarán sujetos á los mismos derechos que bajo las leyes Mexicanas deberian pagar en tales casos si se hubiéran importado en tiempo de paz por las aduanas maritimas, y hubiesen pagado en ellas los derechos que establece el arancél Mexicano.

6. The owners of all merchandise, effects, or property described in the first and second rules, and existing in any port of Mexico, shall have the right to reship the same, exempt from all tax, impost, or contribution whatever.

6. Los dueños de efectos, mercancías y propiedades designados en las reglas primera y segunda, y existentes en algun puerto de México, tienen derecho de re-embarcarlos, sin que pueda exigirseles ninguna clase de impuesto, alcabala ó contribucion.

With respect to the metals, or other property, exported from any Mexican port whilst in the occupation of the forces of the United States, and previously to the restoration of the custom-house at such port, no person shall be required by the Mexican authorities, whether general or State, to pay any tax, duty, or contribution upon any such exportation, or in any manner to account for the same to the said authorities.

Respecto de los metales y de toda otra propiedad exportados por cualquier puerto Mexicano durante su ocupacion por las fuerzas Americanas, y ántes de la devolucion de su aduana al gobierno Mexicano, no se exigirá á ninguna persona por las autoridades de México, ya dependan del gobierno general, ya de algun estado, que pague ningun impuesto, alcabala ó derecho por la indicada exportacion, ni sobre ella podrá exigirsele por las dichas autoridades cuenta alguna.

Article XX.

Through consideration for the interests of commerce generally, it is agreed, that if less than sixty days should elapse between the date of the signature of this treaty and the restoration of the custom-houses, conformably with the stipulation in the third article, in such case all merchandise, effects, and property whatsoever, arriving at the Mexican ports after the restoration of the said custom-houses, and previously to the expiration of sixty days after the day of the signature of this treaty, shall be admitted to entry; and no other duties shall be levied thereon than the duties established by the tariff

Articulo XX.

Por consideracion á los interéses del comercia de todas las naciones, queda convenido que si pasáren menos de sesenta dias desde la fecha de la firma de este tratado hasta que se haga la devolucion de las aduanas marítimas, segun lo estipulado en el artículo tercero; todos los efectos, mercancías y propiedades que lleguen á los puertos Mexicanos desde el dia en que se verifique la devolucion de las dichas aduanas hasta que se completen sesenta dias contados desde la fecha de la firma del presente tratado, se admitirán no pagando otros derechos que los establecidos en la tarifa que esté vigente

found in force at such custom-houses at the time of the restoration of the same. And to all such merchandise, effects, and property, the rules established by the preceding article shall apply.

en las expresadas aduanas al tiempo de su devolucion, y se extenderán á dichos efectos, mercancias y propiedades las mismas reglas establecidas en el articulo anterior.

Article XXI.

If unhappily any disagreement should hereafter arise between the governments of the two republics, whether with respect to the interpretation of any stipulation in this treaty, or with respect to any other particular concerning the political or commercial relations of the two nations, the said governments, in the name of those nations, do promise to each other that they will endeavor, in the most sincere and earnest manner, to settle the differences so arising, and to preserve the state of peace and friendship in which the two countries are now placing themselves; using, for this end, mutual representations and pacific negotiations. And if by these means they should not be enabled to come to an agreement, a resort shall not on this account be had to reprisals, aggression, or hostility of any kind, by the one republic against the other, until the government

Articulo XXI.

Si desgraciadamente en el tiempo futuro se suscitare algun punto de desacuerdo entre los gobiernos de las dos repúblicas, bien sea sobre la inteligencia de alguna estipulacion de este tratado, bien sobre cualquiera otra materia de las relaciones politicas ó comerciales de las dos naciones, los mismos gobiernos, á nombre de ellas, se comprometen á procurar de la manera mas sincera y empeñosa á llanar las diferencias que se presenten y conservar el estado de paz y amistad en que ahora se ponen los dos paises, usando al efecto de representaciones mútuas y de negociaciones pacificas. Y si por estos medios no se lograre todavia ponerse de acuerdo no por eso se apelará á represalia, agresion ni hostilidad de ningun género de una república contra otra, hasta que el gobierno de la que se crea agraviada haya considerado maduramente y en espiritu de paz y buena vecindad,

of that which deems itself aggrieved shall have maturely considered, in the spirit of peace and good neighborship, whether it would not be better that such difference should be settled by the arbitration of commissioners appointed on each side, or by that of a friendly nation. And should such course be proposed by either party, it shall be acceded to by the other, unless deemed by it altogether incompatible with the nature of the difference, or the circumstances of the case.

si no seria mejor que la diferencia se terminara por un arbitramento de comisarios nombrados por ambas partes, ó de una nacion amiga. Y si tal medio fuére propuesto por cualquiera de las dos partes, la otra accedera á él, á no ser que lo juzgue absolutamente incompatible con la naturaleza y circunstancias del caso.

Article XXII.

If (which is not to be expected, and which God forbid!) war should unhappily break out between the two republics, they do now, with a view to such calamity, solemnly pledge themselves to each other, and to the world, to observe the following rules: absolutely, where the nature of the subject permits, and as closely as possible in all cases where such absolute observance shall be impossible:

1. The merchants of either republic then residing in the other shall be allowed to remain twelve months (for those dwelling in the interior), and

Articulo XXII.

Si (lo que no es de esperarse, y Dios no permita) desgraciadamente se suscitare guerra entre las dos repúblicas, estas para el caso de tal calamidad se comprometen ahora solemnemente, ánte si mismas y ánte el mundo, á observar las reglas siguientes de una manera absoluta si la naturaleza del objeto á que se contraen lo permite; y tan extrictamente como sea dable en todos los casos en que la absoluta observancia de ellas fuére imposible:

1. Los comerciantes de cada una de las dos repúblicas que á la sazon residan en territorio de la otra, podrán permanecer doce meses los que residan en

six months (for those dwelling at the seaports), to collect their debts and settle their affairs, during which periods they shall enjoy the same protection, and be on the same footing, in all respects, as the citizens or subjects of the most friendly nations; and, at the expiration thereof, or any time before, they shall have full liberty to depart, carrying off all their effects without molestation or hinderance—conforming therein to the same laws which the citizens or subjects of the most friendly nations are required to conform to. Upon the entrance of the armies of either nation into the territories of the other, women and children, ecclesiastics, scholars of every faculty, cultivators of the earth, merchants, artisans, manufacturers, and fishermen, unarmed and inhabiting unfortified towns, villages, or places, and in general all persons whose occupations are for the common subsistence and benefit of mankind, shall be allowed to continue their respective employments unmolested in their persons. Nor shall their houses or goods be burnt or otherwise destroyed, nor their cattle taken, nor their fields wasted, by the armed force into whose power, by the

el interior, y seis meses los que residan en los puertos, para recoger sus deudas y arreglar sus negocios; durante estos plazos desfrutarán la misma proteccion y estarán sobre el mismo pié en todos respectos que los ciudadanos ó súbditos de las naciones mas amigas; y al expirar el término, ó ántes de él, tendrán completa libertad para salir y llevar todos sus efectos sin molestia ó embarazo, sujetándose en este particular á las mismas leyes á que estén sujetos, y deban arreglarse los ciudadanos ó súbditos de las naciones mas amigas. Cuando los ejercitos de una de las dos naciones entren en territorios de la otra, las mujeres y niños, los eclesiasticos, los estudiantes de cualquier facultad, los labradores, comerciantes, artesanos, manufactureros, y pescadores que esten desarmados y residan en ciudades, pueblos ó lugares no fortificados, y en general todas las personas cuya ocupacion sirva para la comun subsistencia y beneficio del género humano, podrán continuar en sus ejercicios, sin que sus personas sean molestadas. No serán incendiadas sus casas ó bienes, ó destruidos de otra manera; ni serán tomados sus ganados, ni devastados sus campos, por

events of war, they may happen to fall; but if the necessity arise to take anything from them for the use of such armed force, the same shall be paid for at an equitable price. All churches, hospitals, schools, colleges, libraries, and other establishments for charitable and beneficent purposes, shall be respected, and all persons connected with the same protected in the discharge of their duties and the pursuit of their vocations.

la fuerza armada en cuyo poder puedan venir á caer por los acontecimientos de la guerra; pero si hubiere necesidad de tomarles alguna cosa para el uso de la misma fuerza armada, se les pagará lo tomado á un precio justo. Todas las iglesias, hospitales, escuelas, colegios, librerías, y demas establecimientos de caridad y beneficencia serán respetados; y todas las personas que dependan de las mismas serán protegidas en el desempeño de sus deberes y en la continuacion de sus profesiones.

2. In order that the fate of prisoners of war may be alleviated, all such practices as those of sending them into distant, inclement, or unwholesome districts, or crowding them into close and noxious places, shall be studiously avoided. They shall not be confined in dungeons, prison-ships, or prisons; nor be put in irons, or bound, or otherwise restrained in the use of their limbs. The officers shall enjoy liberty on their paroles within convenient districts, and have comfortable quarters; and the common soldiers shall be disposed in cantonments, open and extensive enough for air and exercise, and lodged in

2. Para aliviar la suerte de los prisioneros de guerra, se evitarán cuidadosamente las praticas de enviarlos á distritos distantes, inclementes ó malsanos, ó de aglomerarlos en lugares estrechos y enfermizos. No se confinarán en calabosos, prisiones ni pontones; no se les aherrojará ni se les atará, ni se les impedirá de ningun otro modo el uso de sus miembros. Los oficiales que darán en libertad bajo su palabra de honor, dentro de distritos convenientes y tendrán alojamientos comodos; y los soldados rasos se colocarán en acantonamientos bastante despejados y extensos para la ventilacion y el ejercicio, y se alojarán en cuarteles tan

barracks as roomy and good as are provided by the party in whose power they are for its own troops. But if any officer shall break his parole by leaving the district so assigned him, or any other prisoner shall escape from the limits of his cantonment, after they shall have been designated to him, such individual, officer, or other prisoner shall forfeit so much of the benefit of this article as provides for his liberty on parole or in cantonment. And if any officer so breaking his parole, or any common soldier so escaping from the limits assigned him, shall afterwards be found in arms, previously to his being regularly exchanged, the person so offending shall be dealt with according to the established laws of war. The officers shall be daily furnished by the party in whose power they are with as many rations, and of the same articles, as are allowed, either in kind or by commutation, to officers of equal rank in its own army; and all others shall be daily furnished with such ration as is allowed to a common soldier in its own service—the value of all which supplies shall, at the close of the war, or at periods to be agreed upon between the re-

amplios y comodos como los que use para sus propias tropas la parte que los tenga en su poder. Pero si algun oficial faltare á su palabra, saliendo del distrito que se le ha señalado, ó algun otro prisionero se fugare de los límites de su acantonamiento despues que estos se les hayan fijado, tal oficial ó prisionero perderá el beneficio del presente artículo por lo que mera á su libertad bajo su palabra ó en acantonamiento. Y si algun oficial faltando así á su palabra, ó algun soldado raso saliendo de los límites que se le han asignado, fuére encontrado despues con las armas en la mano ántes de ser debidamente cangeado, tal persona en esta actitud ofensiva será tratada conforme á las leyes comunes de la guerra. A los oficiales se proveerá diariamente por la parte en cuyo poder estén, de tantas raciones compuestas de los mismos artículos como las que gozan en especie ó en equivalente los oficiales de la misma graduacion en su propio ejército; á todos los demas prisioneros se proveerá diariamente de una racion semejante á la que se ministra al soldado raso en su propio servicio; el valor de todas estas suministraciones se pagará por la otra

spective commanders, be paid by the other party, on a mutual adjustment of accounts for subsistence of prisoners; and such accounts shall not be mingled with or set off against any others, nor the balance due on them be withheld, as a compensation or reprisal for any cause whatever, real or pretended. Each party shall be allowed to keep a commissary of prisoners, appointed by itself, with every cantonment of prisoners in possession of the other; which commissary shall see the prisoners as often as he pleases; shall be allowed to receive, exempt from all duties or taxes, and to distribute, whatever comforts may be sent to them by their friends; and shall be free to transmit his reports in open letters to the party by whom he is employed.

parte al concluirse la guerra, ó en los periodos que se convengan entre sus respectivos comandantes, precediendo una mutua liquidacion de las cuentas que se lleven del mantenimiento de prisioneros; y tales cuentas no se mezclarán ni compensarán con otras; ni el saldo que resulte de ellas, se rehusara bajo pretesto de compensacion ó represalia por cualquiera causa, real ó figurada. Cada una de las partes podrá mantener un comisario de prisioneros nombrado por ella misma en cada acantonamiento de los prisioneros que estén en poder de la otra parte; este comisario visitará á los prisioneros siempre que quiera; tendrá facultad de recibir, libres de todo derecho ó impuesto, y de distribuir todos los auxilios que pueden enviarles sus amigos, y podrá libremente transmitir sus partes en cartas abiertas á la autoridad por la cual está empleado.

And it is declared that neither the pretence that war dissolves all treaties, nor any other whatever, shall be considered as annulling or suspending the solemn covenant contained in this article. On the contrary, the state of war is precisely that for which it is provided, and during which its stipulations

Y se declará que ni el pretesto de que la guerra destruye los tratados, ni otro alguno, sea él que fuére, se considerará que anula ó suspende el pacto solemne contenido en este artículo. Por el contrario, el estado de guerra es cabalmente el que se ha tenido presente al ajustarlo, y durante el cual sus estipula-

are to be as sacredly observed as the most acknowledged obligations under the law of nature or nations.

ciones se han de observar tan santamente como las obligaciones mas reconocidas de la ley natural ó de gentes.

ARTICLE XXIII.

This treaty shall be ratified by the President of the United States of America, by and with the advice and consent of the Senate thereof; and by the President of the Mexican republic, with the previous approbation of its General Congress; and the ratifications shall be exchanged in the City of Washington, or at the seat of government of Mexico, in four months from the date of the signature hereof, or sooner if practicable.

In faith whereof, we, the respective plenipotentiaries, have signed this treaty of peace, friendship, limits, and settlement; and have hereunto affixed our seals respectively. Done in quintuplicate, at the City of Guadalupe Hidalgo, on the second day of February, in the year of our Lord one thousand eight hundred and forty-eight.

N. P. TRIST, [L. S.]
LUIS G. CUEVAS, [L. S.]
BERNARDO COUTO, [L. S.]
MIGL. ATRISTAIN. [L. S.]

ARTICULO XXIII.

Este tratado será ratificado por el Presidente de la república Mexicana, previa la aprobacion de su Congreso General; y por el Presidente de los Estados Unidos de América, con el consejo y consentimiento del Senado; y las ratificaciones se cangearán en la ciudad de Washington, ó donde estuviere el gobierno Mexicano, á los cuatro meses de la fecha de la firma del mismo tratado, ó antes si fuére posible.

En fé de lo cual, nosotros los respectivos plenipotenciarios hemos firmado y sellado por quintuplicado este tratado de paz, amistad, límites y arreglo definitivo, en la ciudad de Guadalupe Hidalgo, el dia dos de Febrero del año de nuestro Señor mil ochocientos cuarenta y ocho.

BERNARDO COUTO, [L. S.]
MIGL. ATRISTAIN, [L. S.]
LUIS G. CUEVAS, [L. S.]
N. P. TRIST. [L. S.]

THE END.